DATE DUE

1 2 2007

GAYLORD			PRINTED IN U.S.A.

DOUBLE TROUBLE

TRANSGRESSING BOUNDARIES

Studies in Black Politics and Black Communities
Cathy Cohen and Fredrick Harris, Series Editors

*The Politics of Public Housing: Black Women's
Struggles Against Urban Inequality*
RHONDA Y. WILLIAMS

Keepin' It Real: School Success Beyond Black and White
PRUDENCE L. CARTER

*Double Trouble: Black Mayors, Black Communities,
and the Call for a Deep Democracy*
J. PHILLIP THOMPSON, III

J. Phillip Thompson, III

DOUBLE TROUBLE

Black Mayors,

Black Communities,

and the Call for

a Deep Democracy

OXFORD
UNIVERSITY PRESS

2006

OXFORD

UNIVERSITY PRESS

Oxford University Press, Inc., publishes works that further
Oxford University's objective of excellence
in research, scholarship, and education.

Oxford   New York
Auckland   Cape Town   Dar es Salaam   Hong Kong   Karachi
Kuala Lumpur   Madrid   Melbourne   Mexico City   Nairobi
New Delhi   Shanghai   Taipei   Toronto

With offices in
Argentina   Austria   Brazil   Chile   Czech Republic   France   Greece
Guatemala   Hungary   Italy   Japan   Poland   Portugal   Singapore
South Korea   Switzerland   Thailand   Turkey   Ukraine   Vietnam

Copyright © 2006 by Oxford University Press, Inc.

Published by Oxford University Press, Inc.
198 Madison Avenue, New York, New York 10016

www.oup.com

Oxford is a registered trademark of Oxford University Press

Library of Congress Cataloging-in-Publications Data
Thompson, J. Phillip.
    Double trouble : black mayors, black communities, and the call for a deep democracy /
J. Phillip Thompson, III.
        p.   cm.—(Transgressing boundaries)
    ISBN-13 978-0-19-517733-6
    ISBN 0-19-517733-9
        1. African American—Politics and government. 2. African American mayors.
    3. Dinkins, David N. 4. Municipal government—United States. 5. Pluralism
    (Social sciences)—United States. 6. Political participation—United States.
    7. Power (Social sciences)—United States. 8. Social change—United States.
    9. Democracy—United States. 10. United States—Race relations—
    Political aspects.   I. Title.   II. Series
    E185.615.T554 2005
    352.23'216'08996073—dc22   2005004944

9 8 7 6 5 4 3 2 1

Printed in the United States of America
on acid-free paper

To Dayna, James, and Calvin

Preface

My first direct experience with black mayors was in the early 1980s, when I worked soon after college as a community-organizing consultant for Clarence Coggins, Mayor Kenneth Gibson's chief of staff in Newark, New Jersey. Being exposed at a young age to civil rights activism through my parents and the church, and, later, with thousands of other young black activists in my generation, moving from (and between) black nationalism to Pan-Africanism and then to Marxism in student and community movements, I approached black electoral politics skeptically, thinking that black politicians chose electoral politics to avoid community organizing and working for the empowerment of the black poor. Working with Coggins, with the late David Richardson, a community leader and state representative from my hometown of Philadelphia, and then with New York Mayor David Dinkins, I arrived at a more complex view. There were many black politicians who saw political office as a job rather than as a means of serving a broader cause, and there were many working hard for their neediest constituents, but many, perhaps most black elected officials swirled between these poles. Many black officials seemed frustrated they could not make a difference in their neediest constituents' lives, and most activists I knew were pessimistic about building broad coalitions, with other racial and ethnic groups, around poverty issues. It was hard to avoid the conclusion that electoral politics was a trap for black activists. It offered a steady job, and fame and fortune for those willing to be team players with increasingly conservative white Democrats, but it had diminishing relevance for the cause of liberating the poor from the shackles of poverty. In the low-income neighborhoods and public housing developments where I worked, it was obvious that black politicians were no longer revered, especially among the young people, and it was clear that few black politicians were actively seeking their support. Dinkins became an exception; his margin of victory over Rudolph Giuliani was so slim in 1989 that he could not politically afford to ignore the black poor. The insistence, on the one hand, that Dinkins live up to his own lofty rhetoric of serving the poor, and, on the other hand, that he serve the needs of financial investors and middle-class taxpayers gripped his administration like a vise. Among Dinkins's black staff, there was constant talk about whether the administration was standing up or caving in to the Establishment, but the conversations were conducted in whispered tones. We staffers all implicitly understood that open and frank talk about race and class problems in the city was a sure path to political ostracism in the mainstream media and political estrangement from middle-class white voters. But without open and frank talk, our conversations with constituents were superficial and evaded the real issues. Mayor Dinkins seemed to struggle with the same frustration; occasionally his habitual graciousness would wear thin and a biting remark would slip through.

In my view, the lack of accountability of black officials to their neediest constituents, the lack of open talk about race and class on the part of black mayors, and the absence of meaningful change-oriented coalitions across racial divides, in short, the shallow discourse and special-interest dealmaking character of much of urban pluralist politics, leads to the absence of voice and participation of poor blacks and other marginalized groups in society. Getting black mayors to challenge conservative public policies and their roots in the majority public's negative opinions of the inner-city black poor requires strong political pressure to be applied on the mayors. Strong political pressure, in turn, requires the mayors to be vulnerable during elections to pressure from their poor and marginalized groups. Mounting such pressure on big-city mayors is not easy; it takes substantial organization, sustained political participation, and coalitions across sharp class, gender, and ideological divides within black communities. This requires an openness to political debate and greater inclusion within black politics, but discussions about the limits and failings of black politics, and about whose in-terests have been included and excluded by black mayors and other black leaders, is as rare as frank race and class talk in the mainstream media and political discourse. For blacks to increase their power to more effectively challenge opinions and public policies supported by the white public, there is a need for greater political inclusion and open political discourse within black communities. I call this concept "deep" pluralism because it begins with unveiling painful *internal* oppressions and exclusions within black pol-itics for the purpose of increasing the black community's power to compel similar unveiling in broader interracial politics.

Several advantages derive from a deep pluralist approach. Learning how to bridge intra-black conflicts and broaden black political participa-tion provides important political skills for blacks attempting to unite with other racial and ethnic groups. Increasing political solidarity and the po-litical power of black communities can increase black organizations' con-fidence that they can hold their own in coalitions with non-black organi-zations, and the more power blacks have, the more they can lend it in support of potential allies. With increased group political strength and al-liances with other groups, black activists are in a better position to chal-lenge dominant norms and public policies. Without power, it is hard to see how blacks' grievances can be addressed democratically. At the same time, power without an appreciation of its corrupting influences can be dangerous. Acknowledging that one's own group, even though it is op-pressed, may nonetheless be led to oppress some of its own group mem-bers or other weaker groups—even when it is not in the oppressor group's overall political interest—deep pluralism helps blacks to understand the existence of oppression among whites, and also to appreciate many whites' unwitting oppression of blacks. Such a critical self-awareness permits more insightful understanding of others and can contain dangerously sharp edges of interracial conflict. While the perspective of this book is an in-ward look at black politics, it is not meant to suggest that deep pluralism applies solely to blacks, indeed, such an approach would contradict the book's emphasis on opening up rigid understandings of political identity. At heart, deep pluralism is a call for limits on the claim of moral superior-ity by both those demanding and those dispensing justice; it is an appeal to recognize our shared fallibility and capacity to inflict terrible harm on oth-ers; it is the suggestion that the best way to broaden democracy is to prac-tice it internally.

Outline of the Book

This book is divided into two parts. Part I develops the discussion of deep pluralism within the context of black mayoral politics. The early chapters discuss political and administrative structures that shape black mayors' political interest (either in hindering or in enabling grassroots black mobilization), black political ideologies, the state of black civic participation in cities, and differences between the types of interracial coalitions black mayors form. The chapters contrast an emerging deep pluralism, a broad interracial and substantive change-oriented-movement building approach to black politics exemplified by civil rights leaders such as Dr. Martin Luther King Jr., Ella Baker, and a few black mayors, with more conservative and instrumental political strategies pursued by most black mayors. Part II traces these same threads in New York City's black politics before, during, and after the Dinkins administration. It shows how a fragmented local governance structure weakened efforts to build black political coalitions until the late 1980s, when centralization of power in the mayor's office encouraged formation of a citywide black political coalition that led to Dinkins's mayoralty. The black civic organizations that helped elect Dinkins pressured him to be accountable to his largely low-income constituents. He did so by challenging the conservative policy orientation of the city council, by creating a civic coalition to organize community residents and to run candidates against council opponents, and by taking creative administrative steps to organize poor black voters. These moves led to a conservative white backlash and to sharp debates over the legitimacy of ideological frames that demonize poor blacks and Latinos. A profound racial divide persisted in the city long after Dinkins's loss to Rudolph Giuliani in his reelection bid in 1993. The Democratic party remained divided along racial and class lines during the 2001 mayoral election and this led an unusual number of black and Latino voters to support a Republican candidate, Michael Bloomberg, who wooed Latino and black Democrats to succeed Rudolph Giuliani as mayor. Despite the appearance of conservative ascendance, it was an emerging deep pluralist politics that undermined the old political edifice (the city's Democratic Party coalition), however, it did so without solidifying a new one. Chapter 8 reviews the arguments and evidence of the book and discusses whether deep pluralism might emerge as a trend in other large U.S. cities.

Data and Methods

Double Trouble mines evidence from notes and interviews I conducted over fifteen years, including interviews with more than sixty civic activists, mayoral administration officials, and black elected officials deeply engaged in black politics. Because issues such as increasing voter registration and maintaining black solidarity are normative in black communities, for example, many people profess to engage in both even if they do not, the interviews were especially valuable for assessing whether or not political actors were engaged in political organizing and mobilization. I also selected interviewees from different sides of intra-black conflicts in order to gain a perspective on how each side viewed the other's political strategies. Interviewees were asked to suggest additional people the author might interview to get a sense of the networks of black activists and to avoid overlooking unfamiliar networks.

Part II draws on my notes and participant observations over eight years of work for David Dinkins—from his campaign for Manhattan borough president in 1984 to the end of his mayoralty in 1993—and my many conversations with him since 1993. The role of participant observer raises the issue of my objectivity. While working in the administration undoubtedly influenced my selection of issues and interviewees, I view this as mainly a positive experience. Being directly involved in events gave me a good opportunity for close observation and to assess the meaning of events in highly complex cultural and political environments. I also made note of persons around me who had interesting observations or critiques; most of them were not familiar names in the media. I also explored files from Dinkins's personal archives, from the archives located at the Municipal Research Library in New York City, and from the archives of the Jewish Community Relations Council in New York City. Newspaper articles (cited in the text), census data, government documents, and policy reports have provided further context for recounted events. I decided not to formally interview David Dinkins directly about still sensitive issues, in part because he is still active in politics, but also because I thought his "speech-in-action" while mayor best reflects his thinking at the time particular events occurred. Were this book a biography of David Dinkins, I probably would have made a different choice.

The method I employ in the book is process-tracing, suitable to case studies that involve complex combinations of variables (Bennett 1997;

Bennett and George 1997; Mahoney 2000). None of the individual factors I emphasize, taken in isolation from the others—whether political structure, black civic organization, or interracial dynamics—can account for Dinkins's approach of deeply pluralist organizing and grassroots coalition building. I hope that other students will pursue close process-tracing in other cities to determine whether the dynamics fostering deep pluralism in New York are emerging similarly elsewhere.

Acknowledgments

This book would have been impossible to write without the insights of many dozens of urban political activists who were generous in sharing their time and perspectives with me. They have been my greatest teachers, and I feel privileged to know them. Dave Dinkins and Bill Lynch were especially open and candid with me during our many conversations.

I received financial support in the early stages of writing from the Russell Sage Foundation and the Open Society Institute, to whom I am deeply grateful. I had the benefit of careful reads from Michael Dawson, Fred Harris, John Mollenkopf, Wilbur Rich, Alethia Jones, Gerry Hudson, Bob Shapiro, and anonymous reviewers from Oxford University Press. Jeanette Hopkins was invaluable. Aside from her helpful editorial suggestions, she challenged me to think and re-think my ideas and to reach for more generalizable conclusions. My colleagues at MIT, especially Bish Sanyal and Larry Vale, gave me the space I needed to complete the book. LaTonya Green and Maeghan Fennelly helped with the research.

Dedi Felman at Oxford University Press stood with this project from the beginning and has been its strongest supporter, offering wise advice at just the right times. I also owe Laura Lewis, Rene Leath, and Gwen Colvin at Oxford University Press many thanks for their help along the way.

My wife, Dayna, my children, James and Calvin, and my mother Mabel Latta Thompson, gave me tremendous support through the years, and often good ideas. I cannot leave out the inspiration and moral support I have recieved from Marilyn Gittell. Marilyn first encouraged me to pursue a Ph.D. in political science and her persistant focus on the importance of popular political participation is echoed in this book.

Contents

Part I

Black Mayors and the Quest for Democracy

Part I analyzes three factors that play a major role in shaping outcomes in black mayoral politics. It discusses local political and administrative structures that either hinder or enable black civic coalition building by enhancing or hindering the ability of black mayors to be accountable to their constituents; by creating incentives in the latter case for black mayors and other officials to *de*mobilize the black poor, or in the former case by providing patronage resources to mayors who want to encourage black mobilization. Black mayors are strongly affected by black community pressure, when applied. Another chapter analyzes contours of black political ideologies and divides between them, the state of black civic organization and black civic participation, and problems of accountability and anti-democratic tendencies in intra-black coalition-building efforts. A third influence on black politics are the presence of non-black allies. Black mayors have differed in the kinds of non-black allies they seek. Some mayors sought to build bottom-up class alliances of the multiracial poor, as exemplified by Dr. Martin Luther King, Jr. In the 1960s. Others organized more conservative multiracial coalitions with downtown businesses and upper-middle class whites. The key argument of this section is that the centralized structure of local government and strong capacity of black civic organizations in some cities leads black mayors in those places to pursue bottom-up multiracial political coalitions that favor substantive policy changes. Such pressure on mayors is more difficult to assemble and harder to sustain in less centralized cities.

Introduction

Black Mayors

and Social Change

The election of black mayors was one of the most dramatic and abrupt changes in urban politics in the last century, yet scholars and activists alike are divided as to whether it represented a giant step toward racial equality or blacks' political cooptation in exchange for a hollow prize.

The most immediate impetus for the election of black mayors was demographic shifts in cities as blacks moved North in the 1940s and 1950s from the rural South and whites moved out to the suburbs. Between 1950 and 1960, 1.2 million whites left Chicago, Philadelphia, and Newark, New Jersey, and 301,000 blacks moved in. In New York City, between 1950 and 1965, one million whites left and a nearly equal number of blacks and Puerto Ricans entered. White suburbanization was fostered by federal and state transportation policies that favored the automobile over public transportation and by federal housing and tax policies that benefited suburbs most by subsidizing new homeownership. The Federal Housing Authority (FHA) and Veteran's Authority (VA) initiated mortgage-underwriting policies that covered 90 percent of the cost of purchasing a new house and stretched payments over thirty years (Powell 2002, 78). White racial homogeneity of the suburbs was maintained by the real estate industry's systematic discrimination against black homebuyers and by resistance from white residents—some of it violent (Dreier 2001, 108)—and by the federal government's mortgage underwriting criteria discouraging investment in black city neighborhoods while encouraging investment in white suburbs (Jackson 1985; Judd 1999, 129).

Most black mayors were elected in highly racially polarized elections, garnering the lion's share of energized black voters and winning small but critical sections of the white vote—usually drawing liberal white or downtown business support. Two waves of black mayors were elected over the last thirty-five years, and both waves have crested. The first wave consisted of "civil rights" mayors. These mayors were elected in highly racially polarized elections taking place in cities that had become majority black or were approaching a black majority.

The election of black candidates to the city halls of America's most important cities began in 1967, two years after the passage of the Voting Rights Act, with the election of Carl Stokes in Cleveland, Ohio, and Richard Hatcher in Gary. Two years later, Kenneth Gibson was elected mayor of Newark; four years afterward, in 1973, Tom Bradley of Los Angeles, Coleman Young of Detroit, Maynard Jackson of Atlanta, and Walter Washington of Washington, D.C., blacks began to occupy other political offices and leadership positions as well, becoming everything from members of Congress to local sheriff and police chief.

This first wave of black mayors made tremendous changes in ordinary black citizens' perception of city government as millions of blacks voted enthusiastically for them and cities like Atlanta—racially segregated a decade earlier—now became black-run. One of the first things on these mayors' agendas was to rein in police departments that had been considered brutal and oppressive to blacks. Although the value of this action was mostly symbolic, it had real consequences to blacks in cities. So, too, black mayors greatly increased the number of African Americans working for city government and expanded government contract opportunities for black-owned small businesses. But, with the election of Ronald Reagan in the 1980s and subsequent cutbacks in federal aid to cities (Caraley 1992; Caraley 1996), the ability of black mayors to improve conditions in their cities was dramatically curtailed. Mayor Kenneth Gibson (1970–86) of Newark, concluded bitterly in 1983 that "progress is maintaining the status quo" (Biles 1992, 116).

Black voters who had been initially excited by the election of blacks as mayors now became increasingly disenchanted. Conditions in their neighborhoods and lives changed little. This created, in turn, incentives for black officials to demobilize the black poor, or to allow demobilization to occur. Those most disheartened by their conditions failed to or ceased to participate (Reed 1999, 121). Alienation of the black urban poor from politics set in motion a cycle of political withdrawal. Black political participation declined, particularly in poor neighborhoods (Gilliam and Kaufman 1998). As poor blacks' political participation weakened, the black middle class, which had gained in numbers and power in the aftermath of the early civil rights era, in turn, suffered a loss in bargaining power. And because the black middle class tends to live in close proximity with the black poor, they, like the poor, directly suffer the impact of high unemployment, high crime, and neighborhood decline (Pattillo-McCoy 2000). Although the black middle class made substantial economic, political, and social progress between the 1960s and the 1980s, its progress stalled with the tightening conservative domination of America's national politics and with the decline of black political participation. In 1999, the net financial assets of the highest fifth of African American households was $7,448, only $448 above that of the lowest fifth of white American households (Shapiro 2004, 50). The black middle class became increasingly angry and politically alienated (see chapter 3).

A legacy from first-wave civil rights black mayoral elections has been intense racial conflict. Black mayors' elections were strenuously opposed by large majorities of white voters, labor unions, and, frequently, by white businesses (Colburn 2001). When Tom Bradley, one of the most moderate black mayors, was elected in the first wave as mayor of Los Angeles, blacks, unlike most black-led cities, were a small minority of the population. Although Bradley was not a civil rights mayor, he had built a strong biracial coalition emphasizing racial moderation, and the politically influential Jewish community provided substantial support (Sonnenshein 1993). And yet, the racial conflict surrounding his election was so intense that Bradley, in his inauguration in 1973, wore a bulletproof vest (Payne and Ratzan 1986, 133). Bradley's biracial coalition allowed him to reign as Los Angeles's mayor for twenty years. Unlike Bradley, many black mayors were accused of maintaining the bitter racial atmosphere that surrounded their elections as a way to rally black voters to their side in reelection campaigns. Coleman Young, Detroit's first black mayor, was often accused of pitting city blacks against white suburbanites and white businesses in order to hold onto his working-class black support (Applebome 1993; Rich 1989).

By the mid-1980s, high levels of violent crime, drug abuse, homelessness, school failure, and job loss undermined black civil rights mayors. By 1990, Detroit, New Orleans, and Atlanta, which had continuous black mayoral administrations for more than a decade, were three of the five cities with the highest poverty rates in the nation. Black mayors were increasingly criticized for assuming a role of race leader rather than as city manager, and accused of antagonizing white businesses and failing to entice them to their cities (Ross and Levine 2001, 120). New, younger, black mayoral candidates replaced the mayors of the civil rights era, promising to de-emphasize race, promote efficient government, and offer strategies to lure investors to strengthen downtown businesses and create jobs. One of the most prominent of these new technocratic mayors was Mayor Mike White of Cleveland, elected in 1989, the first black mayor in that city since Carl Stokes declined to run for reelection in 1972 after two terms in office. White ran on a platform of hiring more police officers, attracting business, and relieving Cleveland of court-ordered busing to integrate the public schools, but also offered plans to improve conditions in low-income neighborhoods. Stokes had won in 1967 against a white candidate by winning nearly all of the black votes and a small share of liberal white and downtown business support. In 1989, White won the Democratic primary with only a third of the black vote and 80 percent of the white vote, defeating a black competitor, former council president and longtime black community leader George Forbes (Larkin 1993). White was hailed as one of a "new breed" of black politicians. As Andrew Cuomo, secretary of Housing and Urban Development (HUD) put it in 1997, "You have a new breed of mayor, they are entrepreneurial, pragmatic, and intelligent" (Samuel 1997). Many observers celebrated the seeming transcendence of racial divisions evidenced in the de-emphasis on race. David Axelrod, a prominent political campaign consultant who worked on Mike White's 1993 reelection and on Dennis Archer's successful mayoral run in Detroit that same year, said, "I think people desperately want leaders who will make cities work, and they take them in whatever shapes, sizes and colors they come in" (Pierce 1993). Carl Stokes said of White, "He sees himself not as a [black] leader, but as a manager. The current black mayors have gone out of their way to distance themselves from civil-rights era leaders" (Moore 2002). To the *Wall Street Journal,* White was "stronger in Cleveland's boardrooms than in its back streets." Even George Forbes, who lost to White in the 1989 Democratic primary, admitted that, "I've got to tell you something. There's been a shift in politics. . . . White people are not going to vote for the black civil rights types. Mike White found a new solution on how to get into office and serve blacks and whites at the same time. It's a new era" (Larkin 1993).

Dennis Archer's election in Detroit in 1993 was greeted with a similar enthusiasm as White's election in Cleveland in 1989. Archer came to city hall after serving as a Michigan supreme court justice. He had been Coleman Young's campaign manager in his first reelection campaign in 1977. Archer now drew a sharp distinction between himself and Young: "My end-game is the same as the previous mayor, but my approach is different" (Samuel 1997). "We need to become a pro-business city," he pledged in his campaign, running as an interracial coalition-builder trying to mend relationships with the business community, the state legislature, and the whites suburbs, the groups that had been very hostile to the previous Young administration (Peirce 1993). Archer defeated Sharon McPhail, whom Coleman Young had endorsed to succeed him as mayor. McPhail suggested in the campaign that Archer represented outside "forces plotting to take over the city of Detroit" (Edmonds 1993). The day after his electoral victory, Archer said, "What used to be used as a race card in an effort to perpetuate business as usual has received a long-term burial" (Applebome 1993).

William ("Bill") Campbell, elected mayor of Atlanta in 1993 with 73 percent of the vote in a runoff against another black candidate, former Fulton County Commission Chairman Michael Lomax, was another of the new wave. Cynthia Tucker, editorial page editor for *The Atlanta Journal-Constitution* and herself African American, described Campbell, a Vanderbilt and Duke graduate, as "a successful attorney and a former federal prosecutor. Here was an example of the new breed of post-civil-rights black mayors, a well-educated and competent manager who would get things done" (Tucker 1998). According to a survey of Atlanta business leaders, Campbell was more popular with the downtown business community than Mayor Andrew Young, civil rights hero and close associate of the Reverend Martin Luther King Jr., or Maynard Jackson, Young's entrepreneurial predecessor, had been (Holmes 1995).[1]

Other second-wave technocratic mayors—Philadelphia's first black mayor was Wilson Goode, who served from 1984–92, and businessman Ray Nagin of New Orleans, who was elected in 2002—came to office promising greater efficiency in government. Another respected technocrat, Anthony Williams, won election as mayor of Washington, D.C., in 1998, coasting into victory over a weak Republican candidate, Carol Schwartz, after his African American competitor, Marion Barry, who had served four controversial terms as mayor, bowed out of the Democratic primary. Williams, a Harvard-trained lawyer, had served as the chief financial officer of the financial control board, which was authorized by Congress in 1996 to assume control of the district's finances when the city failed to balance its budget.[2] Williams's election marked an abrupt turning away from Barry's administration. A well-known civil rights leader in the 1960s, Barry had struck a defiant posture as mayor, championing home rule and thumbing his nose at Congress. Barry opened up local government to blacks for the first time, expanded the ranks of the black middle class, and delivered services to the elderly and summer jobs to youth. But Barry's regime was widely viewed as a dysfunctional patronage mill; the public housing authority and foster care program were put under receivership, and Barry himself was criticized for persistent confrontational racial rhetoric and for his personal behavior (Palmer 1998; Williams 1998). He embarrassed the city after hidden cameras caught him smoking crack cocaine.[3] Juan Williams, a *Washington Post* columnist, long-time Barry critic, and himself black, wrote that "Barry—having sold out the city's political independence and self-respect, having divided the races and chased off the middle class, having raised taxes and frightened off commercial enterprise, having trapped the poor in shameful schools and having left the city with inadequate and inefficient services—is now left to protect the only two things he truly cares about: his pension and his political future" (Williams 1995). Once in office, Anthony Williams promptly fired workers deemed as incompetent or lacking a proper work ethic (Cottman 1998).

What has the second wave of black mayors, the generation of technopoliticians accomplished? Cleveland's Mayor Mike White, who left office in 2002 after twelve years as mayor, the longest term of any mayor in Cleveland's history, had backed a sin tax to pay for the "Gateway" development, home of Jacobs Field and the Gund Arena, hosts of Cleveland's professional baseball and basketball teams, respectively. The project created sixty-five hundred jobs and gave the downtown area six new hotels and five hundred apartments. More than twenty-three hundred homes were built in the city in the 1990s, more than in any decade since the 1940s. Voters approved a $380 million bond issue and levy to repair schools (Quinn and Vosburgh 2002). But White's solicitation of business could not revitalize downtown Cleveland. Dillard's, the city's last downtown department store, closed in 2002, and the once bustling Euclid Avenue storefronts remained empty. City residents went to shop in suburban department stores. A hostile city council accused White of favoring downtown businesses over the welfare of the city's neighborhoods. In 2001, White supported a slate of candidates against council incumbents, and all but one lost (Quinn and Vosburgh 2002). A columnist for the *Cleveland Plain Dealer* wrote that "many business and civic leaders finally tired of him. And Cleveland lost any semblance of a reputation as a good place to do business," because "the political climate is so unsettled" (Larkin 2001). In 2004, the U.S. Census Bureau reported Cleveland's poverty rate at 31 percent, among the highest in the nation. So, too, White's commitment to transcending racial conflict was also largely unfulfilled. Before White left office, the police department accused his administration of leaking charges of police racism to the press. White fired and hired nine police chiefs in twelve years (Quinn and Vosburgh 2002).

Dennis Archer's record in Detroit paralleled Mike White's. Under Archer, economic development initiatives brought more than $13 million in new investment to downtown. The Detroit Tigers baseball team built a forty thousand-seat stadium, and three gambling casinos opened, boosting tax revenues. But under Archer, Detroit's long-standing problems of high unemployment, persistent poverty, high crime rates, and school dropout continued. Archer was criticized for being out of touch with the city's neighborhoods and inner-city youth. His successor, State Representative Kwame Kilpatrick, a young, black man who had run for mayor at age thirty-two, won the election in 2002. Mark Grebner, an urban analyst sympathetic to Archer, was pessimistic about Kilpatrick's chances: "The whole city administration is screwed up, the bureaucracy is completely corrupted and rotted and Kwame has inherited this." He added, "If Dennis Archer, whom I greatly respect couldn't do it, I don't know if Kwame can" (Marks 2002).

Atlanta's mayor Bill Campbell left office in 2001, at the end of his second term, under the cloud of a corruption scandal.[4] Even before the scandal broke, some of Campbell's early enthusiastic supporters had turned against his administration, in part because he had not de-emphasized race. Cynthia Tucker, the *Atlanta Journal-Constitution* editorial page editor, wrote:

> Campbell is allowing this period of relative urban prosperity
> to slip by without doing much about the tough problems:
> homelessness, crime, infrastructure decay, downtown revitaliza-
> tion. Though he can claim credit for a new downtown basketball

arena and a favorable citywide vote to raise money for infrastructure, too much remains undone. . . . He also frequently
resorts to race-baiting, charging his white critics with racism.
(Tucker 1998)

Mayor Anthony Williams of Washington, D.C., was also in hot water.
In September 2004, three veteran city council members were trounced in
their bid for reelection by three insurgents who charged that these council
members had failed to ensure that the poor get a piece of the city's expanding economic pie. One of these insurgents was former Mayor Marion
Barry, who ran in the poorest district in the city. Barry accused the city
council and Mayor Williams of focusing on rebuilding downtown while
neglecting affordable housing and neighborhood development. All three
insurgents opposed Williams's priority of raising taxes to build a Major
League Baseball stadium (Montgomery and Woodlee 2004). Soon after
this election, Mayor Williams indicated that his city agenda was "subject to
change based on things that have happened over the last couple of days. . . .
I mean, I'm not stupid" (Montgomery 2004).

In short, the nation's technocratic black mayors have suffered fates not
unlike their predecessors. They came to office promising change and significant improvements, and they were often blamed when they could not
stem the tide of urban decline; their primary success seemed to be providing grander facilities for professional sports. Neither the "civil rights" black
mayors nor the technocratic managers addressed two characteristics of
government structure that consistently undermine efforts to improve cities:
the first, the fiscal and political isolation of cities within larger regional and
state governments; and the second, the lack of empowerment of black civic
organizations. The first, related to race, is not a consequence of the agendas or style of black mayors but of the attributes of whites. Suburban voters, who tend to dominate state politics, are predominantly white—more
than half of the white population lives in the suburbs' inner and outer
rings—and ill-disposed to share the fiscal burdens of low-income central-
city residents. Less than a quarter of the white population and a majority
of the black population live in central cities (a large minority live in inner-
ring suburbs).[5] The departure of large numbers of more affluent taxpayers
to outer-ring suburbs, and the concentration in cities of large numbers of
poor black and Latino residents has heightened fiscal stress in central
cities. Tax burdens on city residents have increased, further stimulating

taxpayer flight, with a repetitive pattern of cause and effect. Political impediments to cities' ability to annex suburbs to create a wider region and distributed costs, particularly the rising voting power of suburbs, have helped suburbs insulate themselves from state-imposed cost sharing to maintain services in cities (Danielson 1976), even as whites drew their own livelihoods from the business core of cities they fled each evening. With the majority of virtually every state's population now residing in suburbs,[6] so James Caraley, editor of *Political Science Quarterly*, wrote, "there is no good political reason for governors or state legislatures to give priority to programs that benefit the poor, especially the urban poor" (Caraley 1996, 253).

Urban mayors are hamstrung as well by changes in the economy that put a premium on highly educated workers. Manufacturing employment, which had been the key source of upward mobility for earlier generations of urban immigrants, has become less and less available.[7] Service industry jobs in fields like health care, finance, insurance, real estate, and tourism have replaced manufacturing in the central city, but even service jobs are highly segmented between well-paid, high-skill jobs requiring college education or even graduate degrees that few blacks have, and low-paid, "dead-end" jobs (Levy 1998; Wilson 1978 [1980]). Central-city mayors who make marginal improvements in schools through school-based management and other efficiency techniques lack the substantial financial resources for major improvements in failing schools. Financial resources are concentrated in suburbs whose schools have superior facilities and superior services. As a consequence, upwardly mobile employment prospects for inner-city black youth are diminished.

Despite dramatic reductions in racial inequality over the last thirty years—including the end of de jure Jim Crow segregation, the emergence of a significantly larger black middle class, and the creation of a black political class—profound racial inequalities in conditions of daily life persist, particularly for the lower-middle class and the poor. In the thirty-year period from 1973, when Atlanta, Detroit, and Washington, D.C., elected their first black mayors, to 2003, the black youth jobless rate rose from 70.1 percent to 78.3 percent.[8] Many unemployed inner-city black youth turned to drug dealing and became entangled in the criminal justice system. Nationwide, 28 percent of black men will spend time in a state or federal prison during their lifetime (Brown et al. 2003).[9] Efficiency measures introduced by technocratic mayors were insufficient resources to counter these trends of a generation of inner-city black youth caught in a tangle of unemployment, drug dealing, incarceration, chronic disease, and lower life expectancy rates. Carl Stokes, commenting in 1994, noted that, "the greatest concern of mayors today is meeting their budgets and not increasing taxes. It is not the social needs of the city. . . . You can't decimate your city health department and then wonder why you're getting more cases of tuberculosis" (Sharkey 1994).

The other significant problem of governmental structure impeding the effectiveness of black mayors is the connection between their election and the broader empowerment of disempowered black civic organizations (Kilson 1987, 528). At best, black "civil rights" mayors put in place small networks of black businesses that gained city contracts, and small networks of government employees who benefited from patronage, as well as limited summer jobs programs, all of which generated a political base for their own reelection campaigns. The more technocratic black mayors who followed them, faced with cuts in federal aid and limited by their aversion to the appearance of racial favoritism, have been even less effective in empowering black civic leadership. Mike White's political weakness, for instance, was reflected in his thoroughly unsuccessful attempt to run a competing slate of candidates for Cleveland's hostile city council. Anthony Williams's similar political weakness as mayor of Washington, D.C., was reflected in former mayor Marion Barry's comeback to the city council. Williams has been respected, especially by the Congressional leaders who control much of the District's affairs, as an apolitical "numbers cruncher." Yet his political skills were so undeveloped that in 2002 he was nearly disqualified for a race for reelection because he failed to gather the required number of signatures to get his name on the Democratic primary ballot (Dionne 2002).

The lack of a strategy for grassroots black civic empowerment to shore up elected black mayors has weakened black political participation and, in consequence, has weakened black mayors in their struggles with white-led state legislatures and suburbs, and federal officials. Today, few political candidates—white or black—for national or state offices want to be known as urban liberals, and improving cities and addressing longstanding issues of racial inequality have been off the core national Democratic Party agenda for more than a decade.[10] Despite, or perhaps because of, the Democratic Party efforts to reposition itself to the center to counter a rightward trend in the Republican Party, blacks, feminists, and other traditional Democratic constituent groups are marginalized as "special interests" whose priority is not the common good. Even many progressive political analysts now argue that the Democratic Party, and progressive Democrats in particular, expect too much from black politics, that the black poor cannot be expected to participate at high levels, and that the emphasis of progressive and Democratic politics should be squarely on class-based needs, that is, principally on poor whites (Teixeira and Rogers 2000).

In short, the structural governmental issues confronting black mayors are, on the one hand, how to overcome municipal boundaries that create regional inequality and political weakness in state political bodies that starve cities of needed resources, and, on the other hand, how to use the administrative powers and resources available to mayors to strengthen systematically the political capacity of black civic organizations (and members of other poor groups) in order to tackle structures of inequality at the regional, state, and federal levels.

Neither the first nor the second wave of black mayors has had an effective strategy for overcoming racial conflicts in the electorate, no small endeavor at best. First-wave "civil rights" mayors, like Marion Barry of Washington, D.C., Coleman Young of Detroit, Richard Hatcher of Gary, and Maynard Jackson of Atlanta had won office in majority-black cities in highly racially polarized elections, all were fierce racial advocates known for their frequent denunciations of white racism and they, aside from their small core of liberal white voters, anticipated white hostility to their administrations, But because of their secure electoral base in majority-black cities, it was unnecessary to appeal to white voters in order to stay in office. They did not need to develop strategies for making significant inroads among white middle- and working-class voters.

Many technocratic black mayors, on the other hand, such as Mike White of Cleveland, Dennis Archer of Detroit, Anthony Williams of Washington, D.C., and Bill Campbell of Atlanta, came to office after running against other black candidates, often veterans of civil rights struggle, and relied on white voters to edge out these competitors. This "new breed" of mayors initially tended to argue that race was a distraction from the more important fiscal and managerial issues facing cities, and their stance reassured and hence made inroads among moderate white voters and businesses that shared that perspective. Urban analysts have called this political approach a "deracialized" strategy (McCormick and Jones 1993). The deracialization strategy to avoid racial conflict by tampering it down is a difficult posture to sustain within a public that is itself highly racially polarized.

In such a public, conservatives often scorn social-welfare programs, in cities as elsewhere, as interfering with taxpayers' freedom to spend their own money, and as instead rewarding a group that does not respect American values and has no capacity to earn their way to upward mobility.[11] Linking the undeserving poor with stereotypes of black laziness, reinforced by some urban sociologists, provided considerable momentum to critiques of urban social-welfare programs. In their wake, unserved inner-city residents have become apathetic, politically isolated, and programmatically abandoned at the city, state, and federal levels.[12] The successful popular framing of urban problems as attributable to an overly generous, racially favoritist, and excessively permissive urban liberalism devastated the ideology of progressive political liberalism in the eyes of the predominantly white and racially nervous public. But the deracialization approach of the second wave of black mayors has done little to transform the negative ideological framings of urban black poverty that perpetuate racial inequality and attribute racial inequality to black culture. Technocratic black mayors who fail to solve the problems of urban social decay often fall prey to charges of incompetence or poor leadership of their own people and are expected to perform miracles that white mayors are not asked to perform. Kurt Schmoke, black mayor of Baltimore from 1987 to 1995, cited a "kind of a prejudice against urban [black] officials running statewide," a *Denver Post* columnist then wrote. "I believe the inefficient management of cities by the so-called 'best and brightest black politicians'—like former Mayor Dennis Archer of Detroit and Mayor Marc Morial of New Orleans—may be a good reason why the idea of electing minority politicians to a higher office leaves an unpleasant taste in voters' mouths" (Hamblin 2002). When technocratic black mayors have complained of a racial double standard applied to their administrations, their complaint has been exploited as evidence that they have regressed back to the race-baiting tactics of their predecessors. Thus, when Atlanta's Mayor Bill Campbell accused the mainstream press of treating his administration in a racially biased manner, the editorial page of the *Atlanta Journal-Constitution* accused Campbell of "still playing the politics of the 1970s" (Tucker 1997). Actually, both charges have merit. Black mayors are often judged by double standards. Yet by avoiding conflicts and debates on the broad issues of a racialized governmental structures of regional inequality and racialized popular ideologies, the newer technocratic black mayors undermine their own defense against charges of incompetence and underachievement, and sometimes revert to racially polarizing rhetoric to increase black support for their reelection. Speaking of the inability of such black mayors to escape the racial context of urban problems, Ron Walters, a University of Maryland political scientist, noted that Dennis Archer, Mike White, and Marc Morial of New Orleans retired from politics or stepped down from city hall rather than seek higher office. "Essentially, because of race," Walters maintains, "they don't have any future" (Kiely 2002).

Transformative Black Politics: A Third Wave

A third kind of black mayoral politics does not fit either the "civil rights" or "technocratic" mold. Such mayors attempt to restructure government to strengthen the connection between holding office and grassroots black civic empowerment; they rely on grassroots civic empowerment for re-election, work to provide services for the poor rather than consolidating ties to downtown business elites at the expense of developing programs for poor neighborhoods, and confront white racism at the same time that they attempt to build ties with low-income whites and Latinos around substantive common issues. While none of these mayors has developed sufficient capacity to establish regional or state coalitions to pursue broad policy reforms at the regional or state level, their political direction and strategies might eventually enable others to do so. Chicago's Mayor Harold Washington, who served from 1983 and died in 1987, shortly after winning reelection, Baltimore's Mayor Kurt Schmoke, who served from 1987 to 1995, and New York's Mayor David Dinkins, who served from 1989 to 1993, and was defeated in his run for reelection, were mayors who moved, to varying degrees, in this direction.

The third wave in black mayoral politics is more rare, at least so far, in part because it is difficult to win transformative victories when the power and resources to improve the lives of the poor are largely out of the reach of mayors, and when the black poor are negatively perceived by the broad public. So, too, it is also easy to disappoint black constituents with unkept promises of change, when one's efforts are often thwarted by the fact that advocacy for the poor tends to arouse fright in businesses and taxpayers whose principle concern is to avoid higher taxes. It takes a high level of pre-existing black civic political capacity to assure black mayors their strong advocacy on poverty and race issues will be a feasible political project. In no case of "transformational" mayoral administrations have mayoral candidates themselves been the initial driving force. In each case, coalitions of community groups, unions, churches, and civil rights groups pressured and enticed black mayoral candidates to pursue an alternative "transformational" political strategy focused on changing the living conditions of the city's poorest citizens.

Some cities, with much greater black civic political capacity than others, have made it more feasible for black mayors to pursue transformational politics with some level of impunity. In the "union towns" of Chicago, New York, Baltimore, and Philadelphia, for example, African Americans have gained substantial power in municipal unions. When labor unions ally with black community groups, they can together exert effective pressure on black mayors to pay attention to the concerns of low-income blacks and support them when they do. This is especially true of cities where blacks are neither a large majority nor a small minority of the total city population, as is true of each of the four cities listed above. In cities with a substantial majority of blacks, like Atlanta, on the other hand, black mayors can ignore low-income blacks' efforts by demobilizing the black poor and by building or relying on alternative middle-class and business coalitions to support their regimes (Owens and Rich 2003). Where blacks are not a commanding majority of the electorate and where mayors' offices are strongly contested between blacks and whites, low-income black voters, ironically, have greater leverage over black mayors. None of the four cities listed above have large black majorities and all have had racially contested elections for the office of mayor in the past, and may well again. Three of the four—Chicago, Baltimore, and New York—have had "transformational" black mayors, at least to some extent, and there are signs that Mayor John Street of Philadelphia, reelected in 2003, too, may be in the process of establishing a transformational regime anchored in his relationship to city trade unions and community-church coalitions.[13] The small size of black populations in certain other large cities has precluded black civic organizations from playing a leading role in mayoral politics. Several major cities with small black populations have had black mayors but none of these elections were racially contested, and each of these mayors, Norman Rice in Seattle, who served from 1989 to 1997, Sharon Belton in Minneapolis, who served from 1994 to 2001, and Tom Bradley in Los Angeles, have taken a technocratic or deracialized approach to city governance.

Black mayors seldom pursue transformational strategies because such strategies require winning policy battles to reward the poor for their political participation and this eventually means establishing majority political coalitions with sections of the white middle class and white working class at the regional and state levels of government. Many black leaders and black intellectuals doubt these requisites can be met in view of the fact that quite a few black mayors were elected to office over strenuous white working-class and middle-class opposition and could make little headway in breaking down such racial divisions (Orr 1999; Powell 1999). Mayor Wilson Goode of Philadelphia, who was elected in 1983 and 1991, and who was a technocratic black mayor and a racial moderate, garnered only 18 percent of the white vote in his 1987 reelection campaign. The dismal track record of black candidates, particularly former mayors, who have run for statewide office also generates pessimism that broad interracial coalitions can actually be built beyond cities. Tom Bradley, the racially moderate black mayor of Los Angeles, twice lost later campaigns for governor of California (1982 and 1986). Andrew Young, the black mayor of Atlanta who made a transition from "civil rights" activism to deracialized-technocratic black mayoral politics, was trounced, 62 to 38 percent, by conservative white Democrat Zell Miller in a runoff election for the Democratic nomination for governor of Georgia in 1990 (Edsall 1993).[14] Moreover, black mayors in Chicago (where Richard Daley has repeatedly defeated black opponents), New York, Los Angeles, and Philadelphia—four the five largest cities in the United States—were successively replaced by more conservative white mayors (Judd and Swanstrom 2003, 413–14).

Nonetheless, while caution is warranted, there are reasons to challenge the view that low-income whites cannot be won over to interracial coalitions that consciously help poor blacks as well as whites. One is that black mayors, including those who have run for governor, have tended to run on platforms that do not offer substantive reasons for the poor—black, white, yellow, or brown—to support them. Both Tom Bradley and Andrew Young, who relied on close ties to downtown corporations to support their political careers, avoided strong advocacy on class and poverty issues that would jeopardize their business support. Most black mayors, discounting the possibility of building a base among low-income whites, have pursued similar strategies; they have failed to articulate openly a structural critique of economic and political institutions and policies that perpetuate black and white poverty and a class inequality that affects all races, and they have made weak efforts to organize the poor of any race. A different kind of black politics, such as the interracial coalition of the poor advocated by

Rev. Martin Luther King Jr., in the 1960s, could address these issues directly, including the view that racial inequality is attributable to the behavior of blacks themselves, and set out to organize and unite poor and marginalized groups on an interracial basis.

Another reason to believe that whites may join interracial coalitions is that many suburbanites, including large numbers of whites, are now experiencing sharp declines in their quality of life. More than ten million Americans in 2000, 18 percent of all suburbanites, lived in poor suburbs (a suburb with a per capita income of less than 75 percent of its metropolitan area) compared with only 8.4 percent of suburbs considered poor in 1980 (Swanstrom et al. 2004). Suburbs now suffer many of the same poverty-related problems as central cities, and without the amenities, central business districts, and professional services that central cities possess. So, too, the rapid rise of the Latino population in cities and suburbs changes the equation and may change the dynamics. Nearly one in four residents in the largest U.S. cities now considers himself or herself Latino, compared with one in ten elsewhere in the nation (Berube 2003, 140). And, a majority (54 percent) of U.S. Latinos live in suburbs, where the suburban Latino population grew by 71 percent in the 1990s. Together, white workers in poor suburbs and Latinos (and to a lesser extent, Asians) offer prospects for strong city-suburban coalitions that could become a political force in many states in the future (Drier, Mollenkopf, and Swanstrom 2001).

A strategy of organizing for power beyond the borders of the city, for trying to win over working-class whites to fight racism as well as their own class oppression, for utilizing the powers of city government to strengthen and sustain neighborhood and labor organizing, and for seeking alliances with Latinos (and Asians in some cities), could be a return, in many respects, to a kind of movement politics. Such politics involves a high risk of initial failure, long-term effort, and, no doubt, a contentious struggle over racial ideologies and a sorting out of group identities. It is a difficult politics of last resort, but the easier alternatives have largely run their course. The "civil rights" model has reached its demographic limit and "civil rights" candidates seem to have lost the enthusiastic support of the black poor (Elliot-Banks 2000; Frank D. Gilliam 1996; Mollenkopf 2003, 136). Cities with large black majorities have already elected black mayors, and in many of these cities—Detroit, Cleveland, Washington, D.C.—black "civil rights" candidates have been defeated by technocratic black candidates who forged coalitions with disaffected black and white voters. Few other large cities, including New York, Los Angeles, Chicago, and Houston are likely to develop black majorities in the future. The technocratic alternative to "civil rights" politics obviates the need for a "black" politics with its traditional emphasis—even if only token or symbolic—on advocating for the black poor, and it does not envision organizing the poor to change dominant policy rules and political alignments. Constrained to "efficiency" within fiscal and political structures that put them at a disadvantage, the technocrats offer improvements over civil rights mayors that are marginal at best.

There is another practical reason for black mayors and civic leaders to pursue a "transformative" path in black politics: as a practical matter, there is no way to rejuvenate the nation's ailing cities without structural changes in the way cities are financed, but structural change cannot come about without fundamental change in the political isolation of the city's neediest residents—the black, and increasingly, the Latino poor—from mainstream white America. Black mayors and other electoral officials cannot separate their declining political status, increasing insecurity in office, and their abortive, near impossible political future beyond city hall from the condition of cities they govern.

Is Empowerment Possible?

In the mid 1970s Richard Cloward and Frances Fox Piven argued, in an analysis of power, that the black poor lack resources for sustained participation in politics and public policy.

> Much Negro leadership exists largely by the grace of white institutions: white political parties and government agencies, white unions and businesses and professions, even white civil-rights organizations. Everything in the environment of the Negro politician, civil servant or professional makes him attentive to white interests and perspectives. If black leadership were based in separatist institutions—particularly economic ones, such as black labor unions—it might be capable of some independence, but those separatist institutions do not now exist. (Cloward and Piven 1974, 252)

Cloward and Piven said, in addition, that the poor were not readily organized because many were out of the workforce, geographically dispersed, without economic incentives to participate in organizations, and socially conditioned to believe in their powerlessness. "People who know they cannot win do not often try" (Cloward and Piven 1974, 78). They concluded that a traditional mass-membership organization was not an effective model for organizing the poor because the poor had no resources to sustain such an organization. Leaders of mass organizations, they said, promote the false belief that the poor can alter politics and policy through regular political channels and that external resources made available to the poor in the 1960s were a response to poor people's organization rather than "widespread black unrest" (Piven and Cloward 1999, 336). Once leaders become "enmeshed in a web of relationships with governmental officials and private groups . . . external resources become a substitute for a mass base." As mass unrest subsides, the external resources are withdrawn and the result is "organizational collapse" (Piven and Cloward 1999, 317, 331). To Cloward and Piven, disrupting the operation of mainstream economic and political institutions was the poor's only effective option to gain the attention of elected officials, so they therefore viewed the post-1960s ascension of blacks into elected office and bureaucracies as actually depleting the strength of black movements (Piven and Cloward 1999, 255). Except during periods of economic, social, or political crises, the poor could not be expected to engage in political action. "Cadre organizations" should be networked together to plan disruptive strategies in the periods between structural crises (Piven and Cloward 1999, 284). Disruption risks violent repression, and although Cloward and Piven play down this possibility, they acknowledge that to their fellow organizers in the welfare-rights movement, a cadre-elite steering the poor masses toward potentially harmful disruption was a manipulative and antidemocratic process: "Our emphasis on mass mobilization with cadre organizations as the vehicle struck organizers as exceedingly manipulative. Their perspective on organizing was imbued with values which they considered democratic. The poor had a right to run their own organizations, and to determine their own policies and strategies" (Piven and Cloward 1999, 284). Piven stated recently that, "we were pessimistic, but the subsequent losses in all of the policy areas championed by these [1960s poor people's] movements shows that we were correct" (Piven 2004). The thrust of Piven and Cloward's persistent argument: that the poor cannot be empowered within the present political-economic structure, remains highly influential in urban and black political studies.[15]

Social movements of the poor have declined since the early 1970s, yet effective black politics has not declined in all cities and at all times. The exceptions call into question some of Cloward and Piven's theses. While transformative political movements are not the dominant trend by any means, the fact that some emerged nonetheless suggests that generalizations about the poor's incapacity to achieve power or make substantive change in cities are too sweeping. Greater attention needs to be addressed to local political structures and local political dynamics to understand why organizations of the poor gained power in some places and not others, or in some time periods in some cities and not in others. By understanding how poor people's power has been assembled in some places and exploring the motivations of actors who assembled that power, the obstacles they faced and overcame and those that they did not overcome, we can read more fine-grained analyses of the actual dynamics of city and political structures under diverse circumstances, and offer more grounded—and perhaps more adjustable—conclusions about the prospects for change in U.S. cities.

Three decades ago, Cloward and Piven did not anticipate government serving to empower poor organizations, thus their insistence on mobilizing the poor for acts of disruption (following the earlier Saul Alinsky model of disruptive political action for the oppressed) rather than organizing the poor for regular participation in voting and policy making. If no subsequent examples of elections of blacks to office had led to grassroots empowerment, Cloward and Piven's theory would remain valid. But in Harold Washington's victory in Chicago in 1983, for one, poor people gained political attention and leverage through voting (see chapter 2). Fortunately, disruption (risking one's life or limb) is not the only way for the poor to get the attention of elected officials (and especially if an elite does not do all the planning). Democratic rights in the South were achieved also in the extraordinarily successful civil rights revolution of the 1950s and 1960s, largely through huge sacrifices by poor people who, through nonviolent protest, not disruption—the disruption was caused by civil authorities and angry whites—won moral, legal, and political victories.

Political machines have been opposed by black political movements because of their exclusion of all but a few token blacks and their control of blacks, but political machines are not the only forms of organization available to the poor. Cloward and Piven considered labor unions more effective than other kinds of poor people's organizations because labor unions could disrupt the economy, had resources, and could protect workers' right to strike, but, they wrote, "It is our view that this organizational form is not available to the contemporary poor" (Piven 1974, 81). Cloward and Piven rightly argued that labor unions of the 1960s (as for generations earlier) provided few leadership opportunities for blacks. The emergence of black-led unions would be an event of potential consequence for Cloward and Piven's thesis.[16] Thirty years later, racial transition has occurred in many predominantly black and Latino union locals across the country; it is not unusual to see minority-led unions wearing "two hats": working within umbrella black or Latino political coalitions while operating also in inter-racial labor federations. This opens the possibility that racial solidarity might lead some unions to align with, and provide political resources for, other people of their race, such as welfare recipients or immigrants, and seek to persuade their larger interracial labor federations to do the same (see chapter 3). It is worth noting that if minority labor leaders depended on a "new outbreak of mass defiance" and a spurning of "the rules and authorities of the union system," as Piven and Cloward suggested, they would not be in a position to support poor people's organizing and mobilizing today (Piven and Cloward 1999, 175).

I argue that, contrary to withdrawing from civic organizing and engaging in the political system in favor of a search for the right moment to mobilize for disruption, the greatest risk for effective black politics is to withdraw from the political process and from civic organizing. Without broad political participation, African Americans, at 12 percent of the national population as of 2000, will be too small a group to wield decisive impact on politics in many states and in the nation as a whole. Withdrawal from any action also threatens gains—including growing strength in labor unions and control of local governments—that blacks have already won. Broad, regular, and persistent civic participation provides a range of experience and potential upward mobility and encourages deeper democracy within black politics—an important gain, since learning how to overcome internal differences itself, including domination of women and other sub-group advocates, prefigures democratic approaches to overcoming deep divisions in broader interracial coalitions.

Cloward and Piven noted that the prevalent American ideology disadvantaged the black poor "because the contemporary poor are isolated and marked off as deviant by a predominantly middle-class political culture," but they did not explore the possibility that public debate on highly contested race and class issues might enlarge understanding of poverty among the white nonpoor, and, therefore, enhance the possibility of interracial and interclass political cooperation and resource sharing (Cloward and Piven 1974, 84). These are still vital and problematic issues. The poor, especially the black poor, are unpopular with the nonpoor, especially whites (Gilens 1999). While political theorists argue that in an ideal world, democratic deliberation (public political debates) values all voices equally, and also that the power of a good argument outweighs the superior resources of strong groups, it is dangerous to confuse either with the real world. Yet disruption often leads to less understanding and more hostility and fear on the part of opponents, which is why it is so dangerous. In real politics, marginal groups must struggle mightily to have their voices heard in opposition to prevailing ideologies of majority groups, and to enlarge their opponents' understanding of marginal-group demands. Strong black organization and regular and persistent participation increases a minority's ability to be noticed in broader political coalitions, and this, in turn, increases political confidence in the value and the promise of working with and sometimes resisting other groups. The process can be seen clearly in cities, such as Baltimore and Philadelphia, where strong community-church-labor coalitions have gained a voice in politics for blacks and won significant concessions, as well as moral recognition, from city officials. I call "deep pluralism" the process through which marginal groups attain roughly equal power in intra- and intergroup political deliberation, and gain consideration of issues previously ignored or suppressed, such as the legitimacy of established political, social, and economic institutions and policies. It does not avoid the dynamics of race, class, or gender but confronts them directly in order to overcome the disability they impose on minorities or on others without access to established power.

Participatory Democrats argue that organizing people is a counterweight to the power of organized money in the political process and maintain that participation can give citizens a sense of their own power and can lead them to revise their self-interests and enhance their recognition of others. In the absence of participation, Peter Bachrach and Aryeh Botwinick write, the "power gap between ruler and ruled increases, the masses can become alienated, disaffected, and mean" (Bachrach and Botwinick 1992, 32). A crucial practical dilemma for deep pluralism is how blacks can achieve power in competitive struggles with whites and other groups for available resources, and how to debate deeply held ideologies of difference and inferiority, a difficult task in itself, while, at the same time, avoiding racial bitterness that derails deliberation about a politics of common (cross-racial) good. The solution for strong political disagreements, as on matters of race, Robert Putnam maintains, is greater civic engagement (Putnam 2000, 355). Regions of the country with the most civic participation are the most tolerant of racial integration, civil liberties, and gender equality. But Putnam makes a clear distinction between good and bad kinds of civic engagement, extending the view that "social capital" (norms of trust, cooperation, and reciprocity) has two forms: "bonding," or exclusive social capital differs from "bridging" or inclusive social capital. White opposition to metropolitan busing to achieve racial integration and the defense of the racially exclusive neighborhood schools has been largely based on white *bonding* social capital; support of school desegregation, by contrast, on building social capital of the *bridging* type between racial groups. But Putnam offers no solution other than building more bridging social capital for conflict between tightly bonded groups. His limited proposal of supporting groups that seek to "bridge the racial, social, and geographic cleavages that fracture our metropolitan areas" seems to suggest that these divisions can be overcome entirely on a volunteer basis. Putnam does not, for example, promote government reform to enforce compliance with metropolitan integration. Some political scientists see dangers in contemporary political activism. Morris Fiorina believes that democratic discourse can be harmed by "emotional and excessive" activist rhetoric (Fiorina 1999). Fiorina suggests that the only democratic corrective is to encourage more participation by average citizens to dilute the influence of political extremists from the right and left. But a focus on political moderation does not take into account the radical critique shared by a significant majority of blacks and a small minority of whites that U.S. institutions discriminate by class and also that racial equality will be not achieved in their lifetime, if ever (Harms 1994). Fiorina's proposal for increased political participation, without a concomitant development in democratic understanding and skills, could, contrary to his expectations, increase racial confrontation and bring little hope that increased participation will make government more accountable to, and more effective for, less powerful minorities.

One other criticism of participatory democracy needs to be taken seriously, that popular participation may make majority domination of minorities worse and generate more group conflict. In response, deliberation theorists propose a participatory process in which the affairs of political or civic associations are governed by respectful public deliberation among its members (Cohen 1997, 67). John Dryzek writes that it invokes, "persuasion rather than coercion, manipulation, or deception." Dryzek goes so far as to say that, "the essence of democracy itself is now widely taken to be deliberation, as opposed to voting, interest aggregation, constitutional rights, or even self government" (Dryzek 2000, 1).

In *The Miner's Canary*, Lani Guinier and Gerald Torres take a deliberative approach toward overcoming racial conflicts and transforming democracy. Guinier and Torres offer a three-dimensional process for building cross-racial alliances that can overcome racial conflicts as well as transcend the limits of public policy. They begin with protecting the "canaries," particularly, black movements who warn of dangerous problems, arguing that although a cross-racial politics of common good must respect the dignity and autonomy of individuals and groups, black solidarity provides resources and a "political space" for blacks to affirm their worth in the face of oppression, to develop notions of group and self-interests, and to struggle for those interests (Guinier and Torres 2002, 100). Unless the canaries are protected and heard, dominant or hegemonic ideologies that hide structural causes for distributional inequalities will continue to blame groups for their own conditions and pit poor groups against one another in zero-sum competition for limited resources. Guinier and Torres would move from local group to interracial forums, where blacks should "shift" from "mere solidarity and group consciousness" to "strategic deployment of race consciousness," seeking to align themselves with the white poor and other groups with whom blacks share a substantive interest in redistribution and against oppression.

Groups need to engage internal hierarchies of power, both to promote critical over narrow competitive ideologies and to develop the confidence and the listening and speaking skills needed to participate on a more equal and effective basis in larger "risk-taking ventures." They say that "a participatory framework needs to address internal, not just external, racial and political hierarchies and emphasize democratic practices and accountability from the inside out" (Guinier and Torres 2002, 153). How this can be concretely achieved is left open. They do not discuss where bridge-building leaders, those who lead the shift from competitive relations to cross-racial alliances, come from. It is not clear whether they see few or many such leaders, where others might come from, or whether and why similar movements have failed.

Archon Fung and Erik Olin Wright's Empowered Participatory Governance (EPG) focuses on community representatives and government officials' collaboration on and debates about problems of common local concern such as high levels of crime. Fung found a broadening of formal participation in civic activity among inner-city residents in Chicago and successful collaboration with police. But the scope of deliberation he reviewed was narrow, limited to nuisances such as drug dealing. Fung and Wright maintain that problems of broader scope, and considerable black criticism, had to be sidelined for collaboration to work and they criticize "many adversarial groups and their constituencies," by which they mean labor unions, the NAACP, and some feminist and environmental groups for embracing "cognitive frames," that is, strongly felt perspectives, "that do not lend themselves to collaborative problem-solving approaches" (Wright 2003, 282). These groups "assign culpability," and "depict Manichean protagonists and antagonists (e.g., brutal police officers and defenseless youth), and prescribe simple and direct policy solutions":

> Participatory collaboration, by contrast, requires much less rigid diagnostic, prognostic, and therefore motivational cognitive frames. . . . [and frequently] depends upon sustained and deep cooperation between diverse parties such as police officers and minority residents, parents and educators, workers and managers, and environmentalists and developers. "Injustice frames" that demonize or recriminate adversaries again obstruct such joint action. . . . Unsurprisingly, many adversarial organizations resist such revolutionary transformations. They not only erode bases of solidarity and support, but also call into question the deep purposes of leaders and the very reasons that these organizations exist. (Wright 2003, 282)

In effect, Fung and Wright require black advocates to adopt a noncritical attitude toward government authorities and larger structural inequality as a condition of their participation in collaborative projects. This clearly shows a power inequality between local government representatives and community representatives. Yet Mayor Harold Washington came to office in Chicago in 1983 on the shoulders of a black and progressive white civic movement dedicated to overturning decades of centralized white machine control and transferring power to neighborhoods (Clavel and Wiewel 1991; Gills 1991; Mangcu 1997). Without a connection between EPG and broader city politics, it is difficult to envision how civic groups can gain power to contend with city authorities in EPG-type initiatives. It is hard to imagine that a relatively conservative mayor (in contrast to Mayor Washington) would allow citizen participation initiatives to assume a broad and critical political character.

For Fung and Wright, strong criticism of government programs and representatives is disruptive to local problem-solving collaboratives with government and is to be avoided. To Guinier and Torres, critical black perspectives on the economy and politics are a strategic resource for exposing dominant social narratives that justify current inequality to its victims and promote cooptation. From a critical perspective like that of Guinier and Torres, Fung and Wright are suggesting a strategy that may lead to broader cooptation of black activists. However, Guinier and Torres say little about how long-term movements can be generated or sustained. Nor does Fung and Wright's local problem-solving approach suggest mechanisms for overcoming race and class cleavages to assemble the political power necessary to change policies of broad scope. Deliberation, in theory, offers a counterweight to the powerlessness of resource-poor and weaker groups in politics. But deliberation theory lacks a view on how marginal groups gain and leverage power. In "deep pluralism," marginal groups must attain power to have a voice in political deliberation. Unlike processes like EPG, authoritative figures like local government authorities do not gain an upper hand. The crucial dilemma for my theory of deep pluralism is how marginal groups are to achieve power in competitive struggles with other groups while still striving for a politics of common (cross-racial) good. And how can a deep interracial pluralist politics appeal to black political actors (and others) so as to be applied in specific practical political contexts. *Double Trouble* considers how black mayors might turn from a politics of symbolic representation to building internally pluralistic black grassroots movements and interracial coalitions that achieve substantive changes in public policy.

Power and Deep Pluralism

Local problem solving and local participation more generally operate within the structural context of city politics and the broader context of state, regional, and national politics. Devolution of power to the community level, and increased community participation, does not solve resource problems in cities. Indeed, increased black political participation may exacerbate already considerable tensions between inner city and suburbs (Orr 1999). A credible political strategy cannot ignore these broader power issues at higher levels in the political structure and the need for multiracial alliances across racial divides. Nor can it ignore important variations in political structures from city to city and region to region. It is no accident that the EPG case studies are taken from Chicago, which has a legacy of strongly centralized government and exclusion of blacks from policy making. In Chicago a strong black citywide coalition arose in opposition both to elite concentration of power and white control of the city and elected a black mayor, Harold Washington, who strongly supported government devolution of power to the neighborhoods. But some cities, of the reform type, are highly decentralized and activists have difficulty organizing across boundaries. In other cities, a few blacks have been incorporated into parts of the city government but have little power, leading to internal struggles within the black community between incorporated and excluded elements over the importance of governmental reform and community participation.

So, too, the characteristics of the voting population and their history of conflict and cooperation (political demography) matter. Black politicians running for mayor or governor in predominantly white districts, and those running for mayor of large-majority-black cities require differing strategies. The former tend to have low support among white voters and need a high voter turnout from all sectors of the black community; the latter do not need high black voter turnout.[17] These electoral requirements create differences, in turn, between black politicians' advocacy of broad substantive policy change to gain needed support of poor blacks in need of jobs, housing, healthcare, and other big-ticket items, and politicians who can win without strong support from the black poor and therefore support policies that might scare away downtown business taxpayers.

Gear Shifting: The Strategic Use of Civic Power in Building Coalitions

Deliberation theories tend to frame deliberation as a positive alternative to power struggles where resources are decisive and the poor and weak groups are considered to be at a disadvantage; they tend to frame power negatively. Joshua Cohen and Joel Rogers write, "In ideal deliberation, the only power that prevails is, as Habermas puts it, the 'force of a better argument'—and that is a force equally available to all" (Cohen and Rogers 2003, 242). It remains unclear how the ideal of deliberation emerges from the practical world of power. Contrary to the generally negative concept of power in deliberation theory, power may play a positive and necessary role in encouraging interracial coalitions that can form an initial basis for cross-racial deliberation. For racial minorities, interracial political deliberation is not always best advanced by direct engagement with the majority: neither group may be able to withstand the tensions created by unequal power, mutual distrust, suspicion or enmity, and poorly developed skills of self-reflection and persuasion on both sides. In fact, blacks have tended to withdraw from such processes, some retreating instead to an essentialist notion of black solidarity that they hope will protect them. Internal group power can increase blacks' confidence that they will not be manipulated in coalitions with other more powerful groups.

One of the fears of treating black or other racial group activism positively is that it will antagonize whites and impede interracial coalition building. Habermas, for example, explicitly distinguishes between the white feminist movement, which has "long been anchored in the acknowledged universalistic foundations of morality and law" and black movements since the civil rights movement that he says are immersed "in a particularistic self-affirmation of black sub-cultures" and are "of a defensive character" (Habermas 1987, 393). But the assumption that black politics emerges from a shared black identity, or that it is an apolitical expression of racial pride, whereas other movements are more genuinely political and less particularistic, bears little relation to contemporary politics. Habermas's view reflects lack of familiarity with black movements: black civic groups have had continual difficulty gaining allies for broad "universalistic" structural changes of the type originally sought by the civil rights movement (Hamilton and Hamilton 1997). In this regard a focus on the *substance* of black demands is critical. Blacks want from politics the basis of racial advocacy, the same things that other groups have sought and continue to seek: equal rights, good jobs, education, decent housing, and safe neighborhoods (Hamilton and Hamilton 1997). Blacks do not engage in politics simply, or even primarily, in order to socialize with members of their own group (or others), to make friends, or even to establish trusting relationships and social capital with strangers. Much the same can be said of other groups' motivations in politics. This is not a bad thing, because if warm social feelings were required to forge interracial coalitions in politics, as some social-capital theorists seem to suggest, or if attitudes and hearts had to change before progress is possible, as some religious advocates maintain, it is doubtful that interracial coalitions would ever get started in many cities.[18] In fact, if these things were required, there would have been no civil rights legislation or court decisions. The simple truth is that behavior often changes before attitudes change, and, even working with one's enemies can make sense if both sides have something to gain or if they are interdependent. Warm feelings, trust, alliance building, and a renegotiation of group identity as the lines between friend and enemy get redrawn, are all important to sustaining relationships, but they do not have to precede political and economic progress and they alone cannot overcome initial hostility.

A focus on the substantive outcomes of black politics, on who gets what and why, also serves as a healthy corrective to the manipulative use of overheated appeals for racial solidarity within black politics itself. A focus on substance prompts the question of whether electing black mayors, or electing blacks to governmental office generally, is necessary or sufficient for changing the daily lives of most blacks. I argue that it is neither. Experience has demonstrated that electing black mayors or members of Congress is not sufficient to produce observable social change in the lives of most blacks. And, provided blacks have strong civic political organizations, it is not necessary to elect African Americans to ensure that black interests are protected in politics. This is not to say that electing blacks to office is unimportant for its own sake and as evidence of inclusion, or that having the capacity to elect a member of one's own group to govern a city has no strategic value in bargaining with other groups or in empowering black civic groups. But treating the election of black mayors as an intrinsic and sufficient good for all blacks, regardless of substantive outcomes for blacks generally, contributes to grassroots cynicism and despair, and reinforces black demobilization, which, in turn, facilitates political ascendancy of forces in the society whose goals are inimical to the interests of the poor. Race pride with token rewards and no positive consequences for the lives of the people is too high a price to pay for the protection of black mayors and other black officials.

Another of the most influential theories or urban politics since the early 1970s has been urban regime theory. Regime theory takes a middle position between the pessimistic structural determinism of the Cloward and Piven argument and the dismissal of structural obstacles found in traditional pluralism.[19] Clarence Stone, a leading political science proponent of regime theory, moves down the ladder of generality from Cloward and

Piven to argue that poor or excluded groups do have opportunities to achieve power in cities, but that those opportunities have limits that vary from city to city. In his study of Atlanta, Stone argues that voting gave blacks access to power and resources through government with black mayors able to negotiate over city development policies with the city's permanent power bloc, the downtown business community. City policy did not come about through government commands or business-directed prerogatives but through informal political negotiations between political leaders, business, and key powerful civic organizations (such as the press). Because this informal coalition in Atlanta secured the resources needed to generate and complete agreed-upon projects over time, Stone characterized Atlanta's governing arrangement as a "regime" (Stone 1989), stable because black mayors won white business support and ensured that their black business supporters secured a share of city-funded contracts. These black businesses were core supporters of black mayors in Atlanta's black communities.

Stone argues that Atlanta's regime has been conservative because black leaders did not extend benefits to poor blacks, and because poor blacks lack sufficient organization and resources to hold black mayors accountable. But he believes that if poor blacks could find ways to organize and garner resources, they could push regimes to become progressive, for example, to manage downtown expansion in favor of neighborhood-oriented policies. Stone more recently refers to El Paso, Texas, as an example of an "opportunity expanding" or progressive regime. Thus his regime theory is not structurally deterministic. Business is vital to the economic health of cities, and has ample resources to engage in politics and policy making, but it does not have the power to run cities on its own and it must win government approval and civic support for major initiatives that it favors. The poor can exert leverage if they gain capacity to weld it.

Stone subordinates ideology or "value consensus" as central to regime and public-policy formation simply because he finds it unlikely to be achieved and too diffuse to be effective:

> Problems big enough to contend for priority status on a city's
> governing agenda are unlikely to evoke value consensus as a
> basis for action. Hence regime analysis should look to coalition
> politics rather than shared values as the path to explanation.
> Any consensus is likely to be too general to explain a concrete
> course of action. (Stone 2004, 11)

Criticizing pluralist political economists, like Paul Peterson, who assert the primacy of unitary economic interests based on a particular ideology of economic self-interest over the primacy of political contestations, Stone cites the political theorist Benjamin Barber: "There must be citizens before there can be common truth" (Stone 2004, 6). Politics comes before ideological consensus around public and private interests. But, I would say that Barber's point misses a key step because before there are "citizens," at least in the sense of active participants in a society, there must some shared concept of who deserve to be treated as citizens, that is, at least one ideological "common truth" is necessary (Smith 1997). An adequate analysis needs to incorporate ideology as well as political structures and civic organizational formations. Part 1 of this book examines the role of local political structures, black civic power, and race in influencing the course of black mayoral administrations. Part 2 of this book focuses on the case of New York City, with illustration of how racialized ideologies of deserving and undeserving citizens have played an important role in that city in decisions on budget priorities and on attributions of blame for crime and other forms of urban social decay. From a different angle, the political scientist Adolph Reed has highlighted the degree to which black solidarity, itself based on a concept of group identity, hence a form of ideology, has blunted black criticism and protest against urban policies and institutions in cities that are predominantly black run (Reed 1999). Reed maintains that there is a "conceptual bias in black political discourse against accounting for intra-racial stratification." Reed also argues that given the high fiscal and political costs of incorporating the needs of the poor, it is easier for black administrations to reward politically active upper-strata blacks (Reed 1999, 98–99). Reed's remedy is "greatly increased and informed pressure from the black electoral constituency, which in sum implies proliferation of public, policy-focused debate" (Reed 1999, 110). Political and economic structures and the power of civic groups are central to urban political power, and so are ideological presumptions and conflicts—for positive or negative consequences— including those of race. The analysis in this book focuses on all three, with deep pluralism at the core. Some of the questions the book engages are: What are current structural obstacles to black political participation and what kinds of structural reforms would be helpful? How do marginal groups assemble power needed to contend with dominant ideologies and form coalitions with sufficient power to alter political and economic barriers? Why haven't interracial class coalitions emerged over last thirty years? What opportunities exist for deep pluralist discourse and coalition building, and what role can mayors play?

Regime theorists maintain that voting and civic organizing does give the poor access to power, but there nevertheless is a near consensus in the urban politics field that the power thus far achieved by inner-city blacks or Latinos falls far short of that needed to enact major social change. I agree with that consensus. Some leading urbanists are advocating the formation of central-city/suburban coalitions of the poor and sinking middle class as a way of gaining the power needed to sway urban policies. I do not dispute these findings and I share the advocacy of interracial regional coalitions. But deep pluralism goes further and asks who will build and cement these coalitions. The third, "transformative," trend in black politics is one that has been essentially overlooked by the field. It is the intent of this book that those who study urban politics take into account the success and analyze causes of failure of transformative politics that can be remedied and that those who live in inner cities engage in the practice of deep pluralism that has the potential of transforming their lives.

From Coalitions to Alliances

Abraham Lincoln argued in 1854 that the "universal feeling" of the great mass of white people, not justice and "sound judgement," must guide state action on race. Slavery was not acceptable but "we cannot . . . make them equals":

> What then? Free them all, and keep them among us as under-lings? Is it quite certain that this betters their condition? I think I would not hold one in slavery, at any rate; yet the point is not clear enough for me to denounce people upon. What next? Free them, and make them politically and socially, our equals? My own feelings will not admit of this; and if mine would, we well know that those of the great mass of white people will not. Whether this feeling accords with justice and sound judgement, is not the sole question, if indeed, it is any part of it. A universal feeling, whether it is well or ill-founded, cannot be safely dis-regarded. We cannot, then, make them equals.[20]

Lincoln's argument cuts to the core of theoretical and practical dilemmas facing a democratic republic. How does such a republic, based fundamentally on the will of the majority, ensure freedom and justice for a minority that the majority disdains or despises?[21] How can the minority in this circumstance become more than "underlings"? How, if ever, can minorities be considered "equals"? What can be done about dissatisfied minorities? Can their allegiance to the rule of the majority be assured? How can it be assured?

Lincoln understood the practical fallacy of the standard response to racial division: in circumstances where the majority does not believe in the equal worth of persons and does not want to treat denigrated persons or groups fairly, procedural guarantees will provide limited protection.[22] Government cannot ignore the attitudes and opinions of the majority without losing its own legitimacy, or even risking political instability. Certainly, government cannot legislate that individual citizens or groups regard one another favorably (Johnston 1994). The majority is the foundation of political authority in democracy; in a republic, the majority is limited but still holds dominant power. If the majority bears ill will against a minority, the minority may lack reliable protection because, in the words of legal scholar Frank Michelman "rights ultimately are nothing but determinations of prevailing political will."[23] Political theorists are well aware of this problem, and have not solved it. And there is always concern that contempt, hatred, and violence may break through the surface of near consensus in pure democratic societies. "In the real world," writes the liberal pluralist Robert Dahl, " . . . what constitutes 'a people' for democratic purposes are far more likely to come from political action and conflict, which will often be accompanied by violence and coercion, than from reasoned inferences from democratic principles and practices . . . in solving this particular problem democratic theory cannot take us very far" (Dahl 1989, 209).

This book argues that there is no consensus in the United States about treatment of racial minorities, certainly no agreement to treat blacks in particular, in the United States, equally to whites, and that Lincoln's dilemma is of urgent contemporary relevance. Where deep moral conflict or prejudice separates groups, oppressed minority groups have two essential choices: either to accept or propose separation into distinct territorial units defined by race, or in effect, by race—a proposal seriously considered by Lincoln, by black Pan-Africanists, and by the apartheid regime in South Africa—or to an ideal for a politics of common good, through "political action and conflict."

Some activists make a distinction between coalitions and alliances. The coalition relationship is captured in a slogan promoted by the Industrial Areas Foundation (IAF), a leading community organizing group, "no permanent friends, no permanent enemies." An alliance is more of a permanent friendship. The problem with the "no permanent friends" idea is that it precludes reimaging one's political identity and original commitments so as to decide on forming an alliance with another group. The original group never broadens its concept of "self" as a result of its dealings with others.

How, then, do groups make the transition from coalitions of convergent self-interest to alliances, or, as in friendship, to a politics of shared commitment to participation in a relationship and to efforts to understand others' points of view even if disagreeable? There is little empirical research on this central question. Political deliberation that aims to bring together blacks who deeply distrust the police and police representatives cannot succeed by requiring adversarial blacks to change their views or excluding them from the process. Guinier and Torres correctly point out that excluding critical adversaries undermines the entire value of political deliberation for transcending racial conflicts. To serve the purpose of transcending deep conflicts, the boundaries of deliberation cannot be set by authoritative powers. In my view it must be a *deep* pluralism, a pluralism that causes powerful individuals and groups to rethink their self-identities and strongest value commitments.

Political theorists tend to describe the process of unifying groups around a common good as a matter of agreeing around first principles, or of pragmatic negotiating to reach tolerable compromises, or of agreeing to disagree. In the end, it is true that groups must find rational procedures to construct agreements. But real alliances, like real conflict, do not emerge from sterile procedures and rational arguments alone. African American activists have tended to put little stock in the ideas that powerful white groups will listen to blacks or that the nation is mostly free of irrational white prejudice. Frederick Douglass's statement that "power concedes nothing without demand" is one of the most frequently cited admonitions in black political rhetoric. Bridge-builders therefore tend to build their own group power for competitive politics while looking for opportunities to leverage their power for building coalitions and alliances.

Power can be used to attract coalition allies, but it can also be deployed to help groups re-form their emotional commitments and political identities. Many examples provided in this book suggest that groups begin to identify strongly with other groups when those others lend power and make sacrifice for one's own cause. Adopting another group's issues as one's own does not mean that one takes up all of another group's agenda or fully understands or agrees with all of the various aspirations or points of view of another group. Rather than wholesale agreement or rational agreement on the specifics of a common good, it demonstrates an awareness of intertwined destinies between groups and an emotional desire for an alliance, as was the case when white students worked to help register blacks to vote in Mississippi. Some died in the process. The students added their power and sacrifice to the civil rights cause, and thereby helped many blacks imagine that interracial alliances might really be possible. Supporting the causes of others, lending power, and sacrificing for others are not irrational, and instead demonstrates reasoning beyond narrowly construed self-interest.

How do structures, building civic power, and creating interracial alliances relate to black mayoral strategies? Georgia Persons observed in 1993 that cities with large black majorities such as Newark Washington, D.C., and Detroit, elected black mayors who stayed in office for a long period of time and stifled broader "democratization and accountability, and may thereby hinder the move towards institutionalization of substantive black interests and participation " (Persons 1993, 49). Yet the structural position of some black mayors, particularly those in racially contested cities, sometimes produces a need to organize and mobilize alienated and critical sections of the black community. In summarizing a 1981 study of black voting by Richard Shingles, political scientist Cathy Cohen wrote that "it seems that although many blacks were willing to participate in potentially transformative (of the distribution of resources and power) political behavior, they were unwilling to engage in acts seen as largely symbolic and legitimizing of a political structure which they overwhelmingly distrusted" (Cohen 1998, 15–16). The task of engaging alienated blacks in the political process has reemerged as central to black progress. This can be done most effectively on a internally, deep pluralistic basis that includes all segments of black communities, and also on the basis of substantive promises and practices that go beyond symbolic black representation politics. The need to produce substantive policy change can make appealing the formation of interracial coalitions with groups sharing similar substantive concerns. Yet a history of interracial conflict can make the formation of such coalitions extremely difficult. Building a group's civic power, particularly in a pluralistic manner, can aid the process of coalition building between groups. Mayors can use the resources of local government to strengthen community civic power where it is weak. Groups that are better organized are likely to have more confidence that they can enter coalitions without manipulation by other groups. Groups that have bridged deep conflicts internally to achieve deep pluralism are better able to handle deep conflicts with other groups, making the transition from coalitions to alliances easier. And groups that have power can lend it to support the causes of others as a means of demonstrating a desire for friendship and alliance. The strategy of building multiracial coalitions around issues of substance, as with low-income whites, Latinos, environmentalists, and other groups who share broad substantive interests with African Americans, is a departure from current black mayoral strategies that tend to be confined, at best, to coalitions with downtown businesses (to retain jobs) and with middle- and upper-class white liberals. But internal crises in cities may increase the appeal of multiracial coalitions as a power-building strategy that can weaken conservative opponents and provide resources that are beyond the reach of the city.

"The Dirty Little Secret" of Black Politics

2

Harold Washington, Chicago's first African American mayor, elected in 1983, was asked the following question by a reporter for *Crain's Chicago Weekly:* "I hear from some business leaders . . . [that] they lament the divisiveness of the city and they worry about the image that projects beyond our borders, and they wish that Harold Washington would do more to overcome that kind of divisiveness. . . . You're down there in the gutter with these guys . . . and they wish that we had the kind of mayor that could somehow bring the city together again."

Washington replied, "They can wish unto hell. Let me tell you something very bluntly. You've had two kinds of mayor in this city. One who watered the Machine . . . and milked this city dry. The others were like me, trying to clean it up. Now you cannot clean it up unless you get down in the mud with these suckers and fight 'em. . . . You cannot compromise with a person who says give me all of it. You can't do that. And the sooner the media in this city understand that, and the sooner the business people understand that, the sooner we can get over that hump (Miller 1989, 123–24).

Mayor Washington's comments were remarkable. They contrasted sharply with the prevailing image of black mayors, since the 1980s, as captive agents of powerful business interests. A leading urban politics textbook concludes that "most African American mayors have supported a pro-growth, downtown development agenda. . . . Studies provide little evidence . . . that the incorporation of blacks and Latinos into political systems has led to significantly different taxing, spending, and service delivery policies. For the most part, African American mayors have not significantly altered development trends favoring downtown areas over the neighborhoods" (Judd and Swanstrom 2003, 389, 390). Mayor Tom Bradley of Los Angeles, Mayor Richard Hatcher in Gary, Indiana, Mayor Coleman Young in Detroit, Mayor Andrew Young in Atlanta, Mayor Michael White in Cleveland, and Mayor Wilson Goode in Philadelphia have all been so described by political scientists and others (Keiser 1997; Lane 2001; Rich 1989; Sonnenshein 1993; Stone 1989a). The dominant view in urban political studies has been that these men and other black mayors had little choice but to accept co-optation.

Co-opted mayors are those adopting a "pro-growth" orientation to urban policy. Since the New Deal, cities had been governed by "pro-growth" coalitions of "real estate developers, lawyers, design professionals, newspapers, service sector businesses that benefited from population growth, and unions, particularly those in the construction trades that relied on federal subsidies for public infrastructure to promote private investment and economic growth" (Clavel and Wiewel 1991, 3–4). Hence, the name "growth" coalitions. In the 1960s, strong minority community opposition effectively halted some pro-growth initiatives, such as Urban Renewal and major highway construction. Thus, the Embarcadero and Central Freeway projects in San Francisco were thwarted in the late 1960s by such opposition. By 1970, four hundred communities were fighting against highway plans that could disrupt city neighborhoods (Boyte 1980, 11). Pro-growth coalitions' other major project in the post–World War II period was promoting suburban development, ironic in view of the fact that the successful construction of suburbs created spatial and municipal boundaries between races and promoted the election of black mayors in the cities who, in turn, have been critical of pro-growth coalitions' exclusion of black interests from their projects (Mollenkopf 1983).

When blacks began to win mayoral elections in major cities in the late 1960s and early 1970s, many resisted their white predecessors' allocation of priorities, such as the improvement of downtown central business districts. These newly elected black mayors demanded that primary attention be given instead to more jobs, to low-income neighborhood development, and to business contracts for blacks. They were more successful at getting contracts for black businesses than in the former demands. Many did not have the staff resources to generate alternatives to the development ideas proposed by private developers, or the private investment partners it takes to produce new development projects. Large white-owned businesses were the source of such investments (Stone 1993). Black mayors who sought new private investment had to cooperate with the white business community and adjust to their priorities. Even though many black mayors worked to avoid racial confrontations that might frighten business investors, many white businesses moved out to the suburbs, further depleting jobs and tax revenues in the cities. To minimize racial conflict and the risk of business flight to the suburbs, these mayors seldom mobilized black communities in local policy making and politics.[1]

Chicago's Mayor Washington was an exception to the prevailing stance of black mayors: he did not accept co-optation by the business community, choosing instead to mobilize Chicago's poor black constituency. Washington, unlike most other black mayors, made little effort to conceal Chicago's deep racial antagonisms.[2] He worked hard to develop alternative models of community building and economic development that might encourage low-income blacks to participate in the political process. His administration determined its own development priorities, producing many creative proposals for addressing urban poverty. His Department of Economic Development established a research and development division (R & D), its mission to find innovative ways to implement the jobs platform to which the mayor had committed himself in his initial election campaign. The R & D group worked with community organizations and academic think tanks to shape alternative economic development policies, including the creation of loan funds, resource recycling, business incubators, planned manufacturing districts, and worker buyouts (Giloth 1991). Washington's administration also sought to leverage downtown business investment through measures like a commercial exaction tax on downtown business development to fund neighborhood development. While this particular initiative failed, and many of Washington's economic ventures did not survive in subsequent administrations, and although his administration lasted only four brief years (Washington died shortly after his election to a second term) and produced too few jobs to satisfy the black unemployed, it did succeed in, "changing the lives of the poor of the city . . . [by] making their issues a part of the debate," in the words of his commissioner of planning, Elizabeth Hollander (Hollander 1991, 144). He had highlighted the possibilities for innovation in city economic policies to produce greater equity, and he sought to make the city's policies accountable to its black poor.

Washington framed his administration in terms of accountability to the public—and particularly, to those parts of the public habitually ignored by the earlier white machine. He undertook, as Hollander put it, "the cultivation of community organizations and citizens" to mobilize support for neighborhood improvements. In 1985 he proposed a $250 million general obligation bond issue to fund community demands for improvements in streets, sewers, and sidewalks. The Chicago City Council opposed it, as it did most of Washington's other proposals during his first term, but, in response, rather than negotiate directly with the council, he involved community groups in the debate. His office prepared simple brochures explaining the local benefits of the bond issue, and Washington took reporters and local officials by bus to see broken sewers, potholes, and collapsed sidewalks. A few weeks later, the bond measure passed under strong community pressure.

In 1987, in a clear effort to generate public controversy over unemployment in Chicago's poor neighborhoods, Mayor Washington issued an executive order requiring all companies that received city subsidies or contracts to give first priority to employees referred through city hall. The mayor's "Chicago First" order provoked a storm of criticism in the business community, and he later made the program voluntary (Green 1989, 68), but he strongly signaled his intention to link city purchases and investments directly to increasing employment in Chicago's poorest neighborhoods. That same year, after a long teachers' strike, the mayor held an all-day open meeting on the state of the schools, after which he set up a parent community council, urging that it convene parent and community forums citywide. The reform coalition Washington initiated led to legislation to create school decentralization and greater parent participation through a system of local school councils. Clarence Stone, in his study of the politics of urban school reform, argued that Washington played a "facilitative" role in initiating school decentralization. Mayor Richard M. Daley, Chicago's current mayor, has played more of a "top-command" role, and civic power regressed (Stone et al. 2001, 17).

Washington's mayoralty had defied the widely held cynicism of black politics experts who believe that most black activists, discouraged by government repression of progressive black movements and induced by expanding personal opportunities to work through the process of government in the late 1960s and early 1970s, had abandoned social justice claims.[3] Robert C. Smith writes that, "the results of incorporation are that blacks have lost the capacity to effectively press their demands on the system and that the system has consequently responded to their demands with symbolism, neglect, and an ongoing pattern of cooptation." Smith believes that incorporation has not been able to empower black politics because "the black community has not been effectively mobilized" to effect change for the black community, and because, at the same time, a "progressive coalition of whites and other ethnic minorities . . . has not materialized," and the Democratic Party, which has been the more responsive to blacks, either failed to win national elections in the 1970s or 1980s, or, when they did, "tended to ignore black demands or respond with symbols" (Smith 1996, 23).

Washington's regime, brief as it was, offered a model of progressive policies that other black mayors could adapt and implement; it sought black political participation, and it built a broad progressive coalition with Latinos and liberal whites (Grimshaw 1992). None of that invalidates Smith's general point, but it does suggest that there are exceptions. The regime of Mayor David Dinkins in New York was also an exception, at least in part (see part 2), as was Mayor Kurt Schmoke's administration in Baltimore. Thus, several black mayors, including those in two of the nation's three largest cities, had been able to move beyond conventional caveats of the fiscal limits on city policy making and demobilization of the black poor. It is important to understand why they were able to do so, but also why other mayors have not yet followed their example.

Washington's unusual achievement was not a consequence of personality and temperament alone. Experience had also stamped him. Washington spent most of his career as "a lifelong patronage employee and a machine minion" (Green 1989, 3). When he ran for mayor in Chicago in 1977, he carried most middle-class black wards but lost in poor black wards (Grimshaw 1992, 167). Washington then built a powerful alliance with Chicago's community activists to mobilize the black poor, expanding on his base in the black church. The continued pressure on him from that community to adopt strategies and policies that would be accountable to the poor was the result of the mobilization he engendered. He benefited from a rich civic capacity in the city that spanned race and class to some degree, and, in turn, helped strengthen it to support his reform agenda and to secure his political position.

From the start, Washington's mayoralty was unusual: his first mayoral campaign relied on an extensive parallel mobilization effort led by black nationalists and by People United to Save Humanity (PUSH), a black activist organization headed by the Reverend Jesse Jackson. An electoral campaign training school, established by Lu Palmer, a leading journalist and black nationalist, had turned out twenty-two hundred community activists (Mangcu 1997). PUSH and the Charles A. Hayes Labor and Educational Center, named after the local black labor leader, organized weekly pep rallies to mobilize thousands of community residents for political activity. More than 100,000 new black voters were registered in the year before the election; by 1983, 600,000 of 665,000 eligible black voters had been registered. Washington won the Democratic primary in 1983 by 36,145 votes and the general election by 48,250 votes. More than a million voters participated in each election, nearly half of Washington's black votes coming from poor wards. That huge turnout, especially from the black poor, was vital to his election and to his reelection in 1987. In both elections he won 54 percent of the total vote (Grimshaw 1992, 192); in 1983, roughly 98 percent of the black vote, 19 percent of the white vote, and 79 percent of the Latino vote (Miller 1988, 12). The 1987 election was nearly a replay of the 1983 election. Chicago's black activists now had a critical mass of constituents and a single target for their social justice demands.

Washington's campaigns and his administration, as well, were motivated and rewarded by the centralized power of the mayor's office over city resources. Washington described the mayor's office as a "great prize" (Miller 1988, 63). Chicago's machine was as furious about losing the power of the mayor's office as Washington's supporters were exalted. Despite the impressive election, the mayor faced stiff opposition from twenty-nine of the city council's fifty members throughout most of his first term. Washington maintained that his city council opposition had gained office through the previous machine's manipulation of council redistricting: "they were able to get their '29' in City Council only because they had manipulated the electoral process—by working with the previous mayor to manipulate the mapping of ward lines after the 1980 census" (Miller 1988, 120–21). Both the machine and anti-machine forces vied for influence in Chicago neighborhoods. While the power of the mayor's office enabled Washington to unite significant elements of the black community into a coalition to seize that office, the machine controlled the city council that fought Washington's supporters every step of the way.

The political structure of the mayor's office and city council organized, so to speak, the contours of Chicago's political battlefield. Still, the outcomes were not determined by political structure arrangements alone. Washington's victories and defeats were, more generally, the outcome of power struggles between political factions using the power and resources of different institutions. Washington emphasized that one of the unifying ideas of his campaign had been to snatch the power of the mayor's office away from the political machine and then empower the neighborhoods. "My election," Washington said in his inaugural speech, "was the result of the greatest grassroots movement in the history of the city of Chicago. It may have been equaled somewhere in this country, I know not where. . . . One of the ideas that held us together said that neighborhood involvement has to take the place of the ancient, decrepit, and creaking machine" (Miller 1988, 3). Washington's victory enabled him to use full-time staff resources to communicate with constituents and control city-funded programs to encourage ongoing participation in communities that supported him to maintain a base of power. Washington also fired patronage workers who had been hired by previous administrations, this to weaken his opponents.

The persistence of struggles for and against the old machine created deep political divisions in Chicago's black communities. Just four years before Harold Washington's election in 1983, in a first campaign for mayor, he had lost 70 percent of the black vote to Jane Byrne, a machine-backed white candidate. He concluded that his first priority in a future campaign had to be organizing an intra-black political coalition that could unite black voters solidly against the machine (Miller 1988, 11). He did so not just by appealing to machine-aligned black politicians but by aligning himself with grassroots activists to launch massive voter registration drives and political education efforts in black communities in order to pose an electoral threat to black politicians who supported the machine.[4] Thus Washington and his supporters skillfully combined bridge building in black communities with the threat of political confrontation. Washington's strategy and skill had been to choose deep pluralist grass-roots organizing—opening discourse, developing grassroots leadership, and including as many groups as possible—as a means of challenging government policies that create and reinforce poverty. His citywide organizing strategies may well have been less effective, and made less sense, on other battlefields in other cities, as, for example, those in which the mayor's office is not a "great prize" and offered few tangible benefits for groups that take action in electoral campaigns.

Similarities and differences in political structure between cities are as important in political campaigns as different terrain, such as mountains and the desert, is in fighting military battles. Yet considerable weight must be given to the skill and courage (agency) of the political actors, especially Harold Washington himself.

Accountability as a Political Imperative for Black Mayors

First-time election campaigns of black mayors are often misleading indicators of accountability to the black poor because other communitywide issues take precedence. Particularly in the 1960s and 1970s, black mayors won their initial elections not on platforms of accountability to the poor but on issues of fighting police brutality, hiring more blacks in government, increasing minority shares of city contracts, along with improving service delivery in black neighborhoods and creating jobs for the poor. Progress was often made on hot-button issues of police brutality and black control of police departments and other key city institutions, and on the whole, black mayors tried to be faithful to the other goals as well (Reed 1986b), but accountability to the black poor on economic issues like jobs engendered considerable criticism and alienation within the black community. As it happened, the election of black mayors coincided with other economic and political trends—like deindustrialization, suburbanization, and conservative ascendancy to power in the White House—that had significant impact on city finances, hence on the capacity of black mayors to improve the quality of services in urban black communities. With escalation of crime, homelessness, and other poverty-related social problems, demands on black mayors became more acute, but at the same time, it became increasingly difficult to maintain the capacity of city institutions to cope with such problems. Black mayors were lauded by white leadership according to their willingness to give less attention to the needs of the black community or their incapacity to do so. Political scientists described "new black mayors" Michael White in Cleveland (1990–2002), Kurt Schmoke of Baltimore (1987–99), Marc Morial (1994–2002) and later Ray Nagin (2002–) of New Orleans, Dennis Archer of Detroit (1994–2001), Bill Campbell of Atlanta (1994–2000), and others as "technopoliticians," because they changed the moral tenor of urban politics, as these political scientists saw it, from issues of race and class advocacy to fashioning closer ties with the business community and keeping bond ratings high (Eisinger 1998, 321).

In contrast to an enthusiastic response from white leaders, techno-politicians received a lukewarm response from black voters. In their study of black voting in mayoral elections in Los Angeles, Cleveland, and Atlanta, Franklin Gilliam and Karen Kaufmann found some evidence that blacks voted for a black mayor on symbolic grounds, that is, because they were black, and that black voting increased during racially competitive elections, as in Cleveland and Atlanta in the 1970s. However, the overall trend, they report, was one of declining black voter turnout over the decades. Los Angeles presented the starkest case with a 38 percent drop in black voting in mayoral elections between late 1969 and 1993. Gilliam and Kaufmann attribute the drop to blacks' "frustration over local government's inability to improve the relative status of blacks." The initial election of black mayors boosted blacks' interest and political participation in all three cities, but that interest declined because, so they suggest, with, "each iteration of the empowerment life cycle, the consequential symbolic effect [of electing a black mayor] is not likely to be as robust or durable over time" (Gilliam and Kaufman 1998, 754–59). What they meant was that symbolic representation was losing its grip on black voters.

A predictable result of the civil rights movement's failure to wage a political battle over fundamental economic injustice issues after the assassination of the Reverend Martin Luther King Jr. was another source of decline in black voter turnout. Andrew Young, the two-term mayor of Atlanta, from 1981 until 1989, U.S. Ambassador to the United Nations during the Carter administration, and a principal aide to the Reverend Martin Luther King Jr., in 1991 reflected on his experience in the 1960s civil rights movement and the limits of its effectiveness:

> The civil rights movement was not aimed at ending poverty. It did not focus on economic issues; not because we didn't think economic issues were important, but because we didn't think we would win on economic issues. If you talked too much about class and poverty, you were characterized as a communist, therefore very few wanted to raise economic issues at that time. . . .
> The primary battle in the 1950s and 1960s was to right the wrongs against a population that was already qualified and middle class,

but was still denied the basic right to public accommodations in America. . . . But we always knew that we would have to deal with poverty someday. (Orfield 1991, ix)

Black mayors and other black leaders have not mobilized urban blacks to fight political conservatism, and to make the Democratic Party, with which they were closely associated, more electable and also more responsive to neglected black demands. To do either or both would have required broader progressive coalitions of blacks with whites, as well as Latinos and Asians, a daunting challenge that few black mayors attempted. Black politicians may be willing to advocate progressive politics and accountability to their neediest constituents—mobilizing the black poor, forming interracial coalitions to support major policy changes, confronting the dominant conservative framings of racial problems, and advocating policy changes that could redirect greater public resources to the poor—when they believe that they must do so to remain in office. But black mayors have not been "natural progressives," independent of the structural limits of their offices and reelection calculations. Black mayors who believe it is in their deepest political interest to increase the political participation of the poor often try to do so. If they do not see this as a political necessity, they do not try.

Many students of black politics have agreed with political scientist William Nelson's suggestion that black mayors ought to "establish mass-based political formations at every level of the political process that will be actively and effectively involved in setting and implementing the civic agenda" (Nelson 1990), but few have done so. Black mayors may well find it in their interest to *re*-mobilize the black poor, and to respond to their demands, in circumstances where a large turnout of all sectors of the black community could be the means of returning the mayor to office *and* when *low-income* black communities could compel mayoral accountability by threats of political opposition to their reelection.

The strongest supporters of black mayors tend to come from the black middle class, not the poor. Clarence Stone, in his study of Atlanta, attributes this support to the "small opportunities" black mayors have been able to provide to black businesses. Heather Parker's study of Mayor Tom Bradley pointed out that "middle-class, moderate blacks comprised a vocal support network for the mayor. While they acknowledged poor and working class blacks' frustration with Bradley's approach to their concerns, they encouraged all African Americans to recognize advances, such as affirmative action, that the mayor had initiated. They asserted that his presence in city hall as a symbol of African-American success was far more important than any controversy regarding his methods. Supporting the mayor, they maintained, was an exercise in self-affirmation—a way to demonstrate pride in black accomplishments, not merely an expression of approval for Tom Bradley" (Parker 2001, 171). Supporting Bradley for "self-affirmation," which uses racial solidarity to connect a black mayor to black supporters, is the opposite of accountability. It reflects instead the black middle-class strategy of hegemonic control of group identity discussed by Partha Chatterjee (see discussion of "black power" in chapter 4).

While there is always a possibility the black middle class could be radicalized by issues such as racial profiling or municipal layoffs, leading them to abandon a black mayor, black mayors offer material incentives to sections of the black middle class, gaining their support thereby. It is far easier to address middle-class demands for business contracts, for high-profile patronage appointments, or for the removal of threatening elements from neighborhoods, such as homeless shelters, drug rehabilitation clinics, or public housing units, none of which require additional revenue, than it is to meet poor constituents' demands for jobs, affordable housing, and increased services.[5]

Black-led cities differ by the degree of black mobilization needed to win election of a black mayor. A few large nonpolarized cities—Denver, Seattle, Minneapolis—have elected black mayors despite a small black population whose votes were not their primary base. And in black-majority cities, where black voting power is already sufficiently high to discourage white contenders, black mayors may not need to mobilize the black poor to win reelection, since the support of moderate "pro-growth" political coalitions of middle-class black voters, white businesses, and white middle-class voters may suffice without a mobilization of the black poor. This is the kind of coalition Mayor Andrew Young established in Atlanta in the 1980s, and in many of the heavily black populated cities that elected black mayors several decades ago. But in cities where black voters are a large enough bloc to contest for power on their own terms but not large enough to secure power on their own, mobilization of nonvoting blacks, as well as reducing intra-black political conflict, may be essential for the election of a black mayor. Political scientist Diane Pinderhughes found in this vein that:

> in the case of African Americans, cities with majority black populations, especially those over 65 percent, are especially likely to

have elected black mayors on a sustained basis. Examples are: Detroit; Washington, D.C.; Atlanta; and Gary, Indiana. When the black population is under 65 percent, the coalition is much less secure and more likely to be subject to the vagaries of partisan politics and/or intragroup fission. Black electorates in Cleveland after Carl Stokes, Los Angeles after Tom Bradley, and Chicago after Harold Washington's death were unable to maintain control of the mayor's office. Cities with black populations above 40 percent and below 65 percent find it possible to win control of city hall if they can minimize conflict within the group. Where the black electorate is a minority or only a narrow majority, possibilities of internal conflict *may* be more easily controlled, because the stakes are clearer. Even cities with minorities of 38 percent or less may elect a black mayor, as Charlotte, Hartford, Los Angeles, Kansas City, and New York have done. That individual, however, must rely on a significantly broader multiracial coalition to win election. (Pinderhughes 1997, 149)

Black mayors first won election in cities that were undergoing transition to a majority-black population. Black candidates—Maynard Jackson in Atlanta (1974–82, 1990–94), and Coleman Young in Detroit (1973–93)—mobilized the black poor, along with the black middle class, but in highly racially polarized contests. As their city populations became increasingly black, and as the fears of white voters and white businesspeople that they would be victimized by a black mayor diminished, fighting black mayors became both less feasible and also perceived as less essential (Franklin 1989; Watson 1984). Such black mayors now did not need the poor black vote to defeat a strong white candidate; they could win with support of the black middle class and white allies. There have also been signs of "strategic voting" for black candidates by white voters—rather than supporting a white candidate, becoming a decisive bloc of support to lift the weaker of two or more black candidates to victory—in majority-black cities in black-on-black mayoral contests (Liu 2003).

On the other hand, in black-led cities where blacks were strong but not dominant, racial contests for control of city hall have led either to successful challenges by white candidates against incumbent black mayors or an inability of black mayors to ensure the election of handpicked black successors. Of the twenty largest cities, only Detroit, Philadelphia, and Memphis had black mayors in 2004. It is striking that among large cities in 2004, black mayors were in office only in cities with a 40 percent or more black population. In the twelve large cities with a substantial (25 percent or more) black population, only three have black mayors. There are none at all in cities with less than a 25 percent black population. New York, Los Angeles, Chicago, Houston, and Dallas, the four largest cities and the eighth largest city, had black mayors earlier in the 1990s and no longer do. This suggests that black mayors in large cities have had difficulty building and sustaining interracial coalitions. Of the forty-two cities of fifty thousand or more residents that had black mayors in 2004, the majority had more than a 40 percent black population, and only eight had less than a 25 percent black population (see tables 2.1 and 2.2).

Table 2.1

Black Percentage of Total Population in Twenty Largest U.S. Cities

City	Total Population	Black %
New York	8,008,278	26.6
Los Angeles	3,694,820	11.2
Chicago	2,896,016	36.8
Houston	1,953,631	25.3
Philadelphia	1,517,550	43.2
Phoenix	1,321,045	5.1
San Diego	1,223,400	7.9
Dallas	1,188,580	25.9
San Antonio	1,144,646	6.8
Detroit	951,270	81.6
San Jose	894,943	3.5
Indianapolis	781,870	25.5
San Francisco	776,733	7.8
Jacksonville	735,617	29.0
Columbus, Ohio	711,470	24.5
Austin	656,562	10.0
Baltimore	651,154	64.3
Memphis	650,100	61.4
Milwaukee	596,974	37.3
Boston	589,141	25.3

Source: U.S. Census 2000

Table 2.2

Black Mayors and Black Percentage of Total Population in Cities with Population More Than 50,000

Municipality	State	Population	Black %
Miami Gardens	FL	100,000	90.0
East Orange	NJ	69,824	89.5
Irvington	NJ	60,695	81.7
Detroit	MI	951,270	81.6
Birmingham	AL	242,820	73.5
Jackson	MS	184,256	70.6
New Orleans	LA	484,674	67.3
Macon	GA	97,255	62.5
Atlanta	GA	416,474	61.4
Memphis	TN	650,100	61.4
Monroe	LA	53,107	61.1
Washington	DC	572,059	60.0
Mount Vernon	NY	68,381	59.6
Richmond	VA	197,790	57.2
Savannah	GA	131,510	57.1
Wilmington	DE	72,664	56.4
North Miami	FL	59,880	54.9
Southfield	MI	78,296	54.2
Newark	NJ	273,546	53.5
Flint	MI	124,943	53.3
Camden	NJ	79,904	53.3
Trenton	NJ	85,403	52.1
Portsmouth	VA	100,565	50.6
Pontiac	MI	66,337	47.9
Inglewood	CA	112,580	47.1
Hampton	VA	146,437	44.7
Durham	NC	187,035	43.8
Saginaw	MI	61,799	43.3
Philadelphia	PA	1,517,550	43.2
Compton	CA	93,493	40.3
Rochester	NY	219,773	38.5
Fayetteville	NC	121,015	34.9
Chesapeake	VA	199,184	28.5
Jersey City	NJ	240,055	28.3
Columbus	OH	711,470	24.5

Municipality	State	Population	Black %
Toledo	OH	313,619	23.5
Alexandria	VA	128,283	22.5
Evanston	IL	74,239	22.5
Kalamazoo	MI	77,145	20.6
Dayton	OH	166,179	19.9
Richmond	CA	99,216	9.4
Oceanside	CA	161,029	7.4

Source: National Conference of Black Mayors (2004). Available at http://www.blackmayors.org.

In the twelve contested cities such as Cleveland, Baltimore, Philadelphia, or New York, black candidates may be able to mobilize the black poor to win office in racially polarized elections; alternatively, if they can attract sufficient white support, they may run for office as "deracialized" candidates.[6] Harold Washington in Chicago, elected in 1983 and 1987, and Carl Stokes in Cleveland, elected in 1967 and 1969, pursued the first strategy; Wilson Goode in Philadelphia, elected in 1984, the second. David Dinkins, elected in 1989 in New York, started like Wilson Goode and then hesitantly switched strategies in the direction of Washington's grass-roots mobilization approach. In Cleveland in 1989, Michael White took an opposite tack from Stokes and ran on a deracialized platform, winning the mayoralty over George Forbes, the more popular candidate in the black community. While White received only about 30 percent of the black vote, he gained 76 percent of the white vote.

A black mayor's political strategists may conclude that poor black communities are too disorganized to be mobilized in large numbers—either for or against the mayor—and that winning higher levels of white support is both an easier and a more reliable route to reelection. In such a case the mayor will be encouraged to "deracialize," if he or she has not already, in order to attract white voters. Where strong white voter opposition prevents black mayors from consolidating control of the mayor's office, however, black mayors may be forced to rely for reelection on a high voter turnout of the black poor. Since voter behavior, particularly involving race, is often difficult to decipher, a decision to mobilize poor black voters or pursue a deracialization approach may come down to a candidate's gut preferences.

Black mayors may also be convinced to mobilize the black poor if the low-income black community has the potential strength to hold their black mayors accountable by threats of opposition or by offers of strong grass-roots support. Writing soon after the election of David Dinkins as mayor of New York and of Michael White in Cleveland, the political scientists Joseph McCormick and Charles Jones argued that three factors would determine whether black mayors in majority-white districts would "sell-out" blacks: the racial composition of the electorate; the local culture (degree of race polarization); and the "extent to which the African-American community is politically organized and prepared to make race-specific demands on these officials" (McCormick and Jones 1993). I largely concur, although I do not think politically organized black organizations need to make race-specific demands in order to hold black mayors accountable. Poor black communities often lack this capacity, however, and in some, the civic infrastructure, as in the presence of stores, bars, churches, and banks, already has been so weakened by economic impoverishment as to be near collapse (see chapter 4) (Cohen and Dawson 1993; Marable 1983; Wilson 1996). In other cities, black community organizations and black-led labor unions may have been fragmented by the administrative and political structure of government.

There are many examples of weak black political capacity under favorable structural conditions because structural pressures alone do not explain political outcomes. The skill and strength of local actors and the history of local conflict also matter. Black mayors (and other black officials) under certain conditions may have strong political incentives to suppress the political capacities of their poor black communities. So, for example, once a mayor decides on a deracialization strategy, that mayor has an incentive to discourage the participation of groups most likely to oppose and disrupt that strategy. In such a case, there is a political logic to deliberate demobilization of the black poor.

"They May Be Vulnerable Themselves": The Logic of Demobilization of the Black Community

Deliberate black demobilization is not new to black politics. Southern Jim Crow had, for more than a century, cultivated compliant black leadership in the South. Richard Arrington, a University of Oklahoma zoology professor who became Birmingham's first black mayor, experienced that white strategy in his efforts to mobilize blacks against horrendous police brutality. In 1972, Arrington, then a city councilman, met with A. G. Gaston, a wealthy black businessman and confidant of the city's white establishment, to seek support for organizing the black community to press the police department to rein in abusive police officers. Gaston, according to Arrington, "dashed cold water on the idea of calling black leaders together," urged him to "take it slow," and sought to rein in activist black ministers then organizing against police brutality. Arrington comments that:

> the failure of so-called black leaders in this community to speak out about police brutality simply reconfirms my belief that there is really no such thing as black leaders in this community—they are people who are used by the white power structure in this community, who take an ego trip because they are called upon by some powerful white citizens to fit black folk into an agenda that has been set up by the white community, particularly the business structure here. (Franklin 1989, 104)

Although Birmingham's established black community leaders were not overtly opposed to Arrington's goals, they quietly tamped down or sought to repress black protest and political mobilization. Gaston, who had become a millionaire during segregation, had achieved a secure position within the city's white-dominated power structure, and did not want that structure disrupted.

The incorporation of blacks into elected office has established secure positions in government for blacks who once were community activists, and the political structures in which they operate encourage them to demobilize poor blacks in order to stay in office themselves since black demands for jobs, for affordable housing, for quality public schools, and community health facilities have not been welcomed in Congress or in state legislatures, where black legislators are in the minority. Nor can such demands be sufficiently met by city governments.[7] Although states have the discretion to allow local governments to collect taxes, only the federal government and the states are constitutionally authorized to raise revenue to pay for these demands, and the rise in the number of black elected officials has not been translated into political power sufficient to direct significant public resources to poor communities.[8]

With black legislators generally elected in majority-black voting districts (Swain 1993), white competition is unlikely and a black elected official may have a secure office. Particularly in legislative districts in which district lines have been drawn deliberately to ensure that a black candidate wins the election, a rarely noticed effect is that the absence of effective white competition reduces the need for incumbents to mobilize beyond the black middle class to include the poor.[9] In these typically single-member districts, two-party competition, too, is rare, and the candidate who wins the most votes in the Democratic primary wins the seat without having to seek to boost the margin of victory or voter turnout. Whether three hundred people vote or thirty thousand, the candidate with the most votes gets the reward. The safe and resource-effective way in such circumstances to win reelection is for a candidate to get by with no (or virtually no) competition and low voter turnout.

The combination of political co-optation of black elected officials, the government's lack of response to substantive black demands, and the increasing incidence of majority-black voting districts and winner-take-all elections creates a certain political logic. Why mobilize poor black voters in elections when you will not be able to deliver the most substantial benefits that they need and when they will blame you for failing to provide them? Why not concentrate on mobilizing those parts of the black community that need less from government, such as black middle-class homeowners who primarily want their representatives to protect their home values by keeping homeless shelters and other NIMBYs ("Not In My Back Yard" nuisance facilities) out of their neighborhoods. Steven Gregory's ethnography of the black neighborhood of Corona, Queens, New York, found that homeowner block associations had, "proven to be the most powerful neighborhood interest group in the black community" (Gregory 1998, 151). Not that black homeowners were unsympathetic to the black poor, but they did believe that the city had compelled black middle-class neighborhoods to accept more than their fair share of subsidized housing for the poor. In terms of opposing aid for the black poor, Gregory notes that black politicians in Queens were careful not to attack the poor but to couch their opposition to low-income housing in terms of fighting racist tendencies of local government to assume that blacks of all classes should be clustered together in the same area, thus effectively constricting upward mobility of the black middle class itself. In raising NIMBY issues, legislators can sometimes be effective since such questions are usually matters of administration discretion.

The same logic applies to black mayors even in cities with large majority-black voting populations. It is easier to deliver benefits for black businesses who seek a share of existing city contracts than to raise taxes or float bonds to meet the needs of the black poor. In a majority-black city with no effective or likely source of non-black political opposition, officials see a pragmatic political logic in limiting their political appeals and agenda to sectors of the middle-class black community they consider most likely to perceive real benefits from having a black mayor in office. It does not make sense to expand political capacities and spend scarce resources in poor black neighborhoods in such political circumstances, where residents' votes are not needed and where residents are the most critical of black officials' inability to achieve substantive progress in improving ghetto conditions. Indeed, mobilizing the black poor may even generate a capacity, and a zest, for insurgencies among the poor themselves. When asked why black political leaders would want to stifle "black awareness," one longtime New York black political activist, Audrey Bynoe, said, "Because they may be vulnerable themselves. Once you have a heightened black electorate—[you have] insurgents, young candidates—you have all of that happening. And I don't think that the [Congressman] Charlie Rangels and the [Manhattan county leader] Denny Farrells and those people want to have insurgents" (Bynoe 1988).

And in majority-white cities, political logic may persuade a black mayor to provide resources first to members of the coalition that led to that mayor's victory, most usually white business leaders, white middle-class progressives, and black middle-class leaders.

Many of the political activists cited in this study made similar references to such dynamics. They saw black politicians' avoidance of the poor as contradicting in practice, through acceptance of the status quo, what their progressive rhetoric and their posture has insisted that they believe. Esmerelda Simmons, a well-known black Brooklyn voting rights attorney and veteran community activist, has called demobilization of the black poor "the dirty little secret" of black politics (Simmons 1988). Larry McNeil, West Coast leader of the Industrial Areas Foundation (IAF) for more than a quarter century, has noticed stark contrasts between black legislators in safe black districts who eschewed mobilization, and black candidates for citywide office without a strong interracial coalition of support who sought to mobilize the black poor to provide a compelling political base (McNeil 2004).[10]

Another Brooklyn election attorney, Paul Wooten, points out that in that borough, except for first-time campaigns or candidates running for higher office, few black politicians have been active in registering black voters because to do so may increase pressure on them to produce:[11]

> High voter registration and high turnout and voter education means they have to work harder and be accountable to more people. So low voter turnout is a tool to keep them in [office], but the [black] rhetoric is [to promote] voter registration. If you look at [the figures], voter registration has only been utilized as a tool to develop the machinery either [for a politician] to run for somebody else's [seat] or go for higher office, but [voter registration] never has been truly used as an avenue of political empowerment. Voter registration has been used to manipulate [the black community] and give the perception that they want to do something, but [it] has always been [a] guise [for] someone's personal agenda and never the agenda of the community.

A clear example of a black mayoral political strategy bifurcated by class is Atlanta after the 1980s, touted as a mecca for the black middle class, and as the preeminent example of consolidated black political, economic, and cultural power. Atlanta is also a glaring example of demobilization of the black poor. Maynard Jackson, elected Atlanta's first black mayor in 1973, belied his early image as an advocate of Atlanta's predominantly poor black community,[12] when, after the white business community loudly protested the aggressive tactics of his commissioner of administrative services, Emma Darnelle, in seeking to bring minorities into major positions in political and economic life in Atlanta, Mayor Jackson fired her. Darnelle, very popular in the black community, had been the only prominent black woman in his administration. Soon after she was ousted, she sued Jackson for race and sex discrimination, though she later dropped charges and Jackson changed the firing of Darnell to accept her resignation (Persons 1978, 279). Darnell unsuccessfully opposed Jackson in the 1977 mayoral election.

In late 1976, in the middle of the Darnelle controversy, Jackson fired one thousand predominantly black sanitation workers, members of American Federation of State, County, and Municipal Employees (AFSCME), who were on strike over the issue of a five-hundred-dollar annual increase for workers making less than seven thousand dollars per year, as most of AFSCME's small local membership of fewer than three thousand did.[13] In Atlanta's low-income black communities, seven thousand dollars at the time was considered to be a good salary, and hence large numbers of unemployed blacks applied to replace the striking workers. Although Mayor Jackson gained notoriety several years earlier, while serving as vice mayor, as a strong supporter of striking sanitation workers, he now portrayed the strike as an unwarranted attack on a struggling black administration during a national recession.[14] With unions in Atlanta traditionally segregated by race and the white leadership unconcerned with poor blacks' economic advancement, no large black union constituency existed who could oppose Jackson's charges. John Lucas, a long-time administrator for the Fulton County Commission, protested that such actions left a residue of distrust among Atlanta's poor population:

> What did (Jackson) do for [poor blacks]? Not a lot. They were poor in 1973, they were poor eight years later at the end of his term, and they're still poor. So they don't have the great love [for black mayors] that a lot of us might think that they have. . . . Maynard threatened to fire and eventually did fire a couple of thousand garbage workers . . . those were low income people. He was a union buster. (Lucas 1988)

After Jackson's second term ended in 1981, Andrew Young was elected mayor. At the end of Andrew Young's second term as mayor of Atlanta, in 1988, the percentage of high-poverty census tracts was 46.6, far above Atlanta's 27.7 percent level in 1970 (Owens and Rich 2003, #1470). Job opportunities had increased but primarily in the white-collar sector, and for jobs for which most poor blacks were unqualified. Large numbers of blacks had been displaced from their homes by business development projects supported by the city's black mayors. Development in Atlanta's mostly black south side was minimal. Substandard housing had increased during the 1970s to encompass, by the late 1980s, at least 25 percent of the total housing stock (Bullard and Thomas 1989, 77–86). To protect his pro-growth agenda, Mayor Young had failed to support community participation in neighborhood development, continuing a trend begun toward the end of Mayor Jackson's administration (Stone 1989a). According to Emma Darnelle, there had been close to 160 black community organizations when Jackson was first elected in 1973 with the help of these groups. Thereafter they received little support from the city, and, by the end of Young's term, most had disbanded (Darnelle 1988).

In a widely publicized speech in the spring of 1988, Atlanta City Council member Jabari Samama, an independent-minded community activist, characterized Young's philosophy of economic development as, "voodoo politics, you know, magic to open up the floodgates of the city and let them [white business] all come in and in some kind of way it's going to trickle down" (Samama 1988). That summer, another Atlanta City Council member, the former civil rights leader Hosea Williams, complained that Young had opted to placate the white business community at the expense of the black poor (Harris 1988) and Earl Shinholster, NAACP regional director, said, "His [Young's] administration has been run . . . primarily for the benefit of the power structure. And if there's any benefits to accrue as a result of that, then fine. [Poor black] people get the scraps from the table" (Shinholster 1988).

A poll conducted by *The Atlanta Constitution* in May 1988 found that significant numbers of poor blacks disapproved of Young's performance as mayor; the black community was polarized by class. Among those with less than a high school education, 29 percent said the city had moved forward, 37 percent that it gotten worse, while 48 percent of college graduates said the city had moved forward, and 13 percent that it had gotten worse (Wells 1988). Class conflict within the black community does not, however, trump black racial loyalty in Atlanta's black community.[15] This was evident during the 1993 mayoral race, when Mayor Bill Campbell was opposed for reelection by black City Council President Marvin Arrington. Campbell's campaign accused Arrington of being a stalking horse for white suburban leaders' ambition to regain control of the city when he pushed for a regional body to oversee water and sewer projects (Alexander 1997). Maynard Jackson, campaigning for Campbell, labeled Arrington's supporters "Lester Maddox types," and Arrington said that Campbell supporters had called him a "handkerchief-headed Negro." In response, Arrington accused the light-skinned Maynard Jackson of failing to take active part in the civil rights movement, and of spending the sixties, "in Cleveland, passing," that is, pretending to be white (Fears 1997). The attack on Arrington's motives was a smokescreen for the black regimes' failure to address chronic black poverty in the city, but it was effective because black activists and voters in Atlanta were still deeply suspicious of joining coalitions with white suburbanites. Campbell was reelected in a runoff with 53 percent of the vote to Arrington's 47 percent.

The political scientist Clarence Stone has written that the persistent business-oriented character of Atlanta's city government worked for Atlanta's black regimes as well as for white businesses because black entrepreneurial opportunity, wide business prerogative, and assurance of black business participation in city contracting were a glue that bound Atlanta's biracial governing coalition together. According to Stone, "These regime arrangements satisfy each partner: white business executives gain needed black allies; and black political leaders are able to cultivate a useful and visible black constituency [black businesses]. Furthermore, black contractors and other business executives are a principal source of campaign funds. Overall the system is reinforcing" (Stone 1989a, 15). Stone asserts further that, while city contract requirements may mandate minority participation, they do not specify *which* minority businesses, and that, in Atlanta white business leaders continued to determine which black subcontractors to choose, thus retaining considerable leverage in building alliances and in rewarding black businesses that were presumably most amenable to white business interests. Atlanta has a secure black middle class and has maintained a hold on the mayoralty from Maynard Jackson's election in 1973 to Mayor Shirley Franklin's election in 2000, but its positioning remains dependent on powerful white business "growth" leadership. This biracial political-economic coalition has largely ignored the city's black poor.

When, in his 1991 reflection on his experience, Atlanta's former mayor, Andrew Young, said that "elected officials, white and black, are going to have to be more accountable" to the poor (Orfield 1991, ix), he was clearly troubled by what had transpired in Atlanta. Even committed black mayors had chosen accommodation with white downtown business interests and had supported demobilization of poor blacks who might have stood in the way.

Many of the black activists interviewed for this study witnessed black elected officials transition from insurgents to established incumbents; they uniformly attested that it does not take long for black elected officials to realize the limitations of their power to effect fundamental social change. They find it immensely difficult to explain to disgruntled poor constituents, year after year, why more is not being accomplished. Not that officials would not like to do more for the poor, but rather, like white officials, they are pragmatic realists who are playing the cards the political structure has dealt them. Political incorporation of blacks into top positions in cities can be actively destructive of political capacity in poor urban communities because of the difficulty in achieving serious social change. If black politicians could better understand how the mechanisms of power weaken or strengthen black civic political capacity, they might feel less helpless and more able to leverage their offices to restructure broader political arrangements to produce greater incentives for mobilization of the poor. Some black politicians have had to confront this question because they do not operate in "safe" majority-black voting districts, nor do they avoid accountability to the poor. Some black mayors (and other candidates for high office) mobilize poor blacks, as Harold Washington did in Chicago, because they need them and because they have at their disposal administrative resources to help develop the capacity and interests of black organizations to engage in city politics. These mobilizing officials are more likely to encourage political reforms to facilitate voting in poor neighborhoods, though, ironically, when they do so they frequently encounter subtle resistance from other black officials who fear the consequences to themselves and to the city's equilibrium of arousing the black poor (Hudson 2003).

Resources for Mobilization: Old and New Forms of Patronage

The old political machines were mainly backed by working-class and immigrant organizations. As hierarchical organizations run by a party boss, they reached their heyday at the turn of the twentieth century, and lost much of their power in many cities by the 1930s. In exchange for political support and votes, patronage consisting of entry-level managerial jobs, unskilled labor, clerical, and public safety jobs, was disseminated to supporters (Katznelson 1976; 1973; Rich 1982). If the concept of patronage includes the broader nexus between the exchange of money for votes, patronage did not end with the demise of the party bosses. Other forms of patronage took their place, supplemented by patronage networks of business development ("pro-growth" coalitions), and what can be called "community-labor" patronage.

The Chicago machine was the classic example of early machine patronage, long dominated by Irish politicians who excluded blacks from political power and from significant patronage. The lone exception to Irish control in Chicago was a black machine sub-boss William Dawson, but in 1963, Dawson's control, which had been limited to two or three black wards in the city, was taken over by Mayor Richard J. Daley (Grimshaw 1992, 34–35). Unlike New York, which has five county machines, one for each borough within the city, Chicago had only one machine. Also, unlike New York, where civil-service reform under Mayor Fiorello LaGuardia eliminated most machine-controlled city jobs by the 1950s, in Chicago many of its forty thousand patronage jobs, as in the Park District, were machine controlled until the 1980s. The machine worked in close tandem with the Chicago Federation of Labor, and especially with its predominantly white construction craft union affiliates, which supported the Daley organization's downtown development initiatives. Blacks garnered little of the city's patronage, though "white ethnics used the machine as an instrument of upward social mobility" (Gills 1991, 38).

As black protests escalated in the streets, during the 1960s and early 1970s, the Daley machine abandoned alliances with even moderately independent black leaders like Dawson and recruited black ward leaders with little attachment or support of their own in black neighborhoods and hence much more dependent on the machine. Political scientist William Grimshaw noted that, "as the racial demands escalated, the machine increasingly took on the retrograde character of a southern white supremist Democratic party" (Grimshaw 1992, 117). During a 1968 black riot after Martin Luther King Jr.'s assassination, Mayor Daley gave police officers orders to "shoot to kill," and Chicago police were widely considered in the black community to have deliberately murdered Black Panther leaders Fred Hampton and Mark Clark on December 4, 1969 (Commission of Inquiry into the Black Panthers and the Police 1973). The Daley organization was deeply hated in the black community and especially by black nationalist activists. When Mayor Harold Washington came to power in Chicago, he did so after defeating, as did many other black mayors in the Midwest and Northeast, an established white-led political machine.

A second kind of patronage system, "pro-growth" coalitions, supported by development projects and their beneficiaries, garner campaign resources for the administration then in power. In pro-growth networks the beneficiaries are private businesses rather than public employees, with development contracts allocated according to certain minimum performance standards with machine patronage and pro-growth patronage operating in tandem in some cities. The Chicago machine, under Mayor Richard Daley, not only controlled city jobs but influenced the distribution of federal development funds through the pro-growth coalition (Ferman 1996).

A third form of urban patronage is the contracting out of large sums of money to nonprofit community-based organizations, community-development corporations, churches involved in community building; and the awarding of contracts to municipal trade unions that represent city workers. Many states and cities contract out social-service delivery to nonprofit organizations; in 1977, twenty-five states spent at least half of their state's human-service budget allocation on contracts with nonprofit providers (Smith and Lipsky 1993, 56). Officials can come to rely on non-profits to undertake voter registration to educate residents about various issues, to lobby other officials, or, in the case of officials who want to discourage low-income-voter mobilization, to refuse to conduct any such civic activities. Since nonprofit service providers and community-development corporations are concentrated in low-income minority communities, and are frequently staffed by minority professionals, some political scientists argue that black officials gain legitimacy in poor black communities not directly but through black middle-class professionals who staff such agencies and encourage broader black support for incumbent politicians (Kilson 1996; Reed 1999). Local governments support community-development corporations that build and manage subsidized low-income housing or that undertake local economic development projects. As clients of government patrons, such groups depend on the government for revenue; and government authorities can exercise pressure on them by renegotiating their contracts at lower rates, by paying them late, or by initiating frequent harassing investigations of their performance.

Municipal unions, the formal organizations of public city workers, often also receive patronage. In all but nine states, seven in the South (Arkansas, Louisiana, Mississippi, North Carolina, South Carolina, Virginia, West Virginia), and two in the Southwest (Arizona and Colorado), state legislation has granted certain state and local government employees the right to organize and bargain collectively. Thus, Georgia grants collective bargaining rights only to teachers and firefighters (Kearney 1992). In some cities, like New York, from before World War II and still to this day, municipal unions with collective bargaining rights have played a major role in local politics (Meier 1987). In other cities, especially in the South, where state laws prohibit collective bargaining, few city workers are organized, and for that reason, among others, municipal unions, like labor unions generally, are weakest in the southern states and strongest in the Northeast, Midwest, and on the West Coast, where such collective bargaining is permitted.

To increase a city's power in state politics, municipal trade unions have at times supported efforts to increase voting among the black and Latino poor. But, because, unlike the construction trades, municipal unions derive little direct benefit from private "pro-growth" downtown business development projects, they are squeezed financially by powerful suburban white voting constituencies that are unwilling to shore up increased state spending for urban programs that union employees implement. As city employees in large cities have become increasingly black and Latino, municipal trade unions, too, have tended to become predominantly black and Latino, and in some cities, these unions have led election and reelection campaigns of black mayors. Municipal unions, for example, provided critical support for the reelection of Chicago's Harold Washington, who assiduously courted the unions, extending collective bargaining rights to twenty thousand city employees during his tenure (Green 1989, 153). Washington won the coveted endorsement of the Chicago Federation of Labor (an earlier white machine ally). Where labor unions have collective bargaining agreements with the city, black control of a municipal labor union can make black workers' organizations the most powerful black political organizations in the city, in resources, in numbers, and in political mobilization capacity.

In contrast to the declining strength of labor unions in the national labor force over the last half century, municipal labor unions at the local level have become increasingly central as fulcrums for black organizational power (Williams 2002), and, according to the U.S. Bureau of Labor Statistics, African Americans are more likely to belong to unions than any other major demographic group. With a unionization rate of 18.2 percent in 2002, compared with 13.8 percent for whites, 12.9 percent for Asians, and 11.9 percent for Latinos, African Americans have become the most unionized group in the United States; but black membership in municipal unions varies dramatically by region, in accordance with state laws and, particularly, with the legacy of historical opposition to integrationist unionism in the South (Honey 1993). Black unionization rates are three to four times higher in New York, Chicago, and Oakland than in southern cities such as Atlanta and Houston (see table 2.3). The high black unionization rates in New York and Chicago reflect both high concentration of black workers in public-sector employment and prevalence of collective bargaining in non-southern regions.

Strong black municipal unions have the capacity to alter the balance of power between poor and middle-class sectors of the black community and, therefore, to alter black mayoral politics itself, a combination most likely found in present circumstances outside the South.

Black mayors, historically, were opposed to machine patronage because blacks themselves did not benefit from it, but they have since tended to participate actively in the "pro-growth" patronage system. Some mobi-

Table 2.3
Union Density in Cities

	Employed (in thousands)	Members (in thousands)	Percentage Union	Percentage Public
Buffalo	497.8	154.8	31.1	73.1
New York	8,756.6	2,042.8	23.3	70.1
Sacramento	774.7	173.3	22.4	58.2
Detroit	2,629.4	571.5	21.7	57.6
Milwaukee	909.0	188.3	20.7	68.2
Las Vegas	620.8	123.4	19.9	43.7
Pittsburgh	935.5	178.9	19.1	55.1
Seattle	1,641.5	310.0	18.9	46.8
Chicago	4,096.3	750.7	18.3	50.2
Minneapolis	1,421.4	253.3	17.8	58.2
St. Louis	1,267.9	224.1	17.7	36.1
Philadelphia	2,703.9	471.1	17.4	55.1
Grand Rapids	579.8	97.3	16.8	58.5
San Francisco	3,359.3	552.7	16.5	53.7
Portland, OR	1,072.6	172.8	16.1	58.3
Cleveland	1,419.8	223.8	15.8	54.7
Hartford	516.0	81.2	15.7	50.8
Los Angeles	6,621.1	989.0	14.9	51.6
Louisville	508.9	74.2	14.6	31.7
San Diego	1,199.7	165.7	13.8	44.1
Columbus	779.3	106.0	13.6	50.4
Boston	2,555.0	332.8	13.0	52.3
Cincinnati	887.2	107.0	12.1	34.7
Washington	3,533.0	415.2	11.8	29.0
Indianapolis	704.7	78.6	11.2	26.4
Kansas City, KS	891.2	97.7	11.0	23.5
Jacksonville	502.7	47.8	9.5	40.2
Denver	1,231.2	109.8	8.9	27.6
New Orleans	590.5	51.9	8.8	20.8
Miami	1,635.9	143.0	8.7	39.7
Nashville	567.8	45.9	8.1	22.6
Salt Lake City	655.9	52.7	8.0	22.8
Phoenix	1,370.4	90.9	6.6	20.9
Orlando	810.7	53.8	6.6	25.8
Houston	2,002.4	122.7	6.1	21.0

	Employed (in thousands)	Members (in thousands)	Percentage Union	Percentage Public
Atlanta	2,122.0	124.3	5.9	17.2
Norfolk	610.1	34.3	5.6	10.7
Tampa	1,010.1	52.1	5.2	23.6
Charlotte	661.2	34.0	5.1	13.7
Dallas	2,669.0	134.5	5.0	18.2
Greensboro, N.C.	604.9	26.7	4.4	13.3
San Antonio	710.1	25.6	3.6	11.7
Austin	522.5	15.8	3.0	10.2
Raleigh	581.4	14.1	2.4	6.3

Source: The Labor Research Association (2001). Available: http://www.laborresearch.org.

lizing black mayors have sought to develop political capacity in poor black communities by supporting community and labor patronage, as Mayor Washington did in Chicago, and Mayor Dinkins did in New York. But the existence of municipal unions and extensive publicly funded community-nonprofit organizations does not mean that mayors necessarily control actual contracts since the political design of cities varies tremendously in the degree of power and patronage allocated to their mayors. Decentralization of patronage has a negative effect on black civic attention on mayoral politics. Generally, as blacks attained mayors' offices, the available patronage declined and with it the power of the mayor's office and its access to patronage.

Centralized city governments, or "strong mayors," manage the budget and personnel of city agencies, bargain with unions, and contract out services. Mayoral elections in strong-mayor cities provide opportunities for building citywide coalitions across neighborhood and "special issue" cleavages and for distribution of power in return.[16] In decentralized city governments, or "weak mayor" cities, in contrast, where the city council usually appoints a city manager who manages city agencies and prepares the city budget for council approval, and where the mayor may have a vote on the city council but does not directly manage city affairs, power hangs more on the decisions of the city manager than of the mayor, and on the cumulative results of individual council elections than on the mayor. The mayor's office is less of a political prize. Candidates for council elections tend to focus more on local neighborhood issues than on the welfare of the city as a whole. While a strong political organization (or party) may be able to organize slates of candidates to run on a common program of citywide issues, without strong organization, city elections become highly localized events that seldom engage citizens in broad coalition building.

City political structures differ in other dimensions as well, as, for example, on whether elections are partisan or nonpartisan, and on the established structure for service delivery (city, county, special district, or state-administered). Nonpartisan elections allow candidates to cross-file with either party, leaving no single organization for a party to control and the candidate's party affiliation not even appearing on the ballot. California, for example, has no legally defined party organizations below the level of county committees. California's party organizations, as a consequence, are extremely weak and do not serve as a venue for bringing political activists together. Nor does it have an equivalent of New York City's district leaders, whose job it is to collect petitions for club-endorsed candidates and then to distribute machine patronage (however limited) to club members (Ware 1985, 38).

Organization of service delivery also affects local city politics, as, for example, in cases where it is run mostly by the city or by a larger county government or by the state government directly, and when it is directly provided by government agencies or contracted out to private vendors or parceled out to quasi-public or wholly appointed special authorities, who may, in turn, generate independent revenues through fees for services (such as bridge tolls). Not uncommonly, city services are provided through a dizzying maze of all of the above. Whether the organization of services has a unifying or fragmenting effect on unions, community nonprofit organizations, and civic organizations depend on the structure of local government. Where, as in California cities such as Oakland, schools are managed by independently elected schools boards, social and health services are provided by the county, and land use is dominated by special authorities and the state, with fire, police, and sanitation provided by the city and private vendors, individual unions and civic organizations focus primarily on the relevant elections and public procedures and tend to be single-issue oriented. By contrast, in a city like New York, where these functions are united under the control of a strong mayor, unions and civic organizations are more likely to engage in coalition building and in negotiating with other organizations to influence mayoral elections and mayoral decision making. None of these organizations is strong enough individually to determine the outcome of an election, but together they may.

Thus, a centralized design of city government *encourages* citywide black coalition building, and coalitions strengthen black civic capacity. While decentralized local government, on the other hand, fragments black organizations and tends to hamper citywide black political mobilization in mayoral elections, with less compelling reason to focus on a mayor who does not control organizational resources, fragmentation undermines the potential cooperative efficacy of intra-black coalitions. With city reform movements to "modernize" local governments weakening the power of mayors and political parties and balkanizing service delivery, political demobilization in general, but particularly of non-elites, tends to be the result (Alford and Lee 1968; Bridges 1997a; Welch and Bledsoe 1988). The effect of this process probably is stronger in low-income African American communities, where resources for civic engagement are scarce. Hence what seems like beneficent government reform to progressive white-led organizations may retard the access of blacks and Latino minorities to political power and seem repressive in their effect on minority communities.

In a city with a weak mayor, nonpartisan elections, and a balkanized service-delivery structure, it will be difficult to hold black mayors accountable to black poor without a substantial investment in building citywide organizational capacity and without concerted efforts to establish an ethos of cross-organizational cooperation.

Some regions in the United States are more fragmented than others, and some cities within regions are also more fragmented than others. Nor is the trend necessarily unintentional. As political scientist Amy Bridges has shown, California's nonpartisan elections, its weak-mayor reform local governments, and its fragmented service delivery were, in fact, deliberately designed to undermine dissident social movements and to insulate and sustain elite control of public decision-making processes (Bridges 1997a, 216–21). A recent study of California municipal elections found that cities with greater centralized control of services had higher voter turnout (Lewis 2003). Fragmented authority weakened citizen participation.

Oakland, California, is a study in contrast to Chicago's strongly centralized mayoral control of service delivery. In 1973, when Oakland elected Lionel Wilson as its first black mayor—Wilson was succeeded by Elihu

Harris, another black mayor, and then by the white former governor of California, Jerry Brown—the victory was largely symbolic because the machinery of government rested in the hands of the city manager. With a part-time position, Oakland's mayor had a weak role in city government, presiding over the city council; the mayor neither managed the city on a day-to-day basis nor prepared the city budget for city council ratification (King 1988). Both important tasks belonged to the city manager who was appointed by the council. The mayor also had little control over the delivery of services; a host of specially elected bodies and other branches of government delivered services, and the schools were run by an elected seven-member board of education, with transit, water, and parks services run by separately elected boards for each department. Many other local governmental functions in this largest of the eight cities within the county—the courts, jails, public defender and district attorney's offices, and the county sheriff's department—were overseen by the five-person Alameda County Board of Supervisors, three of whom represented parts of Oakland but also the smaller cities of Berkeley, San Leandro, and Alameda. The supervisors administered the entire welfare system and two hospitals and funded many of the community-based programs in the county. Changes in city government structure after the 1998 election of Mayor Jerry Brown only slightly strengthened the office of the mayor.

Nevertheless the black community of Oakland was organized in various respects. Under the earlier—black—mayors, one of the most prominent community organizations at that time, the Oakland Community Organization (OCO), recruited mainly black and Latino low-income memberships with more than 2,500 families in 165 communities involved by the late 1980s (Miley 1988). Black OCO Director, and—as of 2004—County Supervisor Nate Miley said at the time that black Oakland activists were as involved in community organizing as in the 1960s when the Black Panthers were active, but with this difference: after the expansion of government-funded service programs, "most people tend to be [single] issue-oriented" (Miley 1988). As other research has suggested, black "single-issue" activism in Oakland was dispersed along the balkanized lines of regional-government service delivery (Oden 1999, 60). With so much authority over delivery of key services for black constituents provided by the county or by semi-autonomous authorities, and with black mayors themselves holding little power despite twenty-one years of governance of city hall, black community and labor activists divided their political efforts between the diverse levels of government (Oden 1999, 60). A civic alliance of five hundred members, the Oakland Progressive Political Alliance (OPPA), formed in 1983, banded together explicitly to overcome the divisions between issue-oriented activists in the city (Huen 1988). "Unfortunately that hasn't happened," said Oakland activist James Vann (Vann 1988); OPA was so divided among "single issues" that its members were never able to develop a central focus. Although individual OPA members were critical of Mayor Wilson, who served from 1977 to 1989, they did not speak with a unified voice (Huen 1988), and gradually drifted back into their separate issue niches, the organization suffering a slow death (Vann). Labor unions experienced a similar fragmentation. While Oakland had (and has) a unionized municipal workforce, its municipal unions were (and are) more focused on county and state government than on city government (Huen 1988). The Alameda County Central Labor Council, attending primarily to county issues, did little to encourage political activism in Oakland itself (Ford 1988). When Oakland's unions did get involved in local politics, they tended to focus narrowly on their members' jobs and did not link up with community organizations for broader citywide political campaigns (Rubin 1985). Oakland union leader Pat Ford summed up what many activists repeated, "Unions have not become the force in Oakland politics that they could be and should be" (Ford 1988).

Joe Brooks, a long-time participant in Oakland black politics, said that Mayor Jerry Brown won in Oakland because black activists failed to recognize the political trap of their single-issue orientation and did not organize a unified political coalition: "[T]here was no [black] venue to talk through how to win—issues, program, voting participation, etc. Eleven folks jumped out there [ran for mayor] with no real connection to any base, therefore making it easy for Brown to win" (Brooks 2002). The lack of well-organized community groups and black-led labor unions has been less crucial in Oakland than the lack of strong organizational incentives to coalesce politically. The design of California's political system thus works to diffuse community and labor activism.

Does the Institutionalization of Black Politics Preclude Disruptive Politics?

Black mayoral politics has followed multiple paths, but the dominant one appears to be a traditional one of supporting downtown business development, enhancing affirmative action for the black middle class, and providing little system change for the black poor. Yet some black mayors, like Mayor Washington of Chicago, have pursued nontraditional neighborhood-development policies in poor neighborhoods, attempting to steer greater public resources toward the poor, and found innovative ways to use public resources to strengthen the civic and political capacity of low-income black communities. The reasons for their movements in this direction success have been twofold. One is their continued need to mobilize the black poor both before and after their mayoral election in order to prepare the way for reelection. In Chicago, racial polarization was too high and the size of the total black vote too low for Harold Washington to win reelection with a coalition of liberal whites and middle-class blacks alone. Hence, Washington proclaimed his intention to respond to the needs of the poor, prioritized this goal to his administration, and sought innovation in policy and procedures to implement pro-poor initiatives. The second, related, reason concerns the capacity of poor black communities to hold black mayors accountable by threatening opposition or by offering support for reelection. In this light it would have been perilous for Chicago's Harold Washington to lose the support of black activists in poor communities. I have argued that community civic capacity is more likely to develop (or persist) in cities with strong-mayor structures because many black civic organizations in such cities have a common interest in forming citywide coalitions that empower them to influence mayoral elections and policies—despite ideological differences and spatial separation of neighborhoods. So, too, strong mayors have patronage resources to enhance the power of black civic organizations in poor and working-class communities to help get them reelected. Washington was squeezed from two ends, his regime fiercely resisted by most white Democrats in Chicago, and confronted with potent pressure for substantive results from his core black constituency, yet, despite and because of such pressures, his administration sought innovative ways to be accountable to the black poor. Washington became a national tribune for organizing and mobilizing communities to take control of government. He told the Democratic National Committee in 1983 that "the time has passed for politics as usual because the voters nationwide, like the voters in Chicago, want meaningful change, participation and involvement, reform and, above all, the chance to seize the big decisions about government with their own hands" (Miller 1988, 10).

The structural considerations, or mechanisms, that led Harold Washington to an unconventional political path—to pursue black votes and to respond to organized pressure from the black community for accountability to the black poor—exist in other cities as well. Government centralization strengthens black civic capacity for politics in other cities, as it did in New York City where the city centralized its political structure in the late 1980s, with sharp before and after effects. Mayor Dinkins in New York moved in a direction similar to Washington's. However, outcomes in Chicago and New York were different, due in no small part to differences in the strategic choices of Washington and Dinkins.

The presence of more than one path in black mayoral politics suggests that it is too sweeping a generalization to maintain, as does Robert Smith, that post–civil-rights-era black politics is "trying to achieve a nonsystemic [radical] demand by routine, systemic methods" and therefore, that its focus is limited to "neglect, or at best, symbolism" (Smith 1996, 23–24). Institutionalization has altered the balance of power in many cities to the disadvantage of the poor, but, in some cases, as, for example, in highly unionized cities, it has strengthened the political capacity of poor black communities. Moreover, if the mechanisms that encourage a more relevant and accountable black politics are better understood, activists may learn deliberate strategies to cultivate such politics in other cities. Activists wanting to prod black officials to take a greater interest in engaging the black poor in politics might support the creation of metropolitan governance structures that would have the twofold effect of increasing the racial competitiveness of elected offices, thus forcing black politicians to pay more attention to mobilizing black voters, and, simultaneously, expanding access to regional resources to address the needs of the poor after elections. The downside of this strategy is, of course, the risk of diluting the black vote as was the case in several recent regional consolidations:

> The consolidation of governments in metropolitan areas almost always served to weaken the power of racial minorities in the new electorate as compared to the old central city. In Jacksonville the percentage of the electorate that was black dropped from 44 to 25 percent as a result of the reorganization; in Indianapolis the drop was from 27 to 17 percent, and in Nashville from 38 to 20 percent. (Ross and Levine 2001, 355)

Activists seeking to overcome the effects of vote dilution and fragmented government-service delivery systems could form standing civic coalitions for the explicit purpose of creating shared understandings and shared capacities for political action.[17]

Even where a city's structure favors strong black civic coalitions, they do not always materialize or may not be sustainable. Thus, in Chicago, Harold Washington's death was followed by a splitting apart of the black coalition Washington led and by a machine-endorsed black mayor and then by a moderate white Democrat. While political structure plays a crucial role in the organization and deployment of power, ultimately, in a democracy, the key political considerations for mayors and other officials have to do with the power and direction of informal civic associations because organized constituents have the power to change political structures—and to change elected officials. Thus black civic power is a critical determinant of whether—even in cities where the political structure favors formation of black citywide political coalitions—black mayors will organize and be accountable to the black poor.

Acquiring, Building, and Sustaining Power

Black Civic Organizations
in Urban Democracy

3

On December 14, 1994, the city of Baltimore passed an ordinance requiring companies bidding for service contracts with the city to pay employees on city jobs a minimum of $6.10 an hour, with annual increases totaling up to $7.70 an hour by July 1999, and, after July 1998, with wages tethered at 110 percent of the poverty income for a family of four. In July of 2000 this ordinance provided $8.03 an hour, $2.88 above the federal minimum wage of $5.15. For each day a new wage was unpaid, employers would be fined $50 per worker (Fine 2003, 227, 229). The Baltimore "living wage" ordinance was the first in the United States. Over the subsequent six years, similar ordinances passed in dozens of U.S. cities. The leading force in the living wage campaign was Baltimoreans United in Leadership Development (BUILD), a showcase demonstration of the power low-income groups could wield if organized and focused.

Formed in 1977 by nine black ministers, BUILD grew out of an Interfaith Ministerial Alliance (IMA), a black church coalition organized in the 1940s and active in the civil rights movement of the late 1960s. By the 1970s, frustrated with the declining activism of their Baltimore neighborhoods, the clergy sought professional organizing assistance from the Industrial Areas Foundation (IAF), a group founded by the bold Chicago activist,

Saul Alinsky.[1] BUILD was the result. In the 1980s, it gained a broader following through grassroots organizing and successful protests against bank redlining of black neighborhoods, making it easier for blacks to get home mortgage loans.

With more than fifty member churches at the end of the 1980s, BUILD was widely considered one of the most powerful and independent groups in Baltimore—its member organizations paid dues, it accepted no government funds and foundation grants for its core projects, and accepted these funds only for non-essential individual projects (McDougall 1993, 126). BUILD fought against discriminatory bank lending, utility rates, auto insurance, and housing (Orr 1999, 39–40), and attracted the support of several labor unions, including the Baltimore Teachers Union (BTU) and the American Federation of State, County, and Municipal Employees (AFSCME).

The mayor's office in Baltimore was an important target for citywide black political organizing in a city with a "strong-mayor" political structure. The city council cannot appropriate funds without the mayor's recommendation; it can subtract from, but cannot add to, the city budget (Fine 2003, 215). In 1987, BUILD played a key role in the campaign of Kurt Schmoke to become Baltimore's first elected black mayor. At the time, Baltimore was 60 percent black, with blacks a majority of registered voters (McDougall 1993, 95), yet a low black voter turnout rate had recently led to the defeat of another black mayoralty candidate, Billy Murphy. Blacks held only eight of sixteen city council seats in Baltimore and no African American had ever won a seat in a majority-white political district. In 1987, BUILD conducted a voter registration drive that added ten thousand new voters to the rolls; it collected fifty-five thousand signatures on behalf of a sweeping and focused "municipal agenda" that called for school-based management and neighborhood-school autonomy, for job enrichment centers to upgrade skills for unemployed workers, tenant management of public housing, community-oriented policing, and a commuter tax to help meet city financial obligations (McDougall 1993, 129–31).

Kurt Schmoke was without grassroots activist experience. His opponent was another African American, Clarence "Du" Burns, appointed acting mayor in 1986 after Mayor William Donald Schaefer, a powerful white machine politician, was elected governor. Schaefer supported Burns and so did the "white political clubs that were the framework of Schaefer's machine" (McDougall 1993, 97). Schmoke won in a close election, and told a mass meeting of volunteers that, "the real winner was BUILD's agenda. And

BUILD's agenda is Baltimore's agenda" (Orr 1999, 133; Fine 2003). BUILD became an informal partner in the Schmoke regime and stimulated black community pressure for actions to meet its needs (Orr 1999, 141).

Schmoke took a number of controversial steps in his first term to strengthen his support in poor black neighborhoods (McDougall 1993, 118). For example, he provided a $4.6 million contract to provide security guards for four crime-ridden public housing developments to a company linked to the Nation of Islam (Valentine 1995b), and, in his 1995 Democratic primary reelection campaign (the general election in Baltimore was a token election in the heavily Democratic city), distributed "Vote for Schmoke" bumper stickers in red, black, and green, the traditional Black Power colors. Explaining Schmoke's emphasis on grassroots black organizing, Elijah E. Cummings, a close Schmoke ally and a West Baltimore state legislator, said that, in a conservative national political climate, black activists did not want to "lose another black mayor. . . . We just did not want to be a New York and lose David Dinkins" (Valentine 1995a). At the same time, Schmoke sought to boost his support among white constituents and downtown corporations (Valentine 1995b). Pre-election polls indicated that Schmoke had only a four-point lead over his white challenger, City Councilwoman Mary Pat Clarke. Nevertheless, after a strong black grass-roots mobilization effort, Schmoke won a landslide 59 to 39 percent victory. The black turnout was 60 percent of registered voters, compared with a 40 percent white turnout. Observers noted that the election was strongly polarized by race, with several black precincts giving 92 percent of their vote to Schmoke and several white precincts 96 percent to Clarke (Valentine 1995a).

BUILD, in addition to its key role in Schmoke's mayoralty, continued to pay attention to marginalized groups in local decision making and in protest activities. It also sought to cultivate democratic participation within its own organization and within its participating organizations. It promoted women leaders, previously often unrecognized, and did the homework and organizing after the election that was necessary to translate community grievances into policy demands on government. The Reverend Vernon Dobson, leader of Baltimore's Interfaith Ministerial Alliance in the 1960s and a prominent BUILD leader, explained its philosophy and its challenges: "You must share your vision with people by making them partners in the process. . . . We've done well in the larger arena, but we find that *within* our member churches, power is not being shared. We don't have justice *inside* the church. The clergy are mobilized to attack power inequities in society at large, but they're not prepared to give up any of the power that they wield inside their own churches. It's not just the churches, of course. . . . That's why there is a possibility of conflict between the ministers and the base communities" (McDougall 1993, 179–80).

BUILD's membership reflects the more stable and secure elements of the black community, not the most poor and marginalized, and has often been less than bold. Its black ministers opposed some measures supported by other grassroots black civic groups and school activists, as when it successfully resisted the removal of a heavily criticized black school superintendent, Richard Hunter, two years before his contract was due to expire. Also, worried lest it alienate the Catholic cardinal, BUILD backed off from organizing Head Start workers at Catholic Charities who had sought a living wage (Catholic Charities administered half of the Head Start program and strongly opposed unionization) (Fine 2003, 278). The BUILD churches themselves, "with significant resources are middle class, and many have little contact with marginal people," so Harold McDougall, public policy and law professor, reports (McDougall 1993, 134). But Darnell Ridgley, a Schmoke staffer, community advocate, and go-between with BUILD, expressed BUILD's desire to reach more deeply into marginalized sectors of the black community and to draw them into its orbit:

> It's very important to find and cultivate the informal leadership of the community. . . . The formal leaders are the homeowners, the stable folk–the people who are articulate, the people who have something. They're very important—they are the traditional leadership of the black community, and we're lucky to have them. Too many of them leave the community, abandoning the struggle. But the only way the process of empowerment can continue is if new leadership continues to surface, not always to stand out in front, but also to fill in the gaps, to maintain communications and dialogue among all the people in the community. (McDougall 1993, 149)

A BUILD internal paper written in the early years of the new millennium—discussed in Janice Fine's astute dissertation on its labor-organizing efforts—notes that Baltimore's poor are already informally organized in numerous ways through churches, unions, Narcotics Anonymous groups, prisons, temporary employment agencies, the child-care network, check-cashing agencies/predatory lenders, and even in hospital emergency rooms.

Fine writes that organizing such poor people into broad coalitions might provide a new arena of recruitment for BUILD's coalition: "Temporary jobs and the need for child care, health care, loans and other financial services are examples of programs and services that people need and that can be provided in an much more fair and just way if organized as cooperatives" (Fine 2003, 281).

Such innovative thinking, inclusive coalition-building orientation, and sustained black civic participation in citywide politics are rare in American cities. But, why aren't there more BUILD-like coalitions in other cities, considering its record of success? In numerous other cities, political fragmentation, ideological divisiveness, lack of resources, and nondemocratic styles of leadership account for the lack of black organizational development and cooperation (Marable 1995, 164; Pinderhughes 1997; Polletta 2002; Reed 1986a; Smith 1996, 122). The structure of government and service delivery fragments black organizations in some cities more deeply than in others: Baltimore is a strong-mayor city; weak-mayor cities like Oakland may have strong black civic organizations but their political efforts are diffused into different political arenas. Yet not all strong-mayor cities have black civic coalitions that participate strongly in politics. Chicago and Cleveland, which had black civic coalitions in the 1970s and 1980s, no longer do as of 2004. Nor is weak-mayor structure the sole cause of black political division; ideological divisiveness and other problems matter as well. BUILD's accomplishments in Baltimore are all the more impressive when considered within the context of that city's black ideological conflicts, its resource problems, its diverse leadership styles, and its interorganizational competition.

Contours and Divides in Black Political Thought

The historian Manning Marable points to several trends that characterize African Americans' political organization and strategy: "inclusionism" or "pragmatic integration," "black nationalism," and "radical multicultural democracy" (Marable 1995, 209). Inclusionists are those who assume that African Americans are basically "Americans who happen to be black" and, therefore, inclusionists "seek affirmation and legitimacy within established institutions to influence public policy." Marable lists William Julius Wilson, Henry Louis Gates, Thomas Sowell, and Shelby Steele as inclusionists, all associated with the black managerial and professional elite, with public-sector employees, and stable elements of urban blue-collar workers. Yet, in my view, social democrats like Wilson, liberals like Gates, and conservatives like Sowell and Steele cover too wide an ideological spectrum. Michael Dawson distinguishes between black liberal inclusionists and Marxist-leaning inclusionists—all of whom acknowledge the reality of racism and support remediational programs such as affirmative action—and black conservative inclusionists who don't (Dawson 2001; Wilson 1999). According to Marable, "Black nationalism assumes that 'race' is a historically fixed category, which will not magically decline in significance over time; it suggests that blacks very much define themselves within their own autonomous cultural context; and it is deeply pessimistic about the ability or willingness of white civil society to transform itself democratically to include the demands of people of color" (Marable 1995, 210–11). He identifies as black nationalists the Nation of Islam, cultural nationalists such as Maulana Karenga and Amiri Baraka, academics like Malefi Asante, and among revolutionary nationalists, the former Black Panther Party of Oakland, California. Marable identifies black nationalism, too, with the hip-hop generation and the marginalized black working class, but also with, "a strong segment of the entrepreneurial black elite." He sees "black-nationalist" and "inclusionist" visions as balancing each other in momentum: "one usually advances in influence within black political culture when the other retreats." The third trend Marable identifies is "radical democracy" (Marable 1995, 212). "It differs from inclusionist and black nationalist perspectives, in that its chief objective is the dismantling or destruction of all forms of inequality. It seeks to challenge the institutions of power and privilege, and the ownership patterns, of the dominant society." Marable identifies as proponents of this perspective theorist Lani Guinier, Angela Davis, Cornel West, and himself, all academics, and he fixes its base among radicalized black intelligentsia, progressive middle- and working-class individuals, and marginalized youth. According to Marable, radical democrats argue for multiracial coalitions but believe that blacks should organize themselves as a separate group at the same time.

Black identity needs to be clarified. Black "social identity," as used here and in studies of black identity, is not the same as black "nationalism"; the former is a broader category of black nationalists, liberals, radicals, and conservatives who do not renounce an association with other blacks. Proponents of black social identity believe that all African Americans share a linked fate,[2] although they disagree significantly about whether whites are friends or enemies of black progress (Dawson 1994; Herring et al. 1999). Black nationalism, for example, is one of several black *political* identities; black nationalists are pessimistic about the effectiveness of existing laws and institutions in bringing about racial justice in light of what they regard as entrenched white racism. Not all blacks who identify socially as black share black nationalist political views. Nor should black social identity be confused with the affinity blacks feel, or do not feel, toward other blacks. Blacks who believe that all blacks share a common destiny may not feel close to other blacks and may not feel antipathy toward whites in general. Because they are convinced their individual lot will be determined by what happens to blacks as a group, they define their self-interests in group terms, a cognitive shortcut. Yet their perspective is not the same thing as black nationalism (Dawson 1994). Nor does black social identity mean that blacks trust all black leaders or other blacks (Robinson 1997). Black nationalists tend to feel affinity, for example, for the black poor but not for the black middle class or for black political conservatives as a group (Davis and Brown 2002, 247).

Black nationalists and multiculturalists often give quite different reasons for building black organizations; black nationalists are likely to view separate black organizations as the foundation for black progress in an unalterable racial climate, while black multiculturalists view them as necessary but only transitionally and in the context of an alterable though racialized climate. Both tend to have a common interest in black political independence, but differ, too, on the importance of interracial alliances. Malcolm X, particularly in his earlier years, was highly skeptical of interracial alliances between blacks and whites. He argued that blacks should only cooperate with those "whites who recognize the racism built into the structure of the United States" (Borden 1973, 429). A. Philip Randolph was, in his younger years, a radical multiculturalist. When Randolph organized the Brotherhood of Sleeping Car Porters and Maids in the mid-1920s, he faced stiff opposition from black newspapers, including the *Chicago Defender* and the Pittsburgh *Courier*, funded by the Pullman Company owned by George Pullman (Marable 1985, 81).[3] He sought to establish a national black civic coalition that could counter the conservative political influence of such white corporations in black communities. In 1935 Randolph agreed to chair the National Negro Congress (NNC), a new broad-based black coalition of civil rights, labor, and community-based groups, insisting that, "the National Negro Congress should be dependent on the resources of the

Negro people alone. The grounds for my belief is that history shows that where you get your money you also get your ideas and control." When, in 1940, the Communist Party took control of the National Negro Congress, and then engineered an affiliation between the CIO and NNC, Randolph left the NNC. John Lewis, the white head of the CIO at the time, was a firm opponent of independent black political organization,[4] and Randolph believed the NNC had "lost its soul" by losing control of its own agenda.[5] He struggled against domination by white leftists and white conservatives alike. Unlike black nationalists, however, Randolph did strongly support blacks joining the interracial labor movement.

Black nationalists and multiculturalists may have a common interest in holding black elected officials accountable, though black nationalists worry lest leaders sell out to whites (of any class) and black radical multiculturalists worry lest black leaders sell out to rich and powerful whites. Thus, while most blacks see the necessity for black organizations, they may disagree on their organizations' political direction. Substantial political tensions exist on such matters as to whether to form coalitions with Latinos or poor whites within black organizations and black coalitions, and this may weaken the black community's overall political effectiveness in some cities.

Popular Support for Differing Black Political Strategies

Michael Dawson, in *Black Visions*, identifies poles among black survey respondents based on questions about separate ideologies: black nationalism, black feminism, black Marxism, disillusioned liberalism, and black conservatism. Dawson's poles were "true believers" and "true haters," his assignment based on survey responses to sets of questions about these diverse ideologies. "True believers" were those who agreed on all issues used to construct each of the five ideological categories; "true haters" rejected all elements of a particular ideology. Even granting that a researcher's design can influence patterns of responses and interpretations of responses, Dawson's study did discover considerable diversity in political thinking among African Americans, and also a collectively strong opposition to "black conservatism" (Dawson 2001, 83) (see table 3.1).

Dawson's questions to respondents on black nationalism measured support for black community control of government and of the economy

Table 3.1

Black Ideological True Haters and True Believers

Ideology	True Believers %	True Haters %
Black Nationalism	37	4
Black Feminism	19	2
Black Marxism	34	2
Disillusioned Liberalism	40	2
Black Conservatism	1	20

Source: Michael C. Dawson, 2001. *Black Visions: Roots of Contemporary African-American Political Ideologies.* Chicago: University of Chicago Press.

(Dawson 2001, 363); on black feminism he sought to measure whether women should share leadership with men and whether women suffer from racism *and* sexism; his questions on black Marxism measured whether respondents thought the black middle class has abandoned the black poor, if the American economic system is fair to poor people, and whether blacks have common interests despite their economic differences.[6] He inferred a "disillusioned liberalism" in those who held broad egalitarian attitudes but were gloomy about reducing white/black economic differences and who also believed that the fate of blacks was tied to race (Dawson 2001, 303–7). Black conservatives, the ideological opposite of Marable's radical multiculturalists, were identified by Dawson based on their agreement that in certain circumstances, there are enough jobs but that poor blacks do not want to work, and that racial progress has made antidiscrimination programs unnecessary and counterproductive.

Dawson concluded that there is clearly considerable overlap in opinion among African Americans, but that since many blacks simultaneously strongly support aspects of black nationalism, black Marxism, and disillusioned liberalism, at the same time significant disagreements among them were masked by the polarity of his true believer/hater scale. Black feminists and nationalists, he said, "hold severely conflicting views on coalitions [with non-blacks], the applicability of characterizing blacks as a nation within a nation, and their attitudes toward immigrant groups in the United States" (Dawson 2001, 170). So, too, blacks, Dawson said, were divided on a separate black political party (Dawson 1996), roughly half supporting the formation of such a black political party, and strongly feeling so (Davis and Brown 2002).

Other surveys of black opinion have found strong support among blacks for moderate black nationalism, which is what Dawson calls "community nationalism," and what James Jennings calls "black empowerment politics" (Jennings 1990). Darren Davis and Ronald Brown, in a 2002 study of black opinion report that while African Americans "overwhelmingly support the various components of a black nationalist ideology . . . [the] more practical or realistic aspects of black nationalism win greater support. For instance, a large percentage of African Americans support the notions that blacks should shop in black stores when possible (84.0 percent), should rely on themselves (83.3 percent), should control the economy in their communities (73.9 percent), that black children should study an African language (70.7 percent), and that blacks should control government in their communities (68.3 percent)." Least supported were statements that blacks should vote only for black candidates (26.5 percent) and least of all that black Americans should form a separate nation (14 percent) (Davis and Brown 2002, 242). Dawson argues that what he calls "radical egalitarians," a group in which he includes Marable's liberal inclusionists and integrationist-oriented multiculturalists, are likely to have difficulty attracting popular black support. His analysis on this point is consistent with the pattern of black withdrawal from electoral activity I report on in U.S. cities.

Given that 71 percent of African Americans in 2000 believed that racial progress in the United States would either not be achieved in their lifetime or would never be achieved (Dawson 2001, 318), and given the strong black support for community nationalism, it is noteworthy that sharp disagreement exists among blacks on their relationship to non-black groups in the wider society. In Dawson's survey, a third of those he identifies as black feminists believe that "other minorities and poor make good allies," while less than 10 percent of blacks supporting other ideologies agree (Dawson 2001, 344). His report indicates that 65 percent of blacks believed that blacks best represent majority-black election districts, but more than a third of blacks were convinced that whites could do as well (Dawson 2001, 131). Thirty-four percent of African Americans reported in a 2001 National Urban League survey that a multiracial identification (identifying blacks as African American or as African American and something else) will boost African American political power, while 40 percent believed that it would lessen African Americans' power (Stafford 2001, 55–56). Although strong community nationalism would suggest that most African Americans favor black solidarity, blacks are strongly divided on how deep this solidarity should be. Black rap artists, for example, have been the target of widespread criticism, including protest rallies led by Rev. Calvin Butts, the influential pastor of Harlem's Abyssinian Baptist Church, who calls rap degrading to women and a harmful force in black communities (Miller 1996). Rap artists and a number of black intellectuals respond in turn that rap artists represent authentic voices of alienated poor black youth.[7] With blacks divided over major questions such as whether whites can capably represent black communities, whether other minority and poor groups make good allies, or whether rappers should be denounced or engaged seriously in black politics, the case can be made that black politics should be conceived as intra-black *coalition* politics.[8] However, strong essentialist currents within black nationalism, as well as black liberals' tendency to exclude black nationalists and poor blacks from their political coalitions (see discussion of the National Rainbow Coalition in this chapter) mitigate against sustained coalition building.

Based on the examples of the success of Mayor Schmoke in Baltimore and Mayor Washington in Chicago, I argue that, when black community organizations exercise power through black coalitions, these organizations seem better able to hold officials accountable to substantive community demands. There is a risk, however, that civic capacity and resources are so low in poor black communities that the interests of the poor will be neglected within black coalitions, and that even black mayors who encourage poor blacks to vote will have difficulty organizing civic activity in poor communities.

Trends in Black Civic Participation and Capacity

Since the surge in black registration and turnout in 1984, the electoral participation of African Americans has continued, like other Americans, generally to decline. Except for those history-making local elections, where a black mayor or congressional representative is elected for the first time, increasing numbers of African Americans are making a decision not to participate in the electoral process. Thus, contrary to the belief of some scholars that African-American turnout would eventually equal the turnout of white Americans, this equality has yet to be reached. . . .
When you take into account the purported overestimates of

registration and voting on surveys by African Americans, the
disparity between whites and blacks, especially those living in
the South, is even greater than generally reported. (Cohen 1998)

Decline in one form of urban political participation, the central one of
voting, has been cited as a major contributing factor to anti-urban tilts in
federal and state politics. Urban voter turnout for the 1992 presidential election was 5.8 percentage points lower than suburban turnout; in 2000 9.8
points lower (Dreier et al. 2001). Much of the difference in suburban/urban
turnout is attributable to lower black voter turnout. Although African
Americans are as active in civic affairs in the first decade of the new millennium as in the 1960s, most blacks today are involved in neighborhood-
improvement efforts that do not involve protest activities, unlike Baltimore's BUILD. BUILD continues its Alinsky confrontational style of protest
politics. Civic participation is also far less evident than in the 1960s among
poor black communities. Cohen and Dawson's 1993 study of black participation in central-city Detroit neighborhoods found that, where poverty
rates exceed 30 percent, blacks were at least 20 percent less likely than more
affluent blacks to belong "to a church organization or community group."
The poorest blacks had the least contact with public representatives; and
residents living in severe poverty provided the least support to "the working class and their organizations" (Cohen and Dawson 1993, 291, 294).
Fredrick Harris similarly reports "a steady level of black community participation since the 1960s" that "changes when you look at participation by
class" (Harris 1999b, 332). Harris argues that the black poor are becoming
increasingly isolated from mainstream black civic institutions and, from
this, he concludes: "The institutions of civil society among the poor can no
longer sustain an oppositional civic culture, leaving open the possibility
that the 'organization of discontent' might lead to 'uncivil,' disruptive alternatives. Without the institutions to instill the twin virtues of civic engagement and *organized* opposition against forces that perpetuate racial-
economic inequalities, prospects for civic renewal for those at the margins
of American society seem dim" (Harris 1999b, 334). I agree with this analysis though I am more hopeful about the chances for change.

The sociologist Sharon Zukin describes Brooklyn's Brownsville, center of the divisive Oceanhill-Brownville school decentralization struggle of
1967 to 1969, as a socially disorganized community similar to Harris's description I discussed above:

From 1970, Brownsville has been almost entirely black, with a major concentration of housing projects; high welfare, unemployment and crime rates; large areas torn up by putative urban renewal plans; some rebuilding since 1985 in the form of a large development of new single-family houses [created through advocacy by an IAF affiliate]. . . . There are few stores, no banks and no bars. . . . I am not ignoring such organizations as local development corporations . . . community anti-drug coalitions and neighborhood safety patrols; or social service agencies that continue to serve the community. They simply have not been important in Brownsville. Neither have churches, despite the historical significance of the black church in America. . . . It is almost as though residents of this neighborhood have an unmediated relation with the state. (Zukin 1998, 517–18)

Why are the black poor in 2000 or 2004 participating less in civic organizations than they did in the 1960s? Diverse explanations have been offered: that the black poor are becoming increasingly spatially, and socially, isolated (Cohen and Dawson 1993; Wilson 1987); that the black poor are distrustful of neighbors in dangerous and resource-deprived neighborhoods (Rosset al. 2001); that they are not encouraged to join organizations; though they do participate where organizations are available for them (Berry et al. 1993, 95); and that they may, in fact, belong to informal organizations (such as gangs or street corner groups) that survey questionnaires looking for "good" forms of civic association tend to ignore (Cohen 2004). It is possible that, as a result, the decline in participation of the poor is an artifact of the bias of social scientists studying the poor, not of the behavior of the poor themselves. For example, Zukin's description of Brownsville does not mention gang activity. While gangs are often considered apolitical criminal enterprises, they are not always such: two notorious gangs in Los Angeles, the Bloods and the Crips, declared a truce in the wake of the 1992 Los Angeles riot and issued a document called, "Give Us the Hammer and the Nails and We Will Rebuild the City," calling for $3 billion for neighborhood improvements and health clinics; $700 million for schools; $20 million in low-interest loans for small businesses; and $6 million for training Los Angeles gang members to accompany police on patrols through the community. Its recommendations were ignored by black Los Angeles mayor, Tom Bradley (Kelley 2000, 610). Certain social scientists themselves have designated much of the activity of the poor as "deviant." The black conservative Thomas Sowell has argued that a history of sub-servience to whites has led to "foot-dragging, work-evading patterns" that persist among poorer blacks today.[9] More formal, more middle-class community organizations, churches, and labor unions are generally considered, on the other hand, emblematic of positive civic activity. Poor blacks often appear to be shut out of such respectable groups.

Community-Based Organizations

There is considerable evidence that poor blacks are seldom asked to join local community-based organizations (CBOs) and community development corporations (CDCs) though much of the common wisdom about successful inner-city community-development efforts tells a different story of the strategies pursued by CDCs and many other community-based organizations that go back to the 1960s. Growing out of the Southern civil rights movement and out of resistance to displacement of the black poor threatened by federally funded slum clearance and urban renewal programs, President Lyndon Johnson's administration in the late 1960s initiated the "maximum feasible participation" policies of the War on Poverty (Weir 1999, 141). These programs encouraged direct participation of the poor in policy making and program implementation. A key component of the War on Poverty, the Community Action Program, provided support for local community organizations' involvement in public action. Direct federal funding of the CAP groups ended, in large part, because mayors feared their own power was being eroded and became apprehensive about growing sophistication and style among the poor (Clark and Hopkins 1970, vii; Gittell 2002, 8). In response to the confrontation and activism of the 1960s, the federal government and certain private foundations had shifted their funding from grassroots organizing to encouraging community advocacy organizations to become service providers (Gittell 2002). In describing the reason for Ford Foundation funding in 1967 of the first CDC, the Bedford Stuyvesant Restoration Corporation of Brooklyn, Ford program officer Mitchell Sviridoff wrote two decades and more later that, "though never explicitly stated, the partnership concept implied a collaborative style of leadership, a sharp contrast to the contentiousness associated with its predecessor—community action" (Sviridoff 1994, 93).

Despite the harsh funding environment that followed the election of President Ronald Reagan, CDCs did find a way to survive, through participating in housing development programs.[10] In 1980, the Ford Foundation created a financial intermediary, the Local Initiatives Support Corporation (LISC), to support private partnerships with CDCs in housing and community development and, around the same time, a similar organization, the Enterprise Foundation, was spun off by the Rouse Corporation of Baltimore. CDCs got a boost, too, from low-income housing tax credits included in the Tax Reform Act of 1986, which provided tax credits to corporations that invest in low-income housing in poor communities (Weir 1999, 151). By 1997, LISC and the Enterprise Foundation had raised more than $7 billion in private equity capital for housing development (Vidal 1997). As of 2004, there were at least two thousand CDCs in low-income communities across the nation, a large proportion of them in black communities. Ninety percent of all CDCs engage in building housing, more than 75 percent overall provide resident services, such as homeowner and tenant counseling, and 60 percent provide human services such as health counseling. More than 70 percent conduct advocacy and organizing activities (Vidal 1998, 34–35). Why then, given the growing incidence of active CDCs in low-income black communities, do researchers report declines in civic political participation of the black poor? Don't CDCs ask the poor to participate in political action?

The urban policy analyst Peter Dreier responds to this question that many "CDCs that view themselves as vehicles for community mobilization among the poor are reluctant to bite the hand that feeds them, even if the meal consists mainly of scraps from the corporate or government table.... CDCs are often reluctant to engage directly in political action—whether it means mobilizing community residents around elections, protesting public policy, or advocating for different policies—for fear that they may not receive (or lose their existing) government subsidies" (Weir 1999, 179–80). The law limits the political involvement of groups that receive 501(c)(3) tax status from the Internal Revenue Service and Dreier suggests that groups hesitate to test the limits of the law because "enforcement of these statutes can be somewhat arbitrary and political." Marilyn Gittell's 2002 study of CDCs' nonpolitical focus concludes that local governments and funders generally have discouraged CDC involvement in political coalitions, that local groups compete for limited funding, while local politicians often pit community groups against one another, and that many CDCs in black communities are run by whites who live outside the community. According to Gittell, too, most CDCs support gentrification and pro-growth policies in their cities and neighborhoods. CDCs may also fail to mobilize the poor because nonconfrontational CDCs single out middle-class and stable working-class residents for their organizing focus.

Trade Unions

But, while decline in the participation of the black poor seems to be a general trend, at least as measured in social science surveys to date, there are important exceptions. Certain labor unions have bucked this trend.

Blacks, including poor blacks, participate in trade unions at a higher rate than other racial or ethnic groups (see chapter 2). The 1995 victory of John Sweeney as president of the AFL-CIO represented a shift in the labor movement's prior lack of commitment to organizing low-income service workers, to recruiting women and workers of color, and also to collaborating with community-based organizations. Before winning the AFL-CIO presidency, Sweeney had been head of the Service Employees International Union (SEIU), which launched several successful organizing campaigns—including the national Justice for Janitors campaign begun in the late 1980s and the unionization of more than sixty thousand homecare workers in Los Angeles, campaigns that particularly targeted immigrants among people of color while deploying community-based organizing as a core tactic. SEIU, UNITE (Union of Needletrades, Industrial and Textile Employees), and HERE (Hotel Employees and Restaurant Employees International Union) are among the service unions that, in the early years of the new millennium, have increasingly turned to community-organizing strategies (Fine 2000–2001).

Unlike most CDCs and CBOs, unions do tend to encourage their members to participate in politics, including even contentious politics.[11]

Industrial unions, especially in the 1930s and 1940s had served as an early training ground for some black activists as black workers took advantage of openings for organizing within industrial unions to establish militant local labor organizations (Hill 1996). The biggest advance in black unionization in that period came about through the activities of the Congress of Industrial Organizations (CIO), after its formation in the Depression, with black unionization rising from 150,000 in 1935 to 1.25 million in 1945 at the end of World War II. But, despite such gains, the CIO had, at best, a mixed record on race.[12] While its stand in favor of black civil and voting rights earned respect from black leadership, it did little to fight discriminatory hiring practices or occupational discrimination against black workers, and, in the 1940s, abandoned its grand plan (Operation Dixie) to organize Southern black workers (Goldfield 1997; Hill 1996; Kelley 1998). By 1956, when the CIO merged with the American Federation of Labor, which was historically based in more racially exclusive craft unions, it had backpedaled substantially on civil rights.

"Free" labor and freedom itself has been historically associated in the United States with being white, and, for much of U.S. history, with white male workers only (Kelley 1998). The U.S. labor movement historically exhibited considerable hostility and exclusionary behavior toward black (as well as to Asian and Latino) workers. Indeed, many white labor movements were forged with the goal of blocking minorities from gaining a foothold as citizens as well as in industry (Roediger 2002). As Earl Lewis writes, in his study of Norfolk, Virginia: "Even white workers who may have shared a similar class position enjoyed a superior position because of their race. Thus, although it appears that some black workers manifested a semblance of worker consciousness, that consciousness was so imbedded in the perspective of race that neither blacks nor whites saw themselves as equal partners in the same labor movement" (Lewis 1991, 58). Because of a long history of racial discrimination against blacks, Latinos, and Asians in the U.S. labor movement, one could describe black workers in interracial unions as having chosen "class over race," but this would be inaccurate (Hill 1996). The framework through which labor unions viewed "class" interests was itself off-putting to black movements. The U.S. labor movement in the twentieth century was characterized by a large divide between workplace and community struggles, and between union economic battles and broader struggles for equal rights (Katznelson 1981). Most labor leaders did not organize the unemployed, and they disconnected welfare rights and the criminalization of large numbers of underemployed black and Latino youth for "hustling" in the informal drug economy from "labor" issues. So, too, labor organizations seldom linked the history of exploitation of blacks as slaves to underpaid southern Jim Crow workers, or of blacks' social oppression and political disenfranchisement to U.S. workers' political weakness (Thompson 2004).

Many black labor leaders themselves understood the connections between labor and community struggle though most white labor leaders did not. A. Philip Randolph, for example, was both a trade union leader and a leader of the civil rights movement. Coleman Young, elected Detroit's first black mayor in 1973, had been a veteran of the United Automobile Workers (UAW) and executive secretary of the leftist National Negro Labor Council in the 1950s. Civil rights leader E. D. Nixon, Oakland political leader (and uncle of Oakland congressman, Ron Dellums) C. L. Dellums, New York's labor, electoral, and black power leader Vickie Garvin, North Carolina labor and community nationalist leader and, later, Milwaukee education activist Howard Fuller, and many other black leaders were simultaneously labor and community leaders.

Black activists and organizations like black churches, fraternal orders, and community organizations often supported black unionization efforts early. "Black workers turned union gatherings into revival meetings," Kelley reported of organizing drives (Kelley 1998, 5). Randolph's Brotherhood of Sleeping Car Porters (BSCP) maintained a women's auxiliary that provided crucial support for the union (Chateauvert 1998), and the Brotherhood was a major distribution network for northern black newspapers banned from sale in the South (Nelson). Industrial unions were, despite their racial contradictions, interracial meeting places, providing rare spaces for common conversation and socializing between white workers and black labor and community associations. Such communal common spaces have shrunk dramatically in recent decades as production processes moved overseas to take advantage of cheaper labor, lower taxes, less regulation, and anti-union political environments. Manufacturing jobs have been replaced by service jobs in health care, education, office maintenance, entertainment, food services, and retail, divided sharply between high-paid professionals (such as physicians) and low-paid, lesser skilled workers (such as homecare attendants), both groups less likely to be unionized, and the lower income jobs more likely to be held by women and brown and black workers. White male membership in unions dropped to below 50 percent in 1995, the vacuum filled by women and minority workers, who became the majority.

The renewed interest among some labor unions in working with black community organizations has, as with BUILD in Baltimore, altered black politics. Alliances have emerged in Philadelphia, Los Angeles, and New Haven, Connecticut, with such growing labor interest and activity in organizing in low-income black communities a potentially significant countertendency to the general decline in civic organization, in black voter turnout in poor black communities, as well as decline in labor union membership nationally. Since the mid-1980s, there has also been a significant growth in the number of powerful local unions headed by African Americans (Marable 1999, 190).

As black-led trade unions gain more access to significant political resources and large numbers of dues-paying members, black and Latino communities have moved to the center of efforts in the new millennium to rebuild labor unions, especially in the service industry, where they dominate after the substantial exodus of manufacturing jobs to low-wage developing countries. It is even conceivable that black- or Latino-led trade unions may increasingly transcend the historical parochialism of American trade unionism and initiate, or join, organizing efforts in poor black or Latino neighborhoods. This might indeed occur if the jobs of blacks in municipal trade unions—such as welfare and school service providers—are threatened by cuts in federal funding directed at the poorest of the black poor. Unions standing alone in the face of such loss seldom have enough power to win battles in local, state, or national elections. In Baltimore, the head of the teachers' union explained why the union joined BUILD: "We wanted to align ourselves with a group that had some power. It was that simple" (Orr 1999, 86). The earlier dominant trade unionist ideology of framing workers' interests in terms of the "self-interest" of individual workers, and of individual union contracts, is increasingly viewed by black worker activists as inappropriate and insufficient in the black urban context (Lynch 2000). Thus, following a strategy of group self-interest, a strong local municipal health care union may be able to win some wage increases from a city or state government while other less powerful unions fail in this effort. If, however, the money to pay for a health care contract is generated by cuts in funding for daycare and education, the health care union will have won a questionable victory since members of the union themselves are likely to rely on public schools and daycare services. In this context, framing black workers' interests in ways that connect to those of other community organizations that advocate for community needs makes more sense.

Black Churches

The black church, the first civic organization to be owned and controlled by African Americans, during much of the history of the Jim Crow South was the only place where most blacks could hold meetings, pray, and protest. Many churches provided a wide array of services, from aid for the sick and elderly to insurance to the establishment of colleges. The churches were, in effect, *public* institutions (Higgenbotham 1993, 11, 65). Although not all black churches were or are active in their communities, many remain the primary civic institution not only, as traditionally, in towns and rural communities of the South that made the civil rights movement possible but also in inner-city black neighborhoods across the country. In 1993, roughly twenty million African Americans, half of the U.S. black population, reported that they belonged to a black church (Harris 1999a, 31–32). Eighty percent of blacks in 1993 said that religion was "very important" in their lives, and an additional 16 percent that it is "somewhat important" (Tate 1994, 95).[13] These church members are divided among more than a half-dozen major denominations and numerous smaller sects, and are theologically and socially diverse, but with the largest denomination, the Baptists, entirely autonomous in governance. While other significant denominations within the black community—for example, the Methodists (African Methodist Episcopal [AME]) and Pentecostals (Church of God in Christ [COGIC])—are more hierarchical, many individual churches exercise considerable autonomy in local affairs; generally, black churches are quite independent of external control though they vary greatly in the extent of involvement in civic and political affairs.

Black churches have been a significant organizational resource for civic participation and political mobilization. According to political scientist Katherine Tate, nearly 60 percent of black church attendants in 1984 said their churches encouraged voter participation (Tate 1994, 97). Church members visit other churches and build networks across and between communities. In church social networks, politics is discussed and church services are key events for black (and white) politicians in search of votes. A positive signal from a pastor in support of a candidate usually carries great weight with a church congregation. Carl Stokes, mayor of Cleveland, wrote in 1973, "Having a preacher mention your name favorably to his congregation is worth any number of union endorsements" (Stokes 1973, 55). Black churches are also schools for civic education and training; many black leaders can trace their first public-speaking event to reciting Bible verses or poems in Sunday school, reading the minutes, or testifying about God's work in a church service. Church members learn how to raise money through church suppers, raffles, and building drives. So, too, black churches provide important moral motivations and cultural resources for civic and political involvement (Calhoun-Brown 1996; Harris 2001; 1999a). Black Christian theology has long linked freedom to deliverance into heaven and God's kingdom but also to deliverance from racial oppression in the material world (Lincoln and Manning 1990, 234). Many, perhaps most, black pastors refuse to blame the black poor for their circumstances, as many whites do, and place primary responsibility for racial inequality on societal institutions (Lincoln and Manning 1990; Warren 1998).[14] But, from the standpoint of deepening pluralism, in some respects black churches are a troublesome model. Thus, for example, most of the traditional churches are hierarchical, with the minister (usually male) wielding autocratic power (Morris 1984, 9). They are almost universally patriarchal. Although black women far outnumber men as members and in attendance in all denominations except in the Nation of Islam, and they shoulder most of the work in churches, few churches promote or permit women to be ministers (the Methodists being one exception). So, too, a problem for inclusiveness and community unity, many black churches are intolerant of openly gay and lesbian lifestyles in the ministry and among the laity.

Although African Americans are diverse ideologically, and although different black civic organizations and churches have varying constraints and imperatives, the tendency toward charismatic, hierarchical, and male leadership, much of it historically rooted in black churches, has been a recurring obstacle to establishing durable wider black coalitions. Positive or negative, the influence of church traditions on black civic and political organizations is, nevertheless, substantial.[15]

Black Coalitions

Stokely Carmichael and Charles V. Hamilton wrote in *Black Power* that blacks should form coalitions with whites only under certain conditions. They argue it is not "possible to form meaningful coalitions unless both or all parties are not only willing but believe it absolutely necessary to challenge Anglo-conformity and other prevailing norms and institutions" (Carmichael and Hamilton 1967, 62). Blacks ought, they said, to take a skeptical view of whites' "goodwill." They insisted that blacks cannot work productively within larger multiracial associations if they lack an "independent base of power."

The sub-group will have to acquiesce to the goals and demands of the parent.... Coalition between the strong and the weak leads ultimately only to perpetuation of the hierarchical status: super-ordinance and subordinance.... Black Power simply says: enter coalitions only *after* you are able to 'stand on your own.' Black Power seeks to correct the approach to dependency, to remove that dependency, and to establish a viable psychological, political and social base upon which the black community can function to meet its needs. (Carmichael and Hamilton 1967, 74, 81)

Black Power called for "organizing and developing institutions of community power within the black community." Blacks were to form interracial coalitions based strictly on group "self-interest" (Carmichael and Hamilton 1967, 77): "Let black people organize themselves *first,* define their interest and goals, and then see what kind of allies are available" (Carmichael and Hamilton 1967, 80). The long-term goals of blacks and whites tend to conflict, they argue, and coalitions should, therefore, be approached cautiously, and only for "specific goals." Although Carmichael and Hamilton supported coalitions between poor whites and poor blacks as "the major internal instrument of change in the American society," the principal responsibility for "creating a poor-white power block dedicated to the goals of a free, open society ... falls upon whites" (Carmichael and Hamilton 1967, 82–83).

Carmichael and Hamilton were advocating a kind of black interest-group pluralism, in which blacks would focus on internal organizing and on identifying their interests while remaining deeply cautious about joining organizations or coalitions with whites until whites have become aware of the depths of racial oppression and are committed to changing it. They specified conditions under which blacks *could* safely form coalitions with whites: when blacks had organized themselves internally, when blacks have become psychologically and socially independent, when they have defined their own interest and have identified specific goals to achieve in coalitions. In the early 1970s, the popularity of this view was registered in the Congressional Black Caucus's motto, "No permanent friends, no permanent enemies, just permanent interests," a slogan that assumes, as do many nationalists, that black interests are held in common and are permanent. After the mid-1980s the Caucus became increasingly diverse (Swain 1993, 39–41) but surveys of black opinion in this period reflect an upsurge in black nationalist sentiment, particularly within the black middle class, a finding that corresponds with the increasing prominence of nationalist leaders in black politics. In October 1995, when Nation of Islam leader Louis Farrakhan organized the Million Man March on Washington, attracting close to a million, mostly middle-class, African American men, a Howard University survey conducted at the march itself indicated that only about 8 percent were Muslim (Walton and Smith 2000, 131; McCormick 1997).

Unlike theories that white racism is largely a relic of the Jim Crow era, the Carmichael-Hamilton argument does not minimize the depths of racial conflict. In contrast, the political scientist Paul Sniderman and colleagues write:

> Racial prejudice is no longer the paramount factor dominating the positions that white Americans take on issues of race. . . . Simply put, a significant part of the explanation over why Americans disagree about the politics of race is that they disagree about the politics of equality. . . . Once one acknowledges the central role of equality in the politics of race, one acknowledges in the bargain the continuity between racial politics and the larger politics of social welfare. . . . In saying this, we are far from denying that racial politics has a distinctive component. But we are contending that some of its deepest and most enduring cleavages are defined by the clash between competing conceptions of the obligations of government and the responsibilities of citizens. (Sniderman et al. 2000, 267–68)

Put differently, these authors maintain that it is whites' principled (nonracial) beliefs about equality that shape the racial views.

My argument is the reverse (see chapter 7).[16] Carmichael and Hamilton emphasize the importance of organizing black communities at the grassroots level for effective representation of black interests. I do the same but Carmichael and Hamilton's criteria as applied to interracial coalitions are problematic. They place on white activists alone the burden of changing racial attitudes of white Americans, and of racial self-introspection, and insist that there can be no black progress in interracial coalitions without such attitudinal change among whites. Blacks, in my view, cannot wait for this. The Reverend Martin Luther King Jr. acted, and white attitudinal change followed black activism and related federal legislation.

Problems emerge, too, if Carmichael and Hamilton's coalition criteria are applied to intra-black coalitions, as their own writings do not attempt to do. From the Carmichael-Hamilton perspective, and in black interest-group pluralism more generally, there is an implicit assumption that black communities are internally non-antagonistic. The black community is treated metaphorically as one, as an individual entity. Blacks are urged to "stand on your own" as if the community were a single body—a naturally unified organism. Thus Carmichael and Hamilton wrote:

> There is a terminology and ethos peculiar to the black community
> of which black people are beginning to be no longer ashamed.
> Black communities are the only large segments of this society
> where people refer to each other as brother—soul-brother, soul-
> sister. Some people may look upon this as *ersatz,* as make-believe,
> but it is not that. It is real. It is a growing sense of community.
> It is a growing realization that black Americans have a common
> bond not only among themselves, but with their African brothers.
> (Carmichael and Hamilton 1967, 38)

While the sentiments Carmichael and Hamilton cite are no doubt broadly shared among blacks, they are far from universal, and conflicts within the black community continue. Black communities were not naturally unified in the 1960s or now. They are composed of people who have been thrown together by dominant institutions—controlled by whites—most of whom believe that they share a similar destiny but who also have different and also conflicting interests. Some blacks exercise power over other blacks and oppress other blacks within black institutions.

The view that the black community is a unified and undifferentiated body easily leads to the conclusion that black leaders need never consult with diverse elements of black communities to negotiate their representation of blacks. United States Representative Louis Stokes (D-OH) said, for example, that "when I vote as a black man, I necessarily represent the black community. I don't have any trouble knowing what the black community thinks or wants. . . . They have a blind faith in me" (Fenno 2003, 32). The concept of essential, or natural, black unity, by definition, appears to obviate the need for black individuals to participate in politics in order to hold black leaders accountable. The veteran NAACP Southern Director Earl Shinholster has said, of this context, that, "what [the election of blacks] does is relieve us [community residents] from responsibility for acting ourselves . . . once we elected somebody they stopped going [to civic meetings]" [Shinholster 1988].

When the black community is thought of as having a natural essence, internal black political differences logically must not be about the substance of black interests because the substance is seen as held in common. Differences among blacks are attributed, rather, either to effects of white control over certain blacks (co-optation) or to selfish power plays of black individuals to replace existing black leadership. More ominously, if the black community is like a single body it can only have one true voice. This view can lead, and has led, to intense rivalry, even political violence, between black organizations over who represents that authentic voice of black people, as it did on January 17, 1969, when members of the cultural nationalist United Slaves Organization (US) killed Black Panther leaders John Huggins and Alprentice "Bunchy" Carter (Brown 1992; Churchill and Vander Wall [1988] 2002, 42). More commonly, the essentialist strand of black nationalism combines with already existing hierarchical tendencies in black organizations and leads to the exclusion of political opponents from coalitions, and to the eventual fragmentation of those coalitions.

So, to illustrate, black nationalists who led the Jesse Jackson presidential campaign in New York in 1984 blocked regular machine Democrats, including Jackson's Brooklyn campaign coordinator, Congressman Ed Townes, from meeting with Jackson (Williams 1988) and New York nationalists clashed with prominent ministers who were supporting Jackson over control of the slating of Jackson delegates to the Democratic National Convention (Jetter 1987).

The case of black women, perhaps more than any other, demonstrates the danger of presuming the reality of a black unity. Black feminists have sharply opposed black nationalist and black pluralist discourse that projects an image of a unified black community made coherent by a single racial identity. They have argued that there is no single meaning of race for blacks, rather that there are many. The unitary notion of racial solidarity masks patterns of patriarchy and the domination of male-centered frameworks on race. Thus, many black feminists severely criticized prominent black organizations and leaders who supported, at least initially, the nomination of Clarence Thomas, a black archconservative, to the U.S. Supreme Court simply because he was black, despite Thomas's recognized opposition to popular black civil rights demands, let alone the accusations of Anita Hill, a former aide and African American attorney, of sexual harassment. Thomas invoked race to defend himself against the charges, stating that Hill's charges were part of a "legal lynching" (Crenshaw 1992, 433).

Black feminists have maintained that they are marginalized by any black discourse that ignores gender oppression within black communities, and also by white feminists who minimize the role race plays in shaping the lives of black women, and marginalized, too, by labor (class) advocates who have traditionally paid little attention to black women's struggles. Many black feminists, as a consequence, have insisted on asserting their own "black feminist" perspectives. Rather than framing race, gender, and class as competing frameworks, they have stressed the ways in which these categories of oppression intersect and reinforce one another. In response to the criticism that black feminism is a divisive attack on black men that undermines the power of the black community to fight racism, black feminists maintain that black communities cannot build collective political power as long as women leaders are sidelined and as long as the issues vital to black women are suppressed. This is no small matter because there is a sizable feminist orientation among black women: 36 percent of black women identity themselves as feminist and 17 percent more consider themselves strong feminists (Dawson 2001, 164).

Were Carmichael and Hamilton's criteria for coalition building between blacks and whites to be applied to intra-black coalitions, one would conclude that black women should either not form coalitions with black men or only form them with extreme caution and after developing separate women's organizations. While some black women do advocate gender separatism, most have tended to support efforts to unify black communities across gender lines. They have insisted that male-led black organizations and coalitions engage in serious discussions of gender issues, and that black leadership be shared across gender. The author Toni Morrison put it this way:

> In matters of race and gender, it is now possible and necessary, as it seemed never to have been before, to speak about these matters without the barriers, the silences, the embarrassing gaps in discourse. It is clear to even the most reductionist intellect that black people think differently from one another; it is also clear that the time for an undiscriminating racial unity has passed. (Morrison 1992, xxx)

If black communities are not like a single human body, naturally or reductively united, then what kind of a group are they? The concept of intersectionality suggests that blacks are more like a group thrown together in a condition of famine, with part of the group also without access to water, and some without medicine. While lack of food is a defining condition for the whole group, so is the lack of water and lack of medicine for some. It makes little sense to the latter to argue whether food, water, or medicine is more important: without each they are weakened and many will die. From their perspective, it would be more productive for others in the group to consider whether the lack of water and medicine for part of the group contributes to the group's overall inability to generate food and survive famine. Famine has more complex causes and related consequences than the lack of food. Acknowledging that does not minimize the fight against famine; quite the contrary.

Other causes must be addressed if racism is to be fought effectively. The strategy of black feminism has not been to deny the salience of racism but to reframe its meaning from within black discourse, to encourage blacks to rethink the multiple causes of racism and strategies to overcome it. Accordingly, black feminists are far more likely than black nationalists to support black coalition building with non-black immigrants and other groups. Black feminism has challenged black organizations and coalitions in general to be more open-minded, to provide space for gender criticism, to share leadership between men and women, and, for some, to rethink additional categories of exclusion or ostracism within black civic institutions and political discourse: of gays and lesbians, single black mothers (including those on welfare and teenagers), incarcerated black men, and those engaged in unlawful behavior like drug dealing. In so doing, new understandings of contemporary racial oppressions, as well as possible paths of resistance, may emerge. The African American political scientist Cathy Cohen writes, in this vein, that, "only by listening to their voices, trying to understand their motivations, and accurately centering their stories with all of its complexities in our work can we begin to understand and map the connection between deviant practice, defiant behavior, and political resistance" (Cohen 2004, 33).

Recent National Coalition Efforts

National efforts to build coalitions across political trends in the black community, however desirable, in recent decades—Jesse Jackson's Rainbow Coalition, the NAACP's "Summit," the Million March movements—have been short-lived and torn by splits over the role of nationalists, gender, and the participation of grass-roots activists. Jackson's 1984 and 1988 campaigns for the Democratic presidential nomination attempted to unite black organizations.

In 1984, Jesse Jackson's presidential campaign, strapped for money and time to collect signatures or to file papers to get on the ballot in many states, relied on Jackson's ties to black churches or on his PUSH organization to establish the campaign infrastructure. The fact that black ministers were self-financed provided a needed financial reprieve for the Jackson campaign (Williams and Morris 1989, 239). But involving local area ministers put them in conflict with local black politicians who assumed they would control political campaigns in their area. At the end of the campaign, Jackson declared his intention to "institutionalize the Rainbow, state by state and nationally." However, when the primary campaign ended with a debt of $1.4 million, with no resources immediately available to institutionalize the Rainbow Coalition, activists quickly drifted back to their local networks and organizations. "Money was only part of the problem, however." Jackson, comments author-activist Shiela Collins, "seemed incapable of lending himself to the kind of careful, patient, systematic work involved in organization-building. As soon as colleagues pinned him down on commitments, he sabotaged their plans with others of his own" (Collins 1986, 307). Jackson himself had not seemed deeply interested in a real Rainbow Coalition. Many of his close black political supporters, liberal elected Democrats, worried that a strong Coalition might drain support away from them, and the Rainbow Coalition was organized, in 1986, only when Rep. Ron Dellums (D-CA) and Rep. John Conyers (D-MI), two of the most outspoken black leaders, moved to pull it together themselves (Collins 1986, 308). At its founding convention were a number of labor leaders and liberal politicians (such as Rep. Charles Rangel of New York) who had not endorsed Jackson in 1984. Conflicts emerged at that initial convention over the Rainbow Coalition's independence from the Democratic Party, over Jackson's handpicking of the leadership, and over the lack of involvement of grass-roots and poor people in the organization. After debate, these issues were postponed for a planned convention the following year in 1987.

The tensions between activists who wanted a more open and participatory movement and established black elected officials who were pushing toward a top-down style of election campaigning, continued through Jackson's second, 1988, presidential primary. There was palpable uneasiness among community activists who had been involved in the militant grass-roots campaign of 1984 with 1988's top-down control and avoidance of heated racial issues. Former Harlem district leader and WLIB radio producer Chuck Sutton said, "I think the last time [1984] you had a lot of students who were involved. You had a lot of grass-roots community organizing types who were in the campaign. The grass-roots types are the ones that I don't see this go around. I don't think they know how to integrate [grass-roots nationalists and liberal Democratic officials] . . . there hasn't been a mending of the two together" (Sutton 1988). Harlem district leader Peggy Shepherd blamed Harlem elected officials who were leading the 1988 New York State Jackson campaign for the lack of grass-roots participation: "You have a Rangel or somebody and they're not that interested in community participation" (Shepherd 1988). The New York political strategist Audrey Bynoe, who had played a key leadership role when nationalists led the New York 1984 Jackson campaign, accused liberal black Harlem officials of *planning* to derail grassroots participation in the 1988 Jackson campaign— to forestall the emergence of political upstarts who might challenge their authority. Asked why black political leaders would want to stifle black participation, Bynoe replied, "Because they may be vulnerable themselves. Once you have a heightened black electorate—[you have] insurgents, young candidates—you have all of that happening. And I don't think that the Charlie Rangels and the Denny Farrells and those people want to have insurgents" (Bynoe 1988).

The divisions in New York City reflected a national split in the direction of the Rainbow Coalition. Jackson wavered between the two competing poles. By 1989, Jackson came down firmly on the side of the Coalition's moderate wing. According to Manning Marable:

> Jackson called for the right to appoint all Rainbow Coalition
> leaders at the congressional district level. In effect, he wanted
> to block democratic elections of Rainbow local leadership,
> muzzling socialist and black nationalist dissenters from above.
> Ron Daniels [a key national 1984 Jackson organizer] left the
> Rainbow, as did thousands of local and community-based
> activists who were disillusioned with Jackson's autocratic
> tactics. . . . Rainbow organizers in the leadership were replaced
> because of Jackson's reservations about having strong assertive
> people around him. (Marable 1995, 58, 61)

The Rainbow Coalition rapidly became a shell organization incapable of supporting a reported Jackson presidential run in 1992. Instead, Jackson vied with Rev. Ben Chavis, a well-known civil rights leader and a North Carolina political prisoner for four years during the 1970s, for the post of executive director of the NAACP. Chavis won and moved quickly to reach out to gang leaders and rap artists of the "hip-hop" generation of black youth born after the triumph of the civil rights movement, and younger African Americans who considered the NAACP largely out of touch with the problems of joblessness, school failure, mass incarceration of black youth, and poverty. To open a dialogue among leaders across the black political spectrum, in 1994 Chavis invited a broad array of black organizations to a Summit of African-American Leadership. His invitation to the Nation of Islam leader Louis Farrakhan, who is well known for anti-Semitic, misogynist, and homophobic views, sparked a wave of criticism both within and outside the NAACP, although Farrakhan had won wide respect in black communities for the Nation of Islam's work in prisons, its campaign against the spread of drugs in black communities, and against inner-city gang violence.

Few black elected officials, trade union leaders, or other nationally recognized civil rights leaders showed up at the NAACP summit Chavis had called. Representatives from black fraternities, local activists' organizations, and religious leaders did attend, along with scholars associated with radical multiculturalism, among them, Cornel West, Julianne Malveaux, Roger Wilkins, and Marable (Marable 1995, 163). The NAACP itself was divided about a dialogue with conservative black nationalists like Farrakhan, on its right, and black radicals, on its left, yet Chavis withstood the criticism and was reelected executive director the following month. But the dialogue he had initiated, along with his leadership of the NAACP, was cut short one month later by revelations that he had used $332,000 of NAACP funds to pay a former assistant, Mary Stansel, who was threatening him with a lawsuit on charges of sexual discrimination and sexual harassment. Like Clarence Thomas's response to the Senate, Chavis responded that he had been the victim of an orchestrated "lynching" (Best 1994). He resigned and subsequently moved closer to Farrakhan, the following year, serving as the national spokesperson for the Million Man March; he later became a minister in the Nation of Islam, and in that role, endorsed the call that women remain in the home.

The Million Man March was a phenomenal success in numerical terms; the black think tank, the Joint Center for Political and Economic Studies in Washington, D.C., whose origin was in the original meetings of black elected officials, credited it with boosting black participation in the 1996 presidential elections (Dreier 1995). Farrakhan's speech at the march had encouraged participants to join local civic organizations, including the mainstream civil rights groups that had opposed him in the past (Harris 1999b, 329). Still, the overwhelming endorsement of an exclusive male march—gays, as well as women, were explicitly dis-invited—was deeply troubling for many black women. It generated little support from black labor leaders, and little sustained organizational follow-up to the march.

Many black intellectuals and activists describe the first years of the new millennium as distinctly different from the era of civil rights progress, with increasing class inequality and continuing racial inequality, with growing class polarization in the black community, and little public support for black interests from either of the two major political parties. National black political leadership, to the extent that exists in groups like the Congressional Black Caucus, the NAACP, and the National Urban League, is fragmented, weak, and seemingly unable to respond effectively to black community demands (Marable 1995, 208; Smith 1996).

Black Mayors and Black Coalitions

In light of the increasing difficulty of sustaining black coalitions at the national level, the longevity of the grass-roots community coalition BUILD in Baltimore is all the more impressive. So, too, are prominent black citywide political coalitions in city politics, the one in Cleveland during Carl Stokes's administration and in Chicago during Harold Washington's tenure.

In 1969, toward the end of his second term, Mayor Stokes formed an all-black civic political organization, the 21st District Caucus, named after the congressional district where most of Cleveland's blacks were concentrated. The first black mayor elected in a large city in the United States needed a strong vote from the black poor to stay in office, and he took bold steps to improve conditions in poor communities. William Nelson explained that, "Cleveland's ward system for the election of city councilmen had established over the years a highly fragmented political structure in the black community"; the immediate purpose of the caucus was to unify black councilmen under a single banner (Nelson 1982, 192). Its long-range goal was "to institutionalize [Carl Stokes's] power base, and to make the

Cuyahoga County Democratic Party responsive to black interests and concerns" (Moore 2002).

Cleveland, at the time of Stokes's 1967 reelection, was 39 percent black; Stokes won by just 2,000 votes out of more than 256,000 votes cast, over his white Republican opponent, Seth Taft, attorney and grandson of U.S. president William Howard Taft (Zannes 1972, 77). Stokes provided a stewardship that was strongly racially contested. After Stokes built 5,496 units of public housing in just four years—Cleveland had built only 6,700 units in the previous 30 years (Moore 2002)—he was confronted by resistant blacks and hostile whites. To Mayor Stokes it was a matter of "power":

> when you start dealing with the basic fundamentals of housing and schools and jobs, then you are talking about fundamental change and you are dealing with a resistance that is not going to yield peacefully. How do you deal with it? There is only one way: power against power. That's what I did. I took the power of the mayor's office and a solid constituency and went head on against those [middle-class blacks] who didn't want the poor in their neighborhood, [whites who] didn't want the blacks in their neighborhood, were determined to exclude blacks from jobs and new economic opportunities. (Stokes 1973, 252)

Stokes did not hesitate to acknowledge his insistence on loyalty and his tight personal control over the 21st District Caucus:

> The motivation came from my wanting to leave my people a vehicle to continue the political thrust I had taught them and to leave my brother [Louis Stokes] a solid political base not dependent on my presence and muscle. All black elected officials who had been loyal to me were named to the executive board. A number of ward leaders were also elected to the board. Later, we expanded the board to include ministers of different faiths and civic leaders. Louis was chairman. I was honorary chairman. (Stokes 1973, 241)

The Caucus's members—between seven hundred and one thousand of them—each paid a $2 membership fee. Its general meetings attracted about five hundred (Nelson 1982, 194). It declared itself nonpartisan, presented demands to the county Democratic Party as a condition for support, and when its demands were not met, swung nearly half the black vote over to a Republican candidate in a county commissioner race, leading to defeat of the Democratic candidate. The Caucus also took over control of legislative races within its congressional district from the Democrats. In 1971, the year Stokes left office, the Caucus capsized the Democratic Party organization's favorite candidate to succeed Stokes as mayor, the white city council president, Anthony Garafoli; 95 percent of the black vote went instead to a young white liberal real estate developer and political upstart, James Carney, in the Democratic primary (Moore 2002, 185).[17]

"Much of the success of the caucus turned on the personal popularity, charisma, and political sagacity of Carl Stokes. It was therefore inevitable that political momentum would be lost and organizational prowess diminished in the wake of Stokes' dramatic announcement in April 1971 that he would not seek a third term as mayor of Cleveland" (Nelson 1982, 195). The support dissolved when Carl's brother, Rep. Louis Stokes, virtually demanded to be made chair of the Caucus and subsequently that all administrative authority within the Caucus be placed in his hands: "I'm the leader, and when you are the leader, people expect you to lead," Louis Stokes said. "As the highest elected official in the district, I can't let anyone lower in the hierarchy get the idea that I'm not the leader" (Fenno 2003, 44). Thereafter many black leaders left the Caucus (Nelson 1982). Carl Stokes's similar control had been sustained because of the strength of his personality and leadership skills. Such control could not be sustained without them.

The Caucus was weakened also because it was held together primarily by patronage resources. Carl Stokes's urging black voters to support white candidate Carney in the primary against the Democratic party candidate was a political miscalculation in the 1971 mayoral race. Stokes's favored candidate was an African American independent, Arnold Pinkney, running in the general election. Confused by Stokes's complicated double-barreled strategy, black voters split their votes between Pinkney and Carney, giving the election to Ralph Perk, the Republican candidate. Without patronage from city hall, many caucus members drifted back to their earlier home, the county Democratic Party. Louis Stokes regarded those who did so to be "traitors" to the black community: "The Democratic Party owns them now. They have to do what the party wants and what the party tells them to do" (Fenno 2003). The trouble was that without the party they had no organized political support and with the charismatic Carl Stokes no longer available, no chance of patronage or for benefits to the black community.

The black coalition that supported Harold Washington for election and reelection in 1983 and 1987 suffered a similar fate. It was a coalition of coalitions that included the Task Force for Black Political Empowerment, Chicago Black United Communities, VOTE, and an assortment of social, religious, and professional groups (Gills 1991; Pinderhughes 1997). It was effective in mobilizing during Washington's election and in opposing the white ethnic-led machine, and also key to enlisting white liberals, who, according to Dianne Pinderhughes, gained "more space to influence policy than they had previously enjoyed" (Pinderhughes 1997, 130). Pinderhughes did note as a weakness of the Chicago coalition that Washington was both the protest leader and electoral leader "elevated above the mass united by organizations of organizations in singular, hierarchical fashion, [he] articulated the political and material as well as the moral goals and interests of the black community to the larger white city" (Pinderhughes 1997, 127). Washington was similar in style, she believes, to the charismatic Adam Clayton Powell Jr., and to the Nation of Islam's Elijah Muhammad; she also pointed to the black coalition's failure to "develop or maintain grassroots interest in governing and policy making, in contacting and communicating with public officials, or in negotiating with or choosing among political leaders within the community" (Pinderhughes 1997, 127). Immediately after Mayor Washington's death in 1987, the coalition fractured over policy issues and leadership succession. The Chicago coalition had coalesced around the personality of Harold Washington and this had negative consequences for their potential successes.

In all three cities, Cleveland, Chicago, and Baltimore, black mayors had faced close, racially contested elections. The mayors in all three cities needed black civic organizations as a channel of communication with constituents and to help with mobilization around policy battles and elections. In all the three cities the mayor's office had enough power to make formation of a citywide coalition worthwhile for community organizations and residents seeking concrete benefits in exchange for participation. But there were differences in civic organization among the three strong-mayor cities. In Cleveland in 1971 and in Chicago in 1987, coalitions fell apart not long after their formation, with the loss of the strong personalities that had motivated and sustained them. Unlike Baltimore's BUILD coalition, in Cleveland and in Chicago, black mayors were the inspirational and political leaders of the black civic coalitions. In both, their coalition dared not establish a critical opposition against the mayor, and that proved to be a problem for the future. More pressing in both was the lack of an agreed upon method for choosing a new leader after the incumbent mayor left the scene. When Stokes decided not to run again and when Washington died, the civic coalitions squabbled over leadership succession, also. There was no systematic training of new leaders; leadership was hierarchical and personality-centered, as in the Rainbow Coalition under Rev. Jesse Jackson. In Baltimore, BUILD, in contrast, was not dependent on a single personality, rotated leadership, shared leadership positions across gender, and focused on training new leaders. Also, unlike Cleveland's 21st District Caucus, BUILD did not rely on city patronage. It could be more independent of elected leadership and hence could survive their loss. Its strategies were disciplined and consistent. It emphasized winning concrete victories, it balanced protest actions with electoral activities, and it also generated more significant dues revenue because it required institutions that join the coalition to pay per capita dues. Because Cleveland's 21st District Caucus had restricted itself primarily to elections as a means of gaining resources, it could not sustain itself when it lost.

Community Capacity for Pluralism

In his 1990 article, "Black Mayoral Leadership: A Twenty-Year Perspective," William Nelson wrote that:

> effective black political incorporation must involve the institutionalization of black influence across broad dimensions of the policy-making process, not merely the election of black politicians to public office. . . . A look across the black political landscape reveals a paucity of stable, black-led political organizations. It is at once informative and heartbreaking to note that after more than twenty years of black control in Gary, no organization exists to lobby for black goals, and to organize black political resources on a continuous basis. (Nelson 1990, #706, 454–55)

Baltimore's BUILD coalition success suggests that stable, black-led, citywide, civic political coalitions can be built, and that *sometimes* black mayors will develop such organizations. Black mayors who do could well succeed in racially contested cities where mobilized poor blacks vote to gain reelection. Strong community activists can be found in strong-mayor cities where it makes sense for citywide politics to have their focused attention. For a while,

Baltimore, Cleveland, and Chicago all had both—strong black mayors who support and engage activism, and activists who hold them accountable.

But not all black mayors in racially contested and strong-mayor cities do support building black civic organizations that will engage in politics. Some black mayoral candidates have, instead, projected a conservative deracialized image to moderate white voters, cobbling together a winning coalition of whites and middle-class blacks without relying on the black poor. That was the principal strategy of Wilson Goode in Philadelphia in 1984, and of Michael White in Cleveland from 1989 to 2001, though other black mayors who have come to office through the mobilizing efforts of the black poor have sometimes sought safe reelection by gaining white support at the expense of black demands, thereby decreasing their reliance on the black poor. In Baltimore, Schmoke attempted to move to the right at the expense of his core black supporters on several occasions, such as on issues of council redistricting and school privatization, but these moves were repeatedly blocked by black civic organizations who held him accountable (McDougall 1993; Orr 1999).

The question remains why there are not more BUILD-like black coalitions in other cities. Black mayors who aggressively block efforts to organize the black poor are in large majority-black cities and do not need to mobilize the black poor. So, too, Gittell, Newman, and Pierre-Louis's six-city study of the local politics of Empowerment Zones, an inner-city development program initiated by the Clinton administration, found that despite the encouragement of community resident participation, "mayors and city council persons and agency bureaucrats guard their powers jealously, and work at keeping large segments of the population outside the process, especially if they are critical of the programs" (Gittell et al. 2001, 92, 94). Gittell's findings are similar, if for different reasons, to the reviews of community action programs in the 1960s. In the 1960s, white mayors sought to hold back black racial mobilization that might lead to political challenges to their regimes. But in the 1990s, in Atlanta and Detroit, large majority-black cities with well-established black regimes, conflict over Empowerment Zone participation was class based between poor blacks and black middle-class-led administrations.

But, in many racially contested cities, such as Chicago, with fairly unresponsive white mayors and no BUILD-like structures, the lack of black coalitions before and after Harold Washington appears to have been a consequence of a lack of black civic leadership as well as of restrictions on, and the perception of, black community organizations that accept government and foundation grants that political activity would be too risky, a form of co-optation. Because Baltimore's BUILD, unlike community development corporations and most community-based black organizations, refused to accept foundation grants and government money for its core operations, and relied instead on dues from member church organizations (Warren 2001, 38), as unions do from their members, they are, like unions, more free to engage in protest and confrontation.

Most analysts tend to agree with William Julius Wilson's class-based observation that very poor black people suffer physical and social isolation, "as more and more city neighborhoods become classified as 'dangerous' by middle- and working-class citizens, the ghetto tracts fall into a seemingly irreversible isolation" (Wilson 1999, 36). Still, we should be cautious not to overestimate disorganization in poor black communities in light of the fact that few studies have yet included within their scope so-called uncivil organizations like gangs that, though negative, are forms of community participation. Nonetheless, there is indeed substantial evidence of decline of participation among the poor in voting, in church attendance, and in other forms of "good" civic activity in very low-income black communities.

Baltimore seems to have experienced a clear countertrend. Its black community is not wealthy in comparison with other large cities and its success is not attributable to an exceptional amount of material resources or to a particularly hospitable racial climate.[18]

Its success seems also to depend, in significant part, on its leadership style. Rather than relying on a single all-powerful leader, as in Chicago and Cleveland, BUILD, as noted above, rotates and shares leadership responsibilities, and, like other Industrial Area Foundation organizations, strongly emphasizes the training of new leaders. It pays some attention to enlisting women in leadership roles and to organizing marginalized black subgroups. BUILD's "relational organizing" approach is a classic "bonding" social capital approach, in which a priority is put on building enduring ties and trust rather than on establishing a hierarchy.

BUILD has also pursued multiracial alliance building without serious fracturing along racial lines. Sociologist Mark Warren has argued that the Industrial Areas Foundation's general approach to creating institutional memberships allows black organizations to maintain their independence and internal bonds even when working in a multiracial alliance (Warren 2001, 138). He argues that IAF member groups have, thus, been able to avoid either/or choices of organizing separately or in alliance. Janice Fine speculates that because BUILD is a predominantly black organization with black leadership, blacks have control over the organization and are not fearful of interracial alliances because they can always leave without loss of power (Fine 2003). Both arguments support the idea I advance in chapter 2, that forming strong black civic organizations that have the capacity to monitor other groups, with sanctions if necessary, creates positive conditions for bridging racial differences.

In challenging patriarchal and hierarchical norms of leadership, in reaching out to the marginalized poor, in developing black-community capacity for deliberation and definition of interests, in holding elected officials and coalition partners accountable, and in engaging interracial alliance building, BUILD appears to be on a path of deepening pluralism, at least within parts of Baltimore. However, its approach has limits and is not yet fully or deeply pluralistic. Thus far it reflects an Alinskyite focusing on local issues, on confrontation, on winning small battles, on building the confidence and capacity of local groups, and on building deep trust among participants—all positive but circumstantial. Its local approach means it does not bridge wider differences between groups—as between inner-city blacks and white suburbanites—that appear to have no immediate or urgent reason for relating to each other or that do not want to. Janice Fine reports that BUILD organizers felt that despite their local success, their efforts were being overwhelmed by broader forces, and that the city itself was failing (Fine 2003).

For blacks, connecting their viewpoints to immediate local reforms (or making them "issuable") means voicing them within political and policy frameworks already accepted as legitimate by other groups and within the normal nontransformational scope of action of local decision makers. In such a framework there is no way to work on demands where fundamental political disagreements exist. Blacks need civic and political organizations, their own if no others exist, to take up issues unpopular with other groups. To its credit, the IAF's organizational approach appears to leave room for this. IAF groups like BUILD serve as an important network that may be able to bridge racial differences among participants over time. As long as significant issues crucial to the black community remain unpopular with the white public, such organizations and coalitions do not obviate organization of black coalitions willing to pursue and act in behalf of their unpopular causes.

BUILD's local relation-building approach, however, has no way to address problems rooted in national structures and in deep ideological divisions like race. Paul Osterman's study of IAF shows that it considers two kinds of power, of "organized people and organized money," but leaves out a third source of power: organized thought, or ideology. Not that IAF leaders ignore the power of ideology, but that they are determined to avoid the destructive potential of sharp ideological controversy.[19] Osterman argues that IAF's "very traditional American values" are one of their core *strengths* because, "it seems clear that there is a strong aversion in the broad American public to anything that smacks of radicalism" (Osterman 2002, 25). Its avoidance of radical difference, in my view, including the radically different opinion of most blacks on the legitimacy of U.S. institutions, is profoundly undemocratic in spirit, and a weakness. Racism is still a prevalent American value, one that underlies political differences between many whites and blacks. The risk of not confronting racially divisive issues is that potentially explosive divisions remain embedded within supposedly racially unified organizations. The fact that the original community organization Saul Alinsky founded in Chicago degenerated into a virulently racist homeowner's association, to Alinsky's chagrin, is telling on this point (Warren 2001).

Black power advocates have argued that internal black organizing is fundamental for black progress. IAF supporters, for their part, argue that interracial organizing is fundamental. I want to argue that neither approach is sufficient or fundamental. Whether to organize blacks separately or in multiracial alliances, or both, is a matter of the strategy of politics and is specific to time and place, sometimes necessary and efficacious, sometimes counterproductive. Right now, if blacks do not have organizations of their own, committed to take up core issues unpopular with the white majority, they will often find that no one else will. Yet, as a minority group, hence usually unable to win in big issues and in fundamental systemic ways, as in economic development and in provision of quality education in nonsegregated settings, blacks in cities must cultivate non-black allies. How to do both simultaneously is the challenge.

Race and Interracial Coalitions

4

On August 8, 1978, hundreds of police officers attempted to evict eleven adults and their children from a house in Powelton Village, a part of Philadelphia not far from Drexel University and the University of Pennsylvania. The adults were members of MOVE, an eccentric black back-to-nature group with a history of violent confrontations with the police. MOVE was an annoyance to its neighbors, with threats, foul language broadcast on bullhorns, running across the adjacent rooftops of their neighbors and blocking the common rear-alley driveway. Its members made little effort to comply with city housing ordinances. While groups like MOVE sometimes find refuge in remote rural areas, MOVE's members feared to leave the city's black community lest they become isolated and even more vulnerable to attack by vigilantes or government authorities.

During the police eviction, an officer, James Ramp, was shot and died from the bullet wound. Whether Officer Ramp was killed by a MOVE member or by friendly fire from another police officer remains unclear. The police claimed they had found guns in the house; MOVE members said the police planted the guns. Despite scant, and sometimes conflicting, evidence, the house was razed and eleven adult members of MOVE were convicted of murder and sent to prison (Boyette 1989, 4). MOVE members now became even more confrontational; they steadfastly denied killing Officer Ramp, insisted on the release of convicted members from prison, and resettled in Cobbs Creek, a black middle-class neighborhood in west Philadelphia, where they angered their new neighbors with similar behavior. Some people speculated that they were trying to draw city officials' attention to their demand to release their incarcerated comrades.

Mayor Wilson Goode, the city's first black mayor, who had been elected in 1983, was hesitant to confront the MOVE issue. He insisted that MOVE had a right to free speech and expression, even if offensive, and resisted protesting residents' requests to evict MOVE from Cobbs Creek. But when Ed Rendell, the city district attorney and Goode's possible opponent in the next mayoral election, reminded him of outstanding arrest warrants for parole violations and assault, Goode authorized that arrest warrants to be served at MOVE's household (Goode and Stevens, 1992, 210). On the morning of May 13, 1985, nearly five hundred police officers evacuated residents in the block and encircled the MOVE stone row house. Around 5:30 PM, a Philadelphia police department helicopter dropped a three-pound bomb of high-grade military (C4) explosive on the roof to dislodge a bunker MOVE had built; inside were thirteen people, six children and seven adults. The explosion shook the house, set off a large orange fireball above the house, and the roof caught on fire. At the scene were Philadelphia's police and fire commissioners and Leo Brooks, an African American, who was the city's managing director and a top Goode aide. Mayor Goode himself was monitoring the scene by television at his home. According to Goode, he decided not to go to the scene because several "people who always provided . . . reliable information" told him he would "'catch a bullet with my name on it'" if he came near the MOVE house. He said he believed the police were determined to take revenge for the slaying of Officer Ramp, and Goode cited a later investigation's finding, that the police at the MOVE house had guns with silencers, as lending credibility to those threats. Members of the Philadelphia police, Goode said he was told, "had targeted me for death" and he said his assassination "would be made to look like an accident" (Goode and Stevens 1992, 218).

Mayor Goode said later that the police commissioner had ignored a direct order from Leo Brooks to put out the fire and had instructed the fire commissioner to allow it to burn (Anderson and Hevenor 1987, 227). Goode telephoned the police and fire commissioners and ordered them to put out the fire, but after forty-five minutes the fire had spread down the block and jumped across the street (Boyette 1989, 195). Six adults and five children in the MOVE house died, most of them burned alive. Several attempted to escape by running into the back alley, but, according to some accounts, they were forced, by police gunfire, back into the burning house. Two hundred fifty others—neighbors of the MOVE members—lost their homes and possessions. Many of the details of what happened that day are disputed, as are the facts surrounding the 1978 MOVE eviction (Anderson and Hevenor 1987, 37).

The disputes about what actually occurred took on racial overtones, much as in the racially polarized reaction to the O. J. Simpson acquittal. Goode wrote, "That afternoon watching the television screens, I saw everything I had worked for all my life go up in smoke. I had worked my entire professional life to preserve life, to build houses, to build communities. This was totally the opposite from everything I ever wanted to happen" (Goode and Stevens 1992, 227). Mayor Wilson Goode admitted errors of judgment on the day of the attack, but asserted that his most serious error had been the prior appointment of Gregore Sambor as police commissioner. He sought forgiveness from MOVE, called for an investigation of the attack, and rejected the substance cited by some for the police hostility toward MOVE: "I don't believe there was evidence to prove that these nine people conspired and then killed Officer Ramp. In fact, I don't believe that there is evidence that any MOVE member killed Officer Ramp" (Goode and Stevens 1992, 301–2).

A number of white law enforcement officers elsewhere praised the actions that Goode himself so deeply regretted. Daryl Gates, then police chief of Los Angeles, sent Goode a letter lauding his efforts against MOVE. United States Attorney General Edwin Meese said that Goode's handling of MOVE was "a good example we should all take note of" (Boyette 1989, 243). Goode himself wrote:

> When I went into restaurants or other public places, people gave me standing ovations. . . . I found the response baffling. . . . I was anything but proud of what happened. I should not be cheered for that. While some people, like Gates, were applauding the action that we took, I could never be proud that police fired ten thousand rounds of ammunition into a house with innocent people inside. I could never be proud of a police commissioner who would drop a bomb on a roof and then when it did not

achieve the desired goal, let a fire burn until it destroyed sixty-one homes and killed eleven people. I could never be proud of a police department that fired their guns at women and children trying to escape a burning inferno. No, we had done nothing to be cheered for. (Goode and Stevens 1992, 235)

The polarized response to MOVE reflected a long-standing racial divide in Philadelphia and in the nation as well, over police handling of black protest, and, of their general treatment of black citizens. When Goode's predecessor as mayor, Frank Rizzo, who served as police commissioner during the turbulent 1960s, and was widely regarded as a white racial populist, campaigned for mayor in 1971, he had, so political scientist Richard Keiser reported, "confined his appearances to working-class white neighborhoods. He promised their residents safe streets, no unwanted public housing projects, opposition to racially motivated school busing, and no tax hikes. He won the endorsement of every union in the city. He ignored the black third of the city's population that had been the party's staunchest supporters" (Keiser 1997, 103). Rizzo had aggressively undercut the city's black leadership, for example, by removing the city's most prominent black ministers from the city's appointed school board (Keiser 1997, 106). And, in his reelection campaign in 1975, Rizzo described the upcoming election as "between the social extremists and the radicals against the people who live within the law. What I am talking about? The Black Panthers . . . the Milton Streets. You could throw in Benjamin Hooks from the NAACP too" (Frump 1978a).[1]

Goode's own brother had been brutally assaulted by police officers and, as mayor, Goode sought fundamental changes in the police department. Like many black mayors elected in racially contested cities, Goode had won office with support of a black, liberal white, and downtown business coalition, and, although taking on the police would alienate working-class conservatives (but they had not supported him in the first place), Goode discovered that this prospect frightened his white liberal and business allies as well, and he did not pursue the changes he desired to make. As a result, the trust between Goode and black Philadelphians eroded; he was perceived in some quarters of the black community as having "gone over to the other side."

Several aspects of the MOVE controversy can be compared with the experiences of other black mayors. Opposition from poor whites and subsequent black leaders' alliance building with downtown business and white middle-class reform liberals has been the strategy of many black-white mayoral coalitions across the country. Goode's selection of coalition partners had not been governed by the fundamental interests of his core black constituency; his electoral strategy was dictated rather by the political reality of the need to counter white working-class racism and its strong opposition to the election of a black mayor. Since liberals and downtown businesses had their own problems with white workers, they had a common enemy with blacks, and this fueled a black-white coalition (Keiser 1997). Goode's decisions on policing were constrained by his need to maintain liberal whites and white business coalition partners and he could hardly afford to appear soft on MOVE with a liberal white district attorney in the wings, calculating his own chances of running against Goode in the next election. To hold his political coalition together, Goode decided, if reluctantly, that he would have to evict MOVE.

Nor did Goode press for an investigation of the convictions of MOVE members. He revealed his true opinions about his tenure as mayor later in a book, *In Goode Faith*, written after he left office, where he said that black officials ought not criticize other black officials publicly but deal with their differences privately to prevent whites' taking advantage of divisions in the black community. Both of Goode's decisions sound like pragmatic politics, but they mislead whites and blacks alike about matters of race. Indeed, as Andrew Young maintained in 1991, "It is far easier to attack white institutions for their failures than to admit that local institutions are unable to solve the problems even when they are led by blacks" (Massey and Denton 1993, viii). It is hard to find black politicians who do speak candidly about race while in office.

Black urban regimes thus are constrained by the structure of the political economy. Yet they are even more deeply constrained by the historical, and the continued, lack of a sustained alliance between poor whites and blacks—a lack that is the political essence of the race problem, and that prevents class-based interracial cooperation to solve common problems. Generations of black leaders have called for transracial coalitions, insisting in effect that only poor whites' resistance to coalition building with blacks (on an equal basis) prevents black activists from joining a multiracial "class" coalition to reform oppressive political and economic structures. Even many black nationalists agree with this finding.

The civil rights movement itself in the 1960s sought to build a coalition with poor whites not only to achieve equal rights but also to effect social-democratic economic reform. The enority of this task, and its failure, led activists to attempt political approaches close to what I am calling deep pluralism. Black mayors, in contrast, typically have sought to join forces with more conservative white groups around superficial common interests. Black mayors seldom sought to mobilize the black poor, even when pressured to do so by a mobilized black poor themselves. Indeed, most black mayors either have distanced themselves from the traditional civil rights economic agenda, or have even sought to silence and demobilize that agenda's proponents. Most have hesitated to engage in honest race talk for fear of alienating liberal white allies or of arousing white conservative opposition.

Ideal and Less-than-Ideal Biracial Coalitions

As the term "civil rights" suggests, the civil rights movement is usually characterized as a movement focused on the attainment of individual rights for blacks who have suffered racial discrimination. The movement, in the South, was, indeed, focused on this issue with peaceful resistance and the filing of suits in the courts. But civil rights as such was only one critical thrust of the original movement. The civil rights movement was, at heart, just as concerned about economic justice as about social and political justice, and tended to see the three as inseparable. Its strategic political goal was a class-based political coalition with poor whites (the white working class), and with support of white liberal elites, to win broad moral and political transformations that could eradicate poverty.[2] The Rev. Martin Luther King Jr., against the advice of many, opposed the Vietnam War as morally wrong. And King said in 1968, months before his assassination in Memphis, where he had gone to support sanitation workers, that poor whites "ought to be out here marching with every one of us every time we have a march." "You're just as poor as Negroes. You are put in the position of supporting your oppressor. Because through blindness and prejudice, you fail to see that the same forces that oppress Negroes in American society oppress poor white people. And all you are living on is the satisfaction of your skin being white. . . . And you're so poor you can't send your children to school" (King 1986b, 264). Seven years earlier, in a 1961 speech to the AFL-CIO, King had said that he looked forward to the time when "there will be no separate identification of Negroes and labor," when "all who work for a living will be one." His American Dream of 1961 was "a dream of equality of opportunity, of privilege and property widely distributed; a dream of a land when men will not take necessities from the many to give luxuries to the few; a dream of a land where men will not argue that the color of a man's skin determines the content of his character; a dream where all of our gifts and resources are held not for ourselves alone but as instruments of service for the rest of humanity—that is the dream" (King 1986a, 260). By 1965, King had translated this dream into a call for a coalition in support of full employment, a new New Deal:

> We must develop a federal program of public works, retraining and jobs for all—so that none, white or black, will have cause to feel threatened . . . the unemployed, poverty-stricken white man must be made to realize that he is in the very same boat with the Negro. Together, they could exert massive pressure on the government to get jobs for all. Together, they could form a grand alliance. (King 1986c, 368)

But the hoped-for coalition with the white working class did not emerge. Civil rights leaders found, as Ralph Gomes and Linda Williams write, that "the group of whites that has been more likely to participate in coalitions with African Americans either as actual members (for example in the NAACP) or as significant supporters (for example in the SCLC [Southern Christian Leadership Conference] or SNCC [Student Nonviolent Coordinating Committee]) has not been African Americans' most 'natural allies'—the exploited white working class—but rather, affluent, more highly educated whites" (Gomes and Williams [1992] 1995, 143). And King wrote about tensions with blacks' white liberal allies: "Many whites who concede that Negroes should have equal access to public facilities and the untrammeled right to vote cannot understand that we do not intend to remain in the basement of the economic structure. . . . This incomprehension is a heavy burden in our efforts to win white allies for the long struggle" (King 1986d, 316).

King had gone to Memphis, Tennessee in a campaign to organize what he called a "Poor People's Campaign" (Garrow 1986). It was to include poor people—sharecroppers, welfare recipients, unemployed people—black, Latino, Native American, and white. More than two hundred civil rights organizations (including SNCC and CORE, organizations that had become black nationalist-oriented) had joined together to lobby for the "Freedom Budget" that called for full employment or a guaranteed income for those who could not or should not work, also for affordable housing, universal health care, environmental cleanup, and more public transportation.

Over the next ten years, the civil rights movement and the Congressional Black Caucus, too, pressed for full employment (Smith 1996; Weir 1992) to lessen racial tensions over affirmative action and job competition, and also to reduce crime and welfare dependency (Hamilton and Hamilton 1997, 200). While welcoming support from white liberals, black civil rights leaders hoped that economic self-interest would eventually convince poor whites to join their cause despite the earlier warnings of W. E. B. Du Bois, Ralph Bunche, Harlem community leader Herbert Harrison, and many other black leaders and intellectuals that white workers enjoyed a compensatory if token economic advantage and a significant psychological boost from racist labor practices and cultural stigmatization of blacks (Du Bois 1995).

King, one of the stronger believers in the power of moral conviction, was not solely reliant on moral suasion as the basis for strategic politics nor did he focus only on economic self-interest as the conceptual building block for a broad political strategy. Thus, regardless of its compelling economic logic, he understood that there could be no united movement of the poor without a determined struggle against the white racial identity that gives priority to continued separation from blacks over economic prosperity for all, and that led white workers to identify even with oppressive employers over their fellow black workers. The decision of King and SCLC in 1967 to take the civil rights movement north, and to create poor people's campaigns, beginning in Chicago, was linked to a decision to confront the prejudices of northern white workers while confronting their common economic problems. But it turned out to be a harder and more uphill struggle than the struggle to defeat pervasive and brutal racial segregation in the South. King saw that the consensus orientation to politics promulgated during the McCarthy period had led to intimidation of progressives in democratic discourse. Aside from its importance in learning from enemies, King's method of nonviolent protest was a self-conscious method to engage enemies in politics without the specter of violence (and without an excuse for repression of "treasonous" radicals):

McCarthyism left a legacy of social paralysis. Fear persisted through succeeding years, and social reform remained inhibited and defensive. A blanket of conformity and intimidation conditioned young and old to exalt mediocrity and convention. Criticism of the social order was still imbued with implications of treason. . . .

Here is the true meaning and value of compassion and nonviolence, when they help us to see the enemy's point of view, to hear his questions, to know his assessment of ourselves. For from his view we may indeed see the basic weaknesses of our own condition, and if we are mature, we may learn and grow and profit from the wisdom of the brothers who are called the opposition. (King 1986e, 645, 638)

King's idea that pluralist democracy must encourage people to cooperate thoughtfully in the political process in spite of fundamental disagreements, instead of insisting first on convergence around a single ideal like the American Dream or socialism, is part of deep pluralism.[3]

Black Mayoral Politics

The Reverend Martin Luther King Jr. was dismissive of the potential of black progress through local elections, viewing it mainly as a psychological boost for a more meaningful national movement. King wrote:

The election of Negro mayors, such as Hatcher, in some of the nation's largest cities has also had a tremendous psychological impact upon the Negro. It has shown him that he has the potential to participate in the determination of his own destiny—and that of society. We will see more Negro mayors in major cities in the next ten years, but this is not the ultimate answer. Mayors are relatively unimportant figures in the scheme of national politics. Even a white mayor such as John Lindsay of New York simply does not have the money and resources to deal with the problems of his city. The necessary money to deal with urban problems must come from the federal government, and this money is ultimately controlled by the Congress of the United States. The success of these enlightened mayors is entirely dependent upon the financial support made available by Washington. (King 1986d, 319)

The politics of building a movement coalition of the poor conflicted sharply with the more limited instrumental coalition politics of winning mayoral elections that emerged in the mid-1960s. Black mayoral candidates generally downplayed deep interracial conflicts lest these mobilize conservative white opposition. They did seek transracial coalitions, as did the civil rights movement, but focused on support of white liberals and business groups, although those interests differed from the coalition of the poor that the civil rights movement had envisioned. They saw such coalitions as a pragmatic first step. Liberal political reformers tend to have more limited goals than blacks, such as an end to machine patronage, a rooting out of unprofessionalism and waste in the delivery of public services, or reduction of violent crime and prevention of riots to enact racial peace and protect business investments in cities. The interracial coalition the civil rights leaders had sought was a long-term alliance thicker and stronger than a coincidental convergence of interests during an election, but black mayoral candidates worked in short time frames of the next election, not for long-term alliances they believed they could not yet achieve, and like their white counterparts running for mayor they gave priority to winning city hall.

Business and middle-class allies often had unrealistic expectations that black mayors could maintain racial peace despite popular racial hostility. In Atlanta, the white business community saw poor whites as so rabidly racist as to scare off northern investors. Atlanta's downtown businesses wanted racial calm above all. They projected an image of Atlanta as "the city too busy to hate" (Ferguson 1996; Stone 1989a). Hence, when dozens of race riots swept across cities in the mid- and late-1960s, many businesses could not get riot insurance, including in Atlanta, and so supported black candidates as a kind of insurance policy against further upheaval (Rich 1989). In Cleveland, Carl Stokes, the first black mayor elected in 1967, said of his business supporters, "Clearly, I was a 'safe' candidate. In the backs of their minds, those white men believed that if they put me out front they would be buying off the ghetto" (Stokes 1973, 96). Similarly, in Philadelphia in the 1980s, Mayor Wilson Goode complained that many whites expected him to maintain racial calm, "No one asked why the MOVE issues hadn't been resolved in the seven years since 1978. They focused only on my sixteen months in office. . . . Somehow as the city's first African American mayor, I was expected to maintain a standard and perform miracles that had never been required of my predecessors. I knew that some people who never wanted a black mayor to begin with were now using these events as a new reason to challenge my competency" (Goode and Stevens 1992, 249).

Had black mayoral candidates been able to forge racial coalitions with white workers they might well have been able to go beyond issues of racial peace and civil stability to address common economic and social issues. But, with moderate business and middle-class coalition partners, rhetoric like Goode's post-mayoral language could have been suicidal. To gain white votes and investments, other black candidates, too, have cast themselves not only as keepers of the peace, but as managers capable of running cities like corporations, as a white mayor would be, helping blacks not by direct confrontation with white conservatives but by working with business to attract new investments.

Lacking a broad, social democratic, economic agenda to gain the allegiance of poor blacks (and poor whites, Asians, and Latinos), black mayoral candidates, because they lacked the power to implement such an agenda against the greater power of white business and social leadership—and taking a stance like that of Carmichael and Hamilton—meshed elements of interest group pluralism with black nationalism into a kind of militant-sounding black electoral nationalism. If the militant anti-white rhetoric and symbolism of black electoral nationalism that sometimes accompanied such campaigns sounded sometimes like the civil rights movement itself, it was, actually, a turn toward a more limited economic and political agenda, one aimed at more conservative white allies, and a deliberate toning-down of civil rights radicalism and an avoidance of the deeply challenging political-economic and moral issues King and others had emphasized. Mayor Carl Stokes made this point clear during his first mayoral race, when he sought to convince the Reverend Martin Luther King Jr. not to come to Cleveland to conduct protest marches like those in Chicago in 1966:

> I explained to Dr. King that I had carefully put this whole cam-
> paign together. I had worked to get actual white votes. I couldn't
> afford to do anything to aggravate the white voter. There was
> too much at stake. We had everything together, and if nothing
> foreign was introduced we knew how to handle the situation.
> "Martin," I told him, "if you just come in here with these
> marches and what not, you can just see what the reaction
> will be. . . . I would rather that you not stay."
> Asking Dr. King not to stay was one of the toughest decisions
> I ever had to make. . . . But it came down to the hard game of

politics—whether we wanted a cause or a victory. I wanted to win. Our people needed me to win. I had been the architect for a unique assembly of interests, and I knew with one wrong move it would be just another house of cards. (Stokes 1973, 101–3)

Thomas Bradley, running for mayor of Los Angeles in 1973, came to a decision similar to Stokes's in his approach to Bobby Seale, a national Black Panther leader, who had endorsed Bradley's candidacy soon after losing a mayoral bid of his own in Oakland. Bradley, running in a city only 18 percent black, moved promptly to reject Seale's endorsement. According to Stokes, who advised Bradley, "He [Bradley] didn't want to do it [reject Seale]. But he had to if he wanted to keep those white voters whose fears he had so carefully allayed over the four years. . . . He had learned the game" (Stokes 1973, 272). It is worth pointing out that Stokes's opposition did not come from an ideological disagreement with black radicals or nationalists. Stokes, like Detroit's first black mayor, Coleman Young, had been deeply influenced in the 1940s and 1950s by social democratic ideas, and Stokes and Young both understood the power of black nationalism in the ghetto.[4] Stokes warned Bradley that black mayors may not be able to function in government at the same time keeping pace with the leftward movement among black community activists (Stokes 1973, 279). Coleman Young embodied these tensions in his own person, himself not a candidate of the black middle class but rather a black labor radical. He relied on his notoriety in appealing to Detroit's largely blue-collar black working-class constituency (Rich 1989, 120), but his past was a liability with his white supporters, and in response to repeated questioning from reporters about his leftist past, Young stated, "I am not now and never have been a member of any organization that was subversive or whose design was to overthrow the United States in any way" (Rich 1989, 99). He cultivated close ties with conservative businesses and politicians: "Young has reconciled himself to the fact that whites control the economic lifeblood of the city, and he is not prepared to cut any essential arteries or refuse proffered transfusions" (Rich 1989, 150).

To blacks, Young explained his traditional downtown business focus as the only practical way to focus on the needs of the black poor and he described his local tax increases as efforts to stave off white control of the city. Operating in Detroit, a heavily majority-black city with a large blue-collar working-class voting base, Young could win without the votes of whites.

He made little effort to hide his appeals to black workers and did not seek instead to win over either working-class whites or middle-class blacks. He maintained the trust of many black workers, yet he was careful not to support organizing in the black working-class community itself. Rich wrote of this: "When Mayor Young articulates the economic aspirations of the poor, they appreciate his attention to their situation. Thus, in the 1981 income tax vote, they overwhelmingly supported him. Prudently, the mayor has not tried to over organize or over promise this group, yet his care and nurturing of this constituency has also allowed him to safely ignore the criticism of the white-collar middle class" (Rich 1989, 274). Rich explained that "the white residents do not support him in his reelection bids, nor do they subscribe to his policies, and this is particularly true of working-class whites. Those who have remained in the city do not think that the mayor is doing enough for them. They dislike his racial references in speeches, and they believe he is driving whites and middle class blacks out of the city" (Rich 1989, 275).

Mayors Stokes, Bradley, and Young, in different contexts and with differing strategies, simply did what they thought was necessary to win, just as white mayoral candidates would do. Today, generations later in a more conservative national environment, winning elections by relying on votes or investments from moderate white coalition partners requires most black mayors to silence what they know are legitimate black demands. The interracial campaigns black mayors organized in, for example, Los Angeles, Atlanta, or Philadelphia, were not coalitions of conscience predicated on eradicating deep-seated problems of poverty and racism, for black politicians were not, like King, martyrs willing to sacrifice their careers, even their lives, for a cause. Some, equating their personal victories with those of the movement, no doubt believe that their successful careers would advance the broader cause of racial justice and equality. In the process a number neutralized black activists who threatened the viability of their electoral coalitions. Their political language of civil rights protest, which some used and others eschewed, was not used to build the kind of people's movement the civil rights activists endorsed. Stokes put this bluntly: "Underneath all the high talk, the campaign promises, the idealist theories, politicians are mostly interested in perpetuating their privileged positions. No matter how well a man understands this, no matter how hard he is, if he fights for the have-nots he will find himself alienated from most of his fellows, and they will do their level best to wear him down, to break him. He may, if he is good enough or sharp enough or powerful enough, win some particular and even important victories. But eventually he will be driven out" (Stokes 1973, 20–21).

Mayor Wilson Goode made a similar statement after he was out of office in Philadelphia. Like Stokes, Goode had been elected in a racially contested city and considered it critical to promote black community involvement in politics and governance, particularly with his primary political base, the black church. In this sense Goode was elected by the same forces that organized BUILD in Baltimore. The Baltimore and Philadelphia coalitions differed in that Goode's coalition had little independence from Goode himself and, therefore, less power to hold him accountable. Yet Goode saw the conservative shift in black electoral politics and the consequent movement among black candidates farther away from the civil rights movement social justice agenda. As he wrote later:

> Over the years black politicians had gained significant power. . . . Our reform movement had broken down the racial barriers, but it was threatening to create others as these new "bosses" sought to solidify and hold on to their power, not through merit, but by political control. Among themselves they decided something that should have been the decision of the voters: Who was going to be included in the next level of leadership? Essentially, they were saying they didn't like the way the first wave of reformers had played the political game. It was too altruistic. They didn't like this "common good" stuff—working for the best interests of the community rather than themselves. . . . True, many of the leaders were black, and many had come up through the activists ranks of the streets. The only difference now, though, between them and a James H. J. Tate or Frank Rizzo [former Philadelphia machine mayors] was the color of their skins. (Goode and Stevens 1992, 280)

Not only were black mayors and other elected officials not out to build a participatory people's democracy, they usually discouraged it. Thus Coleman Young of Detroit, as Wilbur Rich put it, avoided "over-organizing" and "over-promising" the black poor, and was harshly critical of black politicians who encouraged movement challenging of the existing political economy. Despite his personal roots in interracial labor radicalism, Young as political candidate abandoned efforts to build biracial coalitions among the poor. Organizing black voters disgruntled by the limits of his downtown development policies would not have added to Young's political capacity. But there was a larger impact of Young's and other black mayors' failure to mobilize the black poor: considerable tension developed between those local black elected officials who actively avoided "over-organizing" black poor and black civic organizations. Black demobilization, or lack of mobilization, like the existing deep divisions between poor whites and poor blacks, sapped the potential power of African Americans at both the state and national level in politics.

Goode and Stokes argued, in their behalf, that mayors who try to change direction of dominant black politics won't last long. Black mayors who survive, if free of strong pressure from the black community, can make deals with moderate white liberals or business groups that help blacks and can enable the mayor to stay in office. If confronted with overt pressure from the organized black community, they risk having to take a stand on controversial issues that may cause them to lose the next election as well as support for progress. Both the winner-take-all election structure and the dependence of local government on private investments discourage risk taking and are inherently limiting (see chapter 2).

Black mayoral interests thus tend to break with the interest of the broader black civic community. Because black mayors do not choose ideal coalition partners but must craft coalitions under the constraints of immediate practicality, they tend to form more conservative coalitions than those sought by the civil rights community historically; and they tend to form coalitions with forces significantly to the right of the black public. They may, anticipating this, seek to silence or demobilize groups within the black community that might disrupt the politically moderate coalitions that got them elected in the first place. Because of such constraints, black mayors cannot present a substantive economic program to the black community, and instead, must or believe they must rely on a form of black electoral nationalism ("vote black") to gain the votes of blacks through symbolism not substance. In predominantly white communities, black mayors tend to frame race as traditional American pluralism, "blacks are just like the old Irish," or they utilize a deracialized "color-blind" rhetoric. The conflicting messages lead many in the black community to criticize black mayors as duplicitous on matters of race. Yet, when black mayors confront racial differences openly, as they are sometimes forced to do in contested cities, they run a strong risk of defeat. At least in large cities, no civic coalition has been strong enough to make a mayor who engages in honest racial discourse politically secure.

Black/White Racial Dialogue

The obstacles black mayors face in attempting to discuss racial differences openly, and to act to resolve them, are formidable. In additional to facing coalition problems, mayors have little confidence that black racial views will be fairly aired, in the media and elsewhere.[5] But this is not the most daunting challenge of black/white racial dialogue. With black mayors seen by the daily press as primary black leaders, but pursuing conventional social and economic policies and promoting black nationalism in elections (electoral nationalism) or conventional pluralism (if they address race at all), and with the condition of the poorest urban blacks dismal and worsening, it is not surprising that many observers believe that black political representation, at least in city hall and perhaps also in Congress, has lost its earlier compelling appeal. Some suggest even that charges of racism are cynically used by some black middle-class aspirants to win political office or job promotions, that these candidates are not primarily out to help more needy blacks but to address their own cause, and therefore that whites have no reason to respond to such need—with compassion let alone guilt.

The difficulty in racial communication is compounded by the reluctance of black mayors to speak openly about blacks' historical and still-prevalent conviction that the political-economic structures in the United States are fundamentally unfair from both a race *and* class standpoint. Without such a structural critique, black advocacy for race-specific rights appears oblivious to the plight of the white poor and other groups. If blacks can narrowly assert a middle-class self-interest, why should white liberals be ashamed to protect their own material gains and safe neighborhoods from incursion by blacks and other groups? Raphael Sonnenshein writes that the theory of black power "set out a highly dignified role for Blacks, based on the pursuit of their group interest, but then confined whites to a role that is highly unrealistic and close to demeaning. . . . Liberal whites who defended their own interests were defined as betrayers" (Sonnenshein 1993, 276). Conservative racial populists attack the hypocrisy of black leaders who appeal directly to black interests but also cry foul whenever poor white leaders appeal to the interests of the white poor and who thereby make themselves vulnerable to attack on racial grounds. During his reelection bid for mayor of Philadelphia, Frank Rizzo said, "Vote *black,* vote *black, black, black*—all I hear are black politicians getting up and saying 'Vote black, vote black.' *Well,* I'm gonna tell everybody to *vote white.* And the people who think like me, and there's a lot of them, will help us. Okay, see how easy it is. That's how the lines are being drawn and I welcome it" (Frump 1978b).

In the civil rights movement, in contrast, middle-class black leaders were fighting not only for themselves but for the poorest group in society—the black poor—and were widely perceived as fighting for a higher cause, the welfare of all oppressed people. But once the black middle class accepted the practical limits on advocacy and policy change required by their new, often fragile, coalitions with business and white liberal reformers, they could seldom address in an effective way the fundamental needs of the poor. They began to pursue the time-honored tradition of boosting their own success and rationalizing that the benefits would trickle down to their black poor constituents. Yet, as Sonnenshein suggests, charging liberal whites with betrayal and racism in such a context is indefensible and hypocritical. If the black middle class is acting just as other upwardly mobile self-interested groups do, if, for example, middle-class blacks have fled the ghetto for the suburbs in large numbers, if they, too, want to avoid crime, failing schools, and social disorder—and the poor would follow them if they could—then why is it racist for middle-class whites to want to avoid such problems, as well? The desire for a middle-class existence is American, not racist on the part of either whites or blacks. Abandonment of the plight of the black poor on the part of middle-class blacks may be a moral flaw for their unwillingness to sacrifice their own security, but it is a behavioral failing. There is still a general difference between the white and black middle class in responsibility for the poor; most middle-class blacks would like to see government do more for the poor, especially the black poor. The constraints on their ability to help the poor themselves do not reflect a class selfishness or a general lack of will.[6] Moreover, blacks who advocate for the poor and seek elected office with that agenda do have a special responsibility. Yet, black mayors almost never address fundamental issues of the need for reform of the economic structure to bring greater equality, and have found themselves unable—in the main—to address fundamental connections between the economic concerns of blacks and white workers, nor have they played a leading role in building multiracial political coalitions to redress deep-seated economic impoverishment. Their own need for survival has pre-empted their sense of purpose. They have behaved, as a result, as white mayors historically have, if for reasons of a racial and class bind, not for reasons of seeking personal gain. This is a matter of lack of sufficient power to cope with white majority clout.

The lack of substance on the part of black mayors has contributed to a critique of black politics on the part of white progressives who question if antiracism today is merely a form of narrow identity politics that de-tracts from an effort to meet more substantive economic problems and that hinders broad classwide interracial solidarity, and even if there is sub-stance to charges of racial unfairness. Indeed, measured by the assumptions of the Jim Crow era—the conviction among most whites that blacks are in-herently and biologically inferior to whites—white racism has declined dramatically over the last half century; whites are far more willing to inte-grate socially with blacks and to support race-neutral public policies that assist blacks. However, since the 1960s, popular racism has continued in a new form that substitutes an assumed cultural inferiority of blacks for the earlier concept of biological and cognitive inferiority (Bobo and Smith 1998). The premise of this new "cultural racism" is that the economic and social gaps between blacks and whites, for example, persistently high jobless rates, involvement in the criminal justice system, lower academic achieve-ment, and alarmingly high HIV/AIDS infection rates are all the result of culturally defined and deficient characteristics of African Americans them-selves, such as lack of discipline or promiscuity, not of systemic failure in public policy and in institutions. Critics of this cultural racism assert that, to the contrary, economic and social gaps between whites and blacks are caused principally by the structure of the political economy and the un-equal resources and services made available by government and the pri-vate industry to the black community. After centuries of the consequences of such inequality, accumulated disadvantage in education, homeowner-ship, business ownership, wealth accumulation, life expectancy—and con-comitant and unequal advantage to whites—blacks remain severely handi-capped competitively in the economic marketplace. In politics, as well, blacks are still a weak political minority in a majoritarian white society. When they gain office they lack the power that historically goes with that office.

Those in the majority who consider the social structure neutral, color-blind, and hence fair to all, conclude that blacks who fall behind whites must be inferior by objective, factual, analysis. Supporters of the cultural inferiority argument maintain that their views are not racist but simply the logical conclusion of social scientific findings. The critiques of this new cultural racism bear a resemblance to neo-Marxist class critiques of equal opportunity that have criticized the American Creed for ignoring class-based obstacles to black advance. But, the critique goes beyond a neo-Marxist analysis to examine cultural beliefs and institutions and the continuing impact of concepts of racial inferiority/superiority on political alignments. Arguing that race is a political and "social construct," that it has no essential biological or natural meaning, and that concepts of racial inferiority are advanced because of their relevance to powerful economic and political interests, the struggle is not only one of the economic effect of capitalism but of political isolation on the basis of race and the outcomes of that struggle are not predetermined by economic class. The principal adherents of racism today in urban politics are not economic elites or capitalist bosses, but representatives of working-class whites.

Economic elites may benefit from racial divisions, but to ignore the impact of white working-class racism and the responsibility that working-class whites bear for their own social and political commitments minimizes the power poor whites have achieved in their struggles and exaggerates the power of economic elites. A key to multiracial class solidarity may be to confront the white proletariat's racism, not the bourgeoisie, recognizing that the white working-class attitudes and civic organizations are instrumental in making, and in resisting, broader social change. In chapter 3, in a similar vein, I suggested that to strengthen their civic political capacity, black communities themselves must take political responsibility for their internal discrimination against women, gays, lesbians, and other black urban subgroups. The critique of cultural racism opens up theoretical space to consider this possibility because it is not satisfied by an economically determinist analysis, but works to account for the actual political behavior and consciousness of workers and other groups, which is largely based on racial and gender identities. Some white progressives attempt to explain white racism as a reaction to the excesses of black advocates unschooled in the superior logic of class solidarity, yet when black mayoral politics is examined within this framework, it is evident instead that the white working class's susceptibility to racism has been responsible for the adversarial attitudes and behavior of many whites to blacks. The deep pluralism idea is that non-elites not only need deliberative space to divine and illuminate the oppressive meta-narratives of dominant groups but that to create that space, blacks, white workers, and other oppressed groups need to challenge the exclusions and oppressions embedded in their own civic and political formations and self-identities. The process of inclusion and social change begins at home.

Intraminority Coalitions

Mayoral elections in Los Angeles and Houston in the 1990s focused national attention on black and Latino coalitions. Black-Asian and Latino-Asian coalitions also have become increasingly important to the course of multiracial coalition building elsewhere in California and in a number of other states. In Texas, in March 2004, a white businessman, Bill White, defeated Orlando Sanchez, a Hispanic candidate, and Sylvester Turner, a black candidate, to succeed an African American mayor, Lee Brown, the former New York City police commissioner and a liberal mayor who worked closely with Latino elected officials (Williams 2004). Had there been a minority unity candidate, White would have lost. In the nation's four largest cities—New York, Los Angeles, Chicago, Houston—and in its fifth largest city, Philadelphia, blacks and Latinos now comprise a majority. Yet only in Philadelphia is there now a minority mayor, John Street. Forging black-Latino coalitions and political alliances could give city hall to this new political majority if the separate groups behaved as a majority coalition (see table 4.1). In terms of the twenty largest cities, black and Latinos together (but not separately) form a majority in six cities, from 62.8 percent in Chicago, 62.7 percent in Houston, 61.5 percent in Dallas, 57.7 percent in Los Angeles, 53.6 percent in New York, to 51.7 percent in Philadelphia. In 2000, Milwaukee was 49.3 percent black and Latino; by now it is probably over 50 percent.

In the 2001 Los Angeles election, Antonio Villaraigosa, a Latino Democrat and former speaker of the California assembly, was defeated in a run-off election by city attorney James Hahn, regarded as a moderate white Democrat; Hahn got 80 percent of the black vote, decisive in his victory, although Villaraigosa was by far the more politically progressive candidate. Blacks and Latinos had competed not combined their power. (This changed in 2005, when Villaraigosa defeated Hahn in the race for mayor.) Unlike the campaigns of two former Latino mayors, Henry Cisneros in San Anto-

Table 4.1

Latino and Black Percentages in Twenty Largest U.S. Cities

City	Population	Latino %	Black %	Latino and Black %
New York*	8,008,278	27.0	26.6	53.6
Los Angeles*	3,694,820	46.5	11.2	57.7
Chicago*	2,896,016	26.0	36.8	62.8
Houston*	1,953,631	37.4	25.3	62.7
Philadelphia*	1,517,550	8.5	43.2	51.7
Phoenix	1,321,045	34.1	5.1	39.2
San Diego	1,223,400	25.4	7.9	33.3
Dallas*	1,188,580	35.6	25.9	61.5
San Antonio	1,144,646	58.7	6.8	65.5
Detroit	951,270	5.0	81.6	86.6
San Jose	894,943	30.2	3.5	33.7
Indianapolis	781,870	3.9	25.5	29.4
San Francisco	776,733	14.1	7.8	21.9
Jacksonville	735,617	4.2	29.0	33.2
Columbus	711,470	2.5	24.5	27.0
Austin	656,562	30.5	10.0	40.5
Baltimore	651,154	1.7	64.3	66.0
Memphis	650,100	3.0	61.4	64.4
Milwaukee	596,974	12.0	37.3	49.3
Boston	589,141	14.4	25.3	39.7

Source: U.S. Census 2000; (* represents cities where blacks and Latinos are individually a minority, but combined comprise a majority of the city population).

nio, and Federico Pena in Denver—both elected with business, white liberal, Latino coalitions—Villaraigosa's campaign was the outgrowth of a community-labor coalition (Meyerson 2001b) of the County Federation of Labor, the Service Employees International Union (SEIU), the Hotel Employees and Restaurant Employees (HERE), as well as a multiracial network of grass-roots environmental groups, women's groups, immigrant groups, and community-based organizations. Logically, he would have seemed an obvious choice for black support; he had been a strong advocate of police reform, traditionally a key means of securing black support in Los Angeles, and criticized the actions of Los Angeles police officers during the Rampart controversy, a far-reaching scandal of police corruption and misconduct involving, among other things, admissions by certain police officers that they had shot handcuffed suspects in a poor immigrant Latino neighborhood. But Villaraigosa was not trusted among many black political leaders. Hahn also took actions signaling his intention to provide prominent positions to blacks in his administration. Los Angeles's police department at the time was headed by an African American, Bernard Parks (apparently to dampen criticism of the police within the black community) (Meyerson 2001a). During the campaign, Hahn emphasized his support for Chief Parks (Barrs 2001). Although Villaraigosa was endorsed by some influential, if relatively young, black community activists, such as Anthony Thigpen of LA AGENDA (Action for Grassroots Empowerment and Neighborhood Development Alternatives) and Karen Bass of Community Coalition (subsequently elected to the city council), and by black elected officials active in the labor-community coalition, Councilman Mark Ridley Thomas among them. However, Villaraigosa was opposed by an older generation of black political activists in South Central Los Angeles. They were loyal to the late Kenny Hahn, James Hahn's father, who had represented the largely black South Central area of Los Angeles on the County Board of Supervisors for forty years from 1952 through 1992, and who had consistently supported African Americans' demands and received their loyalty in return. Thus James Hahn won 59 percent of the white vote and 80 percent of the black vote (Vaca 2004, 104). Villaraigosa won 82 percent of the Latino vote. Latinos made up 46 percent of the Los Angeles population, but low voter registration and high numbers of noncitizens kept the Latino vote to only 22 percent of the total, though 10 percent higher than in the 1993 mayoral election (Meyerson 2001b).

The implications of the Villaraigosa-Hahn results for black politics is best understood in the context of Latino-black political relations. For twenty years, Los Angeles had a black mayor, Thomas Bradley, elected through a black-liberal white coalition. Earlier, in 1969, Bradley had lost a close race for mayor against Sam Yorty, a conservative Democrat and racial populist. Despite this, 67 percent of the Latino vote went for Yorty that year (Sonnenshein 1993, 94). In subsequent elections, Bradley made inroads into the Latino vote, but Latinos were not a significant part of Bradley's long-term coalition. He won the 1973 general election for mayor, with 44 percent of the Latino vote against Yorty, with most of his Latino vote coming from poorer Latino neighborhoods (Sonnenshein 1993, 109). The majority of the Latino vote had gone to Yorty, in large part because Bradley and other black activists had angered Latino political activists by supporting an all-black slate to occupy three vacant city council seats, leaving Latinos without seats on the city council despite their nearly equal numbers in Los Angeles at the time (1963). Black candidates won and held on to all three city council seats for the next thirty years. Sonnenshein wrote that there were "three council seats for Blacks and none for Latinos. . . . Liberal money and support had been flowing to Blacks, most notably Bradley, creating resentment among even liberal Latino activists" (Sonnenshein 1993, 99). Bradley's focus on downtown business development, too, had done little to attract popular grassroots Latino support. His strongest non-black base was among Jews, in 1969 and 1973: "Jews were twenty points more pro-Bradley than either white Gentiles or Latinos" (Sonnenshein 1993, 93). Bradley won easily in 1973 with 54 percent of the vote and a surprising 46 percent of the white vote, but he lost the Latino vote (Sonnenshein 1993, 109).

Although he had received overwhelming black voter support, his popularity in black communities had also steadily declined over the course of his five electoral runs Said historian Heather Parker:

> Anticipating that Bradley would serve as their spokesman in city hall, African Americans expected his election to usher in a bold new era of unprecedented social and economic advancement for black people . . . [but] his five consecutive terms as mayor witnessed a gradual deterioration in his relationship with the black community. . . . Bradley's seemingly color-blind approach to politics and his efforts to distance himself from the black community resulted in some African Americans resenting him for not using his position to pursue their concerns more aggressively. (Parker 2001, 153)

Yet Bradley's political strategy was successful in securing votes to maintain his regime. African Americans under Bradley had secured a disproportionate share of jobs in city and county government, and probably, therefore, he won black middle-class support. Blacks represented 1.3 percent of the total administrative appointments (170) in 1973, but 10.6 percent of the total (220) by 1992. Blacks made significant gains, too, in the protective services (such as police hires), going from 9.5 percent in 1973 to 23.9 percent in 1992, in a city where blacks were only 13 percent of the city population. But Latinos, too, had gained, from 7.8 percent of protective service employees in 1973 to 25.5 percent in 1992, although Latinos were then nearly 40 percent of the city population; whites had declined from 81.5 to 45.9 percent in that job category (Parker 2001, 163). But, despite expectations of his black base, Bradley did not change the leadership of the Los Angeles police department or its reputation for brutality. He provided old-fashioned patronage in lieu of social change.

Bradley is a leading example of a deracialized black mayor. While blacks had quietly made significant incremental gains in city employment and administration under cover of color-blind rhetoric, after the 1992 Los Angeles riot, the bloodiest in U.S. history, when Bradley spoke at the First African Methodist Episcopal Church at a community meeting, "the church reverberated with deafening boos and jeers" (Parker 2001, 170). Bradley had ignored warning signs a year earlier when he was strongly criticized in the black community after a teenage black girl, caught trying to steal a bottle of orange juice, was shot in the back of the head and killed by a Korean store owner. The store owner was convicted of manslaughter but sentenced only to probation, infuriating many in the black community. Soon afterward, a Korean store was firebombed. Bradley visited the store to express his concern, but never expressed sympathy for the Harlins family (the family of the teenager who was shot), whose members subsequently criticized him publicly for lack of compassion for black children (Parker 2001, 165).

Bradley's consistent projections of a color-blind image put him under constant pressure from black organizations and activists to demonstrate identity with them. But he resisted the pressure and as the federal government became more conservative in the Reagan administration, so did Bradley, cultivating an image as a fiscal conservative (Payne and Ratzan 1986). "When left without federal aid and with little public pressure," his administration was, in the words of Sonnenshein, "supportive of the status quo, probusiness, and not very innovative" (Sonnenshein 1993, 174). It was ineffective in providing affordable housing for Latinos, blacks, and Asians, and his downtown business approach produced few jobs for blacks in Los Angeles's poor neighborhoods.

Bradley's coalition efforts focused on holding the confidence of white businesses and organizations. One might say that, except for black middle-class patronage, he was not deracialized but identified with white interests. From an electoral standpoint, it may not have been in Bradley's political interest to spend scarce resources to advocate change in the black community or to incorporate Latinos whose voting power was still weak. It would only be a matter of time before Latino voting power would catch up with the swelling Latino population numbers but that was well ahead of Bradley's timetable for his political career and there was no black civic coalition to compel him to respond to its needs. Although Latinos and blacks (and Asians) in Los Angeles had common economic problems, they were not organized cooperatively to address them. (In 1990, the mean annual family income for black adult workers was $18,576; for Latinos $13,126; for Asians $21,341; for whites $31,826 [Bobo et al. 2000, 19]). Poor blacks and Latinos were increasingly concentrated in the city's cheapest and most deteriorated areas (Bobo et al. 2000, 24). So, too, as in other southwestern cities, Los Angeles's system of governance is highly dispersed, leading to fragmentation among local organizations. Thus many service functions in the city of Los Angeles are administered by Los Angeles County government, presiding over eighty-eight separate municipalities. And, with a long history of mutual distrust between blacks and Latinos in Los Angeles, there were many suggestions that Los Angeles blacks supported Hahn out of concern that a Latino mayor would redirect city job resources away from blacks toward Latinos. Sonnenshein's study of Los Angeles politics suggests that the formation and maintenance of political coalitions generally cannot be explained solely by groups' material self-interests, and Los Angeles was a prime example of that. Ideological commitments and intergroup trust matter, as well. Many blacks in Los Angeles had long espoused the idea, articulated by Lani Guinier and Gerald Torres in their 2002 book, *The Miner's Canary,* that some light-skinned Latinos are "accepting the 'racial bribe'" in trying to become white. Guinier and Torres wrote:

> The racial bribe is a strategy that invites specific racial or ethnic groups to advance within the existing black-white racial hierarchy by becoming "white." . . . Despite inconsistencies within the census groupings, the management of relations between Hispanics and whites has always contained the peculiar promise to some Hispanics that they could become white. Implicit in this promise was the assumption that Mexicans would not be treated like black people and locked into a permanent condition of racial inferiority. And in California in the early twentieth century, it contained the implicit assumption that Mexicans would not be treated like Asians, either . . . [when] virulent anti-Asian racism made Mexicans "whiter." (Guinier and Torres 2002, 225, 226)

Such sentiments might have encouraged black support for Hahn, though there is little direct evidence in this regard; black elected officials justified black support as supporting a winner who, as a white liberal, could potentially generate greater payoffs for blacks. This posture was disingenuous; a more likely explanation is that Hahn, though white, could be more trusted than his Latino opponent to protect middle-class blacks' gains from the Bradley era.

A different way of framing black civic interests might follow the track of the earlier civil rights movement. A black alliance with Latinos would not pay off in prestigious commission appointments for blacks since blacks and Latinos were both competing for a small number of such positions. With the Latino population rapidly rising in the state, African Americans, had they looked ahead, might have achieved greater long-term benefits by cooperating in the present with Latinos on non-zero-sum—hence non-competitive—issues such as lack of adequate state funding for public schools, rather than fighting over who gets a particular elected office or the most elected offices or commission seats. According to the 2000 federal census, California was already a minority-majority state, with whites only 47 percent of the state population, Latinos 32 percent, Asians 11 percent, and blacks 7 percent. Sonnenshein presciently wrote in 1993:

> Los Angeles may have a basis for a Black-Latino coalition that is quite different from the sort of coalition that could be made with whites. This Latino class vote gets pulled out of voting analysis as an "ethnic vote," but it may be important in class terms. In the search for a white working-class base for black politics, observers may tend to miss it. If there is a working-class Latino base for the biracial coalition, its members probably have different priorities than those of white liberals. (Vaca 2004, 98)

Stronger Latino support for a civic alliance of Latinos and blacks to effect basic economic and political reforms in California would matter to the black poor.

Both mayoral election strategies and longer-term civic coalition strategies in Los Angeles embody black interests, but each focuses on different black interests. The black argument for the white candidate Hahn as mayor was directed toward defending the gains of black middle-class officials, civil servants, and some community-service providers. Any advocacy of long-range civic coalition strategy would be directed more toward poor blacks who have not benefited much from black urban empowerment, and also toward the Latino poor who are also unlikely to benefit from similar patronage from a Latino mayor.

Short-term electoral strategies and longer-term civic strategies need not be in conflict, though they were in Los Angeles, where blacks lacked both a longer-term civic strategy and also a workable electoral strategy in the mayoral race. Thus, Hahn, a white political moderate, was able to forge a coalition with blacks and with conservative whites long considered political enemies in the black community. In fact, in the last days of the campaign, Hahn resorted to virulently racist campaign ads of the sort regularly denounced in black communities. In one such ad, Villaraigosa, his Latino opponent was shown standing in front of Watts Towers, symbolic of poor blacks in Los Angeles, suggesting that Villaraigosa was supported by the wrong element of blacks. Soon after the election, Hahn withdrew his support for the black police chief, Bernard Parks, prompting calls of outrage from Hahn's black supporters and quickly eroding the black-conservative white coalition engineered by Hahn. But the horse had left the stable.

Black support for Hahn had also made it easier for middle-class Latinos, eager to displace blacks in local government, to paint blacks as hostile to Latino progress. This could become a more serious problem in the future for blacks as Latino voting rates catch up with their growing population densities. Roger Wilkins, the historian and civil rights leader, has said that, "as the Hispanic population grows, as it remembers the prominent place in the racial dialogue blacks traditionally held and remembers its feelings of exclusion, it's going to be hard for them to modulate their feeling of potency from numbers. That's going to cause real stress for blacks" (Vaca 2004, 107). Wilkins was writing broadly, not of Los Angeles, but the thesis applies. As long as black and Latino interests are popularly framed in terms of securing the limited number of local political offices or other patronage appointments rather than in terms of common social and economic concerns, there is a strong basis for black-Latino conflict not only in Los Angeles but also in other U.S. cities as well, and for the continuance of white plurality power.

When black coalitional efforts are directed instead toward broader political and economic change, the definition of friends and enemies tends to change. One of the principal complaints of Latinos and Asians against black activists and civil rights organizations is that the latter have tended to cast racial-justice issues in narrow black or white terms while ignoring racial discrimination against other groups. Black interests have not always been framed so narrowly, though they were in Los Angeles. When the aim of black political activists is to build broad coalitions leading to structural change, black leaders have tended to frame racial justice issues so as to include others, and indeed, have frequently connected the black racial struggle to international struggles of formerly colonized peoples in Latin America, Asia, and India.

The nineteenth-century slave who freed himself to become the first internally recognized spokesman for African Americans, Frederick Douglass, did not view the black struggle in a mere "black-white" paradigm. Aiming to build as broad a coalition against U.S. slavery as possible, Douglass called the 1846–48 war against Mexico racist and expansionist, a war against freedom and against working people of both countries, and an exercise of "Anglo-Saxon cupidity and love of domination." So, too, during the 1870s, Douglass strongly opposed efforts to restrict Chinese immigration, noting that references to a "Yellow Peril" sounded much like "Black Peril" (Martin 1984, 216–18). He was an outspoken supporter also of Irish nationalists, whose support of abolitionists was returned in kind. Similarly, W. E. B. Du Bois, leader of the newly founded NAACP in the first decade of the twentieth century, attempted to win broad interracial and global support, and he did not frame the black struggle in such a narrow black versus white paradigm. He and others intentionally named the NAACP an association of "colored" people and not "black" or "Negro" people "to promote the interests of dark-skinned people everywhere" (Lewis 1993, 405). In the 1930s, Du Bois argued that the race problem in the United States should be closely linked to labor and anticolonial struggles worldwide. His book, *Black Reconstruction,* outlined the relationship of black oppression to the oppression of white workers and workers of color globally:

> the plight of the white working class throughout the world
> today is directly traceable to Negro slavery in America, on which
> modern commerce and industry was founded, and which per-
> sisted to threaten free labor until it was partially overthrown in
> 1863. The resulting color caste founded and retained by capital-
> ism was adopted, forwarded and approved by white labor, and
> resulted in subordination of colored labor to white profits the
> world over. Thus the majority of the world's laborers, by the in-
> sistence of white labor, became the basis of a system of industry
> which ruined democracy and showed its perfect fruit in World

War and Depression. And this book seeks to tell that story. (Du Bois 1992, 30)

As Robin Kelley writes in *Freedom Dreams*, black activists of the 1950s, too, maintained a global perspective (Kelley 2002), inspired by anticolonial movements in the Third World. The Reverend Martin Luther King Jr., especially, and the African American civil rights movement, broadly, learned nonviolent methods of struggle from their close observation of and solidarity with Ghandi and with India's struggle against British colonialism. Following Du Bois, Huey Newton, the Black Panther leader, asserted in the late 1960s that black Americans must view their own struggle as part of a *world* revolution. There were, he said, no longer national economies and national corporations but a worldwide economy (Brown 1992). Recent scholarship has argued that criticism of racial segregation from "Third World" nations was a principal factor in the decisions of Presidents Eisenhower and Kennedy to act against segregation (Borstelmann 2001; Carmines and Stimson 1989; Dudziak 2000).

But at the local level of city halls in the United States, black political empowerment in government has not encouraged, and has even discouraged, a broadening of blacks' sense of racial identity. The narrow coalitional aims of black political entrepreneurs set as their primary goal winning elections, not long-term alliances with partners who share deep interests. Such a narrow framing of race is unlikely to change in the absence of black civic coalitions with broader goals, and without an intent to encourage diversity among black leaders rather than "a single leader of black people" as a black mayor is often made out to be. Removing the aura of self-serving manipulation from racial discourse requires more than a commitment to consideration of different ideas; it requires a commitment to cultivating diverse organizations, interests, and leaders, not black elected officials alone. Mayoral elections, in practice, do not ensure representation of most black interests whether blacks are the minority or even the numerical majority since they do not control economic power and do not control state and federal governments on whose funding and support cities must depend. It is, I believe, in the broader self-interest of blacks to align with Latinos and Asians, as well as with poor whites, in behalf of their common interests. The political temptation to win elections through racial polarization are great for politicians appealing to a white political majority but also for those blacks or Latinos representing strong minorities. That the temptation has seduced a number of white state and national politicians has been the cause of black frustration. It can also be a cause of Latino frustration when black politicians in majority-black cities do the same, and of black frustration with Latinos in majority-Latino cities.

Black Mayors and Interracial Solidarity

Existing incentives in city politics (winning elections and maintaining civic organizations) have made the black poor expendable. Voting majorities can be constructed without them, and the service-delivery structure of (particularly in weak-mayor "reform") cities may divert black civic organizational focus from the common political interest of mayoral and other city elections. Black civic capacity is further hindered by the collapse of civic life in areas of concentrated poverty, by antidemocratic tendencies among black organizations, and by black organizations' dependency on political and private patrons. Study of BUILD in Baltimore suggests that many of these problems can be overcome with persistent community organizing and a building up of democratic capacity. Black community coalitions that develop independent power in racially contested cities can also bring pressure on black mayors to address the hard and divisive race conflicts that attend efforts to change social policies related to poverty.

Taking on racial conflict, admittedly, is difficult and politically dangerous for black mayors to assume. Because black mayors have tended to win their elections in coalition with moderate white liberals and business elites, and over the strong opposition of working-class whites, the political need to maintain these moderate biracial coalitions with access to financial and state and national political power often leads them to avoid or silence persistent black demands for fundamental economic reform. The same practical process invariably contributes to a continuing impasse with poor whites, and threatens to do the same with Latinos as well. The dilemma is not, in many respects, of black mayors' making. Andrew Young in Atlanta, Wilson Goode in Philadelphia, and Carl Stokes in Cleveland all had deep misgivings about their political roles as mayors but little choice in selecting coalition partners to win elections and to gain business support to keep their cities out of bankruptcy.

Black mayoral styles differ but they are also distinct; each mayor's style corresponds roughly to the electoral and structural dynamics of that city.

I have identified three types of black leadership style of the first thirty-five years of black administrations in medium and larger U.S. cities:[7]

* *Symbolic nationalist mayors:* Mayors in safely majority black cities (usually more than 65 percent black). They have used race symbolically but have been conservative and incrementalist in practice, their focus and policies oriented primarily toward the downtown business community as a resource for jobs and tax revenue. Examples include Atlanta's black mayors Maynard Jackson (1974–82, 1990–94), Andrew Young (1982–90), Bill Campbell (1994–2002),[8] and Detroit's Coleman Young (1973–93).
* *Deracialized mayors:* Black mayors in cities where blacks represent a minority of the electorate, the majority of them poor. Black influence on the mayor to produce in such cities is low because low-income black community organizations are small, disorganized, factionalized, or demobilized. Examples include Thomas Bradley in Los Angeles, Norm Rice in Seattle, and Lionel Wilson in Oakland. These mayors have built stable coalitions with moderate white liberals and with the business community, avoiding racial controversy.
* *Mobilizer mayors:* Black mayors in racially contested cities where black civic organizations are strong and can exert influence upon them. Kurt Schmoke in Baltimore, Harold Washington in Chicago, Carl Stokes in Cleveland, and Wilson Goode in Philadelphia were mobilizers. Because their elections were close, they needed votes of the black poor and responded, in different degrees, to their demands. They also need the votes of white liberals. Such coalitions across race and class are inherently unstable and the mayors tend to be politically vulnerable. Mayors in such racially contested cities, seeking safer reelection prospects, may try to demobilize poor blacks because they are a costly constituency to maintain; they may therefore opt to try to win over moderate whites instead. In effect, unless faced with constant resistance, they generally will try to move into one of the other categories, as Dinkins and Schmoke at times attempted to do.

Black mayors to date have rarely attempted to mobilize the black poor of their cities or to engage in open debate about the political differences at the core of the social construct of race. Mayors who try to be true to the responsibility to representing a broad spectrum of the black public, and who consistently engage the sometimes unruly black poor in that political process, will have difficulty surviving in office. They face resistance from white coalition partners, from a cynical media that is principally white owned, from a skeptical and even hostile white working class, and they risk defections among other black elected officials.

Yet, the conclusion to the question of the effectiveness and independence of black mayors is not that they have no value and no options, and not, one scholar put it, that black electoral politics is "irrelevant." Mine is a different critique. Although black mayors, in their first decades from the late 1960s to the early years of the new millennium, have been unable to deliver substantive improvements in the lives of the black poor, and although a number have avoided what political scientist Wilbur Rich calls, in his study of Coleman Young, "over-organizing" the poor even as black civic organizations decry the lack of black political mobilization and a weakening of black influence in state and national elections, black mayors are not passive. They have responded pragmatically to the pressures they face, and their pragmatism leads them in a variety of directions.

The deeper problem is not that black mayors have been hopelessly coopted or have accomplished no observable improvements in the lives of the blacks of their cities but that they are expected to achieve what they probably cannot achieve, or at least not unassisted. Black mayors can effect fundamental economic and political reform (necessarily on a state or national level) only with coalitions between blacks, Latinos, and poor whites (such as with the support of labor unions). Black mayors cannot survive politically the certain upheaval of political confrontations with poor whites. Other black civic actors, however, can assume that task. New York's black clergy, for example, frequently confronted the police union and white politicians on racial issues during Dinkins's mayoralty when the mayor was reticent to do so (see chapter 7). Black mayors also cannot be expected, without intense black civic involvement, to pursue regional governance strategies that put their own offices in jeopardy. Nor are black mayoral candidates likely, without intense civic prodding, to put their own careers on hold to support a Latino mayoral candidate in order to generate greater solidarity, for the future, between black and Latino civic groups. These are tasks better left to black civic coalitions, but they are essential tasks.

There are important things black mayors can do, and, to some extent, some have done while still surviving in city hall. Black mayors can reform service agencies, such as the police, still seen by many in the black community as an occupying army. They can support efforts to democratize media ownership and access. They can use city-contracting processes to strengthen independent black civic organizations. Such things, including patronage jobs, help to build political power in black communities. While the limitations and constraints on black mayors are frequently noted in urban politics, their role in supporting the transformation of civic organizations that represent minorities and the poor, and in developing democracy, is little discussed.[9]

The process of deepening pluralism as it affects the poor and minorities requires black civic capacity and interracial coalitions, both shaped, in part, by local political structures. The necessity of assembling winning voter coalitions, and of keeping their cities fiscally afloat has led black mayors to restrict their goals in such a way that it causes them to fail to respond to or to censor the most economically substantive aspects of black demands and political thought. This has left on the table mainly race-specific black middle-class demands such as high-profile appointments of blacks or minority business set-asides that steer blacks into zero-sum competition with Latinos, Asians, and poor whites. But can a centralizing of political structure and an enhancing of black civil capacity lead to a fundamental breakthrough in racial consciousness? And if multiracial coalition building is achieved in American cities, would these problems of civic organizational capacity and political structure no longer matter? The answer to the first is "yes" and the second is "no." Deepening pluralism is a long-term process, and, without continued attention to political structure and civic capacity, gains in one period may dissipate in the next. The example of Oakland, California, is a case in point.

Racial Solidarity in Oakland

In Oakland, a strong multiracial movement in the 1960s confronted deep racial differences and, as a consequence, achieved substantial political unity and interracial trust. Ideological agreement and personal trust may still remain, but the interracial coalition did not hold together. As activists engaged in the daily routines of community and union organizing, the fragmented structure of Oakland's governance and service-delivery system fragmented Oakland's civic organizations.

Oakland's city hall of the 1960s, dominated by Republican business-men, was so resistant to sharing power with the black community that even moderate black middle-class leaders were excluded and, as a result, became increasingly radical. By the end of the 1960s even the moderate Oakland NAACP president, Donald McCullum, had begun to advocate black power (Self 1998, 249). In a climate of both racial and class exclusion, black middle-class social workers and educators used the anti-poverty resources of the Office of Economic Opportunities to establish independent black political organizations. In early 1967, two employees of the North Oakland Area Services Center (an outgrowth of the federal anti-poverty program) drafted a ten-point program for a new black political organization. The two, Huey Newton and Bobby Seale, opened the first storefront office of what they called the Black Panther Party (BPP), a new group pledged to build a "people's political machine" of the "poor of the city, of all ethnic backgrounds." The Panthers also demanded "black liberation."

In March 1967, the city council voted 6–3 not even to *hear* the city's own community action agency's report on the need for civilian review of complaints against the Oakland police. Oakland's community action agency disaffiliated from the city later in that year, whereupon, in 1967, black community leadership passed to the Black Panthers.[10] Blacks were a sizable percentage of the Oakland population but previously had had no meaningful political representation; hence the Panthers found "fertile ground" with little organized opposition from the black community. They built a strong base of support in low-income black communities through their "survival" programs: free food, free shoes, legal defense, medical screenings, and a busing program to visit relatives in jail (Bush 1984). The Party published a local newspaper, *The Black Panther,* widely read in black neighborhoods and used for voter education and to promote voter registration. Panther leader Elaine Brown explained that their involvement in electoral politics was "part of the revolutionary process—to build a base of operations to start talking about seizing power in Oakland" (Ware 1985, 132). In the 1972 presidential election campaign, the Panthers strongly supported the candidacy of black Brooklyn Rep. Shirley Chisholm for the Democratic Party presidential nomination. Oakland politician Wilson Riles Jr., recalled that "Chisholm's campaign had an effect on Oakland because the Panthers got to test their system for voter registration" (Riles 1988). The following year, Panther leader Bobby Seale announced that he was running for mayor and Elaine Brown for city council. The Panther announcement caught black Democratic activists off guard, since most black Democratic Party activists were supporting Otho Green, a black businessman, for mayor. Whereupon black supporters of Green met with the Panthers and attempted to persuade Seale to drop out of the race in exchange for Green's endorsement of Elaine Brown's candidacy for the city council. The Panthers were not to be deterred (Riles 1988). Their unwillingness to coalesce with the more politically moderate, and older, part of the black community (including the churches) created a schism within Oakland's black community that subsequently hampered progressive black candidates (Brooks 2002). Liberal white Democrats, for their part, supported John Sutter, an environmentalist, who, in 1971, became the first liberal ever to win a council seat in Oakland (Ware 1985, 133).

One of the effects of Oakland's earlier disorganized (nearly totally absent) local party structure had been notoriously low voter turnout, particularly in black neighborhoods (Pressman 1972), with local election turnout generally ranging between 15 to 30 percent (Goddard 1988). Political scientist Alan Ware wrote that in the East Bay (which includes Oakland), "the institutional framework was about as weak as it could be for a continuous and extensive electoral role for the parties" (Ware 1985, 39). In the 1973 mayoral race a Panther-initiated voter registration drive in East Oakland— the "Flatland"—registered more than thirty thousand new voters before the election. Wilson Riles Jr. said that, "the [the Panthers] did the greatest voter registration ever done in the Flatland before or since. They registered people who had never been in politics, who had never thought of voting" (Riles 1988). The results of the election stunned even Panther supporters. Panther Bobby Seale came in second place, beating out the other candidates by a slim margin and entering a runoff with incumbent Republican mayor, John Reading. Seale lost in the runoff but made quite a respectable showing. The black turnout in that election was 63 percent, spectacular by Oakland standards. "You had a real record turnout in the black community," said Riles. "I don't know if it has been rivaled since, but there was also a record turnout of 90 percent or more in the Hill precincts [an upper-middle-class white area], with white voters voting 10 to 1 against Seale" (Bush 1984, 324).

Political scientists Rufus Browning, Dale Marshall, and David Tabb wrote that Bobby Seale's "extreme militancy" alienated "supportive whites that would have been necessary for a successful challenge to the conservative dominant coalition" (Browning et al. 1984, 114). The Oakland activists interviewed for this study without exception arrived at precisely the opposite conclusion: Seale's candidacy was an essential element in mobilizing the black electorate for a successful challenge to the conservative Republican administration four years later. Oakland activist James Vann reported that "when Bobby ran for mayor, he had tremendous organization, tremendous turnout, and he just scared the hell out of the city. It paved the way for Lionel [Oakland's Mayor Lionel Wilson] to run and be elected" (Vann 1988). Riles argued that the Panthers made liberal whites "deal with the fact that blacks were a significant power force within the politics of the city. Liberal whites then looked for a [more moderate] black candidate [they could support]" (Riles 1988).

Key to the Panthers' engagement in local politics was the support they received from white antiwar activists. The liberal/radical antiwar student movement developed in Berkeley at the same time that the Panthers emerged in nearby Oakland, and the student activists who made the transition to electoral politics earlier than the Panthers had strongly supported the Panther movement. This made a huge impression on the Panthers in Oakland, and led them to debate with black nationalists in the Student Nonviolent Coordinating Committee (SNCC) who were in the process of expelling whites from their organization.[11] In 1966, when Bob Scheer, a radical antiwar activist and former editor of *Ramparts* magazine, ran for Congress in the 8th congressional district (including Berkeley and sections of Oakland), he was supported by many black movement activists, beginning a tradition of progressive white-black nationalist electoral coalitions that culminated in the election to Congress of Ron Dellums, a black antiwar activist and nephew of the legendary labor-civil rights leader C. L. Dellums, running for the second time in 1970 (Weills 1988). Ron Dellums won the race, remaining in Congress for more than two decades in an 85-percent-white district. Dellums had deep roots in Oakland's black community, but his history and political base were equally in the white-progressive movement that grew out of the Berkeley antiwar protests. For many years, he was the only black in Congress elected from a majority-white district (Carson 1988). Dellums won endorsement of mainstream liberal organizations, such as the League of Women Voters, as well as of the black community. He had a strong electoral interest in building a coalition between radical whites and black activists in Berkeley and Oakland, and his office served as an ideological and organizational bridge between the two groups.

When Lionel Wilson, an African American judge and former anti-poverty leader, ran for mayor of Oakland in 1977 with broad black backing and significant radical white allies, the Panthers ran (Riles 1988) the get-out-the-vote effort and deployed scores of disciplined workers on the campaign. Wilson won narrowly but his victory was largely symbolic because the machinery of government was still in the hands of the city manager, the office of the Oakland mayor playing a weak role in a part-time position in city government. The mayor presided over the city council but did not manage the city or prepare the city budget for city council ratification (King 1988). Because so much authority over delivery of key services for black constituents resided at the county level or with semi-autonomous authorities, black community and labor activists tended to divide their political efforts between various levels of government. With declining community oversight and increasing fiscal poverty in the city, Wilson pursued a traditional pro-growth downtown development agenda. The mayor's concern about attracting businesses was heightened by the passage of Proposition 13 in a 1978 state referendum, limiting property taxes in California and creating a massive state budget shortfall. In 1980, the Reagan administration initiated a series of reductions in federal aid to cities and Wilson was pushed to provide aid to downtown so as to maintain the economic viability of the city (Riles 1988).

Wilson's "cozying up" to the Republican business community and his reappointment of Republicans to important boards and commissions angered both Oakland's white-progressive community and also many black activists, yet Wilson used his twenty-year history in the civil rights movement and his former directorship of Oakland's anti-poverty programs to deflect black protest (Rubin 1988), despite strong black-activist criticisms of his regime (Abbot 1988; Miley 1988). In 1990, at age seventy-three, Wilson ran for reelection, opposed by seven candidates, most prominently by Wilson Riles Jr. and Elihu Harris, a state legislator since 1978, and a protégé of Democratic power, former State Assembly Speaker and San Francisco Mayor Willie Brown. Harris ran as a younger and more energetic version of Lionel Wilson (Oden 1999, 94) and came in first. In the subsequent runoff, Harris defeated Riles. When, in 1997, former Governor Jerry Brown declared his candidacy for mayor of Oakland, a group of black ministers formed a group against Brown called "African American Coalition for Social and Political Justice," but Brown had already locked up support from other key ministers (Oden 1999, 227). He emphasized his civil rights record as governor of California, and pledged to put poor Oaklanders first in public policy considerations. His campaign chief of staff was former Black Panther leader David Hilliard. Brown promised to reduce crime, to bring new upper-income residents to rejuvenate downtown Oakland day and night, to increase the visibility of the arts in Oakland, and improve education, with an emphasis on charter schools. Brown won with 48,953 votes, 58.7 percent of the total, with a white majority and a plurality of black votes. Brown had bypassed the black middle-class leadership and had gone directly to low-income black-community (and other ethnic groups) residents for support.

Brown's election showed the dissolution of any semblance of unity in Oakland's black community, as well as the breakdown of the old progressive interracial political coalition initiated by the Panthers and white anti-war activists. Dellums's retirement in 1997 added to the community's sense of leaderlessness. As others have also noted, black "single-issue" activism was dispersed along the balkanized lines of governmental-service delivery, because this is how activists received funding to maintain their organizations (Oden 1999, 60). Although Oakland activists had relatively high levels of interracial trust, and were not opposed to forming interracial coalitions of white, Latino, and Asian progressives, this was not enough for them to focus their political efforts and unite against the local regime. Despite knowing that they "should" be united, collectively they were too engaged in maintaining their particular municipal union and community-service turf to unite for politics, and, as a consequence, they were displaced.

The achievement of interracial solidarity during the height of political movements is not, as Oakland shows, sufficient for a long-term process of social transformation. Attention must be paid to how and whether the political structure can support civic coalition building over time (Nicholls 2003).

Black urban politics does not encounter the same problem in every city. Some cities have fragmented and weak black civic organizations, others do not. Most cities lack progressive multiracial coalitions, but not all do. Cities with similar configurations of political structure, black civic organization, and racial conflicts will have similar political problems. Although case-study research on black mayors and blacks in city politics is too thin at this point for confident predictions, limited generalizations are possible. Many cities have fragmented political structures, few black communities have Baltimore's BUILD civic capacity, and few have a tradition of racial solidarity like Oakland's. This suggests a generally low capacity for deepening pluralism in minority communities across the country. On the other hand, the demographic emergence of Latinos in cities, and the increased labor and civic organizing in poor communities suggest a new pattern of possibility. While outcomes cannot be predicted, inferences can be drawn about the lines of political choice and future conflict.

The recent history of black mayoral politics suggests that some of the most recalcitrant adversaries of blacks, Mayor Rizzo of Philadelphia, for example, were not representatives of economic elites, but grass-roots racial populists. The white working class, in real politics, has often been as much or more opposed to black empowerment than white elites have been, thus how are black activists to make friends with real and powerful opponents without succumbing to their power? I will argue that the problem of deepening pluralism and structural political change is not so much about fighting external class elites that oppress both blacks and poor whites as about developing the capacity of blacks and whites to unite democratically across class lines, whether in their own communities or in coalitions with other groups, and thereby accumulate the combinatorial power needed to confront their powerful opponents.

The Dinkins Experience

Part II

Part II examines New York City's black politics in the context of the city's political structure, the strength and unity of its black civic organizations, and local patterns of racial conflict and cooperation. The section focuses on the emergence of David Dinkins as New York City's first black mayor and the changes in black politics following his administration. Although New York has strong black-led labor unions and savvy community civic organizations in some parts of the city, these organizations were unable to coalesce while the city's Board of Estimate governance structure divided power and administrative authority, and the attention of black civic organizations, among five borough presidents and their respective county political organizations. A city charter change in 1989 that concentrated power in the hands of the mayor and eliminated the Board of Estimate provided black organizations with a strong reason to try to influence mayoral politics and they united to do so. Also in the late 1980s, black activists working on the two presidential campaigns of Rev. Jesse Jackson in New York had evolved from mainly black community organizing, factional power plays within black communities, and racial confrontation with whites in 1984 to a more inclusiveness approach within black communities and bridge-building efforts to Latino, labor, and progressive white groups in 1988. The commitment of black political activists coming out of the Jackson campaigns to grass-roots organizing, bridge building within the black community and in interracial coalitions, and centralizing power and political attention on the office of the mayor were key forces that led to Dinkins's election. After taking office, Dinkins came under heavy pressure from financial elites and the City Council to abandon his low-income black, Latino, and labor union core political base. Dinkins took steps in this direction, but renewed pressure from his core political supporters caused him to reverse direction and to attempt to use local government to build a grass-roots, multiracial movement that championed policy changes sought by poor people. Dinkins's movement in this direction provoked an ideological crisis in the city largely between defenders and detractors of the city's treatment of the black poor. The debate subsided with Dinkins's loss to Rudolph Giuliani in 1993, however a similar political polarization reemerged even more sharply in 2001 as Dinkins's former supporters joined with Latinos to support Fernando Ferrer's candidacy for mayor. Ferrer maintained that a majority of New Yorkers, whom he called the "Other New York," did not have a voice in city politics. His campaign made deliberate efforts to organize the poorest New Yorkers, to build bridges across long-standing political divides between black and Latino activists, to appeal to poor and progressive whites, and, at the same time, to directly address controversial race and class issues. I call the accumulation of power on the part of oppressed groups, and their use of power to democratically contest dominant political norms and policies "deep pluralism."

"Cursed by Factions and Feuds"

Black Factionalism and

the Structure of New York

City Government

5

On September 12, 1989, thousands crowded into the ballroom at the Penta Hotel to hear from the declared winner of New York's Democratic primary election for mayor of New York City. The Reverend Jesse Jackson, at the microphone, linked Dinkins's victory to the city's reaction to a recent killing of a black teenager by a gang of young white men. Voters had decided "to turn pain into power," Jackson declared with the clear implication that Dinkins's victory was for blacks (Bohlen 1989). Dinkins himself seemed perplexed. That was *not* the message he wanted televised across New York as he prepared for the general election. For many among Dinkins's political staff, Jackson's comments seemed out of place for a different reason. He implied that blacks were politically cohesive in New York, yet the black elected officials on the podium did not represent a unified group. The Harvard political scientist Martin Kilson once described New York City's black politics as "cursed with factions and feuds." Although overwhelming black voter support for Dinkins suggested shared grass-roots sentiment among blacks, it seemed overly optimistic to suggest that a cohesive long-term coalition among black elected leaders and activists in New York had emerged.

I agree with Kilson on the "factions and feuds," but not with the causes to which he attributed the fractiousness: personality differences. I propose instead that the cause was New York City's fragmented, weak-mayor polity until the late 1980s, with its incentives to concentrate on county, not on citywide politics. Among blacks as well as white politicians in the city, county politics had fostered distinct political identities, or in Kilson's terms, political personalities, among black politicians. The particular traits that these political personalities embodied were not randomly distributed but focused on whatever it took the different actors to hold onto power in their respective counties, in New York City called "boroughs." With black civic organizations not strong enough to circumvent entrenched machine domination in most of the five boroughs (with partial exceptions in Brooklyn and Queens), the structure of local black politics itself weakened and nearly made citywide cooperation in black politics impossible. The borough governance structure created paths to patronage and resources at the county level, and quite different opportunities and constraints in forming interracial political coalitions. These differences in political context were the basis for contrasting black political strategies and the use of contradictory black political ideologies to justify these different strategies.

Paradoxically, there were upsides both to machine domination and to borough fragmentation. Brooklyn and Queens, the boroughs where machine control was most intense, developed the strongest black civic organizations; they confronted the machine and mitigated its power. The Bronx machine was "friendliest" to blacks and, probably for that reason, never developed strong black civic organizations that could challenge it effectively. In Manhattan, where the machine was destroyed by white liberal reformers in the 1950s, Harlem politicians controlled the county Democratic organization for much of the second half of the twentieth century. Virtually no effort was made to organize a challenge to black Democratic Party leaders. Lack of black civic organization, in turn, undermined the possibility that Harlem's black voters would turn out in large numbers—an incapacity that released Harlem officials from tight accountability to their constituents.

There was an upside to the cultivation of black political divisions. Activists who worked closely with diverse black factions across boroughs could benefit from each faction's critiques of the others. They could imagine a black politics that combined the strengths of the factions without the limitations, practical or ideological, of any one faction.[1] Black factions tended to consider other factions as "enemies." The concept that adversaries should neither be ridiculed nor crushed, and that each could enlighten the others about their weaknesses and strengthen the capacity of the others to achieve their goals is a deeply pluralist idea, one likely to strengthen community effectiveness in the larger political arena. The anthropologist, Steven Gregory calls such action "political heterogeneity" (Gregory 1998). I use the term "deep pluralism" to describe the ideological and organizational resourcefulness (and openness) achieved by activists in efforts to work productively with apparently contradictory and even mutually hostile movements.

Black Political Beginnings in New York City

New York black politics from 1900 through 1960 can be grouped roughly into three periods: pre–New Deal; the New Deal and World War II period; and post–World War II stagnation. Before the New Deal, blacks, largely excluded from the two primary political parties, developed instead strong black civic organizations whose purposes were advocacy and self-help. During the New Deal and World War II, blacks formed alliances with labor unions, Jewish groups, and leftist parties (including, to some extent, the Communist Party) to press their demands. These multiracial coalitions were activist in orientation, some marked by a radical orientation in the sense of looking to deeper causes of both racial and class inequity in economic and in social structures. The New Deal–World War II period was a time of deep pluralism. Protest, debate, and coalition building developed among blacks and also among white workers and immigrant groups as well. During the cold war much of that new energy dissipated in the north. The civil rights movement of the 1950s and 1960s sought to regain that energy and to advance progress of blacks toward political, legal, social, and economic equity, to end Jim Crow and to disrupt the conformity of the cold war period, and it made great strides in that purpose. The Black Power movement that came after that introduced a more confrontational and more nationalist agenda, based largely among young black urban dwellers and black students, but it also extended to parts of the established black middle class (Morris 1975, 227–31).[2] The subsequent turn of black activists from movement insurgency to electoral politics at the end of the 1960s and early 1970s led to another period of intense black civic involvement, this time connected to electoral politics. But by the mid-1980s black electoral participation began to stagnate (see chapter 3).[3]

In the first decades of the twentieth century, both Tammany Hall (the Manhattan Democratic Party machine) and the Republican Party had appointed black political leaders who lacked strong relationships with the Harlem community and were unaccountable to it. Following the creation, in 1898, of the modern New York City through consolidation of Manhattan with Richmond (Staten Island), Queens, and Bronx counties, Manhattan's Tammany made weak attempts to solicit black support to withstand Republican onslaughts from the "outer" boroughs. To this end, it supported a new black organization called United Colored Democracy (UCD), but it was an organization whose leadership was appointed by Tammany (Katznelson [1973] 1976 70). Racist practices against blacks, prevalent in the city, as in the society at large, prevented blacks from gaining much political patronage in exchange for their votes. Blacks had virtually no leverage in the political system of the city.

In the 1920s, the period of the Harlem Renaissance, in New York's African American community several forces combined to produce an extraordinary level of intellectual, political, and artistic ferment. An influx of radical West Indian intellectuals brought "an international, diasporic, and progressive socialist perspective on domestic race and relations" (Gaines 1996, 234). Blacks fleeing southern oppression were exhilarated at their escape from low-paying tenant farming and the searing humiliation of Jim Crow. Black World War I veterans, and blacks generally, had been emboldened by President Woodrow Wilson's promotion of the United States as the world's leader of democracy. "New Negroes" were unwilling to accept accommodationist approaches to racism such as that promulgated by the preeminent black leader, Booker T. Washington (Locke 1968). The momentum of these trends collided against governmental and white civic racism, leading to an unprecedented mobilization in New York's black communities that focused inward toward self-help and intra-black political solidarity; ironically, the former was the same theme stressed by Booker T. Washington.

The NAACP and the National Urban League, in the early years of the century, were established interracial civic organizations that by the 1920s, especially in the NAACP's case, were actively broadening membership among black working and middle classes in state and local chapters (Grossman 2000, 380). Organizing the black working class and black poor around a message of black pride and self-reliance, Marcus Garvey's United Negro Improvement Association (UNIA) established a powerful presence in Harlem alongside the NAACP and the National Urban League, and hence posed a formidable challenge to the United Colored Democracy with its

Tammany leadership (Gaines 1996, 241; Hill and Bair 1987; Vincent 1971, 103). A Jamaican immigrant to the United States, Garvey believed that the government's failure to address racial discrimination and its collusion with Jim Crow led to black self-help organizations and a strong race consciousness that placed African Americans in the United States in the forefront of the African diaspora (Henry 1977; Lewis 2000, 52). In an early example of intra-black pluralism, Garvey built a coalition of diverse black organizations with various ideological agendas, including feminist, socialist, and liberal, a number at sharp odds with Garvey himself (Lewis 2000, 58–59; Robinson 2001, 25; Vincent 1971, chaps. 3–5). The movement declined after 1927, but the organizing skills developed by black activists served Harlem in the 1930s and 1940s.

The New Deal–World War II Era

The Depression eroded the middle ground that separated poor blacks from poor whites, spurring grass-roots community and labor organizing in both communities during the 1930s and 1940s. Many white advocates linked their demands to those of blacks, and black activists reevaluated pragmatically the potential for a radical interracial political movement led by black radical activists and Jews, many of the latter refugees from Nazism.[4] Black support for a radical interracial movement was thus built rapidly following the experience of Garveyism. Black leaders who mobilized in the 1930s looked more explicitly at class than they did earlier and considered more direct confrontations with government, including demands for federal intervention to improve conditions under which blacks lived. Many turned to leftist protest groups, churches, and black nationalist groups as potential allies (Greenberg 1991).

The energy of the political left and the willingness of blacks to switch political parties pragmatically in elections encouraged Mayor Fiorello La-Guardia to offer limited endorsement of the antidiscrimination efforts of the 1930s. Republican support among blacks, staunch since the presidency of Abraham Lincoln, waned in the later 1930s in response to Franklin D. Roosevelt's New Deal. Democrats and the left-leaning American Labor Party (ALP), founded in 1936 by white trade union leaders, vied for black support in Harlem.[5] Certain progressive labor unions and the ALP helped Fiorello LaGuardia gain reelection as an anti-Tammany mayor in 1937.[6]

The coalition they forged won every seat on the city's governing Board of Estimate (BOE) except for the Bronx Borough president's office. The largely Jewish ALP made a practice of boosting anti-racist candidates, including black candidates, for political offices across New York City. Notably, the electoral victories and the gains in black unionization and cross-racial solidarity achieved in this period were achieved in the process of addressing controversial race issues and intense debates over the meaning and significance of race. In addition, many of the black leaders of the 1930s interracial movement honed their debating and organizing skills, and most likely increased confidence in their political abilities, while participating in the Garvey coalition.

Radical black grass-roots organizing had been bolstered through New York City's administration of New Deal social-welfare programs, which not only empowered Harlem's activist churches but did so with few restrictions on their political activities. The churches evolved into centers for political mobilization and protest, and church memberships swelled. The Reverend Adam Clayton Powell Jr., pastor of one of the most activist churches, the Abyssinian Baptist Church, soon became a bold and charismatic political leader. Powell won election to the New York City Council in 1941 in a grass-roots operation that, in the words of political scientist Charles V. Hamilton, "effectively combine[d] protest and election politics in the Harlem community" (Hamilton 1991, 114).

On the strength of organizing around jobs, housing, and social-welfare issues, Harlem's radical black leadership largely displaced machine-affiliated black politicians in the 1930s and 1940s and supplied some of the most outspoken black elected officials in U.S. history. Intensive grass-roots mobilization meant that those elected had to pay close attention not only to Harlem's leadership and middle class but also to the demands of ordinary (poor) African Americans. At the same time, grass-roots support protected them from outside domination both from the Democratic Tammany machine and the white-led leftist parties and associations. The leading black machine politician in Harlem was the independent-minded J. Raymond "Ray" Jones. By the late 1940s, Powell and Jones were widely regarded as the two most powerful black Democrats in New York.

Powell's election to Congress in 1944 was a national symbol of black progress, yet with the beginning of the cold war, it masked what became an escalating political repression that eventually wrecked Powell's radical coalition (Horne 1994).[7] Historian Martha Biondi writes that "the anticommunist crusade clashed head on with the African American rights struggle in New York, which had a significant contingent of left-wing leaders. Virtually every leading activist suffered persecution, investigation, repression or censorship" (Biondi 2003, 137). In the early years of the cold war most civil rights leaders and many white liberals opposed organized anti-communism as an attempt to subvert not only the New Deal but also a growing civil rights movement. The NAACP supported abolishment of the House Committee on Un-American Activities (HUAC) on the grounds that it was being used to harass the wartime Fair Employment Practices Committee; they called HUAC "detrimental to Negroes" (Biondi 2003, 138). The *New York Age,* a local black newspaper, also called for HUAC's abolition. Adam Powell began to modulate his own radicalism in the face of growing hostility. In a move to weaken the influence of leftist parties in 1947, New York State passed the Wilson-Pakula law that barred candidates from entering the primary of any party without approval from that party's county committee, a law that transferred power in the candidate-nominating process from registered party voters to official party leaders. The same law ended proportional representation in city council elections, a move toward control sponsored by the Democratic Party, the chamber of commerce, and the taxpayers association (Horne 1994, 193). New York City's electoral system, in essence, became once again a democratic one-party system with a consolidation of power that weakened electoral mobilization by black radicals and reestablished machine control over black politics. With the radical coalition in retreat and the black vote suddenly up for grabs, Tammany took advantage to regain power in Harlem.

Sensing the changing national political climate and the potential danger to his own career, Powell shifted course to endorse President Truman in 1948 and the incumbent William O'Dwyer's 1949 Democratic mayoral candidacy—in a race that included a left-wing third-party challenger to the incumbent—despite O'Dwyer's political conservatism, and even his regressive actions on race issues. As mayor, O'Dwyer refused to apply anti-discrimination laws to public works projects, and he turned down NAACP requests to investigate claims of police brutality (Biondi 1997, 148).[8] And Powell made deals: O'Dwyer committed himself to a black magistrate of Harlem and Powell and his long-time mentor, Democratic machine boss J. Raymond Jones, "the Fox," ensured Harlem a fair share of patronage jobs and divided additional patronage jobs evenly among Harlem residents and their West Indian and Southern United States bases of black support (Jones

1988).[9] Deal making sharply contrasted with Powell's own earlier protests for broader job opportunities for the poor.

With Jones's help, Powell had become only the second black person to serve in Congress in the period from 1945 to 1953 (Tate 2003, 38). To the generation of black nationalists emerging out of the 1960s, Powell's approach came to symbolize a "Harlem" style of politics: ideologically rooted in protest and grass-roots mobilization implemented through a working arrangement of backroom deal making (Flateau 1988; Simmons 1988). As the cold war took its toll on black radicals, party deal making for limited patronage increasingly replaced popular mobilization for broader demands for jobs and racial equality.[10] Voting in Harlem stagnated, with community mobilization confined to electoral campaigns and attention to protest activity abandoned (Zuber 1969). Jones defended his solicitation of patronage as a practical necessity for blacks. In a rebuke to Democratic Party reformers, delivered directly to a reform club meeting in 1960, Jones said:

> We are not rich enough, if you will, to be idealistic about political
> jobs. We have many able young people whom you will not hire
> in your private enterprises. No one should prevent them from
> serving, and serving ably, in analogous capacities in the govern-
> ment. Your present high socioeconomic status is derived, in part,
> from the fact that your grandparents and parents used the polit-
> ical structures and services of the city, state and nation to ad-
> vance themselves and, necessarily you. . . . If political power
> and place corrupt—and we do not think that necessarily the
> case—we have the historical right, like your forebears, to be
> corrupted. . . . In short, it is not fair to change the rules in the
> middle of the game, especially when it is, for us, not a game
> but a grim struggle.[11]

The moderation of bold civil rights activism was bitterly resented by black radicals, by black nationalists, and by moderate black groups alike.[12] The consequent black demobilization in Harlem meant that new rounds of racial discrimination in employment, housing, and education programs met with little resistance and these forces began to consolidate black communities as permanent ghetto enclaves.[13] The historian and political scientist Ira Katznelson maintains that the limits for reform in the present era were primarily forged in the repressive 1940s:

The contraction of political space for the Left in American politics in the 1940s redefined the social forces undergirding social democratic possibilities in the Democratic party, and changed the locus of political debate from questions of social organization and class relations to issues of technical economics and interest group politics. These alterations to the political landscape defined the features the Democratic party took into the Eisenhower era; in so doing, they set the terms for the modest reform efforts of the Kennedy administration and the more assertive reformist attempt to utilize the state in the Johnson years. . . . The Great Society, in short, is best understood in terms of a larger dynamic of reform in the postwar era that undercut, more than it reinforced, the prospects for an American social democratic politics. The subsequent turn to the Right that culminated in the election of Ronald Reagan on an explicit anti-state platform with significant working-class support thus was facilitated by the way the Great Society embedded the trajectory of the 1940s. (Katznelson 1989, 186–87)

Post-New Deal Stagnation in Racial Progress

Racial resentment soared in northern black communities as blacks' wartime economic and social progress ended. Nine of the largest U.S. cities lost 680,000 production jobs between 1947 and 1963. New York, Chicago, Detroit, and Philadelphia lost 515, 922 retail and industrial jobs (Levy 1998, 139–40). There was also a change among black activists, according to Vincent Harding, Robin Kelley, and Earl Lewis: "a new attitude overtook the movement: no more compromise, no more 'deals' with white liberals, no more subordinating the movement to the needs of the Democratic party" (Harding et al. 2000, 518).

Black activists' disenchantment with the Democratic Party and a more conservative white liberalism led to efforts to build a new anti-racist movement coalition to fight racial segregation in New York's public school system (Taylor 1977, 71). The activists organized two massive school boycotts. On February 3, 1963, in one of the largest organized civil rights protests of the 1960s, 464,361 pupils (45 percent of the total student enrollment) boycotted the public schools and a second boycott of March 16, brought 267,459 children (26 percent of the total school enrollment) out of school. The failure of these significant efforts to integrate the essentially segregated schools led to demands for black community control of schools across the city—as a second-best strategy for improving the quality of education for black children—but the community-control movement, centered in Brooklyn and Harlem, itself failed despite assistance from liberal white groups and foundations principally because of the strong opposition by the powerful United Federation of Teachers, the New York chapter of the American Federation of Teachers (Meier 1987; Perlstein 1994). Its failure left black activists in a state of frustration and disarray at the end of the 1960s. However, many Brooklyn leaders of the community-control movement went on to lead organizing efforts against the borough's political machine in the 1970s and 1980s.[14] In short, cold war repression constrained opportunities for building multiracial coalitions around substantive economic issues, and in the 1960s, the assassination of Martin Luther King Jr. and the fear of political repression dampened civil rights and black power advocates' enthusiasm for pursuing broad economic issues. But new opportunities were created for activism as a result of civil rights success in winning voting rights reform and federal support for eradicating poverty. Government and political structures, as noted in chapter 2, have many sides. The juxtaposition of constraint and opportunity produced shared divisions among black activists in the early 1970s, with some believing government was fundamentally repressive and others believing that it was capable of progressive transformation, and still others attempting to bridge the differences between the two factions into a pragmatic synthesis.[15]

New York's Political Structure and Its Effect on Black Politics

Because New York county (borough) political organizations (especially outside of Manhattan) were determined to control elections in their own borough, the transition from protest to electoral politics that began during the Adam Powell era compelled black activists to focus on fighting machines at the borough level. It was a throwback to the days before the counties surrounding Manhattan were consolidated into the five-borough city. No citywide black candidate could avoid dealing with machine power in Brooklyn, Queens, and the Bronx, and none could bring together Harlem politicians—who led their county Democratic Party (in coalition with white liberals)—with the staunch anti-machine black nationalists of Brooklyn. The overall effect of black electoral incorporation was to segment black politics into four distinct borough-based political arenas (Staten Island, the fifth borough, had almost no blacks);[16] black politicians competed to adopt strategies of survival in their boroughs; each borough faction opposed the political intervention of outsiders in its county affairs. The black community overall had a weak political voice in city politics, and it did not form citywide black coalitions that promoted cooperation across the boroughs, even though the city was led by a conservative racial populist mayor, Ed Koch.

Some have argued that black political mobilization ebbs and flows in response to changes in material benefits or imposition of sanctions.[17] If this were so, the 1970s, a period of massive losses in public benefits, should have seen high levels of black insurgency. The value of Aid to Families with Dependent Children (AFDC) payments, adjusted for inflation, plummeted. Rent burdens for poor female-headed households went from 16 percent of family household income in 1970 to 31 percent by 1980 (Thompson 1996b, 643). The city's basic welfare grant was frozen for much of the period even as overall costs of living increased by 68 percent (Shefter 1987, 147). Funding for many of the "anti-riot" community action programs of the 1960s was eliminated (Gregory 1998, 102–3; Katznelson 1981, 137). During the 1977 mayoral campaign, a time of fiscal crisis for the city when black population was increasing significantly and black employment was highly dependent on local government policies,[18] Ed Koch, the leading mayoral contender, drew sharp battle lines with repeated attacks of blacks in his campaign rhetoric.[19] Even under these conditions, the mayoral candidacy of black Manhattan Borough President Percy Sutton failed to attract overwhelming black support in the face of machine-dominated black politics in much of the city. African Americans also did not mount a unified opposition against Mayor Koch's reelection in 1981 and 1985. This shows the powerful effect of political structure on black movements and political activity beyond that of economic conditions alone.

Political science literature has emphasized the "withering away" of urban political machines since the New Deal, but the words "machine" and "organization," referring to the five county Democratic Party organizations, remained common parlance in local discussions of borough politics at least until the late 1980s when city charter reform in 1989 eliminated the

Board of Estimate (BOE), a quasi-legislative body that voted on city contracts and on the city budget, approved zoning changes and exceptions, and allocated significant power to borough presidents and the county political organizations that supported them. The Board of Estimate was established at the turn of the twentieth century when the modern New York City was created from five county governments. On the Board of Estimate, the mayor, the city council president, and the comptroller each received two votes and the five borough (county) presidents, one vote each (Viterritti 1990).

Although legendary mayors such as Fiorello LaGuardia give the impression that New York is a quintessential "strong-mayor" city, political scientists Wallace Sayre and Herbert Kaufman were right in saying in 1960 that the Board of Estimate "occupies the center of gravity in the city's political process" (Kaufman 1960, 626). Even by the 1970s when offices were reduced in size, they still maintained a staff of 100 people to monitor city agencies and advocate for borough interests. The borough presidents also appointed half of the members of each community planning board, which gave them influence over local land-use issues.[20] Because of the powers of the Board of Estimate, borough presidents were courted by real estate developers, municipal unions, city vendors, and by municipal agency commissioners seeking approval for important projects. The civil service system did prevent large numbers of patronage appointments, but borough presidents learned to trade Board of Estimate votes with the mayor for key appointments in city agencies that affected major policy decisions. The borough presidents and their county "machine" backers could raise significant funds from businesses and unions for political campaigns.

By the 1970s, political machines had not played an important role in bringing large ethnic groups *into* the political process for nearly a half century; they did keep groups *out* of politics, since leaders of the two major parties in each borough selected representatives to the citywide Board of Elections, with extensive power to control ballot access during elections (Hayduk 1996, 307). Machines now had few jobs or material goods to deliver and, therefore, political club activity was generally low, especially in poor black and Latino communities. Yet they did influence selection of candidates with only minimal participation of local citizens, thus shaping popular black consciousness about politics much as earlier political machines had shaped European immigrants' political perspectives (Mollenkopf 1992). But, unlike earlier European immigrants, black communities felt that machines disconnected them from political power rather than incorporated them into the political process. The machines used a significant amount of their resources to discourage insurgent black political movements, hiring election attorneys and using locally elected judges whose election they controlled to challenge election petitions of nonmachine candidates. If candidates were too technically savvy to be removed legally from the ballot, the machine might place additional candidates in the race to weaken the insurgency. If the insurgent won nonetheless, the machine might co-opt the insurgent with small material inducements ("lulus"). If the insurgents resisted lulus, the machine might deplete an insurgent's resources by financing ballot challenges and by fielding opponents in subsequent elections. The machines could also use their influence in the state or city legislature to deny patronage and perks for the insurgent, making it hard for the insurgent to employ even the most loyal supporters. Machines put a lot of pressure on insurgents who lacked financial resources, and wore most of them down (Bynoe 1988; Wooten 1988).

There are two important aspects of local political structure for mayoral politics: one is the degree of power centered in the office of the mayor, the other the political demography of the electorate created through political boundaries. The fact that New York City was divided into five boroughs, each with a vote on the Board of Estimate, created unevenness in the black, Latino, and white liberal/conservative populations across boroughs, with differences between the boroughs' politics reflecting the class and ethnic composition of the boroughs as well as the history of political conflicts between groups in each borough. Significant differences in political strategy developed among black elected officials in each borough over time, evolving into differences in political style and in ideology. Each presented distinctive opportunities for cross-racial alliances and, therefore, different opportunities for political advancement. Major differences in political strategy and outlook hindered cooperation among black elected officials at a citywide level on fundamental and pressing city issues such as who to support for mayor.

In many cities white-led political machines minimized African American political participation. New York, on the other hand, was unique in its *multiple* white-led machines, each with a distinct vested interest, and with different methods for keeping black politicians subservient to its particular borough's organizational hierarchy. Black activists neither had a shared sense of exclusion, nor did they unite to form a bloc able to gain citywide black electoral success. Black elected officials confronted with a popular grass-roots movement calling for citywide black unity—such as the mid-1980s Jackson presidential campaigns—had no strategic capacity to respond. Instead they, and other black activists, were consumed with internecine battles for political survival and influence in their own boroughs.

Black Electoral Politics in Manhattan

Percy Sutton, a product of Harlem's radical left politics of the New Deal era and its subsequent Cold War shift to deal-making patronage politics, served as borough president of Manhattan from 1966 to 1977. In 1977, Sutton decided to oppose incumbent Democrat Mayor Abraham "Abe" Beame in the party primary. With New York's white population declining from a high of 63 percent in 1970 to 52 percent in 1980,[21] Sutton reasoned that he could win the election with a coalition of minorities and white liberals in Manhattan.

Sutton's campaign began in the midst of a city fiscal crisis and a time of heightened racial polarization, after a decade in which, at the height of the 1960s civil rights movement, New York City had poured resources into education, welfare, subsidized housing, and health and social services, which were popularly viewed as benefiting primarily the city's growing black and Latino populations (Shefter 1987, 120). Spending for minorities in anti-poverty programs gave rise to a political backlash among white working-class ethnics, who felt neglected by city hall. In a sign of the changed political mood, in 1971 the New York State Legislature, for the first time since Governor Nelson Rockefeller (a moderate Republican) took office in 1959, rejected a large tax increase proposed by a governor and froze additional aid to the city (Netzer 1990, 41). Mayor John Lindsay of New York City, a liberal white Republican, responded to rising white working-class anger by spending more money for the predominantly white city workers' unions (Cannato 2001, 432), financed by increased borrowing and fiscal gimmicks.

By 1975, with the city's major creditors refusing to underwrite the city's debt, the city experienced a serious financial crisis. Under newly elected Democratic Governor Hugh Carey, the state established a new agency, the Municipal Assistance Corporation for the City of New York (MAC), to redirect some city revenue streams into its own coffers to guarantee new long-term bond issues for financial relief to the city. A second agency, the Emergency Financial Control Board (EFCB)—which comprised the governor, the mayor, the state and city comptrollers, and three members of the private business sector—created that same year, centralized crisis control of fiscal policy making. City officials, suddenly realizing the vulnerability of the local economy, sought to protect city finances from gubernatorial control (Netzer 1990, 53). Democratic mayoral candidate Ed Koch—a liberal congressman from the Greenwich Village section of Manhattan—sensing growing resentment among working- and middle-class white ethnics against social programs for the inner-city poor, resorted to a hard-edged zero-sum "them versus us" fiscal politics that sharpened the city's racial cleavages. The "them" was the city's black and Latino poor and the programs that served them (Shefter 1987). The "us" was whites and the middle class.

Bella Abzug, a well-known antiwar activist, feminist, anti-racist, and the founder of the Taxpayers Campaign for Urban Priorities that supported Mayor John Lindsay (a liberal Republican turned independent) against a conservative Democratic mayoral candidate, Mario Procaccino, declared her own candidacy for mayor. Abzug had just lost the Democratic primary for U.S. Senate to Daniel Patrick Moynihan and was considered a strong candidate. Mario Cuomo, later to become governor, was supported by Governor Carey and was the best-financed candidate. Herman Badillo, a Puerto Rican former Bronx Borough president, congressman, and candidate for mayor in 1969 and 1973, ran again. A seventh candidate, the president of the city club, was not considered a serious candidate.

Percy Sutton, in contrast to Koch, based his own campaign on the suddenly old politics of ethnic coalition building. He called in IOUs from white liberals (especially from among Jews) for his earlier support of Abe Beame, the city's first Jewish mayor, elected in 1973. But Koch outmaneuvered Sutton, exploiting whites' anger toward black "poverty pimps." Abzug had a notorious history of opposing conservative Democrats in New York politics and apparently saw no reason to support Sutton in exchange for his support of Beame, a conservative Brooklyn machine Democrat (McKinney 1989).

Harlem politicians, convinced that they had been double-crossed after supporting Beame's candidacy, complained bitterly that when Sutton's rightful "turn" came to run, "the rules changed" (McKinney 1989). Despite considerable friendly relationships and common cause, relationships between African Americans and liberal reformers deteriorated.[22]

Sutton's black-liberal white coalition strategy now collapsed and Sutton came in fifth in the Democratic primary behind Ed Koch, Mario Cuomo (later Governor of New York), Abe Beame, and Bella Abzug. He won an embarrassing 16 percent of the vote in Manhattan and in citywide totals he trailed Koch by 49,051 votes; he lost by 83,486 votes to Bella Abzug and Herman Badillo in Manhattan alone. Harlem officials reasoned that if Sutton had been able to pick up a majority of Badillo's and Abzug's Manhattan vote, he might have beaten Cuomo and entered a run-off with Ed Koch, the front-runner.[23] While Koch, Badillo, and Abzug each had legitimate grounds to run for mayor—Koch as a conservative, Abzug as a radical, and Badillo as a prominent Latino leader and experienced government official—Harlem's politicians never forgave their previous allies for competing with Sutton in this race.[24]

When Sutton ran for Mayor, black City Clerk David Dinkins ran to fill his seat as Manhattan Borough president. Some Dinkins supporters resented Sutton's long-shot mayoral campaign for Mayor in 1977 as undermining Dinkins's more winnable candidacy for borough president. Sutton and Dinkins were tapping the same limited sources of financial support. So, too, since Dinkins was running for borough president, Sutton could not support a white reformer for the Manhattan Borough president's seat in exchange for liberal white support for his campaign. Likewise, Dinkins could not offer to support a white reformer for mayor to gain white liberal support for his own campaign. The two campaigns negated each other and both candidates lost.

But even with strong white liberal support, Sutton would have had difficulty winning the mayoral election because of his inability to turn out the black vote across the city's fragmented boroughs. Sutton received a bare majority of the black vote, and was unable to win the concerted support of black elected officials (Wilson and Green 1989, 102–3).[25] A successful citywide Sutton candidacy would require a strong and direct appeal to the city's black working class and poor to outflank black political commitments in the other boroughs. But Sutton did not use television advertising as did his better financed rivals Cuomo and Koch, and there was not a citywide political coalition to assist in mounting a citywide grass-roots campaign. To maintain his appeal to white supporters, and to the great dismay of Brooklyn nationalists, Sutton refused to confront Ed Koch's racially charged rhetoric, and, instead, sought to outflank Ed Koch by competing on a "law and order" platform, promising "swift and certain punishment with justice" (Wilson and Green 1989, 120). The strategy did not work; Sutton gained barely 50 percent of the city's black vote and hardly any white votes. Nor did Dinkins prevail in the 1981 borough president race after

Dinkins's defeat for the post in 1977. In 1985, on his third try, Dinkins was elected Manhattan Borough president. Until then, Harlem's black-white liberal coalition politics remained in deep disarray, unable to spark large black election turnouts.

Black Politics in Brooklyn

In contrast to Harlem, Brooklyn black elected officials were rooted in a strong black nationalist insurgency movement that had engaged in all-out "war" with the white-dominated Brooklyn machine. With few white allies, Brooklyn nationalists had to rely on broad grass-roots mobilization and black nationalist agitation to fight the machine. Brooklyn's earlier black politicians had used a more multiracial approach. In the 1940s, Brooklyn's first wave of insurgent black politicians was aligned with the same labor-radical white coalition that supported Adam Clayton Powell in Harlem (Lewinson 1974, 81). In 1948, Bertram Baker, Brooklyn's first black office-holder, won election as an anti-machine insurgent for the state assembly. But Baker soon switched sides and aligned himself with the Brooklyn machine until leaving office in 1962, when Thomas R. Jones, a black lawyer from Barbados, was elected to the state assembly as an insurgent (Jones 1988). Jones had cut his political teeth in earlier radical politics, but soon after his election, his political club negotiated a settlement with Kings County (Brooklyn) Democratic Party leader Stanley Steingut to become part of the regular county Democratic organization.[26] Jones was replaced, in turn, by an up-and-coming community activist, Shirley Chisholm, who had the support of both Jones and Steingut. The Brooklyn machine had formidable power to wear down opponents; black candidates found alliance with white reformers, who were much weaker in Brooklyn than in Manhattan, to win office against machine incumbents, but once in office they regularly switched sides to align with the machine (Jones 1988). Chisholm, too, became a loyal machine politician, whereupon, spared expensive, risky, and time-consuming primary battles to maintain her Brooklyn seat,[27] she opposed anti-machine black candidates and continued to support the machine (Cooper 1984, 42).

Chisholm's machine politics was countered by a coterie of black nationalist activists led by Al Vann, the former president of the Afro-American Teachers' Association and an active figure in the late 1960s school decentralization battle against the United Federation of Teachers, and in similarly tough battles with machine leaders Meade Esposito and Howard Golden in the 1970s and 1980s (Wilson and Green 1989, 104).[28] In 1972, Vann ran for the state assembly on an Independent Party line and lost, but won two years later and set out to organize other insurgencies in central Brooklyn against machine control of Brooklyn black politics. The machine fought back vigorously. A political activist and former chief of staff for Vann said in an interview in 1988: "We were forced every year to register at least 2,500 people because the books were constantly being purged. . . . So we had to do a lot of door-to-door organizing and voter registration, and that helped us. . . . Meade Esposito was then County Leader and he constantly just pummeled us" (Bynoe 1988).

County demographic trends were on the side of the black nationalists. Between 1970 and 1980, Brooklyn's black population had risen by seventy thousand and the white population had decreased by almost three hundred thousand. Blacks by 1980 were 30 percent of the borough's population, twice as numerous as the black population in the Bronx—the borough with the second largest black population. When, after the 1980 census, the state legislature redistricted to reflect demographic changes, the new congressional district effectively minimized Vann's chances of winning a congressional seat (Flateau 1988). Vann and his political organization, "Vannguard," attempted to pick up newly created Assembly districts: "Our thinking was fine—we get elected but we're surrounded, we're on a damn Bantustan—just how far are we going?" (Flateau 1988). Vannguard joined civil rights activists in filing voting rights lawsuits against election districts drawn by the Brooklyn political machine in order to dilute the impact of the black vote.[29]

Vannguard was initially a grass-roots participatory organization concerned with electoral accountability (Lynch 2000). To mount its broad electoral offensive, Vannguard trained an array of "technicians" to develop campaign literature and gather petitions that would withstand the inevitable legal challenges by the county machine. Vann's political club in Bedford Stuyvesant, Brooklyn, joined forces with community organizations in Brownsville to the east of his district and during the 1980's elected two congressmen (Ed Townes and Major Owens), a state senator (Velmanette Montgomery), and four assembly members (Roger Green, William Boyland, Al Vann, and Clarence Norman Jr.). Joe Canason, a savvy political reporter for the *Village Voice,* credited Vann for breaking machine control of black politics in Brooklyn (Conason 1985).

Vannguard's electoral gains led to formation of a Brooklyn coalition, the Coalition for Community Empowerment (CCE), comprising "executive committee members," insurgent-elected politicians from central Brooklyn, and "associate members" recommended by executive committee members (Simmons 1988). This coalition had two purposes and two internal ideological currents. Many of the participants, inspired by the community protest movements of the 1960s, joined CCE as a grass-roots vehicle for "[a] collective [black] political agenda . . . not just political, but a social, economic, and political agenda . . . [to] give politicians an agenda and a script they should all move in sync on" (Flateau 1988). They had hoped to build Vannguard into a larger grass-roots participatory organization like a secular version of Baltimore's BUILD (Lynch 1999). Others joined primarily to gain technical and manpower assistance to win elections. Despite some defections, CCE became a major force in black politics and threatened to take control of the Brooklyn Democratic Party—one of the largest Democratic Party organizations in the country and one with significant influence in city and state politics. After county leader Meade Esposito resigned amid a corruption scandal, several white factions emerged during the fight for his successor along with two black factions, one formerly machine affiliated, the other affiliated with CCE. Bill Banks, a well-known black Brooklyn campaign strategist, explained:

> I tried to orchestrate [selection of a black leader] but couldn't pull it off. . . . In Brooklyn County there are 19 assembly districts [with] 2 district leaders for every district . . . 38 district leaders— 19 male and 19 female . . . we had approximately 12 minority district leaders . . . and had a possibility of getting about 4 or 6 . . . so-called Reform [white] district leaders who are always against the County . . . organization. But there was a fight among ourselves. . . . [T]his was one of the few times the Puerto Ricans . . . said, "Look, we're down with the blacks." But blacks decided to go with Tom Fortune because Tom Fortune had seniority. So we got to fighting among ourselves and we lost our voting power. (Banks 1988)

White borough president Howard Golden, leader of one of Brooklyn's white factions, was elected to the additional post of county leader and, by outmaneuvering his opponent, machine boss Meade Esposito's protégé, Tony Genovese, made overtures to build a coalition with African American district leaders. Golden moved quickly to isolate Vann by making overtures to other members of CCE, and had notable success. District leaders concluded that the opposition could not unite (Banks 1988).

Some of CCE's members originally planned to develop a social, economic, and political policy agenda for Central Brooklyn, but they never did. Instead, CCE became insular and personality centered (around Vann), and, rather than build coalitions, limited its membership to blacks. Though CCE could have targeted some of the heavily black assembly districts represented by Latinos, Latinos were not allowed to join. Nor did CCE attempt to win over black machine politicians or to educate them about important issues for Brooklyn—such as job and contract opportunities in the billion-dollar Metro-Tech/Atlantic Terminal development project planned for downtown Brooklyn. Nor did CCE approach white reform politicians in Brooklyn or white representatives of majority-black districts or even cement ties between Brooklyn's native-born African Americans and sizable West Indian immigrant population (Banks 1988), whose politicians felt excluded by CCE (Wilson and Green 1989).[30] In addition, CCE made little effort to incorporate central Brooklyn churches and community organizations, and, as a result, their leadership felt alienated by CCE's top-down leadership under Vann (James 1988).

Yet, even with meager allies, CCE grass-roots organizing capacity nearly matched the power of the machine.[31] If Harlem had had CCE's grass-roots organizing perspective, or if CCE had had Harlem's broad outlook on coalition building with non-blacks, both groups undoubtedly would have been far more powerful. But, as it was, CCE's bossism, its lack of a popularly supported community agenda to hold officials accountable, and its deep distrust of whites, Latinos, West Indians, and African Americans who had worked with the machine in the past combined to hold its political power to a political stalemate with the machine into the mid-1980s.

Black Machine Politics in Queens

Queens had a small black population (about 8 percent) in the 1960s; blacks, strongly outnumbered by white Democrats, seldom challenged the borough machine, and instead, nearly all black officials settled into junior positions within it. But, by 1970, Queens's white population had declined by 60,000, and the black population had increased by more than 115,000 to 13 percent of the borough's total population; and in 1980 the black population had increased by nearly 100,000 to 18 percent of the total Queens population (U.S. Department of Commerce 1983). Black residents of Queens tended to be more affluent, educated, and more likely to be homeowners than blacks elsewhere in the city. The *New York Voice,* a black-oriented weekly, stated that, in 1980, "The median family income of the 341,000 Afro-Americans in Queens of $15,770 is almost equal to that of the $16,954 median income of white families in Manhattan. The black community in Queens also owned roughly 40 percent of the approximately 108,342 black-owned homes in the city, despite totaling less than 20 percent of its black population." Black residents of Queens, particularly the homeowners, were considered by black activists to be the most conservative blacks in the city (Hart 1988).

The first African American to win elected office in Queens was Kenneth Brown, an attorney, and his success offered no significant insurgent black challenge to the white Democratic machine until the early 1980s. Nearly all black elected officials in Queens won office as loyal county-supported politicians.[32] Malcolm Smith, a state senator and former aide to Congressman Floyd Flake, who was also pastor of the Allen A.M.E. Church in Jamaica, Queens, in the mid-1980s, remarked, "most of them [black candidates] are elected through the party and through the organization . . . they're not really their own people" (Smith 1988). But, despite the Queens Democratic Party's dominating influence, the party itself maintained the veneer of black inclusion. By the mid-1980s, the deputy county leader was an African American district leader, Doris Young, but she had little influence in the party. Many interviewed for this book reported that black political clubs across the city were exclusive, sexist, nonissue oriented, and subservient to white Democratic machine leadership, most noticeably so in Queens. Laura Blackburne, a Queens activist attorney, said, "The clubhouse politics that blacks have been involved in have been the politics of exclusion. . . . If you have been anointed, and have been invited and been permitted to come into the fold of the club it's a big deal. The doors of the clubhouse generally are not flung wide open welcoming people in. . . . The club exists for the purpose of promoting and supporting a politician or a group of politicians who come out of that particular club. It doesn't exist to promote good things in the community in which it exists" (Blackburne 1988).

In Manhattan, black club leaders had learned the technicalities of election law and petition gathering in the 1940s, and used their experience in machine politics against the machine, but similar defections from the Queens machine did not occur. The 1984 congressional campaign of Simeon Golar (a wealthy African American developer and former chairman of the New York City Housing Authority) against Congressman Joseph Addabbo was the first significant black challenge to a machine incumbent in decades (Meeks 1988), but Golar lost miserably despite campaign support from Jesse Jackson, black Illinois Congressman Gus Savage, and the black Deputy New York Assembly Leader Arthur Eve.[33] Only one Queens politician, African American Assemblymember Cynthia Jenkins, supported him (Meeks 1988).

Many observers credited the cohesiveness of the Queens Democratic Party to the tight-fisted control of Donald Manes, county leader from 1974 until his suicide in 1985 in the wake of a corruption investigation initiated by then U.S. Attorney Rudolph Giuliani (Gross 1986). The resulting void in the Queens organization was compounded by the death of Congressman Joseph Addabbo in April 1986, and in a special election to fill Addabbo's seat until the primary election, the Queens machine put forward an African American assemblyman, Alton Waldon Jr. Sensing the machine's vulnerability, five candidates vied for the seat, including African American insurgent the Reverend Floyd Flake, a forceful speaker, and an excellent organizer with ties to Mayor Koch. Flake ran a "people's campaign," but the Queens county machine blocked his name from appearing on absentee ballots. The special election was a cliff-hanger and Flake won a plurality of the voting machines, but Walden, with his way cleared on the absentee ballots, won the election by 278 votes. However, Flake gained the support of Mayor Koch, who needed to cultivate black support in Queens independent of the hobbled machine, and with an intensive get-out-the-vote telephone campaign, he won the general election handily.

Neither an ideological liberal nor radical, and no machine politician, Flake was a socially conservative, politically moderate black power advocate who preached a strong self-help philosophy, not unlike Garvey's, that was popular among his largely middle-class black constituency. Opposed to such liberal causes as abortion rights, he also gained the support of his heavily Catholic white constituents. His mobilization in Queens—middle class, church led, and socially conservative—was the closest campaign in New York to the style of southern black mobilization in the wake of the civil rights movement. The independent black ministers of southeast Queens, with their large and well-financed congregations, had undermined the

Queens machine. Flake displayed shrewdness and tactical flexibility in winning the simultaneous support of Mayor Koch and Jesse Jackson.[34]

Fighting Puerto Ricans in the Bronx

In the Bronx, a majority-black and Latino borough by the 1970s, the machine employed a "divide and conquer" strategy, repeatedly supporting black candidates against insurgent Latinos and vice versa. With the Bronx the poorest of all the boroughs, insurgents had a hard time raising money while the machine used its superior monetary resources to crush opposition. Blacks were 28 percent of the population by 1980 and Latinos 30 percent, but blacks and Latinos did not make common cause even though they would thereby be the majority. The Bronx machine's white leadership held on to power.

As in Manhattan and Queens, the first wave of black electoral empowerment in the Bronx came out of the World War II era multiracial labor-radical coalition. In 1946, the American Labor Party nominated the first African American to run for Congress from the Bronx, labor leader Roy Soden, who lost very credibly with over twenty-four thousand votes (Biondi 1997, 126). A native of British Guyana, Walter Gladwin, was elected to the State Assembly from the South Bronx in 1954, with the Irish-led Bronx machine recognizing the changing population patterns and shrewdly supporting Gladwin (Lewinson 1974, 60). A generally close attachment between black elected officials in the Bronx and the Bronx machine persisted until the late 1980s. With the lone exception of a minister with an independent church base, Councilman Wendell Foster, all of the elected officials in the Bronx were supported by the machine (Joseph 1988).

The Bronx machine strategically incorporated Jewish politicians as well; it passed the baton from Irish to Jewish leadership without opening up the kind of intra-ethnic rivalry among whites that would unlock opportunities for blacks in Manhattan (Lynn 1986). African American elected officials negotiated with the machine on an individual basis rather than as a group (Joseph 1988).

The machine's friendly approach to black politicians inhibited the development of cohesive black elected leadership in the borough, and dissuaded black activists from forming black civic organizations to challenge the machine. There was never a borough-wide black political organization in the Bronx. On several occasions, insurgent Latino or black politicians did challenge machine candidates for borough-wide office, but black and Latino politicians usually worked at cross-purposes. The Bronx machine was infamous for its ability to divide black and Puerto Rican leaders (Meislin 1986). When, in 1965, a Puerto Rican candidate, Herman Badillo, ran as an insurgent for borough president, the county Democratic organization selected a black assemblyman as its candidate to run against him. Badillo won by a scant two hundred votes, but with Latino backers furious that blacks had endorsed the machine candidate instead. In 1977, Badillo got revenge against the black machine supporters by running in the Democratic mayoral primary against Harlem leader Percy Sutton (whose defeat was detailed earlier in this chapter). Over the next five years, African American and Latino factions took turns punishing each other by failing to support the other's borough president candidates. The 1981 candidacy of Puerto Rican assemblyman Jose Serrano for borough president exemplified much of the antipathy and misunderstanding between the black and Puerto Rican communities: "[Serrano] didn't get any black support and he should have . . . the politicians didn't support him [but] it was as much his fault that he didn't get [greater black voter] support. . . . [Serrano] made some statement that he doesn't understand what the blacks in his community want. How difficult is that? You know housing, lack of jobs, teenage pregnancy. I mean there's no [black and Puerto Rican] separation there, and so that when he makes those kinds of comments, people got turned off" (McGee 1988). Serrano blamed his defeat on the machine: "He [county leader Friedman] was able to twist the arms of every black and Puerto Rican elected official in the Bronx to keep me from being elected. . . . I [met] people walking down the street, I would say hello to them and they would turn around the corner immediately" (Meislin 1986).

In 1987, a free-for-all developed after Bronx Borough President Stanley Simon resigned in the wake of a bribery investigation. The year before, the corruption conviction of Bronx machine leader Stanley Friedman had left a void in party leadership, with three African American and three Latino candidates vying for the city council appointment of a new borough president (Lynn 1987a). Cecil Joseph, black acting borough president and a loyal machine Democrat who ran independently of the machine, eventually received the support of all the African American elected officials in the Bronx (Joseph 1988), gaining grass-roots support in the black community and among elements of the white community. It was the closest the Bronx had come to a strong independent black political campaign, but, once again, black-Latino divisions came into play. Mayor Koch was strongly endorsed for reelection by the Bronx machine, received strong support from the Latino community, and wanted a Latino borough president (Lynn 1987b). This, plus the absence of any kind of black insurgent tradition in the Bronx since the 1940s, prevented Joseph from running a stronger campaign. "Grassroots people, yes, they support you," remarked Joseph in an interview, "but they didn't have the type of financing for us to run a formal campaign . . . [to] go out there on the radio . . . have brochures . . . [and] basic stuff you need" (Joseph 1988). Joseph considered the mayor's support for a Latino borough president "inflammatory" and "racist." Joseph, and many other Bronx black officials at the time, was not sympathetic to Puerto Rican concerns that the Latino population outside of the Bronx was too small to elect a Latino to the Board of Estimate. Bronx African American officials believed that black politicians in other boroughs had forced them to pay the price for Latino exclusion elsewhere in the city, and they deeply resented it.

With white and Latino machine members' support, Bronx Councilman and later mayoral candidate Fernando Ferrer won out over two other Latino candidates, Assemblyman Jose Serrano, a reformer, and Assemblyman Hector Diaz, a regular Democrat. Joseph won the support of the usually loyal African American elected officials, and Diaz that of Ramon Velez, the powerful head of the "patronage rich" Hunts Point Multiservice Center. For the first time the Bronx machine was fracturing. At the Bronx judicial convention of 1987, African American and Puerto Rican legislators formed a united front against the county organization (McGee 1988) and an African American judge, the county's candidate for state supreme court the year before, won the election against the machine candidate for Bronx district attorney. By 1988, the Bronx machine was crumbling and Ferrer went to work to rebuild it under Latino leadership.

Harlem liberals and Brooklyn nationalists were at odds on how to view both white coalition partners and black grass-roots mobilization. Queens's black politicians (except for the mercurial Flake) were closely tied to the machine; so were the Bronx's black politicians, but mainly as a way to fight their principal adversary, Puerto Rican politicians. The weakness of black politicians in New York, and their inability to challenge Koch effectively, can be traced directly to the Board of Estimate structure, which gave black politicians different options in their pursuit of resources and power, and led to different political strategies and ideologies used to justify those strategies.

Attempts to Build Citywide Black Coalitions in the 1980s

There were four attempts to establish a citywide black political coalition in the 1980s: the 1984 and 1988 Jackson campaigns for president; the 1985 Coalition for a Just New York; and David Dinkins's 1989 mayoral campaign. Only the last attempt was fully successful.

The 1984 Jackson Presidential Campaign in New York City

The Reverend Jesse Jackson's 1984 campaign for the Democratic nomination for president provided an unexpected boost for the Coalition for Community Empowerment's (CCE) effort to expand militant black mobilization beyond its stronghold in central Brooklyn. Jackson's campaign was a double insurgency: it was directed against the white leadership of the two major political parties and it was directed against established black civil rights leaders and elected officials. The campaign shocked black politicians in New York but aroused interest in the mass media and among politically alienated black constituents,[35] whose political turf it deeply penetrated by mobilizing black voters through black churches. As a Baptist preacher and longtime veteran of the civil rights movement, Jackson evoked many of the movement's symbols and memories. His campaign's special edge was an appearance of genuine militancy, though for Jackson, based on a defiance of the black-liberal political establishment. His candidacy was opposed by many nationally known black leaders including Benjamin Hooks and John Jacobs, executive directors of the NAACP and National Urban League respectively, by Congressman Charles Rangel of Harlem, and by black mayors including Detroit's Coleman Young, Oakland's Lionel Wilson, Atlanta's Andrew Young, Los Angeles's Tom Bradley. The more Jackson was attacked by the black-liberal establishment nationally, the more militant black activists flocked to his campaign and, beyond Congressman Rangel, few other local black politicians dared oppose his candidacy openly (there was little support from labor unions).

Jackson's New York State campaign was led by Brooklyn's Al Vann and CCE with mostly volunteer local campaign organization, little money, and only four paid staff (Bynoe 1988), but a strong platform. (Simmons 1988). In fact, CCE was so determined to demonstrate the power of grass-roots black mobilization despite the campaign's lack of multiracial appeal, that it collected more than seventy thousand signatures to get Jackson on the ballot, and gathered more signatures in Brooklyn than the well-financed Brooklyn Democratic County (machine) organization collected for Walter Mondale (Simmons 1988).

The excitement of the 1984 Jackson campaign caused a big increase in black voter turnout citywide in the primary (Blackburne 1988). More than 293,000 voted, more than 160,000 above the black turnout in the 1980 Democratic primary (Roberts 1984). Blacks increased their proportion of total Democratic primary voters by 33 percent, 10 percent above 1980.[36] Citywide, black voter turnout reached 57 percent, 16 percentage points ahead of whites and 28 ahead of Latinos. Fallout from Jackson's reference to New York as "Hymietown" diminished any possible support from the liberal Jewish community—the most likely source of white support. ABC News exit polls showed that Jackson received only 3 percent of the Jewish vote in the state, compared with 7 percent of the white vote overall (Page 1988).[37] This deeply distressed Harlem politicians, especially David Dinkins, who planned to run for Manhattan Borough president, since white liberals were to be a key part of his political coalition and he could not afford to be perceived as anti-Semitic. But since Dinkins needed black support, too, he could not oppose the Jackson campaign. However, with the campaign over, Dinkins began to distance himself from Jackson and Jackson was not invited to join in as Dinkins initiated his own 1989 campaign for Manhattan Borough president.

The Coalition for a Just New York (CJNY)

Jesse Jackson's 1984 campaign weakened ties with white liberals, who would be needed to defeat Mayor Koch. The CCE campaign strategists still hoped for a black mayoral candidate to head a "third-world" citywide election ticket with a Latino (Jose Serrano) running for Bronx Borough president, an African American (Al Vann) running for Brooklyn Borough president, and David Dinkins running for Manhattan Borough president (Lynch 2000). It was a no-lose strategy, even if the black mayoral candidate lost, as was likely, since a black at the head of the ticket would help elect two blacks and a supportive Puerto Rican to the powerful Board of Estimate.

To Harlem politicians, the citywide "black power" campaign planned by CCE would generate increased racial confrontation in the city, undermine Dinkins's support from white Manhattan liberals, and cause him to lose the borough president's race for the third consecutive time. Intense infighting between Brooklyn and Harlem politicians—about the merits of militant grass-roots black mobilization over coalition building with liberal whites—erased any semblance of unity among black politicians. These differences were fought out in a citywide black organization, the Coalition for a Just New York (CJNY), formed to mobilize blacks around education issues. After Jackson's presidential race, CJNY became a forum for the debate over a black mayoral candidacy. Members of the CCE were at the core of CJNY, but it also included black community activists from the other boroughs and a few of Harlem's black elected officials (Flateau 1988). Noticeably absent were elected officials from the Bronx and Queens, who were most identified with their respective county machines and therefore with Mayor Koch (James 1988).[38]

The CCE tried to entice Harlem attorney activist Basil Paterson to run for mayor. Paterson had served as state senator, New York Secretary of State, and, briefly, as deputy mayor during Koch's first term and was widely perceived as a political moderate with appeal to white liberal voters. He had supported Jackson in 1984 (McKinney 1989) and, unlike black politicians in the outer boroughs, he could raise money (Shepherd 1988). But then, Paterson unexpectedly withdrew his name from mayoral consideration, citing undisclosed personal reasons. There were practical reasons why the race might have seemed unattractive: blacks were only a quarter of the city population, Jackson had won less than 10 percent of the white vote, and had raised only $200,000 in 1984. Paterson, as an African American, had lost any chance of liberal Jewish support because of Jackson's anti-Semitic slur (Roberts 1985) and his showing among Latinos was weak in 1984 (he won only about 30 percent of the Latino vote). Even in the unlikely even that Paterson had won as many black votes as Jackson, he would have had to broaden Jackson's 1984 base of support. Most important, with a black candidate, David Dinkins, running for Manhattan Borough president in the same election, Paterson, in a run for mayor, would have to compete for the same financial resources. The same problem had crippled Percy Sutton's 1977 mayoral campaign. With no Harlem politician on the Board of Estimate since Sutton in 1977, Harlem politicians had diminished political influence and less of a chance at receiving campaign contributions.

With Paterson out of the picture, Al Vann tried to revive the original Paterson strategy by replacing Paterson with Herman Badillo at the head of the ticket to shore up Latino support in Brooklyn for Vann's own borough president race (Simmons 1988). But Harlem's politicians intensely disliked Badillo, whom they blamed for undermining Percy Sutton's 1977 mayoral run and, with CCE having excluded Puerto Rican politicians in the past, Vann's argument for Badillo seemed purely self-serving. The CCE fully expected Harlem politicians to back a liberal white candidate for mayor and were totally unprepared when they suddenly embraced black nationalist arguments and *insisted* on a black mayoral candidate.[39] Harlem politicians, according to then state NAACP counsel and Queens activist Laura Blackburne, initially *did* want a white candidate for mayor in order to broker reciprocal support for Dinkins's own Manhattan Borough presidential candidacy, but their plans were thwarted when Blackburne declared *her* readiness to run for mayor at a secret meeting held in the Bronx before CJNY's formal endorsement meeting.[40] Both Harlem and Brooklyn politicians were willing to destroy the other faction to pursue power in their own borough.

The Third Attempt: The 1988 Jackson Campaign

David Dinkins won the race for borough president in 1985, his support for Jackson in 1984 shoring up his political popularity among Manhattan African Americans. Dinkins's campaign focused on building support among the liberal white "reform" wing of Manhattan Democrats. He won the borough president race with little enthusiasm but no opposition from the black community. Voter turnout in the 1985 Democratic primary election was only 28 percent in central Harlem's 70th Assembly district, well below the 51 percent turnout for Jackson the year before.[41] The "defeated" black "nationalist" mayoral candidate, Herman "Denny" Farrell, commented to the *New York Times*, "Mr. Dinkins was elected through 'coalition politics'— alliances with whites and Hispanic Democrats—'not the black power direction'" (Lynn 1985). Dinkins had not found a strategy for soliciting white liberal support and for generating enthusiastic black support at the same time. His clever maneuver around the black nationalists had increased their wariness of Harlem politicians, and the nationalists were the ones who could mobilize blacks at the grass-roots level. This move would pose a future problem for Dinkins.

Dinkins asked Jackson to minimize campaign appearances for him in New York, and Jackson's willingness to comply (and not denounce Dinkins) helped him win the Manhattan Borough presidency. Jackson was able to convince Dinkins to make a key local Jackson advisor, Bill Lynch, his chief of staff. This proved to be a fateful decision for Dinkins because Lynch had worked in virtually every borough as a political operative and had served as political action director of American Federation of State, County, and Municipal Employees Local 1707. He had participated in all three of the black unity efforts, developing an appreciation for the different political strengths of the various black factions. Along with several other labor and political activists with similar "cross borough" heterogeneity, Lynch had begun to imagine what could happen in New York if these black political talents could be combined. Lynch told me in 1988 that if black factions were to be brought together, blacks could win "unimaginable power." Many activists interviewed for this study—Gerry Hudson, Laura Blackburne, Bill Banks, Thomas Jones, Esmerelda Simmons, Charles McKinney, to name a few—had perspectives similar to Lynch's. His goal, never achieved, was to build a multiracial coalition while still maintaining the grass-roots enthusiasm of the 1984 Jackson campaign in black communities. With David Dinkins the Manhattan Borough president, Lynch encouraged Jackson to move control of the local New York campaign to Dinkins and Stanley Hill, an African American and new head of the largest municipal union in the city, DC 37 of AFSCME. With Lynch on board, the Manhattan Borough president's office became the center for planning Jackson's local strategy for 1988.

Jackson located his 1988 campaign headquarters in Local 1199, a one hundred thousand-member largely black and Latino hospital workers' union led by a newly elected Puerto Rican labor leader Dennis Rivera. Local 1199 had survived five years of intense internal racial conflict in which two black female union presidents had been defeated by a white-led faction of the union made up of the union's original leadership. The white-led faction supported the Puerto Rican Rivera, who moved to consolidate internal black support. Dennis Rivera became head of Jackson's National Rainbow Coalition, and Local 1199 became the coalition's principal major financial supporter. In this second campaign, Jackson avoided a number of hot-button local racial issues: the murder of a black man in Queens by a gang of white youths; the shooting of four black youths by a white subway gunman; and the alleged rape of a black teenager, Tawana Brawley, by a white law enforcement official in upstate New York (Fireman and Murphy 1988)—a cause championed by the Reverend Al Sharpton, who would later become a major figure in New York politics. By switching strategies, Jackson tried to become the leading spokesperson for organized labor. Carol O'Cleireacain, an economist then working for AFSCME Local DC 37, recalls being asked to help develop Jackson's economic message in 1987 "for women, for minorities, for workers, *all* workers" (O'Cleireacain 2000).

In an aggressive effort to win Latino support, Jackson became the only presidential candidate to appear in person at *El Diario-La Prensa,* the leading local Latino newspaper. The local Jackson campaign, distancing itself from a "black unity first" black power approach, deliberately bypassed black elected officials in the Bronx and coordinated the campaign directly with Bronx Latino officials. The Jackson campaign built trust with Latino officials by directly lending the credibility of Jackson's candidacy to Latino candidates attempting to win congressional seats and borough-wide offices with Latino-black coalitions. Jackson's New York campaign manager Hulburt James said, "We may have paid a price for that. I think we paid some price clearly with some of them in the black community on that" (James 1988). Jackson won close to 56 percent of the city's Latino vote in 1988, compared with 36 percent four years earlier.

The New York State Jackson campaign raised $1.4 million, compared with only $200,000 in 1984; $1,084,000 of its total in New York City.[42] Harlem leaders generated much less black grass-roots participation than in 1984. The clubhouse style of leadership and avoidance of heated racial issues in the 1988 campaign caused visible uneasiness among community activists who had been involved in the militant grass-roots 1984 campaign (Simmons 1988; Sutton 1988). Black churches, too, played a far diminished role; long-time political activist Hulburt James said that other than a campaign kick-off event in a church, the campaign had "no sustained [church] activity" (James 1988). Black voter registration declined significantly with neither machine nor black politicians interested in voter registration. Turnout of registered black voters for the presidential primary reached 61 percent, up only 4 percent from 1984. Jackson won New York City, beating Michael Dukakis in the Democratic primary by 4,260 votes (Oreskes 1988).

The New York press correctly perceived Jackson's New York victory as an enormous defeat for Mayor Ed Koch and a big lift for a potential black mayoral candidate. The *Daily News* reported that "Mayor Koch admitted last [primary] night that his relentless attacks on Jesse Jackson backfired, and an NBC exit poll showed a majority of city Democratic primary voters don't want Koch to run for a fourth term in 1989" (Kramer 1988). A *New York Times* reporter observed that Jackson's campaign accomplished something that virtually no politician had achieved in New York City: "the unified support of almost all black and Hispanic political leaders" (Oreskes 1988). The campaign demonstrated that it was possible, in light of damage to the Queens and Bronx party machines caused by anticorruption investigations, to unite a citywide coalition of African Americans, Latinos, labor, and lesbian and gay rights leaders. Experienced black politicians did, nevertheless, recognize the absence of grass-roots black enthusiasm and activist community mobilization. Jackson's coalition, broad in the multiracial sense, lacked depth in the black community. The *City Sun,* a Brooklyn-based black-oriented weekly periodical, criticized Jackson's 1988 campaign for abandoning poor blacks, and, in a front-page editorial entitled, "Jesse, Say It Ain't So," remarked that, "the ideological maverick of 1984 has become a political hostage in 1988, trying to win white approval at the expense of the broader Black imperatives that should have guided him all . . . along" (English 1988). In its dedication to broadening Jackson's support among non–African Americans, the campaign had lost touch with Jackson's original base. The same problem would carry over to Dinkins's own campaign for mayor.

Why a Black Coalition Emerged During Dinkins's Campaign for Mayor

David Dinkins's decision to run for mayor in 1989 was influenced by several factors, the most important being the elimination of the Board of Estimate in the new city charter approved by voters in 1989. The charter change would profoundly alter political power in the city. Borough presidents' offices lost their power over the city budget and city contracting. A Dinkins run for reelection as Manhattan Borough president now became unattractive and the threat that a competing black borough presidential campaign would draw resources away from a black mayoral candidate was now gone (the primacy of county campaigns had had a crippling effect on efforts to organize black mayoral campaigns in 1977 and 1985). Not only was Dinkins encouraged by the strong support of two powerful city unions, DC 37 and Local 1199, the elimination of the Board of Estimate also made its ability to influence the next *mayor,* rather than finding allies among other officials on the Board of Estimate as they had under Koch, critical. So, too, during his term as Manhattan Borough president, Dinkins had gained more white-liberal support. Working closely with Upper West Side Council-woman Ruth Messinger, he had become one of the city's leading advocates for prudent investments in housing and social services to reduce poverty and homelessness. His advocacy increased his name recognition, policy-making influence, and credibility with the liberal press.

Dinkins also had good prospects for Latino support with Bronx bor-ough president Fernando "Freddie" Ferrer as a potential ally because of Ferrer's need for black support to discourage an election challenge by Assemblyman and later Congressman Jose Serrano. The year before, Ser-rano, a Puerto Rican, endorsed Jesse Jackson in order to win those same black supporters in a race for the seat of Congressman Roberto Garcia. While there was a legacy of distrust between Puerto Rican and black politi-cians, some confidence had been established in interracial coalition build-ing during the Jackson campaign. Since it now seemed that black-Latino coalitions might be possible, this created a career motive for the two lead-ing Puerto Rican politicians in the city to support a black mayoral candi-dacy in 1989—and both did so. Just as important, Latino control of the Bronx machine and Borough president's office would mean much less under the new charter. With a large black population in the Bronx, Latino politicians had a better chance of "delivering" the Bronx (and winning in-fluence for themselves thereby) to Dinkins than to Koch. So, too, the cor-ruption scandals that had weakened the Bronx and Queens political ma-chines and helped pave the way for a multiracial Jackson coalition in 1988 had significantly strengthened Dinkins's prospects

Brooklyn had also changed. Congressman Major Owens, a force to be reckoned with, had built a strong grass-roots constituency through his ex-tensive community-service work during the Ocean Hill-Brownsville school control fight. He was strongly anti-machine and closely tied to Dinkins's chief of staff and campaign manager, Bill Lynch, who had served as Owens's first congressional campaign manager and his former chief of staff. With the Board of Estimate eliminated, CCE had two alternative paths to power: to win influence in the city council or to support a black candidate against Ed Koch. With only a limited number of seats to be won from its political base in central Brooklyn, CCE could not pass an opportunity to help select the next mayor.

Charter change provided Dinkins with an unexpected opportunity. His big problem had been his inability to resolve the tension between the muted racial rhetoric dictated by his interracial coalition-building strategy and the need for a strong articulation of black demands and perspectives—a "black testimonial"—to attract activist black volunteers and mobilize grass-roots black communities. Dinkins's campaign staff understood that his fidelity to black interests was questioned by many black community activists. Making matters worse, Dinkins was not a charismatic speaker—his speeches did not stir black (or white) audiences—and he spent much of his time campaigning in white communities.

It was Mayor Koch's inflammatory racial rhetoric that rescued Dinkins's campaign. Black activists' interest was galvanized by Koch's reaction to the murder of a sixteen-year-old black youth, Yusef Hawkins, by a group of white teenagers in the predominantly Italian neighborhood of Bensonhurst, Brooklyn. When black protesters, led by the Reverend Al Sharpton, marched through Bensonhurst, they were greeted by racial epithets and watermelon chunks. Mayor Koch infuriated many in the black (and liberal white) community by asking blacks not to march through Bensonhurst so as not to provoke neighborhood whites. Dinkins appealed for calm in the black community while insisting that blacks had a right to march anywhere in the city. To white liberals, Dinkins seemed a moderate racial healer; to blacks he seemed their champion against Mayor Koch. Dinkins beat Koch in the September Democratic primary by 51 to 43 percent of the vote (Thompson 1990, 146–47).

A month before the November general election, Dinkins led by twenty-four points against Republican Rudolph Giuliani (Thompson 1990), who was damaged in the Republican primary by the negative television ads of a wealthy opponent. With five times as many enrolled Democrats as Republicans in the city, some pundits predicted that Dinkins would win easily. In the preelection weeks, Giuliani's campaign launched a barrage of attacks on Dinkins for failing to pay income taxes eighteen years earlier, and charged that he had undervalued stock in a sale to his son in order to avoid paying gift taxes. The attacks sharply accentuated Dinkins's negative ratings among white voters; one quarter of Giuliani's supporters said they switched from Dinkins to Giuliani based on Dinkins's finances. Dinkins barely won the election, squeaking past Giuliani by 47,000 votes out of more than 1.8 million cast; more than half of Giuliani's supporters said they voted for him because they disliked his opponent. Dinkins came into city hall with only 30 percent of the white vote in the general election, an extremely low figure for a Democrat in New York City. Dinkins captured more than a third of the combined Jewish and white Protestant vote and 18 percent of the white

Catholic vote. Carol O'Cleireacain, Dinkins's finance commissioner who worked with Irish Americans during Dinkins's campaign, maintained that Dinkins's white Catholic support came largely from Irish American supporters of Northern Ireland's independence since Dinkins had become a strong supporter of the Irish nationalist cause (O'Cleireacain 2000). It suggested that race, and not just rumors of Dinkins's personal finance problems, had played a significant part in white Democrats' voting decisions.

The coalition of voters that supported Dinkins in the primary election, his "primary coalition," made up about 70 percent of his vote in the general election. The remaining 30 percent of the Dinkins vote came from Koch voters, Independents, Republicans, and Democrats who did not vote in the primary, voters who might be called Dinkins's "general coalition" who were more conservative and less supportive of Dinkins's attention to the minority poor, and and who contained more whites than the "primary coalition" had (Thompson 1996a, 65–66). Ed Koch surprised many observers by strongly supporting Dinkins in the general election, but, as a U.S. Attorney in New York, Giuliani had relentlessly prosecuted Koch's political supporters in the Bronx and Queens, and Koch appeared to relish the opportunity to oppose him. Koch helped win a share of moderate Jewish support for Dinkins. Anticipating Koch's possible support, Dinkins had taken pains to avoid personal attacks on him throughout the earlier primary.

Dinkins's winning political coalition was held together by a thread: Koch was notoriously mercurial and prone to bombastic racial rhetoric; Dinkins had won strong labor support, but unions' costly demands put the unions at odds with Koch's low-tax fiscal philosophy and Dinkins's "general coalition" allies; black nationalists who had endorsed Dinkins despite strong reservations about his racially centrist approaches now wanted to see him deliver in their communities.

It was no accident that attempts to run black mayoral candidates were dismal failures prior to 1989 but that a successful black mayoral candidacy followed on the heels of local government reform. When the Board of Estimate structure was in place, efforts to build a citywide black organization and black mayoral candidacy were put in the shadow by the contradictory, more dramatic, and closer-to-home borough campaigns of Harlem and Brooklyn politicians. After the elimination of the Board of Estimate, with the borough president's office no longer the most accessible means to power and resources for local black political factions, a unified, citywide black mayoral victory became possible. There was a direct link between the structure of local government and the willingness of black activists to forge a common citywide political organization and strategy, even if tenuous and temporary. But political structure can be overestimated in considering the shaping of black politics. Had, for example, the Bronx's black politicians negotiated with Puerto Rican politicians a slate for mayoral and borough presidents' offices in the 1985 mayoral race, one would probably conclude that the earlier borough-oriented, fragmented structure of New York enabled, rather than thwarted, blacks' political voice. County machines exercised power over black politics because black civic organizations had been weak. Had black civic organization been stronger in the Bronx, for example, it would have mattered less whether a black or a Puerto Rican occupied a particular political seat. Creating a more democratic local politics can be hindered by structures, but the sources of black political weakness went deeper than the structure of political institutions.

But in New York, with the creation of a more centralized governing structure, a new black citywide coalition was born, if fragile and unsure of its identity. In New York in the 1980s, deep pluralists such as Lynch hoped that the combination of grass-roots organizing of black nationalists in Brooklyn, white liberals in Manhattan, Puerto Ricans in the Bronx, black machine politicians repositioning themselves to support a more powerful mayor under the new charter, and rising black leadership in key labor unions might be sufficient to knit together a civic coalition strong enough to transform New York politics and policy.

"Set Up a Think Tank":
A Black Mayor's
Accountability to
the Black Community

The Case of David Dinkins

One day in 1988, Bill Lynch, Manhattan Borough President David Dinkins's chief of staff, met with Basil Paterson, the only black leader in New York City to have served at a senior level at city hall. What should Lynch do first if the opportunity arose for Dinkins to run for mayor? "Set up a think tank," said Patterson.[1]

A think tank may not seem top priority for a pragmatic politician, but to Lynch, a seasoned political campaign strategist and former labor leader, it made sense. Besides, Patterson did not have in mind a detached academic think tank that thinks up policy but has no opportunity to carry it out or take responsibility for results. Paterson urged Lynch to initiate discussions with leaders of local organizations and with academics to help Dinkins develop an agenda, assess what political resources and alliances would be needed, and to begin conversations with those who could help him achieve that agenda. Draw up the agenda *before,* not during or after the campaign, Paterson said. If Dinkins became mayor, "there will not be time to think through issues." But in 1988, fund-raising, the courting of union and party leaders, and polling seemed more important to both Dinkins and Lynch than forming a think tank and a civic roundtable. The wisdom of Paterson's advice became apparent years later when Lynch sought desperately to build a civic coalition to support the mayor's policy goals.

"It takes a different kind of power to implement policy than to win an election" was the clear implication of Paterson's wise advice. Even mayors in strong-mayor systems have limited power. To enact a budget or to initiate major redevelopment projects, mayors usually must get city council approval or, for significant changes in tax or fiscal policy, state legislative approval. New black mayors who have sought to honor campaign promises often found entrenched legislative bodies standing in their way. Few black mayors have had the power to override entrenched legislative opposition, and few mayors, white, black, or Latino, have the political skill or resources to mold their city councils or persuade state governments to abet their plans. Mayors have had to—and still must—choose between working within the limits of what a city council and a state legislature are willing to approve, or attempt to achieve broader changes by putting new and more cooperative members on the city council or in state government, a fundamental course that requires great depth and breadth of political resources, neither readily available to the black mayors of large American cities.

Direct voter contact with, and knowledge of, the candidate matters more in highly local campaigns than in mayoral races. Thus winning city council and state legislative races takes sophisticated local political knowledge, relationships with key community activists, and an ability to persuade these activists to become allies. Newly elected mayors in racially contested cities often lack such knowledge and experience and, therefore, find themselves in conflict with recalcitrant city councils. Black mayoral candidates rarely have sufficient resources to influence important local races in the black community, and even fewer resources to influence races in white or Latino communities, and must reserve their own, perhaps meager, funds to try to outflank or defeat their opponents.

In Chicago, Harold Washington, who served from 1983 to 1987, was virtually paralyzed by council opposition in his entire first term (Holli and Green 1989; Grimshaw 1992). So, too, were Cleveland mayors Carl Stokes (1967 to 1972) and Mike White (1990 to 2002) frustrated by a resistant city council. In response, all three mayors adopted strategies to alter the membership of the council by influencing city council elections. Wilson Goode, in Philadelphia, was similarly hobbled, and concluded in his second and final term that he had no choice but to succumb to the will of machine politicians on the city council (see chapter 4).

Successful black mayors like Stokes and Washington did construct broad civic coalitions in an effort to change the balance of local political power through the use of community-based civic organizations and labor unions that did have constituencies and local political knowledge they themselves may have lacked in the districts of key legislators.[2] But, since the most politically active local civic organizations have usually already received favors from local legislators, they are seldom interested in electing a new representative, and other community organizations, including groups alienated or marginalized and at odds current officeholders, must be brought into the process. Arriving at a common agenda with allies sufficient to achieve such change is deep pluralist work; it may require bridging resentments between "insider" groups and marginalized groups. Overcoming such internal conflicts is the basic building block for larger schemes to alter the outcomes of local elections and hence to effective policy making. The hard work of fulfilling local neighborhood agendas prefigures overcoming similar resentments and conflicts to be encountered in building citywide and cross-racial coalitions, and the second can seldom be achieved without the first.

For a mayor's vision for political and policy change to be credible, a specific agenda of agency priorities and of the revenue sources to pay for them needs to be thought out and articulated in concrete practical ways. It takes political savvy as well as nerve to avoid co-optation by others with agendas of their own at odds with the mayor's. So, for example, large citywide organizations, like labor unions, with the superior resources and the power to dominate citywide coalitions and their policy agendas may exploit such a broad coalition in their own interests, relegating local community groups that are vital in a local legislative district to a role of weak players in the citywide coalition, with their critical interests ignored. For such groups, often too marginalized to join a broad civic coalition, mayors must generate trust (or hope) that their interests will not be abandoned, and if they join the coalition that trust must not be betrayed. Since weaker groups are often excluded from any broad coalition, they risk exclusion throughout later processes of strategy and program development, and a successful leader must see that this exploitation does not occur. So, too, a coalition demands a clear sense of who the opposition is likely to be; few groups can afford to make enemies of their patrons. The Industrial Areas Foundation in Texas, for example, avoids conflict with the hierarchy of the Catholic Church that supports it. Groups asked to confront their patrons must have advance assurances that other coalition partners will shore them up if they take that risk and lose that original patron's support. All of the dynamics of coalition building need vigilant monitoring.

Creating a broad civic alliance strong enough, for example, to remake city councils requires civic organizations to alter their own thinking about their interests and political strategies. Such a process of self-examination is deeply pluralistic. It may be, for example, that a city government cannot solve inner-city employment problems without a major expansion in public works, and, while it may be possible to get agreement among low-income groups and unions that wealthy corporations pay for such public works, making sure that this happens, or that an effective alternative plan is in place so that the inner-city unemployed actually get those publicly funded jobs, is a complex task. It is especially complex because to hire the unemployed usually means to deny preference to unions' existing membership. Or it may require a fundamental revamping of union membership rules, compensation rates, and skills-training programs to include the new employees—a challenge that goes to the core of the internal workings and commitments of the unions and the dynamics of race and class. Addressing existing patterns of exclusion within the union allies may well be a greater challenge for a coalition than confronting wealthy corporations that are not its natural allies.

Existing theories of interest-group pluralism provide little insight into how to change or redirect organizational self-interest, which requires that organizations profoundly rethink their internal structure and commitments. Yet, such reframing of interests to avoid zero-sum conflicts over resources is crucial to civic coalition building. Because interest-group pluralist approaches assume that larger political and economic structures are legitimate, such theories do not propose long-term and broad projects to fundamentally remake policy rules and distribution structures. They, therefore, do not ask large and powerful civic groups to be accountable to weaker civic groups with the rationale that such accountability will build even broader coalitions of power needed to tackle large-scale reforms that are far beyond the reach of unions on their own. When interest-group pluralism is in play, those interested in civic coalition building cannot address core functions of politics: to alter boundaries between groups' conceptions of self-interests to make room for a broader conception of "self"; to open up private, off-limits organizational and personal concerns so that organizations and individuals can adapt themselves to the demands of new political strategies and new intergroup relations; and to reframe relations of power between groups to meet most effectively the power of the identified opponent.[3]

Developing a deeply pluralist process is time-consuming civic work and takes real political shrewdness. Big-city mayors cannot effectively lead such local processes and, at the same time, manage their cities; yet, at the same time, black mayors who support civic alliances will be strengthened by them. In cities where civic organizing is already on the rise (and does not require a major diversion of mayors' energies), civic organizers may provide sufficient political backing for black mayors to alter city and even state policies to meet the city's priorities, and other mayors will be better able to be accountable to the poor, who need them the most. In cities where Latino populations are on the rise, forging multiracial civic coalitions—among blacks, Latinos, and white progressives—that push for rule-altering policies and remake legislative bodies may be more effective than mediating conflicts between blacks and Latinos in a zero-sum contest over limited or shrinking government resources. In cities with low voter participation among the black poor, and where black mayors worry that Latino voters will back their opponents, black mayors must move beyond self-destructive competition for shrinking resources between needy groups (and beyond blaming the disillusioned or apathetic black voters) and establish a more secure multiracial voting base with no group convinced that it will be sacrificed in implementing a coalition agenda.

There are good reasons for black civic organizations to take on time-consuming coalition building that a mayor alone cannot do when black groups fight not only each other but increasingly Latino groups for the same shrinking resources. In Los Angeles, blacks and Latinos have each, at different times, aligned with conservative whites to defeat the other (see chapter 4). This occurred in Houston in the 2001 mayoral election, when a conservative Republican Cuban, Orlando Sanchez, won a majority of the predominantly Chicano Latino vote in opposing a more progressive black Democratic incumbent, Lee Brown. But such victories are likely to be short-lived, and in the end become defeats, since conservative whites seldom support the substantive agendas of low-income black and Latino people.

Rule-altering deep-pluralist politics may be the best way to avoid a major collision between black mayors, black civic organizations, and black city residents over priorities. Most cities' political structures—unless altered by coalitional strategies—now force black mayors to implement policies and laws that do not reduce racial inequality and that most in the black community consider fundamentally unjust. So, for example, black mayors cite unwanted public facilities in neighborhoods where land is cheapest, usually poor and minority neighborhoods. Yet many black mayors have acted to demobilize poor blacks lest their anger at this continuing racial inequality damage their chances for reelection by alienating white voters or chasing away potential business investors, most of them white. Such demobilization, however useful in the short run, is self-defeating in the long run in racially contested cities since it makes black mayors more vulnerable to more conservative white candidates, and, with the decline of the black vote, weakens their power—as well as the power of black civic organizations—in the state and national arena as well. Black civil rights organizations, seeing the long-term implications, have sought to increase voter registration in city after city in order to reverse lagging participation of poor blacks, which reflects a lack of democratic development within black districts.

In New York City, structural and political pressures after Dinkins's election in 1989 led him to curtail his policy change agenda and to steer city policy toward affirming the status quo. After black civic resistance mounted against Dinkins's accommodationist approach, he attempted to shift direction and engage in civic organizing to remake the city council. His efforts failed and he was defeated in his reelection bid. Was this a consequence of weakness of will, lack of activist power, failure to mobilize the full range of the black community and the Latino community in his behalf, or simply evidence of the difficulties of leading a civic-building process from the office of a sitting mayor? Or was it perhaps all of these together?

Pressures to Conform

In 1989, with the Board of Estimate gone, and with it decline in the power of the boroughs, the New York City mayor's office became the center of power in the city and, therefore, the focus of black politics. Black organizational capacity had increased with the formation of a citywide black political coalition behind David Dinkins, and, within that coalition, a key factor was the ascension of black and Latino/black leadership in the city's most powerful municipal unions. Dinkins entered office in 1990 intending to govern as a political centrist and as a good technician. He was fond of repeating the liberal public-interest managerial perspective of "good government is the best politics."[4] But the forces that provided his margin of victory were sharply divided and made it difficult for him to remain a centrist; he became the main target of black advocacy, and had to contend with the anger of the city's politically efficacious black civic organizations. At the same time, firmly committed to building a strong black-white liberal coalition, Dinkins had to bring white liberals' concerns with fiscal stability into accord with demands of low-income blacks and Latinos for substantive improvements in housing, schools, employment, and health. Though all communities in the city wanted public safety, white and black communities generally had different views about how to achieve it; black communities tended to view crime and civic disorder as reflecting a need for jobs and social programs; whites tended to view crime as showing a need for more frequent and more severe punishment (Arian et al. 1991). Reconciling all these demands was Dinkins's greatest challenge.

Dinkins's post-election rhetoric reflected the mind-set of his campaign and his early administration, describing New York City as a "gorgeous mosaic," with different shapes and colors pieced together to form a unified whole. His vision of a mosaic was less apt than one of a crazy quilt without a unifying theme. His words transformed divisive class and racial issues into a beneficent metaphor of unity and beauty. But the city itself was too divided to come together in such a metaphor. Working in a political process with one's adversaries, as Dinkins tried to do, is deeply pluralist, but engaging in such a civic process need not mean failing to confront or conceding the fight for one's own concept of justice, and Dinkins had no framework to guide him in that process. His selection of staff or his setting of priorities reflected not a policy agenda of how to empower a coalition and at the same time meet his own priorities but reflected rather a balancing of the city's political forces. He initially appointed six deputy mayors, three of them political moderates with ties to former Mayor Koch, including Victor Kovner, a former law partner of Koch, and a well-known figure in the city's business community, media, and Jewish leadership circles, as City Corporation counsel; Norman Steisel, former commissioner of sanitation under Koch, as deputy mayor for operations and the budget; and Milton Mollen, a former judge and Brooklyn Democratic Party politician, as deputy mayor for criminal justice. Only two of Dinkins's appointments had an extensive history of working with him and had close ties to his core political base of labor, minorities, and Manhattan liberals: Bill Lynch, Dinkins's campaign manager and former Chief of Staff in the Manhattan

Borough President's Office, was appointed deputy mayor for Intergovernmental Relations; Barbara Fife, a longtime Democratic Party insider and "good government" reform activist, was appointed deputy mayor for planning and development; and Sally Hernandez-Pinero, a Bronx-based Puerto Rican attorney who had served as deputy Manhattan Borough president under Dinkins and then as financial services commissioner under Koch, was appointed deputy mayor for finance and economic development. The conflict between the outer-borough (outside Manhattan) homeowner-business orientation of many Koch holdovers and the demand for jobs and community investments from Dinkins's own, principally Manhattan-based, primary electoral coalition was repeatedly played out in the administration itself, with frequent feuding and occasional undermining of the mayor by his deputy mayors. Dinkins, nonetheless, rarely fired staff since each deputy represented an important element of his electoral base.[5] The appearance of internal cooperation barely masked the intense internal power struggles.

In 1990, with the country in the middle of a national economic recession (Pagano 1991), Mayor Dinkins encountered the same array of problems that has led many urbanists to call the fiscal structure of big cities unmanageable. On January 5, 1990, the City Office of Management and Budget (OMB) sent the mayor a background memo saying that, "non-property tax growth has dropped from 7 percent in 1989 to 1.4 percent in July through December, depriving the City of $1 billion of revenue growth . . . the virtual halt to revenue growth since July has continued unabated" (Office of Management and Budget 1990). Growth in income was the lowest since 1982; growth in employment the lowest since 1980; and employment in the finance industry (an important source of tax revenue) in 1989 was down from the 4 percent rate of increase in 1988 to an almost 2 percent decline in 1989. Dinkins had several options: increase taxes, fees, and other revenues; eliminate services and programs; contract out services (but with municipal layoffs); adopt "one-shot" fiscal gimmicks—such as restructuring debt payments—or seek relief from the state and the federal government, the last option highly unlikely since federal aid to New York City, which had represented 52 percent of its general expenditures in 1980, was down to 36 percent in 1989 (Caraley 1992, 9; Office of Mayor David Dinkins 1990). The state administration, itself pressed by declining federal government funds, was seeking to off-load many of its own costs onto the city.[6] Nor could Dinkins's team rely on fiscal gimmickry. After the city's bankruptcy of the mid-1970s, the state-dominated Financial Control Board (FCB) had gained the power to take over management of the city's finances if it violated prudent fiscal management practices,[7] and could even reject the city's expense and capital budget (Shefter 1987, 169). What "prudent" fiscal management is, however, was a political issue. The FCB also made judgments about policy decisions, with its staff arguing that balancing the budget was not a mere exercise in "arithmetic budget balance," but required making tough-minded political and administrative decisions. It successfully pushed Dinkins to reduce the city's workforce by ten thousand municipal employees, in the process alienating the municipal unions that had supported his election.

The budget crises and investors' concerns led, in turn, to an internal power play that provided the more conservative former Koch faction in Dinkins's administration with the strongest hand. To assure city investors, Dinkins reshuffled his "rainbow" of deputy mayors, elevating Norman Steisel, former Koch official, to "First Deputy" Mayor with all the other deputy mayors required to report to him. Koch himself had established a reputation early in his tenure as mayor for holding down municipal labor costs, for stinginess on social programs, for keeping a lid on property taxes (particularly appealing to his base of white ethnic homeowners in the outer boroughs), while at the same time providing tax subsidies for real estate developers (Mollenkopf 1992, 190–93). All of these were policies that Dinkins's union and minority constituents opposed and Steisel, who generally supported these policies, therefore became an immediate target of union and community leaders among Dinkins's core constituencies. Despite this resistance, Dinkins proposed $239 million in service cuts and $859 million in tax increases along with pledges intended to meet objectives of Koch's base of constituents, though likely to displease both Koch's and Dinkins's constituents. Dinkins hoped to improve the city's finances by reducing the number of municipal employees and delaying the hiring of more than two thousand police officers, moves that guaranteed controversy since police protection was a favorite expenditure among many outer-borough white-ethnic constituents, and social services was a favorite of minority constituents. But then, negotiations with the city council speaker, Peter Vallone (of Queens), led to hiring an additional five hundred police officers and to cutting more services beyond the staggering service reductions already proposed (Dinkins and Vallone 1990). Vallone, in turn, agreed to an increase of more than $250 million in property taxes. It was again meant to be a balancing act. Dinkins, in effect, agreed to fund half the cost of the additional police officers (roughly $500 million annually) from social service cuts that affected his own primary political base; Vallone to fund the other half from increased property taxes that affected his core political base of real estate companies and single-family homeowners. Dinkins had survived his first budget without a major confrontation with the city council but with substantial risk to his own political core. With the council leadership and the Mayor holding sharply different priorities, the earlier negotiated spirit of cooperation would not hold.

Also in 1990, seven months after Dinkins's election, four child killings from random gunfire occurred in a period of nine days. Nineteen cabdrivers had also been killed that year, and a serial killer, the "Zodiac" killer, had gunned down four people. The press had made the crime-wave a leading story for eight long weeks, with picture after picture of murdered crime victims. The *New York Post* goaded Dinkins to hire even more police than the thousands of new hires he had already scheduled. A *Daily News* series appeared under the banner "City under Siege," and in the same period, in referring to the crime issue, the *New York Post* published a huge headline, "DAVE, DO SOMETHING!" *Daily News* columnist Bob Herbert wrote, "If . . . Dinkins becomes gung-ho for hiring lots of new cops, then he will have taken one step toward bringing sanity back to New York. . . . If he doesn't, look out" (Herbert 1990a). Felix Rohatyn, an investment banker, architect of the city's 1970s fiscal bailout, and a Dinkins advisor, said, "I've never lived through anything like this. This is a lot worse than the '70s. People seem to have given up. There is a sense today that we're prisoners of something that's beyond our control" (Diamond and Nagourney 1990). A Gallup poll conducted in late September showed a 20 percent drop in Dinkins's approval among whites, but no decline in his approval among African Americans (Murphy 1990).

Ed Koch criticized Dinkins constantly, in a weekly television show, in his newspaper column in the *New York Post,* and on his morning radio talk show. City Council President Andrew Stein advised the governor to send in the National Guard (Siefman 1990). Bronx Borough President Fernando Ferrer announced he would call his own summit on crime (Herbert 1990b). Peter Vallone joined the *New York Post's* plea for thousands of more cops immediately, which was no surprise since Vallone's white Queens political constituency was relatively conservative. But Governor Mario Cuomo's clarion call for a massive addition to the already-growing police force was an unexpected and serious blow since Cuomo was one of the most prominent liberal Democrats in the country. Dinkins's staff feared that Cuomo's stance would isolate Dinkins from his white liberal supporters. Cuomo made his comments after Republicans threatened to use the New York City crime issue against *him* during upcoming state elections (Dicker and Steier 1990), but Dinkins interpreted Cuomo's move as implying that because Dinkins was black he was somehow less willing than others to fight crime. Dinkins suggested, to the contrary, that the underlying cause of the crime scare was the lurid publicity of attacks *on whites.* To a mostly black radio audience, Dinkins said, "You are aware the problems of crime and violence in our [black] community are not new. We've had this problem, and now I guess it has gone beyond our borders and others [whites] have become concerned. Fact of the matter is, we have been concerned since day one" (Purdum 1990). And, after all, crime had risen dramatically under Koch. Dinkins told a reporter, "The rest of them have had at least four years . . . Some have had eight years and some have had 12 years [a reference to Koch]. I've had seven months. So I say again, I will be [the toughest mayor on crime the city has ever seen]" (Mooney 1990). Jim Bell, president of the Coalition of Black Trade Unionists, spoke out in defense of Dinkins: "Crime was here before David Dinkins got sworn in and Koch had the last twelve years to do something about it. . . . [Now] Koch has the nerve to say Dinkins is not doing enough" (Anekwe 1990).

Nonetheless, Dinkins and his aides decided, despite his backing in his main constituency, that he could not maintain a leadership position against the combined forces of the city council speaker, the governor, the press, the majority of the white public, and his own police department, and hence, that he had little choice but to yield to the widespread demand for a massive increase in police hiring. He did include also funds for social services as part of the new anticrime package and applied a "community policing" frame intended to make the plan more acceptable to his primary support base, with $153 million for drug treatment, youth education, and other youth-related activities, community-service sentencing programs, work-release programs, and community-based crime prevention (Office of the Mayor 1990). Many black activists complained that Dinkins had caved-in under pressure from the white media, an impression made worse by the state legislature's insistence that many of the social-services programs Dinkins had proposed be eliminated (Lynch 2000). In the competition for resources, funding additional police hires had gained priority over jobs and other social programs supported (and sometimes run) by black activists. Police hires were widely viewed as primarily aiding working-class whites and suburban residents—the demographic of the police force itself. If Dinkins's advisors believed that the initiative had demonstrated to a doubting public Dinkins's management ability and strong commitment to public safety, they were mistaken; the fight over crime carried over into a racialized contest over the 1992 budget.

In the context of the 1991 fiscal crisis, the $600 million annual price tag for new police was an *extraordinary* commitment of funds. New York City's job loss at the time, the third largest since the 1950s (Bureau of Labor Statistics 1991), translated into lower tax revenues (Office of the City Comptroller 1992). Publicly aired concerns about Dinkins's ability to manage the budget were so great that Governor Cuomo threatened to take over city spending through the Financial Control Board (FCB), an immense humiliation for Dinkins, who regarded the governor's threat as a racially motivated usurpation of the authority given to him by voters. When he presented the budget in a speech at city hall, Dinkins told those assembled that the governor, through the FCB, was seeking to reverse the results of his election: "In the days and weeks ahead, the nearly eight million people who are privileged to call this great city home must decide whether we shall make our own destiny or have another destiny forced upon us. Elect the former course, and our generation and the next will be able to hold our heads high as free men and free women in a free city. Give in to the latter, however, and we give up on the dreams we hold so dear, effectively permitting others we do not elect—individuals who are not accountable to us—to do our dreaming for us. To me, that is simply unacceptable" (Dinkins 1991).

Dinkins's reference to "free men and free women in a free city" and his demand that no one "do our dreaming for us" was black civil rights code signaling alarm to the city's African Americans. With his own trust in white Democratic Party liberals at risk, Dinkins was implying that his commitment to political moderation had limits: he would not cave in. In the face of Dinkins's outrage and resistance, it was Cuomo who now retreated; he called the editor of the *Amsterdam News* to say that his takeover threat had been a misunderstanding (Browne 1991b).

Dinkins had to doubt the chances of winning over white voters by his "evenhanded" liberal-pluralist approach. At the same time, he was being sharply criticized by his core minority and union supporters, black and Latino labor leaders, community organizations, and the black press alike. Many said that the black community had been abandoned. Some Brooklyn-based black nationalists, sensing a possible wedge, now sought to force Dinkins's hand by a community boycott of a Korean grocer in Flatbush who was said to have beaten a Haitian shopper accused of stealing. Former Mayor Koch and the white press demanded that Dinkins protect the grocer and denounce "black racism," but since such a course would bolster black nationalists' argument that Dinkins was a race-traitor, Dinkins held back on arresting the boycotters. It was a step that angered the Korean business community and a number of city leaders claimed that Dinkins operated by a double standard: fighting white but not black anti-Korean racism. White and black progressive activists, for their part, accused Dinkins of abandoning the constituencies that elected him by joining with "the traditional establishment" (Haq 1991). An *Amsterdam News* front-page article headlined, "All across the City the Cry to Dinkins Is the Same: 'Spare Us,'" quoted a number of analysts who said the city and state budgets were balanced on the backs of the poor, and the state's Financial Control Board was New York City's "invisible government" run by bankers and conservative policy analysts (Browne 1991a).[8]

But the most dangerous criticism came from black and Latino labor leaders. DC 37, AFSCME President Stanley Hill protested that instead of layoffs of city workers, the mayor should raise the top rate of the personal income tax and close tax loopholes that benefited the wealthy. The mayor "can't afford" to proceed with his budget politically (*Amsterdam News* 1991b). Hill's call for taxing the rich was joined by Local 1199 president Dennis Rivera, whose union filed a lawsuit against the city, charging illegal diversion of funds from hospitals to other parts of the city budget (Boyd 1991). When Dinkins refused to back away from layoffs, AFSCME's Hill and president Barry Feinstein of the Teamsters 237 (Public Housing Authority workers) accused him of "betrayal" and expressed public regret that they had worked for his election (Browne 1991c). A threatened shutdown of municipal hospitals by Jim Butler, the African American head of Local 420 (hospital workers) of DC 37, was headed off only after a marathon meeting at the mayor's residence, Gracie Mansion. Local 1199's president, Rivera, said he would not support Dinkins for reelection in 1993 unless Dinkins changed his direction (Enemies 1991). Since these unions had been the center of Dinkins's effort in the previous election, and since Dinkins had no independent organizational capacity to mobilize voters, they would be key to his reelection.

The power of municipal unions in New York was a reflection of the city and state political structure; cities in southern right-to-work states, by comparison, do not have strong municipal unions. But the presence of formidable black city unions did not automatically translate into a mayor's or union leader's skillful leverage or ability to deploy that power not only to win elections, but, more fundamentally, to meet the substantive goals of black workers or other low-income city residents.

In New York, with the election of a black mayor there had been a number of political mistakes, for example, no plan in place for new political roles for Dinkins's key supporters. Dinkins could have promised his core civic coalition priority treatment in exchange for an agreement to ensure election of a cooperative city council. Instead, with labor negotiations placed under a deputy mayor who knew little of Dinkins's political obligations or priorities, no such bargain was made. The divide between the politics of the campaign and the politics of governance was wide.

In another instance of political bumbling, Dinkins, in labor negotiations soon after the election, offered the United Federation of Teachers (UFT) more money than other city workers. True, the teachers union was a powerful political force (more than seventy thousand members in the city), but it was one of the last unions to endorse Dinkins against Koch and it had a bitter history of conflict with Brooklyn black nationalists and other community activists dating back to the late 1960s community control battles over the schools. When the contract with an early Dinkins supporter, the largest municipal union—DC 37, with 130,000 mostly black and Latino workers—came up for renewal immediately after the teachers' contract, the Mayor offered the union, and also Teamsters 237, another early Dinkins supporter and comprising mainly public housing workers, a 3.5 percent increase over fifteen months and an increase of 1 percent later, compared with 5.5 percent in one year for the UFT. The DC 37 and Teamsters 237 union leaders were embarrassed and angry. Adding insult to injury, in the middle of negotiations DC 37's Stanley Hill complained (apparently accurately) that he had learned about the city's lay off plans from the morning newspapers (not from his "friend" Dinkins). Dinkins had, in effect, placed labor, generally, on the "give-back" side of the budget ledger at the same time that the public sector was a major portion of African American jobs in the city, and the financial and social backbone of the city's struggling black ghettos.

Eric Smertz, Dinkins's embattled labor negotiator, and a longtime Koch adversary, complained that negotiations were being run by a union-hostile mayoral budget staff (led by Steisel) and undermined by the city's budget director (Phil Michel), whom Smertz accused of secret contingency agreements to fire city workers. An embarrassed Dinkins, on the verge of losing the critical labor support that helped him become mayor, dismissed Smertz. By contrast, former New York Mayor Robert Wagner, perhaps the closest among modern New York mayors to Dinkins in personal style, never initiated new labor policy without clearing it first with labor leaders. Since Dinkins wanted to reward the core constituency whose support was now at risk, he could do so only by generating more city revenue, and conservatives would use any such move against him. Dinkins eventually did concede rough parity to the teachers and the other unions but the reductions in the teachers' union contract, in turn, angered the teachers.[9] All of the municipal unions were furious and the business community was sharply critical of the wage increases to boot. If Dinkins now lost the support of equally angry black community groups he would have little chance of making up for these core defections by increasing his backing among moderate and conservative Koch followers.

While Dinkins had eventually paid substantive attention to his labor supporters, his administration's lack of political sensitivity deeply antagonized them. Black union leaders grumbled that Dinkins had handed over management to conservative Koch-supporters, some of whom black union leaders accused of racial bigotry.[10] In fact, Dinkins had sought to demonstrate that his administration would not be dominated by African Americans; Deputy Mayor Bill Lynch recalled he had been warned that appointing too many black commissioners would frighten the bond-rating agencies (Lynch 2000).

Shift in Political Strategy: Community Mobilization and Power

With powerful opposition from the municipal unions a crucial obstruction to his election chances, and with mounting criticism from community activists as well, Dinkins began to reposition himself back to the civic groups that had played a key role in his election. In his second (fiscal year 1992) budget, when Dinkins's political survival required that he do something significant for the city's minority poor, he dug in his heels over social services. But how to muster the political might to win a major political fight with the city council? Dinkins proposed $900 million in new taxes, most to come from increased property taxes, but Council Speaker Vallone and the

Real Estate Board (REB), a landlord lobbying group and major contributor to the council speaker's campaign, brought intense pressure for the council leaders to hold the line. Deputy Mayor Bill Lynch was assigned to a last-minute community-advocacy campaign to shore up the mayor's tax plan.

Dinkins's earlier decision to put budget politics in the hands of a former Koch commissioner had alienated key constituencies, for despite Steisel's budget experience and the bond-rating agencies' confidence in him, Steisel had no feel for black politics; he had been nurtured in a Koch administration that shared an outer-borough, moderate, white-middle-class political perspective. No single person in Dinkins's administration, including Dinkins himself, commanded the respect of both the city's investment community and his minority/labor primary base. Further, Dinkins had been not only outspent in the campaign to influence the council but politically outmaneuvered after his victory. A coalition of groups organized by *ALTERBUDGET,* a progressive community-oriented budget group supported by nonprofit service providers, now staged a demonstration at city hall in late May directed against the city council, and, in a last-minute political ploy, Dinkins announced a list of programs that would be cut if he lost his proposed tax increase, among them programs popular with the council itself, such as the Central Park Zoo, libraries, and museums. But the council outfoxed the mayor, restoring funding for the popular programs and threatening to cut the corporation council and city planning—both agencies that lack political constituencies but that the mayor needed in order to govern. The mayor was forced to come to terms (Seifman 1991); he not only lost but was publicly embarrassed. He would have a difficult time winning reelection with such a confrontational council in place, and Dinkins and Lynch, well aware of this, moved to reorganize their core labor-community coalition to defeat council incumbents who had opposed the mayor's budget priorities.

The Dinkins administration had little fiscal wiggle room to win over city council conservatives while satisfying the service needs of Dinkins's largely poor constituency. Dinkins could have cut services and appealed to moderate white voters and a narrow contingent of middle-class black voters to support him against a more conservative opposition candidate, but the consequence would have been a downplaying or demobilization of poor black communities of the sort chosen by black mayors in a number of other large cities. Political scientist Wilbur Rich found, in a study of black mayors in Newark, Detroit, and Gary, that:

Black mayors did not maintain or nurture effective political organizations. . . . None have devoted time building the infrastructure or creating the preconditions for the development of an effective organization. An effective organization for black mayors would include full-time representation at the precinct levels in city politics, ideological cohorts of leadership of supportive community organizations; mechanisms for mobilizing the electorate (e.g., campaign facilities and transportation); an extensive communication network capable of providing reliable and continual contact with members of the network; a queuing and training system for new recruits; and a reliable sanctioning and purging system. (Rich 1996, 145)

Unlike the mayors Rich studied in majority-black cities, Dinkins tried to establish an effective organization. He had reasons to doubt that he could generate strong support among the city's more conservative and moderate voters and, besides, he was, once again, likely to face the populist "law-and-order" conservative, Rudolph Giuliani, whom he had barely defeated in the 1989 race. Even more crucial, activist trade unions and alienated black nationalists were threatening to run a progressive candidate against him in the 1993 Democratic primary.

Lynch, on Dinkins's behalf, now opened an independent (all-black, excluding the council speaker) dialogue with black council members to come to an agreement on a united course of action. But when Council Speaker Peter Vallone heard about the meetings, he, in Lynch's words, "went berserk," and, to Lynch's amazement, black city council members themselves refused to initiate budget conversations with him unless Vallone himself was involved (Lynch 2000). Both Dinkins and Lynch had assumed that black city council members would collaborate with the city's first black mayor—for the benefit of their common constituents and for reasons of racial identity. Black council members opted instead to work within the limitations set down by the speaker. The entire council, including the six African American representatives, went along in reducing Dinkins's proposed property tax increases intended to pay for social services in poor communities that those same black and Latino council members represented. Dinkins's bewildered staff then discovered that Vallone had promised "lulus" (committee and other assignments that brought salary increases, in some cases very modest) to minority council members. Lynch said that black council members "were so tied to the perks . . . the leadership would give them, like committee chairs . . . [t]hey would never go against him. . . . They never were independent of the leadership. They went along [with] the traditional legislative body where all power resides in the leadership. And they even strengthened it [council uniformity] under Dinkins" (Lynch 2000). Black and Latino politicians were behaving as typical machine politicians. Dinkins and Lynch had expected them to put such politics aside. The minority politicians had actually lost both power and resources by their accommodation.

Bill Lynch said in an interview: "The assumption is that folks have the same kind of progressive vision that you have. That's a bad assumption. I think if you have a black or Latin candidate or a progressive white candidate who is sensitive to those issues, to the issues of [poor and minority] communities, then you can get their support. But, assuming that they [minority legislators] have the same vision that you have . . . is a *bad* assumption. [Lynch also said these minority legislators are in politics for employment.] These are jobs. They're not doing public service, *these are jobs*" (Lynch 2000). Why were black legislators not more progressive? "They don't have to do very much . . . they don't have to deliver very much," Lynch said. "They just [can't] piss anybody off, and they can get reelected forever. There's never any real challenge [in "safe" heavily majority-black districts] and as long as you don't anger anybody, make anybody *really* angry, then you don't have a problem. . . . These safe seats are not good for our [black] community."

Dinkins's staff considered the minority council members' reaction as incredibly self-centered, irresponsible, and even immoral, but these career-minded black politicians were not about to oppose their council leadership and face retaliation or retribution and possible electoral opposition. Black and Latino council members had sized up Dinkins as no threat to them, so many cut individual deals with the speaker, who was a threat to some and offered material rewards to others. Lynch concluded that Dinkins must help elect different members to the council. A possible opportunity to change the city council presented itself—a special council election required by charter-mandated redistricting—to expand the size of the city council from thirty-five to fifty-one seats with required redrawing of all political district lines. Dinkins released Lynch from his city hall duties to work with Local 1199 President Rivera on organizing a new "majority coalition" with trade unionists, elected officials, and community groups to promote candidates in the 1991 council elections. The coalition endorsed thirty-one candidates out of an expanded total of fifty-one seats, concentrating its efforts in eighteen districts; in the special election, they won five races, and came close in several, but seventeen of nineteen incumbents who faced challengers won. Since the majority coalition had made no bones about opposing black and Latino council members beholden to the council speaker, Vallone supported fourteen of the candidates targeted by the coalition (McKinley 1991b). Turnout was abysmal, less than 20 percent of registered voters citywide made it to the polls; in five races the winner had fewer than two thousand votes, in nine of thirty-eight Democratic primaries fewer than 170 votes separated winners from losers. In only half the races did the winner receive 50 percent of the vote (After the Voting; Highlights of the Primary 1991). The majority coalition raised only about one-fifth of the sum it had planned to pump into the races, most of it from Local 1199 (Sack 1991).

Lynch's candid assessment of black politics that he made in 2000—that black officials need to be held accountable and, therefore, should have no "safe" seats; that black politicians cannot be assumed to be progressive; and that, in certain situations, Latino and white representatives may be more progressive than black representatives—is still a highly controversial view. But his observations were based on more than thirty years of daily work with black elected officials, and must be taken seriously. Most minority members of the city council outside Manhattan had been elected through their county machines, and had long ago resigned themselves to a subservient role in city politics. Their longevity in office was based on failing to organize, or in the case of former insurgent nationalist officials from Brooklyn (see chapter 5), on demobilizing any organized poor people in their districts, and on soliciting from the council speaker or the mayor small favors for the most loyal in their districts. Most were so jaded about the potential of political mobilization that, during Jesse Jackson's two presidential campaigns, and, later, in Dinkins's mayoral campaign, unions had to pay legislators to gain permission to register and mobilize voters in their home districts, a practice common enough in New York City to warrant the term "safe passage" in political circles. "Safe passage" meant getting an assurance that local incumbent politicians would not sabotage the broader campaign. Getting safe passage usually required the nonlocal politician to avoid certain groups and to praise the local official in speeches and pamphlets. If the outside politician or campaign was known to have money, local officials were often known to demand "walking around money," ostensibly for local campaign mobilization. But, since only the most naive assumed these local officials would indeed mobilize voters, most donors must have expected their donations to go the local candidate's own political operation (Hudson).

For Lynch to campaign openly against black council incumbents, as he did on Dinkins's behalf, was, in electoral politics, a declaration of war. It was largely unsuccessful for two reasons other than its late start. One was the refusal of a still-angry and very powerful AFSCME leader (Stan Hill) to support the majority coalition, a serious defection since the combined forces of DC 37 and Local 1199 would have created a formidable opposition that would have commanded the attention of every minority member of the council.[11] The second reason for failure was the Dinkins administration's distraction from the election by an explosive racial "riot" in Crown Heights, Brooklyn, ignited when a caravan transporting a Jewish religious leader accidentally struck and killed a seven-year-old Guyanese boy. Three hours later, Yankel Rosenbaum, a Jewish rabbinical student, was fatally stabbed during a confrontation with a crowd of young blacks near the scene of the car accident. Three days of tense confrontations between roaming bands of black youth and the police followed with dozens of arrests (see chapter 7 for the narrative of the episode and its aftermath). This disturbance became the defining issue for the entire Dinkins mayoralty.

Promise and Pitfalls in Using Administrative Power to Organize the Black Community

Mayor David Dinkins, having failed to change the membership of the city council and hence demonstrate his commitment to improving the lives of the poor, sought instead to restructure delivery of government services through community programs like community health clinics and after-school programs in low-income black and Latino neighborhoods. In this effort he asked for the backing of black churches and public-housing tenant associations.

To Deputy Mayor Bill Lynch, housing development was a real opportunity to marry community development and voting increases in poor communities by directing housing development funds away from city's Department of Housing and Community Preservation's coterie of nonprofit technicians and toward community organizations committed to citizen participation and voter mobilization. That effort did succeed. In a *New York Times* feature article, "Neighborhood Report: Harlem; Reborn Brownstones: Phase I," Emily Bernstein wrote that, "Mayor Dinkins and his administration accelerated the housing boom, spending more than $200 million in central Harlem over four years, and brought more community groups into the process. Under Mr. Dinkins and his Housing Preservation and Development Commissioner, Felice L. Machetti, the city began a variety of new programs citywide that allowed community-based organizations to build more easily, either by developing projects themselves or by acting as community sponsor, with substantial say in the final product" (Bernstein 1993).

Community housing initiatives were highly political, with minority nonprofit organizations and contractors vying for control of local projects, the most politically contested being the Bradhurst Redevelopment Plan, a project to redevelop clusters of housing in northern Harlem (Washington 2000), an outgrowth during the Koch administration of the Harlem Urban Development Corporation (HUDC), a subsidiary of the state's major development agency, the Urban Development Corporation (UDC). The HUDC was controlled politically by Harlem's Congressman Charles Rangel but had been financed by the State with support from Democratic governors seeking black support. Its concept was visionary and potentially empowering for low-income Harlem residents, with UDC supplying millions of dollars per year for staff and technical assistance to HUDC, and with board appointments and decision-making power mostly left at the local (Harlem) level. But political loyalty often took precedence over community need and policy effectiveness at HUDC, and many community activists viewed HUDC as little more than a patronage mill. When, in 1986, a group of Harlem clergy demanded a greater role in developing low-income housing, HUDC gave them the Bradhurst Plan (Washington 2000). Sixty members of the clergy group formed a community development organization, Harlem Community Congregations, Inc., (HCCI):

> The clergy [meeting in Congressman Rangel's Harlem office] was looking at pictures [architectural renderings by HUDC of planned developments] on Rangel's wall and saying to each other, "this is a bunch of shit. When are they going to start building something?" Then [Rev.] Linton Gunn said, "Congressman, I don't want to be rude, but all this talking about the churches helping to support HUDC infrastructure wise, [and]

our community looks like shit. Infrastructure wise, you're talking about building condos on the Hudson [River], and building a marina. How many of you [in this room] have a yacht?" Wyatt T. Walker was the only one who raised his hand. . . . Rev. Gunn asked the Congressman to leave the room, and he closed the door. And he said, "Brothers," cause it was all brothers [no women were in the room] "We got a problem. There have been millions of dollars spent [by HUDC] and it hasn't built a damn thing. We have got to get our own independent entity." (Washington 2000)

The sixty-odd clergy had modeled their early efforts on Industrial Areas Foundation's (IAF) organizing in a similar way as Baltimore's BUILD, and drew on their own experience in civil rights organizing.[12] "We began to develop strategies for lay empowerment," said Preston Washington. "We used the power strategies against HUDC. The clergy has thirteen prayer rallies on every fourth Sunday for a year and one month. We got the churches to allow us to have these 'prayer meetings' but they were rallies. We raised a hundred thousand dollars in plate offerings, which is hard to do. We leveraged this for grants from religious organizations and in the course of the year we had a million dollars" (Washington 2000).

In response, the city's Department of Housing and Community Preservation (HCP) had told the ministers that no group independent of Harlem's elected officials had any hope of being supported. "I went to the Department of Housing Preservation and Development (HPD)," said HCCI's Executive Director, the late Rev. Preston Washington, "and they told me point blank, if you are trying to build something in Harlem it will never happen . . . because of 'politics.'" "They wouldn't say 'Charlie' [Rangel], they would just say 'the politics,' which is the same thing" (Washington 2000). Dinkins and Lynch now saw an effective way to enlist the churches in mobilizing voters for Dinkins's reelection, though the Bradhurst plan involved one of the most crime-ridden, drug-infested, and abandoned areas of the city; nearly two-thirds of the households had annual incomes of less than $10,000.

Canon Frederick B. Williams, chairman of the board of Harlem Churches for Community Improvement later told the *New York Times:* "Koch and his people were not unsupportive, they were supportive, just at a minimal level. They said, 'Here's a little crumb.' David Dinkins came in and said, 'I know you can serve a banquet'" (Bernstein 1993). HCCI Executive Director Preston Washington told *Newsday,* "Koch didn't really believe that we had the capacity as churches to pull off this massive plan and he took our plan and was going to give it to another developer, a white developer. We fought it tooth and nail" (Cottman 1991). Dinkins set aside $18.4 million in the capital budget for Bradhurst at the same time he was attempting to cut $3 billion (Cottman 1991; Shipp 1991).[13] E. R. Shipp, a reporter for the *New York Times,* wrote, "As envisioned, Bradhurst would represent social engineering on a scale never before tried by a municipal government. In fact, the mayor, who has made it a keystone of his administration, touts it as a beacon to other cities struggling to revitalize inner-city neighborhoods. . . . The project would create 2,200 new apartments and single-family homes and 300,000 square feet of commercial space over a decade" (Shipp 1991).

The mayor's office's blunt talk about helping to generate a "new generation of political and business leaders" (Shipp 1991) made incumbent Harlem politicians nervous; C. Virginia Fields, one of Harlem's city council representatives, expressed concern that Bradhurst could create a "ghetto within the ghetto" (Shipp 1991) and Lloyd Williams, president of the Uptown Chamber of Commerce, announced that "Preachers acting under the guise of God are fighting for their own agendas" (Shipp 1991). After a series of negotiations between HUDC and Harlem Churches for Community Improvement—with legal memos, charges and countercharges, but no progress on actual construction—construction finally began in spring 1992, nearly two and one-half years into the Dinkins administration, and the first housing units came on line only weeks before Dinkins reelection campaign (Bernstein 1993). Mediating black political conflict in Harlem had delayed construction for too long for Dinkins to be able to cite it as a testament to his accomplishments when it mattered most.

Dinkins supported another significant community development initiative, this one in central Brooklyn, Saratoga Square, a blighted area in Ocean Hill–Brownsville. Mayor Ed Koch had earlier outlined plans to build 858 units of housing and to renovate another 420 units. The local machine-affiliated African American city councilman, Enoch Williams, embraced the plan but his support for low-income housing did not last long; when Dinkins proposed shifting control of the project to community-based organizations and churches committed to community mobilization, Williams reversed course and opposed the plan for houses for his poorest constituents. Whereupon two local groups concerned with low-income housing now reached out to each other and, with community organizations, churches, and local businesses, formed the Twenty-First Century Partnership. Lynch saw an opportunity for generating new political leadership and mobilization in a depressed black community and one with a history of low voter turnout (Lynch 1999). Enoch Williams resisted, perhaps realizing that it might not be long before grateful residents in his district would repay others with votes against him (Lynch 2000).

The city's urban renewal plan for Saratoga Square planned project construction for January 1992 (City of New York Department of Housing Preservation and Development 1990) but the mayor's office became bogged down in long negotiations while trying to soften Williams's opposition. The majority coalition ran a candidate against Williams who nearly defeated him in the 1991 Democratic primary election, but, due in part to Williams's opposition, construction was delayed still further until the spring of 1994, after Dinkins had lost his reelection bid.

Lynch and Dinkins also had high hopes that their appointee to the Housing Authority Board, Laura Blackburne, would institute significant reforms in the governance of that Authority and inspire more of its six hundred thousand residents to vote. Blackburne had increased the number of alternative high schools run by the Authority for students failing public school and received death threats from drug dealers angered by her fight against drug trafficking (she was assigned around-the-clock police protection) (Patrick 1992). She had successfully lobbied for federal funds for affordable housing units from the George H. W. Bush administration ($76 million to build 837 new units) (McKim 1992), and was a powerful advocate of greater political participation by residents of public housing. To promote greater empathy for public housing residents, Blackburne had forced senior housing staff to conduct midnight walking tours of public housing developments in the most crime-ridden areas of the city and had conducted an internal New York City Housing Authority (NYCHA) democracy campaign, eliminating poll taxes charged to residents in some developments in elections for the resident leaders council. Lynch and others in the administration hoped that the Authority's more than six hundred thousand residents would reward Dinkins with their enthusiastic vote at the polls. Lynch himself regularly met with tenant groups who submitted lists of issues to discuss, and Lynch urged agency officials to attend.[14] But changing the large public-housing agency proved more difficult than the efforts to rechannel housing development funds to a new set of community organizations. In addition, Blackburne's tenure produced one of the major scandals to hit the Dinkins administration, erupting just months after the Crown Heights episode and affecting the 1993 election. Dinkins had appointed Blackburne as chairwoman of the Housing Authority Board in late 1990; she was forced to resign over charges of misappropriation of housing funds and, as a result, the emerging process of resident mobilization was disrupted. The immediate accusation was that Blackburne had used funds from a nonprofit foundation, "Friends of Public Housing," to pay for a trip to South Africa; the "Friends" in turn, received $9,000 from the Housing Authority, to which Blackburne said she added $11,000 from personal fund-raising efforts. Jack Kemp, secretary of the Department of Housing and Urban Development, promptly announced the department would conduct an investigation. The *Daily News* reported that Blackburne spent $121,000 for her office renovations, including $3,000 for a pink leather couch. Dinkins asked for her resignation despite an outpouring of support from black community leaders (Gonzalez 1992). Blackburne's case appears to have been more than a simple scandal. A *New York Times* story published after her resignation revealed the existence of an internal Housing Authority effort to see her removed:

> Behind the news reports of Ms. Blackburne's lavish spending was a deliberate and skillful plot to unseat her by disgruntled staff members at the Housing Authority, which she headed, and the Metropolitan Transportation Authority, whose board she served on. . . . Reporters who filed Freedom of Information Act requests for public documents detailing her expenses had lists of which reports and dates to ask for. Still-angry members of Ms. Blackburne's staff said last week that they had helped reporters in order to retaliate for times they had been publicly humiliated. "We vowed to get her back, and we did," said one staff member who, like the others, spoke on condition of anonymity. (Sims 1992)

Blackburne's persistent criticism of the Housing Authority manager's management style had caused a great deal of grumbling among some Authority senior civil-service staff with senior bureaucrats complaining that she seemed intent on replacing whites in senior positions with African Americans. She appointed an African American woman from the private sector, for example, as a budget and finance director.

Unlike most black mayors, Dinkins had, after several years of accommodationist strategies, attempted to mobilize black and Latino communities behind progressive city policies, to remove conservative black and Latino city council members who were blocking his initiatives, and to outmaneuver them in providing services, yet his civic organizing strategy failed. His effort to strengthen BUILD-like coalitions in Harlem and Brooklyn did not materialize in time to aid his reelection campaign.

But, despite the modest impact of Dinkins's civic democratization strategies, and his losing his fight to win a second term, his reasons for attempting such an expansion of democracy are important because if these reasons are thought to be sound, other political activists who are more willing to challenge the status quo and to risk everything may decide to do so, and, with better luck, may make the attempt with strategies more likely to succeed. Dinkins and his principal aide, Bill Lynch, later to be a key aide in Democrat Senator John Kerry's presidential race, moved away from assumptions of black racial unity and toward an agenda-based multiracial (Latino, white, and black) coalition. Such a broad civic coalition would have had the numbers to reelect Dinkins as an accountable and progressive mayor and his electoral prospects would have been more favorable than if he had moved in a more conservative direction to try to appease moderate and conservative white voters.

Whether the ends Dinkins and his allies sought or the means they employed were responsible for his rejection by the voters is a central question. Was the failure of his civic organizing strategy a consequence of lack of preparation—and inadequate orientation of leaders who could provide crucial support? Few leaders of the black community apparently understood what Dinkins was trying to do. Basil Paterson warned Dinkins to establish a think tank and civic roundtable in preparation for a mayoral race. Paterson, who had served as a deputy mayor under Mayor Koch, understood powerful city institutions and the people who run them not as abstract forces that inevitably corrupt or co-opt political insurgents (see critique by Cloward and Piven in the introduction). But he did not consider black insurgent control of these institutions as necessarily ensuring positive outcomes for blacks, as black nationalists do. Everything depended on how these institutions were used, and whether they were used for more progressive ends than previous administrations; effective use required new strategies and tactics on how to use power to create coalitions and to strengthen previously powerless core constituencies. Dinkins's administration slowly came to grips with Paterson's advice and began to implement creative strategies to empower civic organizations and to unite them into a citywide, interracial, labor-community coalition. Dinkins did face problems specific to his being black, problems that would have been less likely or less severe for a white progressive candidate. He had to avoid the suspicion that he, because he was black and trying to help blacks, was trying to shake up the city in a radical way that might cause a loss of investor confidence or racial turmoil and abandonment by close white allies. His natural prudence and delivery on public safety issues were no protection as they would have been for a white political leader. Once in office, Dinkins and his city hall were too busy responding to immediate crises to be able to form an effective civic coalition committed to his election and to counter effectively the power ramped against him. Race was, in many respects, the significant factor in the failure of the coalition to bring about a second term for New York City's first black mayor.

Race, Class, and Ideology in a New York Mayoral Election

7

Back in 1978, when Ed Koch was mayor of New York, a thirty-five-year-old businessman and community leader in Crown Heights, Brooklyn, named Arthur Miller had been "choked to death by a policemen trying to arrest him during a street confrontation." The police had been attempting to issue a summons to Miller's brother (Treaster 1978a). It was the fifth controversial killing in five years of a black man by police officers in Brooklyn (Raab 1978).[1] When the deputy medical examiner said he found, "no evidence of excessive, savage beating" (Treaster 1978b), many in the black community complained of a cover-up. Two days later, a sixteen-year-old black youth, Victor Rhodes, was beaten into a coma by a group of whites "in Hasidic garb" in a largely Hasidic populated block, also in Crown Heights, an assault *The New York Times* quoted the police as describing as one of a long string of incidents in which, "members of the Hasidic patrols, who refuse to join the precinct's patrol program, have become involved in altercations with black residents" (*New York Times* 1978). A black minister, Rev. Herbert Daughtry, with twenty church and civic organizations in tow, led a demonstration at city hall to protest Miller's death. It was evidence, Daughtry charged, of "the powerlessness of black people to affect their destinies. It's more than a single issue of the police. The larger issues are how the city's institutions control and manipulate black people—how when Mayor Koch gets ready to cut the budget, it's the people with the least political power who get their services cut more than anyone else" (Raab 1978). Daughtry vowed to form black patrols in Crown Heights to counter Hasidic patrols.

Mayor Koch had, in response, set up a blue-ribbon committee, "to study and recommend strategies to reduce racial, religious and ethnic tensions in the city" (Raab 1978). And the NAACP later called for a U.S. Justice Department investigation of the "denial of civil rights" (Kihss 1978). The state conference of the nineteen members of the Brooklyn and Long Island Baptist Pastors Union, representing 170 black churches, demanded "immediate suspension of all officers directly involved in the Miller assassination." Police Chief Robert J. McGuire responded that suspending the police officers would cause him to "lose credibility as Police Commissioner" (Kihss 1978). A year later, the U.S. Attorney for the Eastern District of New York found "insufficient evidence" that Miller's civil rights had been violated (Fried 1979).

In the early and mid-1980s, racial tensions in Crown Heights continued to escalate. Housing was at the center of the conflict, at a time when large, mostly West Indian, immigrant families were moving in. Hasidics and blacks were vying for scarce vacant (and affordable) living space (Liff 1987). With no civic dialogue to bridge the chasm, both key black and key Jewish politicians in Crown Heights exploited the explosive racial situation. A Clarence Norman Jr. pamphlet produced for his 1988 primary race for reelection to the state assembly and as District Leader, was cast almost entirely in terms of fighting the Hasidim. It read in part:

NORMAN THE FIGHTER: defeated Rabbi Rosenfeld for State Committeeman in 1986; thereby becoming the FIRST black State Committee man in the history of this district . . . he is under attack by persons who are controlled by and represent only the interests of 7% of our district.[2]

After Rabbi Rosenfeld lost the 1986 race, he charged: "Our opponents hate us, are blatantly anti-Semitic, and do not hesitate to disguise their anti-Semitism or hatred of the Jewish community of Crown Heights."[3]

When in 1989 David Dinkins was elected New York City's first black mayor, Brooklyn, and Crown Heights, in particular, was still a racial tinderbox between the deeply polarized Jewish and black communities. Many blacks considered the police an occupying force. In August 1991, the Reverend Al Sharpton, at the time a freelance racial agitator, urged parents of black children to boycott the first day of classes: "Either you're going to teach it [black history] straight, or you won't teach us at all. . . . If they want a war, come by my house. If they want to fight, then come see Sharpton" (Lowery 1991). Sharpton urged Jewish critics to "pin down" their yarmulkes and, "let's get it on." Two days after that a young Guyanese boy was struck by a car driven by a Hasidic man, and three hours later a Jewish rabbinical student (Yankel Rosenbaum) was stabbed by someone in a crowd of angry black youths. Within minutes of the stabbing, a sixteen-year-old black youth was arrested. The next morning, eight hundred police officers were in Crown Heights, and Mayor Dinkins dispatched his deputy mayor and key political aide, Bill Lynch, to meet with religious and neighborhood leaders. Local black community leaders walked the streets seeking to calm angry groups of young people. By the next day, two thousand police officers had been deployed. Mayor Dinkins went to the scene to plead with black youth for peace and then to a meeting with Hasidic leaders to plead the same. Dinkins had received Hasidic support in his own electoral campaign, but cries of "Traitor! Traitor!" now followed him as he visited the Hasidic neighborhood. That night eight police officers were injured by shotgun pellets. A *New York Post* editorial the next day praised the mayor for "physical courage and civic wisdom in speaking before an angry crowd." *Newsday* reported on the situation in an article entitled "On the Road to Peace Dinkins' Staff Finds Its Legwork Paying Off." Dinkins announced a six-point program to help the black and Hasidic communities in Crown Heights learn about each other. In a family exchange program black and Hasidic families met in each other's homes, block associations and civic associations drawn from both communities were organized, and black and Hasidic newspapers were urged to run columnists from the other community's papers. A speakers' bureau provided speakers, and an organization of religious leaders was created to discuss problems on an ongoing basis. Dinkins emerged from the week of disturbances with strong support from the media and a near audible sigh of relief from the city that a possible borough or citywide riot had been averted.

A little more than a year later in 1992, Lemrick Nelson, the young man who had been charged with the murder of the rabbinical student was acquitted by a jury though police said that he had confessed to the stabbing and had a bloody knife in his pocket, and despite a claim that the dying man had identified him as one of his attackers. The state's criminal justice coordinator, Richard Girgenti, had cited "inconsistencies in police testimony, deficiencies in implementing proper investigative procedures, and the influences of the non-evidentiary considerations" as undermining the prosecution's case (Girgenti 1993a), and some jurors said they thought the police had probably lied about the confession. After the acquittal nearly five thousand Hasidim gathered to demonstrate amid "demands for justice" (Girgenti 1993b). In the past year the Rosenbaum murder had been linked in much public discourse to the Holocaust. A rabbi, who eulogized Rosenbaum, said, "He came here to study the Holocaust, he ended up getting his own holocaust." Mayor Dinkins issued a $10,000 reward for information leading to the arrest and conviction of the killer but the angry community charged that Dinkins himself was motivated by anti-Semitism in his handling of the incident.[4] On the eve of Thanksgiving, in a speech entitled "Reason, Respect and Reconciliation in New York City," Dinkins apologized and agreed to demands for a federal and state investigation: "[T]he Police Department," he said, "did make tactical errors in judgment and deployment of police officers in the early hours of the disturbances which may have delayed a return to normalcy. I know and I accept that when a mistake is made that it is the mayor who is called to account."

The extraordinary state investigation that followed was to have major political consequences. Directed by the New York State Division of Criminal Justice Services, who lent it a high level of credibility, "A Report to the Governor on the Disturbances in Crown Heights" reported powerful "evidence" that Dinkins had improperly restrained the police. While it devoted only three sentences of its 334 pages to the 1978 police slaying of the black businessman, local black activists considered crucial background to the 1991 unrest (Girgenti 1993b, 36). It said, in part: "The Crown Heights disturbance represented the most extensive racial unrest in New York City in over twenty years. It differed from most disturbances throughout the turbulent 1960s, however, as the violence was directed at one segment of the population" (Girgenti 1993b, 9).[5] Whether the disturbance was directed only at the Hasidim or more broadly at the police was the subject of sharp disagreement between certain white and black politicians. According to Michael Kharfen, director of the city's Community Assistance Unit at the time, Rosenbaum was the only white civilian physically attacked during the week of disturbances, but a number of black youth and police officers had been injured as well (Kharfen 2000).

Political momentum rose against Dinkins's administration. The *City Sun*, a black newspaper, carried excerpts of resolutions adopted by The Metropolitan Council of the American Jewish Congress, which stated: "As the public leadership vacuum, for the most part, was filled by Sharptons, Carsons, Masons, Moores and Daughtrys and The *City Sun* and *Amsterdam News*, it is left to the Jewish community alone to assert that Black racism is no less racist than white racism. Only the Jewish community railed against the anti-Semitism of the hate mongers" (Daughtry 1991, 7). The American Jewish Congress highlighted a critical element of the crisis: a leadership vacuum in the black community. Dinkins could not mediate between groups in the city and simultaneously serve as the black community's spokesperson. Yet, many black politicians in Crown Heights who were in a position to play a role in the crisis had been nearly mute and invisible. Black leaders, including protest leaders, were out of touch with black youth in Crown Heights and unable to influence them or to represent their views. Many blacks resented Dinkins's handling of the conflict as too apologetic. Ironically, Dinkins had earlier received mostly praise from Jewish groups and from the mainstream press as well; it was the black community delivered stinging criticism. The Reverend Calvin Butts, prominent pastor of Adam Clayton Powell's Abyssinian Baptist Church in Harlem, told *Newsday:* "I am a supporter of the mayor, but what I do now is state the obvious that the mayor is not enjoying the respect or support of the grassroots in terms of the African-American community. That does not bode well for his [political] future." C. Vernon Mason, an activist black nationalist attorney, said Dinkins had been "politically and racially castrated. Mayor Koch never apologized for being Jewish. He embraced his ethnicity. Dinkins has been required not to be a person of African American descent to be in City Hall. And people all over the city are saying, 'we can't take it anymore.'"

Numerous African Americans, Rev. Butts said, had complained of brutality at the hands of the police during the Crown Heights crackdown; "People will say . . . that the mayor turned the police loose on us and it's further evidence he does not care." The Reverend Herbert Daughtry of the House of the Lord Church, emphasized the economic and political roots of the violence: "Everybody agreed that these youth, mostly of Caribbean background, were alienated, angry, and fearless. A statistic worth noting is that, at one point, of the 90 odd people arrested, 60 or so gave no place of employment. These young people didn't belong to anybody's anything. I have criticized Black leadership, myself included, for allowing such a large

segment of our community to be unattached. We did not start [the distur-
bance] and we could not stop it" (Daughtry 1991, 11).

Central Brooklyn's elected black (nationalist) leadership was not to be
seen during the crisis. Assemblyman Clarence Norman Jr., African American
head of the Brooklyn Democratic Party (the machine leader), once "NOR-
MAN THE FIGHTER," was jeered by a black crowd in Crown Heights.
Even militant protest leaders like Daughtry, who had led demonstration
after demonstration to draw attention to youth unemployment and police
abuse, lost their credibility among black youth. Mayor Dinkins, too, complained of "a failure of leadership at the grassroots level," and said that
youth did not have relationships with "elected officials or members of the
clergy" (Purdum 1991). He told the press he could only resolve the problems of Crown Heights with community partners.

Dinkins's dilemma raises a crucial question for a thesis of deep pluralism. There was no way to construct quick and meaningful exchanges
between blacks and Jews when there had been little effort to include unemployed youth in civic affairs or to consider their voices within a neighborhood civic structure. Dinkins wanted to play the role of peacemaker,
but found few civic organizations who would serve as allies in efforts to
reach alienated youth. Mayoral accountability, particularly for an equitable
urban agenda, required a more inclusive civic politics than Dinkins was
able to find or elicit.

After a 1993 *Amsterdam News* story quoting Republican mayoral candidate Rudolph Giuliani as saying, "It's inconceivable to me that what happened in Crown Heights would have happened if I were Mayor," its reporter wrote in response:

> Giuliani is absolutely correct. With Giuliani as Mayor, dozens of
> Blacks, Hasidics, and cops would have been taken to the morgue.
> Hundreds more would have suffered gunshot wounds, burns,
> and cuts. The commercial strips of Kingston Avenue, Utica Av-
> enue, and surrounding areas would probably have been de-
> stroyed, and scores of Hasidic homes would have been fire-
> bombed. . . . By any standards, to have no one killed during 3
> days of rioting was incredible and unprecedented. (Gumbs 1993)

The separate and distinct white and black narratives of Crown Heights were
captured in that exchange. But black activists were angry that Dinkins would
neither publicly defend his correct decisions nor explain to the public the

reasons for black youth anger at the police, and, especially, why it had seemed wise to him to restrict police action in Crown Heights that turbulent week. Dinkins, as the city's top official, had to be careful that his words would not be used to justify street violence or to attribute blame for street violence. Once again, he could not be the mayor and the voice of the black community at the same time. There was no strong black civic response to meet white conservative attacks on black youth and on Dinkins himself and no leadership to counter the criticism of the black community.

Conservative White Mobilization and Resurgent Black Nationalism

Racial conflict in the Crown Heights neighborhood of Brooklyn from 1978 to 1992 had divisive and wide consequences, creating a public sense that the city was spiraling out of control in the shadow of sinister racial forces. Three of the city's five boroughs—Brooklyn, Staten Island, and Queens were in a state of profound unease and movements for succession from New York City had started up in Staten Island and, to a lesser extent, also in a white section of the borough of Queens.

Several years earlier, in 1989, the U.S. Supreme Court had declared the city's Board of Estimate form of government unconstitutional on the ground that it gave equal power to populous Brooklyn and tiny Staten Island. Fifty-one percent of Brooklyn's residents were black and Latino and the borough had six times the population of Staten Island, an 85-percent-white borough with fewer than four hundred thousand people (Viterritti 1990). The charter reform approved by voters in 1989 that abolished the Board of Estimate in the wake of the Court's decision now allocated more power to the mayor and city council and hence less to the boroughs.

While the Queens succession movement fizzled out, Staten Island, angered by its diminished status in city politics, and the borough's Republican state senator, John Marchi, successfully initiated a drive to secede. In 1989, he urged the state legislature to allow a binding ballot referendum asking Staten Island voters simply, "Shall the borough of Staten Island separate from the City of New York to become the City of Staten Island?" State Democratic legislators assumed that the Republican-controlled Senate would pass the measure as a favor to Marchi but that it would die in the majority Democratic assembly (Sack 1993), but instead assembly Democrats passed the measure, some said after assurances that Governor Mario Cuomo would veto the measure. But Governor Cuomo was up for reelection himself and surprised the state legislature by supporting the succession legislation. In a subtle maneuver that undermined the ultimate power of the referendum legislation, Cuomo insisted on a provision that a final decision on secession would be made by the state legislature after a popular vote,[6] scheduled for November 1993, after his own 1990 reelection campaign and at the same time that Dinkins would be up for reelection as Mayor. Dinkins's advisors considered the referendum a threat to his reelection since it could be expected to increase white turnout on Staten Island, where, on the Republican ticket, Rudolph Giuliani had won close to 80 percent of the vote in the 1989 mayoral race.

According to Allen Capelli, a Democratic campaign consultant and strategist for the Staten Island succession effort, the succession movement gained steam after Dinkins's election, in part, because Staten Island activists thought the legislature might be more willing to approve succession under Dinkins than they had been under Koch (Duggan 1993). (Cappelli did not say *why* the activists perceived the legislature as anti-Dinkins.) Dinkins's office countered by citing a recent independent New York University policy school study, showing that a Staten Island secession would create a $200 million budget deficit for the borough and lead to tax increases there. Staten Island's Republican borough president, Guy Molinari, agreed with NYU's projections but a state commission appointed by the governor surprised many with a conclusion, in early 1993, that secession would, in fact, be economically viable. It said the island could provide roughly comparable services to its residents by increased efficiency and reductions in scope, and without sharp increases in taxes despite the fact that it paid about $170 million less in taxes than the amount the island received in New York City services (Lueck 1993). Some Dinkins supporters began to wonder aloud if Cuomo was deliberately undermining Dinkins; Dinkins's press secretary Leland Jones called the state's findings, "disingenuous, if not dishonest" (Lin 1993).

White voters, generally, are considered to be motivated more by tax and income issues than by "identity politics," but the threat of higher taxes deterred the Staten Island succession movement not at all. The *New York Times* reported, "So strong is the [secession] sentiment . . . that a study conducted by the New York City Charter Commission for Staten Island last year showed that 49 percent of those polled would accept a 25 percent increase in their taxes in exchange for their own city. A more recent, though less thorough, poll taken by the Staten Island Chamber of Commerce found 73 percent in favor, higher taxes and all" (Manegold 1993). The data suggested to some that the borough's white suburban-like identity mattered a great deal more to Staten Island residents than the fear of higher taxes.[7] Arguments about the degree to which the secession movement was racially motivated was itself a divisive issue.[8] Many blacks on the island insisted that the movement had racial undertones and worried what would happen if the island seceded. The Reverend Calvin Rice, the black minister of First Central Baptist Church, said, "We don't have a voice as it is, and I feel that if Staten Island separated from the rest of the city, we would have less of a voice. I would rather stay with the city and have access to the voices of millions of minorities" (Schnieder and Campanile 1993). Sam Roberts, a reporter for the *New York Times* wrote, "That the population is less racially diverse than the city's is not coincidental, either to the challenge by the other boroughs to the Board of Estimate or to the possibilities for ethnic cleansing that secession represents for some Staten Islanders" (Roberts 1993b). Dinkins had angered many in Staten Island when, early in his term, he opposed building a U.S. Navy port for warships on the island (citing his opposition to nuclear weapons) and also because of the city's plan to build a new jail there (Lin 1993). Although the city charter's fair share provision required that unwanted facilities such as jails, drug clinics, and homeless shelters be distributed evenly across city neighborhoods, many Staten Island officials were insisting that such facilities be located in neighborhoods where the criminals and homeless people themselves lived.[9]

The willingness of a dominant social group to listen to the narrative of oppressed groups may come to naught if an oppressed group's leaders are too intimidated to speak (Johnston 1994). An oppressed group may, in consequence, participate in its own marginalization (Archer [1988] 1992; Cohen 1999). This was the main line of black activist criticism of Dinkins, who, along with his principal political strategist, Bill Lynch, had been so frustrated by attempts to promote productive discussions on race through the New York media that they now simply avoided it (Lynch 1999). Dinkins himself studiously avoided mentioning race in connection with the secession movement. It was mayoral candidate Giuliani who brought up the subject, but he did so in a coded manner. By denying the existence of a racial motive behind the successionist movement, he could assert that it was Dinkins, not himself, who was motivated by race. "I know what it is that is making them [Staten Islanders] want to go," Giuliani said. "The Mayor tries to put it in racial terms and that makes things worse . . . [the problem is] [i]n the last few years we have seen the basic quality of the management of the city decline" (Manegold 1993). Dinkins said in response, "I have never, ever come even remotely close" to injecting race in the campaign. Giuliani's press secretary retorted that Dinkins had quoted an anti-successionist statement from Abraham Lincoln, "Comparing the Civil War South to Staten Island Clearly Raises Race." Lynch, trying to isolate Giuliani as a racial provocateur, told the press: "For the good of our city, we cannot allow the injection of race into this campaign for the sake of political expediency" (*Long Island Newsday* 1993). He asked the Partnership of Faith—a group of clergy watchdogs from across the city who assumed the role of ethical monitor over the mayoral campaign—to investigate Giuliani's campaign tactics and rhetoric. The secession referendum, on the same ballot as the mayoral election, was to stimulate an enormous white turnout in Staten Island that sealed Giuliani's victory as mayor over Dinkins.

In the meantime, problems with the police department, or more accurately, the white-led police union, the Police Benevolent Association (PBA), had continued to escalate. In 1991, the Association's president, Phil Caruso, caused a stir in the black community with a public tirade against welfare recipients. African American Queens Congressman Rev. Floyd Flake responded: "By calling welfare recipients 'lazy and shiftless,' the PBA has set the police against the [poor and minority] residents of the city in an 'us and them' situation" (Pryce 1991). The "us versus them" frame, with the "them" accompanied by barely concealed racial stereotypes, was repeatedly invoked by the Police Benevolent Association and by Giuliani.

In July 1992, a white police officer, Michael O'Keefe, shot and killed a young Dominican man, Jose Garcia, in Washington Heights (just north of Harlem), claiming that Garcia had tried to conceal a gun, and had been shot in a struggle. He said that he had found in Garcia's possession a fully loaded .38 caliber handgun. The Garcia family maintained, as did two eyewitnesses, that the officer had shot Garcia without provocation. Five days of rioting followed; protesters burned cars, threw bottles at police, and tossed garbage into the streets of Washington Heights. One protestor died and dozens were injured. Dinkins, Catholic Cardinal John O'Connor, and several city officials visited the Garcia family's home and Dinkins invited the family to Gracie Mansion, his official residence; he arranged for the city to pay for the funeral and to transport Garcia's body back to his hometown in the Dominican Republic. The cardinal lauded the mayor's decision: "Unless tempers cooled, more people could be badly hurt and even killed, including police, and extensive property damage could accrue, with major sustained losses by the poor" (Alexander 1992). But Giuliani, running for office on the Republican slate, fiercely criticized Dinkins for visiting the Garcia family and for paying for the funeral. In a letter to the *New York Times,* he accused Dinkins: "In his haste, the mayor didn't bother to check Mr. Garcia's record. When he declared, 'Justice we will have, but peace I beg you for,' he had already taken sides" (Giuliani 1992). Cardinal O'Connor replied in his weekly newspaper column: "Not once did I hear him [Dinkins] say or imply anything that I considered disloyal to the police force, and I say that as a man fiercely loyal to and grateful for the police force.... [I] refuse to back away from supporting his [Dinkins's] efforts in Washington Heights.... Who else has visited and revisited Washington Heights over and over again since the shooting?"[10]

Giuliani's point—that Dinkins's outreach to the bereaved family had lent implicit credibility to claims that Garcia had been wrongly shot by a police officer—was undeniable but defensible. Giuliani wrote in an "op-ed" article appearing in the *New York Times:* "The Mayor's calculated response to Jose Garcia's death led the public and the media to conclude that the shooting had been unjustified. Sensing political advantage, he rushed to Washington Heights, along with Manhattan Borough President Ruth Messinger, to pose with Mr. Garcia's relatives and perpetuate characterizations of Mr. Garcia as an innocent bodega worker victimized by the police. David Dinkins helped make Mr. Garcia a martyr" (*New York Times* 1992). Dinkins's self-defense was indirect and not persuasive. He did not say, for example, the city's police department had long given ghetto residents reason to distrust the police, nor did he explain that residents in poor communities, including those with criminal records, cannot be assumed to be less truthful than police officers. Deputy Mayor Fritz Alexander sent a letter to the editor of the *New York Times.* Written in abstract, highly legalistic language, it said, in part:

> A mayor is not an investigator, prosecutor, judge and jury. Determining the facts in encounters between the police and civilians that result when a civilian dies is the responsibility of the criminal justice system. The Mayor is responsible for insuring that threats to peace in the city are minimized, if not avoided

entirely. Joining these distinct functions—criminal justice and civic leadership—would jeopardize a fundamental tenet of democratic society. (*Amsterdam News* 1992)

On September 16, ten thousand off-duty police officers chanting "Dinkins must go," "No Justice, No Police" (a parody of Al Sharpton's slogan, "No Justice, No Peace), broke through barricades pushed up to the front doors of city hall. Nearly all the demonstrators were white, some carrying racially derogatory and obscene signs, one depicting Dinkins in a large Afro-style haircut and massive lips, another as a "washroom attendant." A black city council member from Brooklyn, Una Clarke, reported that demonstrators had yelled "nigger" at her and blocked her path to city hall. Inside city hall, rows of on-duty police stood behind metal gates while off-duty police protestors banged on the doors and windows, blocked the main entrance to city hall, and climbed onto first-floor window ledges. The mayor's staff, fearing that city hall would be overrun, issued instructions that black city employees, for their own safety, should avoid the area until the police demonstration was over.[11] The African American N.Y.P.D. Chief of Department (Acting Police Commissioner Raymond Kelly's chief of staff), David Scott, tried to restore order, in the words of *New York Times* reporter, Catherine Manegold, "an imposing black figure in a starched white command shirt with four gold stars"; when he "asked the crowd to disperse" he was "drowned out by cheers and obscured by a sea of white arms and fists" (Manegold 1992). Police demonstrators damaged eight cars in the parking lot outside city hall. Manegold said that Giuliani, "led the crowd in a rousing condemnation of Mayor Dinkins's treatment of police issues" (Manegold 1992), and another reporter said that Giuliani joined the demonstrators on the steps of city hall and shouted into a bullhorn: "Dinkins' appointment of a commission to investigate police disciplinary methods is an attempt by the Mayor to cover his 'political ass'" (Byron 1992).

After the demonstration, Acting Police Commissioner Raymond Kelly issued a report that off-duty officers had been drinking, had used racial slurs, and had clearly violated the law by shutting down the Brooklyn Bridge to obstruct traffic. Giuliani called that report another attempt by the Dinkins administration to scapegoat police officers for political gain, saying, "[t]he real question is, has the relatively minor occurrence of racial epithets, if they occurred at all, been made the major focus of this rally for political purposes?" (James 1992). Dinkins answered that Giuliani was "clearly, clearly an opportunist, he's seizing upon a fragile circumstance in our city for his own political gain" (McKinley 1992). Phil Caruso, head of the Police Benevolent Association, defended the rally with force and sarcasm:

> When a massive gathering of off-duty officers evokes intense feelings of rage, it should not be viewed as totally unreasonable or inexplicable. Nor should it be overlooked that when some of the demonstrators stormed up the steps of City Hall and onto the Brooklyn Bridge, it amounted to an emotional catharsis, a symbolic burst of fury that, in the final analysis, really injured no one. . . . It would appear that Mr. Dinkins, who can understand the root causes of the rioting that occurred in Crown Heights and Washington Heights and even Los Angeles, cannot come to grips with the reality of what is occurring in his own police department. (Caruso 1992)

Dinkins was caught between the hostile groups. Giuliani depicted Dinkins as anti-police; Dinkins denied it but, at the same time, he could not back down from his support for an all-civilian police review board without completely alienating his black community support.

On October 6, a *New York Times* editorial said: "The rally against an all-civilian police complaint review board was an unruly mess, with racial slurs, drinking and rowdy behavior on the part of some officers. Mr. Dinkins's anger was justifiable. But no mayor can afford a feud with his own police." The phrase, "no mayor can afford a feud with his own police," was a clear assertion of a white majority racial perspective and helps explain the chronic anger of blacks with the white press. Many blacks maintain that because the police are biased, they *must* be feuded with. Because the police are always formally accountable to the mayor, many blacks had expected Dinkins to rein in abusive police officers. If the mayor himself could not take on the police, what black person in the city could feel a sense of confidence or security, much less a sense that, as citizens, they could hold the N.Y.P.D. accountable? Many black leaders, including Dinkins, worried that statements, such as that of the *New York Times,* reflected the mood of whites across the city. Some were also concerned that if some police were now willing—in front of television cameras and in broad daylight—to slander the mayor with racial epithets in public, to shut down the Brooklyn Bridge illegally, and to assault blacks walking past city hall, then worse things might be in store for ordinary black city residents when no one was looking. If Dinkins was unwilling to "feud" with the police who stormed city hall, many black leaders saw little hope that blacks' rights would be respected by those same police. Dinkins, who understood these concerns, seemed visibly at great pains to restrain himself when he spoke before the city council in support of the Civilian Complaint Review Board: "Some of those [police officers] who were calling out 'nigger'. . . . Why would the people of our community have confidence that they have the capacity to handle a tense situation in a minority community?" (Roberts 1992).

To Giuliani, however, Dinkins's relationship with the police was "a defining issue, because it tells you a lot about someone's philosophy. . . . At some point people are going to say, how can you have a Mayor who has a Police Department where the overwhelming majority of officers think he's putting their lives at risk?" (Roberts 1992). Asked if the public believes "that Mr. Dinkins is soft on crime or that he was vilified by an unruly mob of white officers who hurled racial epithets," Giuliani answered that it largely depended on "the predisposition people have in the first place" (Roberts 1992). Giuliani had made a shrewd political calculation that voters would rely on their preexisting political attitudes to make sense of competing arguments between the two candidates. In invoking a white narrative he had the clear advantage: the police would enforce the law in a fair and professional manner. He was speaking to those who believed that the police are a "thin blue line" between them and the ghetto.[12] A corresponding black narrative, one Giuliani attributed to Dinkins in his "op-ed" in the *New York Times,* was that the law, the police, and the political structure were all seriously flawed and scathed by racial prejudice.[13]

"Go Black" or "Go White": A Mayor's Impossible Choice

Over a year later, despite a rebounding economy, fiscal stability, and crime rate declines over the latter half of Dinkins's mayoralty, a *New York Times/ WCBS-TV News* poll a month before the November 1993 election reported that 62 percent of New York City residents said life in the city had gotten worse over the previous four years; only 9 percent said it had improved. Sixty-five percent said they viewed the local economy as bad or very bad; 59 percent found the city less safe; 67 percent said race relations were poor;

and 70 percent said they were dissatisfied with the quality of public schools (Finder 1993b).

In a demonstration of strong racial polarization, black New Yorkers were more optimistic than white or Hispanic residents on nearly every measure in pre- and post-election polls.[14] Political scientist Jennifer Hochschild wrote that, "from 1988 to 1993 the proportion of African American New Yorkers who said race relations in their city were good increased from 19 percent to 34 percent. The corresponding proportion of white New Yorkers declined from 28 to 22 percent. In 1994, however, when Giuliani was mayor, a majority of whites who perceived any recent change thought New York's race relations had *improved* recently; a majority of blacks who perceived change thought relations had *worsened*" (Hochschild 1995, 60). Giuliani's message of a city in decline was apparently making more headway among whites, though not among blacks, than the administration's recitals of statistics on actual progress in the city. A number of black observers, including television star Bill Cosby, blamed the public mood on the mainstream media's harsh and persistent criticisms of Dinkins. Cosby said that the mainstream press spent four years harassing Dinkins, trying to "shoot him down" (Finder 1993a).

The Giuliani campaign had offered the public a Ronald Reagan-like vision of a return to good times and traditional values. A *New York Times* reporter covering the campaign wrote of Giuliani: "He listens to the anger and hopes and fears, and tells his audiences that only he can lead a radically changed city back to an idyllic time that may never have been, a time when his biggest worry playing on the streets of Flatbush was that he would be beaten up for wearing a Yankees uniform on Dodger turf" (Purdum 1993a). Stripped of innuendo, Giuliani's campaign rhetoric implied that Dinkins had appeased the black poor, excused the cultural dysfunction that caused their behavior, and, thereby, had fostered a disregard for public authority and wholesome social norms. Giuliani promised to improve the city's quality of life by restoring social order. One vivid symbol he constantly invoked was that of the unlicensed street peddlers and the "squeegee-men" who descended upon car drivers waiting in traffic at tunnels and other spots demanding money for a window wash. Giuliani pledged to rid the city of this pervasive nuisance though promising that his administration would be "color-blind," while holding to traditional moral norms, of hard work, self-reliance, and respect for the law.[15] The idea that white success in the United States was built upon such norms was itself, to the ears of many blacks, many the descendants of slaves, a strikingly partisan and distorted interpretation of history. But blacks were not the target audience for Giuliani's message; whites were.

Dinkins's reelection campaign was on the defensive from the start. Campaign aides worried about liberal white defections and low black turnout. Governor Cuomo's administration had landed a devastating blow on Dinkins's reelection prospects when it released its Crown Heights report, critical of the mayor's handling of the 1991 incident, fewer than five months before the election. The continuing debate about Crown Heights became a national Republican party issue. The month before the election, U.S. Senate Republican leader Robert Dole pressed President Bill Clinton's attorney general, Janet Reno, to decide quickly whether she would open a federal investigation of the Crown Heights rioting or "be accused of playing politics" (Douglass 1993). Although the State report made some questionable assumptions, the political damage was done as soon as the governor released the report in the heat of the reelection campaign. Governor Cuomo could distance himself from Dinkins;[16] he had also dramatically reversed his own earlier evaluation of Crown Heights. At the time he had articulated what I am calling the "black narrative" on Crown Heights: "We are failing in Crown Heights—the city, the state, and the nation, that's what it is. It's not a lot of young people all going crazy at once. It's the failure of this society. It's the anger and frustration at the indignity they feel has been thrust upon them" (*Long Island Newsday* 1991). But no evidence of such understanding surfaced in the State report. Herman Badillo and Susan Alter, two prominent New York City Democrats (Latino and Jewish), each with an ax to grind against Dinkins, decided to form a fusion ticket with Giuliani,[17] with Badillo running for city comptroller, and Alter for public advocate. An impression of citywide unity that transcended party and race now prevailed.

At the same time, press interviews with black ministers, politicians, and neighborhood leaders were suggesting widespread black disappointment in Dinkins. Few blacks were expected to support Giuliani, but Dinkins's campaign worried many supporters lest many blacks simply sit out the election (Hicks 1993); polls close to the election showed a virtual dead heat. The key issue, one about which Dinkins would not speak directly, was race. President Clinton, less restrained, caused a stir at a September 26 Manhattan fundraiser for Dinkins when he said the incumbent was in a tough race because "too many of us are still too unwilling to vote for people who are different than we are" (Mitchell 1993; Roberts 1993a).

Other observers had difficulty explaining Dinkins's flagging white liberal support. A writer for the *Los Angeles Times* wrote that had Los Angeles's Mayor Richard Riordan been able to hire four thousand additional cops in the middle of a severe budget shortage, as Dinkins had, "Riordan would probably consider it his greatest accomplishment" (Brownstein 1993). Instead, Dinkins was plagued with a public perception that he was soft on crime and anti-police. Dinkins chose not to debate Giuliani during the re-election campaign, apparently fearing misinterpretation by the media and the white public on racially polarizing issues Giuliani would be expected to introduce. From the standpoint of deepening pluralism—of openly airing and debating racial differences that were splitting the city apart—Dinkins's decision to avoid a public airing of the issue of race or to defend his administration in such an important public forum was a low point in the entire Dinkins administration. But his campaign thought he could not risk critique by the media in a setting in which blacks had little presence and no control (Lynch 2000).

Dinkins was effectively characterized as presiding over the degradation of traditional values and with demoralizing the city's police department. Because of the publicly timid and legalistic convoluted arguments put forward in his behalf by his representatives, it often seemed in the campaign as if Dinkins were an insecure insurgent and Giuliani a confident incumbent. Reporters almost uniformly attributed an impression of Dinkins as a wavering and weak leader (Purdum 1993b; 1993c). A *New York Times* editorial said, in an opinion equally harsh on Giuliani, that:

> We fully understand why some former Dinkins supporters have drifted to Mr. Giuliani and why others are wavering. His legal background appeals to those who believe Mr. Dinkins has been too relaxed about street crime and government corruption. . . . We know Mr. Dinkins's shortcomings. They have been recited so often as to have the feel of folklore. He is disengaged. He is more devoted to the costumes of office—his tuxedos and dashing tennis togs—than to the tasks of governing. . . . Whether the Mayor can achieve his potential as a healer depends heavily on whether he understands why this election is so close. The voters are warning him that they want to see more discipline and diligence from him, that they want not only care but a higher order of competence as well. (*New York Times* 1993)

Just as Dinkins's message of offering services for the poor and asking for police restraint irritated Giuliani's supporters so his pleas for blacks and Latinos to be patient with ghetto poverty and intransigent city bureaucracies struck many black activists as caving in to heartless white conservatism. Dinkins was between a political rock and a hard place. If he spoke out forcefully on racially polarizing issues, such as police brutality, he risked being regarded as intemperate and anti-white by a city's white voting majority. If he did not speak out, he risked being abandoned by his primary black support base on grounds of caving in to white prejudice. Dinkins, and his advisors, opted, in effect, to respond to the first risk by not speaking out, hoping his black base would remain loyal.

For six weeks in the summer leading up to the primary, Dinkins's campaign debated how to frame what Dinkins "stood for."[18] Campaign manager Lynch framed Dinkins's political options as "go white" or "go black." "Go black" meant espousing the black narrative and making strong response against Giuliani's racial rhetoric. Dinkins could thus draw free media to the intensified conflict and spread a forceful message in the black and Latino media—radio and newspapers. The money the campaign saved on high-cost media could be reserved for heavy field mobilization in minority neighborhoods. Reluctantly, after heavy lobbying from the campaign's media consultants, the campaign "went white," its strategy assuming that black voters would vote for Dinkins anyway out of fear of Giuliani.[19] The bulk of campaign resources was spent on expensive television media buys aimed at retaining white liberal support, portraying Dinkins as a racial moderate and Giuliani as a racial provocateur.

Dinkins's core coalition in his election of 1989 had included the black community, labor unions, Latinos, as well as white (mostly Jewish) liberals. In 1993, with the exception of Local 1199, the hospital workers' union, labor support for Dinkins was noticeably weaker. DC 37, the predominantly black city workers' union, maintained a lukewarm stance. The United Federation of Teachers remained neutral, but ran a series of television advertisements arguing that the mayor's refusal to further increase teachers' salaries was undermining the educational system. Latino support was *nearly* equal to the 1989 election, but the crucial decline in black turnout and the rising white vote for Giuliani in Staten Island were enough to swing the 1993 election to Giuliani (Mollenkopf 1997, 111). Dinkins lost by somewhat less than one hundred thousand votes out of more than 1.8 million cast.

Deputy Mayor Lynch said that Dinkins had lost primarily because, "Brooklyn [nationalist activists] didn't mobilize" (Lynch 1999). Black assemblymen in Central Brooklyn, for their part, complained that Dinkins had delivered for white liberals but not for *them*. A strong Brooklyn mobilization could have swung the tide for Dinkins, but the nationalist activists with the organizational capacity to mobilize in central Brooklyn took the position that Dinkins had not been a strong advocate for black community demands. Lynch has observed that they did not pull out the vote. There were some Jewish and Latino defections from Dinkins's camp, but they were not substantial, and despite press reports that Dinkins had lost support of liberal Jews, he won strong political and financial support from prominent liberal Jewish supporters in Manhattan (McKinley 1993). The campaign's "go white" strategy may have helped maintain their support, but liberals were a minority among whites in the city. In the end it was the inability of the Dinkins campaign to mobilize blacks and Latinos in sufficient numbers, and Giuliani's own heightened mobilization of middle-class whites (in Staten Island, especially) that determined the election. Dinkins's unwillingness to "go black" had undermined his appeal to black activists in Brooklyn and elsewhere.

From Black Nationalism to Multiracial Coalition Building

Rudolph Giuliani, mayor of New York City if only by a slim margin, once in office instituted what most local black activists and officials still consider a racially repressive regime. Because he had emphasized "unleashing" the police department, the police were now authorized to institute "zero-tolerance" policing that included aggressive "stop and frisk" methods to search for concealed weapons; in 1997–98 the police recorded stopping and searching 45,000 persons, two thirds of them black and Latino. (The state attorney general said that he believed hundreds of thousands more "stop and frisks" were conducted but were unrecorded by police [Perez-Pena 1999]). In 90 percent of the cases, no contraband (no drugs or guns) was found (Glasser 1999). It is no exaggeration to say that residents in poor black communities felt they were under a state of siege. The Civilian Complaint Review Board (CCRB) reported a 60 percent increase in complaints between 1992 and 1996, half of the increase coming from just nine of the city's total of seventy-six precincts, all of the nine predominantly black and Latino

(Greene 1999). In Giuliani's first term, civil rights claims against the police rose by 75 percent. In January 2001, in his second four-year term, the city was forced to pay $50 million to settle a civil rights suit on behalf of roughly fifty thousand people strip-searched after arrests for minor offenses during the crackdown on "quality-of-life" violations, such as playing music in subway stations (Weiser 2001). Giuliani said that black perceptions "that police officers are too brutal too often [is] a misperception." "It is driven by a very effective partisan political campaign, and the fact that there's been an obsessive concern in the media about it" (Barry 1999).

For six years, Giuliani refused to meet with New York's Council of Black Elected Democrats. The newly elected African American Manhattan Borough president, Virginia Fields, had to wait two years for a meeting. When, in 1997, Dinkins offered to join Giuliani in trying to calm racial tensions in the city with a private dinner of the Giuliani and Dinkins families, Giuliani refused (Skenazy 2003). With black community residents almost unanimously hostile to the Giuliani regime, and black civic leaders angered by having been snubbed, black nationalist activists saw a vacuum and lost little time in mobilizing black community protests against Giuliani and simultaneously isolating black politicians who were collaborating with the mayor.[20] Despite Giuliani's almost certain reelection in 1997, only three black politicians endorsed him: Congressmen Floyd Flake of Queens, Congressman. Ed Townes of Brooklyn, and Councilman Adam C. Powell IV (son of Harlem's former congressman), all three severely criticized in the black press and by other black officials for doing so. David Dinkins weighed in and attempted to convince Al Sharpton, whom he had shunned during his mayoralty, to run for Congress against Townes as a protest.

Municipal union leaders, too, appeared demoralized and frustrated by Giuliani's political popularity. The city's economy did strongly rebound by the mid-1990s in the midst of the Clinton-era economic boom, but Giuliani's conservative program of low taxes, diminished welfare spending, and school funding cuts left no room for significant increases in labor contracts. The head of DC 37, Stanley Hill, went the farthest among black union leaders in forging a relationship with the Mayor and acceded to wage freezes during that expansive city economic boom. When Giuliani nonetheless decided to employ women on welfare in jobs held by DC 37 members, it was a significant public embarrassment for Hill. During this time, DC 37 came under investigation for fraud while trying to win approval of an unpopular contract (pushed by city hall) during a 1996 contract ratification vote,[21] and the local union was put under receivership by the national union leadership (Greenhouse 2002).[22] Giuliani's $11 million campaign war chest, and his popularity with white voters generally, discouraged the unions from providing strong backing for any candidates for any office in the 1997 Democratic primary or for Democratic Manhattan Borough President Ruth Messinger's contest against Giuliani in the general election. Labor's failure to take a strong anti-Giuliani stand disappointed black nationalist activists, deepening their skepticism about the prospects for alliances with labor. So, too, black activists, and not only black nationalists alone, were deeply appalled at the lack of white liberal criticism of the Giuliani regime's repressive policing of black and Latino communities.

As a consequence of all of the disarray among blacks, a shift toward black nationalist-led mobilization was apparent in the 1997 mayoral primary. Ruth Messinger and Sal Albanese (a city councilman from Brooklyn), both white progressives, were contending for the Democratic nomination with the Reverend Al Sharpton, whose campaign attracted black community activists and the support of a few black elected officials, especially his protest against the notorious police assault on a Haitian immigrant, Abner Louima, who was brutally sodomized with a broomstick by a white police officer in a central Brooklyn police station. Although Sharpton raised less than $250,000 for his campaign, he stunned political pundits by winning 32 percent of the vote to Messinger's 40 percent, her total reached only after tabulation of absentee ballots. She barely avoided the nightmare scenario of having to face Sharpton in a runoff election (mandated if a leading candidate obtains less than 40 percent of the vote). Messinger won fewer white votes than Dinkins had in the 1989 primary. Giuliani, however, had won over many white liberals. Messinger had avoided airing her sharp differences with Sharpton for fear of splitting the city further along racial lines. Former Mayor Koch attributed her low support among whites to her unwillingness to pledge opposition to Sharpton should he win the primary. Koch seemed to suggest that Messinger needed to clarify which side she was on. Black activists had the same criticism of Messinger, but from the opposite direction, that she had courted the black vote, but attempted to moderate her leftist image by deemphasizing her strong past support for increases in anti-poverty spending and by downplaying her black endorsements. Black leaders complained that her campaign had made only token efforts to win black votes (Nagourney 1997). Messinger did not, for example, hold the customary press conference to announce the campaign endorsement of Congressman Charles Rangel, the most influential black official in the city.

Sharpton's near-victory in the Democratic primary established him as the city's foremost black figure and exposed the weakened status of black elected officials, most of whom settled for quiescent deal making with the city council and state assembly leaders. Sharpton's 126,799 votes, close to his 1994 total of 138,118 in his campaign for the U.S. Senate, was rooted in black nationalist-oriented support, all the more significant in the 1997 primary since only 18 percent of eligible voters turned out to vote. Sharpton beat Messinger in Harlem by 52 to 33 percent despite her endorsement by Harlem's leading elected officials. So, too, Sharpton won strong support in Congressman Flake's black middle-class district in Queens, gaining 33 percent of the total vote in Queens (a predominantly white borough) to Messinger's 36 percent. A reflection of the breadth of black middle-class alienation, Sharpton was supported by Roscoe Brown and Luther Gatling, the past president and current president, respectively, of One Hundred Black Men, a seventy-year-old elitist, by-invitation-only organization of successful upper-middle-class black men.

Black community protest against the Giuliani regime heightened after his reelection in 1997. In a demonstration supported by Local 1199, Sharpton and fifty thousand Haitians marched from Brooklyn to city hall to protest police brutality. In 1999, when four white police officers shot an unarmed African immigrant, Amadou Diallo, forty-one times in a doorway on suspicion of having a gun (he had no gun), his killing caused an uproar in the black community. More than twelve hundred mostly black activists were arrested in a protest at N.Y.P.D. headquarters against the Diallo shooting, among them all the leading Harlem politicians, prominent black business leaders, black union leaders, leading clergy, as well as, of course, black nationalist leaders. The center of black politics had moved toward street protest mobilization, with Sharpton at center stage, displacing the city's liberal black leadership and even former black militants like Al Vann of the Ocean Hill–Brownsville struggle (see chapter 5)—now viewed as ineffective and complacent.

But Sharpton was too narrow a black nationalist to win the electoral support of black-led labor unions or Latinos, and he did not move to translate his leadership of an emerging black movement into a multiracial coalition effort to win the 2001 mayoral election, but opted instead for a 2004 presidential campaign.

The person who did seek a multiracial coalition was not an African American. Bronx Borough President Fernando Ferrer, a Puerto Rican who had been a schoolteacher and a political centrist in previous campaigns. Ferrer was, in many ways, an unlikely candidate to head a protest-oriented political campaign. He had had a rocky relationship with Mayor Dinkins and, during the 1991 city council redistricting process, when Dinkins relinquished two probable black Harlem seats to increase prospects for Latino representation in the Bronx, Ferrer publicly accused him of undermining Puerto Ricans.[23] It was no surprise, therefore, that Dinkins chose to support instead in the 2000 primary his former consumer affairs commissioner, Mark Green, a white liberal. Ferrer made a run for mayor in the 1997 Democratic primary in a campaign decidedly centrist in style and substance, but his approach to politics was transformed in the 2001 mayoral campaign by the growth of the Latino vote. It was also transformed by an emerging protest movement in black politics, and by a common feeling of racial alienation among Dominican, Puerto Rican, and black labor and community activists, fostered by the Giuliani administration's treatment of black and Latino communities.[24] Ferrer reached out to Dinkins's political strategist Bill Lynch and to leaders of Local 1199 and they reached a common conclusion: if Ferrer could capture an overwhelming share of the Latino vote, he could win the primary if he had strong black support and no less than 15 to 20 percent of the white vote. Ferrer was also persuaded by Dinkins's, Messinger's, and Sharpton's experiences that energizing the black and Latino vote required giving voice to racial demands and perspectives. With a past reputation as a committed centrist, Ferrer now surprised many by promising to provide a clear ideological alternative to Giuliani's policies and moral vision. He seemed genuinely excited by the prospect of, in his words, "getting out of the box" of past political concern of not risking alienating moderate white voters.[25]

Ferrer was calling for recognizing instead of ignoring existing racial and class polarization. At a forum in early summer of 2001, Ferrer said that he was, "running my campaign on class."[26] He framed his campaign language in terms of the "Other New York," and declared that he was building "a movement." At a press conference he said, "[I am] as pleased as anyone that Wall Street's done so well, that Broadway is teeming with tourists, and Disneyland has come to Times Square. . . . I am happy that motorists can drive, truly unthreatened by squeegee guys, and fewer people are jaywalking," but, the "'other New York' has not enjoyed these benefits and has been left to grapple with a lack of housing for the middle class, deteriorating public schools, an often antagonistic police department and poor health-care policies." "There are those, even in this campaign for mayor, who," Ferrer said, "seem to say that they are satisfied with our progress, that we're headed in the right direction and need only make some minor changes and adjustments in course and speed. These candidates of continuity say, in effect, that they'll be Rudy-lite; or Rudy with a smile; or a kinder, gentler Rudy. But I think our challenge is much deeper" (Nagourney 2001b). A conservative *New York Post* columnist, Eric Fettmann, wrote that Ferrer wants to "lead a revolution of revenge for the 'have-nots against the 'haves'" (Fettmann 2001).

Ferrer's substantive statements and his call for black/Latino solidarity were, unexpected in the context, and so surprising that black elected officials and activists at first seemed uncertain whether he was serious. But his campaign made significant progress, his vision for a multiracial campaign for the "Other New York" won over powerful Democratic Congressman Charles Rangel, who overcame decades of bitter competition and conflict with Bronx Puerto Rican politicians to support him in these words:

> I really think my involvement has a lot to do with the fact that Freddie Ferrer did not build his campaign on bringing together a coalition of black leaders [in the traditional Harlem ethnic deal-making style]. . . . In other words, the coalition followed Freddie Ferrer. I have reached the inescapable conclusion that the African Americans' political involvement in the future of our city must include ties with Latinos. I thought about what happened in Los Angeles [the defeat of a progressive Latino mayoral candidate unable to win strong black support]. . . . I'm not saying that this group of blacks coming together for Freddie is going to eliminate . . . [black versus Latino] tension. . . . Our District Leaders, who were all over the lot [in the mayoral race], are excited now that we are together. . . . They are more excited about where they are now than with where they were heading. (Noel 2001)

Rangel's statement indicated a growing impulse among once demobilizing black politicians to reassess their own past political coalition strategies. Many black officials had already committed themselves to other candidates or declared themselves neutral in the 2001 mayoral race, but the logic and the momentum of a black-Latino-progressive white coalition gradually took hold. The emerging black-Latino camaraderie was heightened by black activist support for Puerto Rican activist protests over the U.S. Navy's bombing practice on Vieques, a small, inhabited island off the main coast of Puerto Rico. Sharpton, Roberto Ramirez (Democratic Bronx County boss), and Local 1199 President Dennis Rivera, among others who joined the protests, were sentenced to month-long jail terms. Immediately after his release, Sharpton endorsed Ferrer. The support black leaders lent to the Vieques struggle, like the support many Latino leaders provided to anti-police brutality protests led by Sharpton and other black activists, had publicly demonstrated a desire on both sides for an alliance and for continued reciprocation.

Ferrer was also competing for the left-of-center white vote with his opponent, Mark Green, a leading liberal and the most prominent and most vocal Giuliani critic in the city. Some of the white liberal press viewed Ferrer's "Other New York" rhetoric with skepticism. His mere mention of the word *race* seemed to make journalists forget his equally impassioned emphasis on class. The *New York Times's* deputy metropolitan editor, Joyce Purnick, wrote that Ferrer's supporters, like Rangel and Sharpton, gave the "Other New York" slogan "a them-and-us quality that, if uttered by an Irish or a Jewish supporter to political confreres, would be denounced by the very likes of Mr. Sharpton and Mr. Rangel. . . . In a city that is home to such an ethnic mash, there's a consensus that blatant ethnic and racial appeals debase politics" (Purnick 2001). Dinkins's earlier decision to eschew the "black narrative" during his own campaigns was precisely aimed at avoiding this kind of liberal-white press reaction to an emphasis on racial justice.

The Purnick piece was mistaken on two counts. There was no "consensus" on how to view race in the city, at least not among blacks, Latinos, and whites. Many blacks considered both Koch and Giuliani blatant racists. Perhaps more important, far from embodying an appeal to a single group, the Ferrer strategy was an effort to build the broadest possible multiracial, multiclass coalition, one the city had not seen since the LaGuardia era. Mainstream black politicians such as Congressman Rangel, and even, to some extent, Sharpton, were moving away from a narrow black-interest-group model of politics that pitted blacks against Latinos to endorse a more substantive and inclusive view of political alliance building across class and race.

Ferrer considered the "Other New York" framework more complex than race or class, taken as separate and categorical identities. In an editorial board interview at the *New York Times* Ferrer was asked, "You've defined your constituency as something you've called 'the other New York.' I wonder if you would talk more about what the other New York is: Who is 'the other New York'? And how is it defined? Is it defined geographically? By ethnic group? By income? By attitude?" Ferrer responded:

> In fact it's all of them. And I really appreciate the question. Because there are so many who would define "the other New York" only in terms of color. Or only in terms of class. Or only in terms of geography. In fact, it's a place where all of those things intersect. So, for example, people who find themselves unable to find a decent place to live in this city at a price they can afford live everywhere. They live in Woodside. They live on the West Side of Manhattan. They live in Throgs Neck. They live everywhere. One-point-one million children in the school system. They are not exclusively of one color, of one class. And too many of them of all colors and classes and boroughs and communities are trapped in schools that can't work, for a host of reasons. One out of four New Yorkers doesn't have health insurance, therefore no reliable access to regular health care, live everywhere. Most of them are working. They are largely white New Yorkers. (Interview 2001)

To Ferrer, racial, class, and geographic (spatial) inequalities were inherent in city policies, and their intersection made "the Other New York"—the poor and marginalized racial and ethnic minorities and working-class whites—extraordinarily vulnerable. Ferrer insisted on including poor whites, a difficult message to convey to the press, which tended to view New York as a city of opportunity that had no hardworking white poor. The strong momentum of Ferrer's campaign shocked the city's political establishment even more than Sharpton's mayoral campaign had in 1997. As Council Speaker Peter Vallone felt his own mayoral prospects fading in the last weeks of the campaign, he unleashed a furious attack on Ferrer's "Other New York" theme, and in a public debate, criticized Ferrer for "racially dividing the city" by suggesting that New York had become two cities under Mayor Giuliani (Nagourney 2001a). "Let us be really honest here," Ferrer countered, "the addressing of these issues is not meant to unite. It's really meant to inflame divisions in this city, to exploit them."

The heated exchange between Vallone and Ferrer was far overshadowed by the events of September 11, 2001, by tragic coincidence, primary-election day. With the city and the country consumed by shock and grief, New York's primary election was postponed for two weeks.

Ferrer won the primary with 35 percent of the vote: 52 percent of black voters and 72 percent of Hispanic voters, but only 7 percent of the white vote. A stunned Green finished second with 31 percent, and was forced into a runoff election. Most political observers had thought Ferrer's primary campaign against Green was a long shot, and so, apparently, had Green, since his primary campaign had ignored his opponents, allowing Hevesi and Vallone to attack each other in their attempt to win over white moderate Democratic voters. His own appeal to white moderates was more subtle, attempting to pick up moderate white support by highlighting his strong endorsement by Giuliani's former police commissioner, William Bratton. Green deeply alienated black and Latino voters by his strong embrace of Bratton, but seemed to assume that in light of years of painful racial battles against police excesses in the Giuliani regime, blacks would see no choice but Green against a Republican. His campaign concentrated, therefore, on winning the moderate white "swing" voters needed to defeat a Republican opponent in the general election. The strategy was considered savvy until Ferrer upset him in the primary. In the runoff campaign, Green lurched to the right, in a series of attacks on Ferrer similar to Giuliani's attacks on Messinger and Dinkins in the two most recent mayoral campaigns.

Three days into the runoff, Mayor Giuliani inserted himself directly into the campaign. Because of the shock and turmoil of the terrorist attacks, he declared, the mayoral contenders must accede to his demand for a several-month-term extension of his incumbency. Otherwise, he would urge the state legislature to lift the statutory two-term limit and to pass a statute permitting him to run for a full third term. Green, once the city's leading critic of Giuliani, promptly bowed to the mayor's demand. Ferrer strongly rejected it, with a surge of support in response to his stand that threw the Green campaign into a panic.[27] Eyeing a Wall Street constituency, Green denounced Ferrer's recommendation to allot ten million square feet of proposed new office space, in the wake of the World Trade Center loss, across the five boroughs—to stimulate economic development in the outer boroughs rather than to rebuild Wall Street. Two days before the election, the Green campaign aired a television advertisement that called Ferrer, "borderline irresponsible," and asked voters, "Can we afford to take a chance?" Green supporters passed out leaflets in moderate white neighborhoods of Brooklyn showing a *New York Post* cartoon of Ferrer kissing the rear-end of a bloated Al Sharpton and urging voters to turn out or "Al Sharpton will be our next mayor." Anonymous phone banks called white voters in these neighborhoods saying, "Stop Al Sharpton. Sharpton cannot be given the keys to City Hall" (Nagourney 2001c).

Green did win the runoff election but by a hair-thin margin: White voters supported him 84 to 16 percent, Latino voters chose Ferrer 84 to 16 percent, and black voters also went with Ferrer 71 to 29 percent. Serious allegations of election irregularities led to the filing of tens of thousands of affidavit ballots that threatened to land the election decision in court.[28] Ferrer's campaign raised heated charges about race-baiting in the Green campaign and Ferrer's supporters insisted that the Democratic Party investigate. Investigative reporters from the New York *Daily News* found that Green's campaign director of field mobilization, Jon Kest, and three other aides, Fran Miller, Ralph Perfetto, and Harry Schiffman participated in a meeting with a group of white Brooklyn Democratic elected officials where the topic of organizing a campaign to discredit Ferrer in Jewish neighborhoods, by linking him to Al Sharpton, was discussed (Cohler-Esses 2001).[29]

Ferrer chose not to contest the election in court, telling aides that the city did not need another Bush-Gore type vote recount debacle after the emotional stress of September 11. As a result, Ferrer's campaign expected Green to embrace Ferrer's offer of support and to begin serious negotiations about the shape of a Green mayoralty should he defeat the Republican nominee, billionaire Michael Bloomberg, in the general election. Instead, Green shocked Ferrer's supporters, responding that he did not need them to win the election (Gonzalez 2001). It was the final straw for Ferrer supporters. Democratic Party stalwarts Congressman Rangel, National Democratic Party Vice Chairman and Ferrer advisor Bill Lynch, and Local 1199 president Dennis Rivera held widely publicized friendly meetings with Bloomberg and firmly rejected appeals from national Democratic Party leaders to moderate their criticism of their party's candidate for the sake of party unity.

In the general election, Bloomberg, universally considered to be a long shot candidate, edged out Green who won about 75 percent of the black vote, a low figure for a Democrat. White voters supported Bloomberg over Green by 59 to 39 percent. Usually strongly Democratic Hispanic voters tilted the election to Bloomberg, splitting their votes evenly between Green and Bloomberg, 48 percent to 48 percent. While Bloomberg's upset victory was a significant blow for the Democrats, the party could no longer hide a deep racial split within its ranks. Ferrer's supporters, unrepentant about the outcome, continued to insist that the Democrats must address racist campaigning and the "silence" about the issue within their own tent (Perez-Pena 2001). Black and Latino activists had rallied behind the concept of "the Other New York" to express their marginalized status in the city, and they were sticking firmly with it. It was a sign that a deeper pluralist politics might yet emerge in New York City.

In the November 2003 issue of *Vanity Fair* magazine, in an interview with New York's new mayor, Michael Bloomberg, the mayor said that, "every single decision [in the Giuliani administration], everybody, every story, everything was always couched in terms of race" (Skenazy 2003). Bloomberg's observation was accurate, equally for Dinkins or Koch as it was for Giuliani. Racial conflict is the major political divide in New York, though the subject of race has generally been avoided and obscured by the myth of color blindness that contends that legitimate racial problems have been transcended.

Race and Ideological Polarization in New York

The concept of deep pluralism refers to the need for open political engagement on major differences that separate blacks and whites on issues of the basic fairness and legitimacy of economic, political, and social institutions. These differences extend, especially in American cities, into sharp conflicts over the causes of poverty and racial inequality, and over the solutions best able to meet these problems and prevent their reoccurrence. I argue that consensus politics, as highlighted in an implicit American Creed, has blurred the reality of racial conflict and has led to marginalization of minorities and suppression of dissenters. I see two principal dangers in the engagement of racial differences in America's cities: conservative white populism that treats poor blacks as the enemy of good communities and good values, and black withdrawal from engagement in politics and from efforts to overcome racially based conflicts with whites.

The way to deepen pluralism, I suggest, is to strengthen local capacity in black communities to hold leaders accountable to the demands of the community. Strengthening black civic capacity presses black political leaders to address substantive community problems that have persisted despite black empowerment and the deracialized technopolitics (see chapter 1) strategies of black mayors, yet it also provides mayors with greater political support when they do risk engaging in contentious racial issues. Holding leaders accountable requires an expansion in political participation far beyond that ordinarily encouraged by black political leaders—whether elected or not. Increasing political participation in black communities requires, too, a willingness to fight gender discrimination and also marginalization of the poor within black civic organizations and coalitions. An internal struggle to achieve greater openness and democracy within black communities, as well as efforts to establish common agendas to which leaders can be held accountable, can serve as a training ground and confidence-builder for blacks in efforts beyond the borders of the black community to coalesce with non-black groups who share similar substantive concerns—such as poor groups of whatever race. The problem of substantive political and economic reform is not so much fighting wealthy elites—whether majority or minority—as it is about developing the capacity of blacks and white non-elites to unite democratically without asserting the primacy and infallibility of their own perspectives.

New York's fragmented local political and administrative structures have made it difficult for black civic coalitions of the past half-century to emerge or to sustain themselves. Mutual distrust between black factions competing for resources or fighting to establish their own preferred political strategy as the norm for the group as a whole has disrupted unity efforts. David Dinkins's encounter as mayor of New York City with the city council, the state government, the investment community, and the mainstream press nearly caused him to sever his links with the broad transracial civic coalition that elected him. He appeared to believe that he could only sustain his position if he assuaged the fears in the white community—elite and populists. But his efforts to strengthen grass-roots black civic capacity in public housing developments and poor neighborhoods through community-church coalitions were either aborted (in the first case) or developed too slowly to assist him in governing or winning reelection. In dealing with racial polarization in the city, a pattern of black withdrawal from confrontation with whites over racial differences followed the failure of the majority coalition (the Dinkins administration's attempt to form a community-labor political coalition) and racial explosions in Crown Heights. The later alignment of Latinos with blacks around substantive race and class concerns and the growing Latino political strength in the city provided an impetus for black leaders to reevaluate defensive black nationalist and petty patronage politics toward a reinvigorated quest for a progressive multiracial coalition that would openly and strongly represent the views and interests of historically marginalized city residents. Such a new coalition—not yet firmly entrenched in any major city—suggests a model that may make it possible in the future to save some core American cities from racial turmoil, class conflict, flight of resources, and isolation of minorities in declining cities.

In New York, nearly half of the city's voters, mainly white working- and middle-class, did not vote for the black mayoral candidate, Dinkins, or for the later Puerto Rican candidate, Fernando Ferrer. Dinkins's supporters were viewed by his strongest opponents as real enemies: a threat to New York's progress and civic order. Ferrer's supporters were outmaneuvered, if barely, by a white liberal-led coalition. Dinkins was handicapped by events, by white racial opposition during the Crown Heights debacle. Still, a higher than usual degree of political awareness and organization was required for black civic organizations to play a major role in policy battles in the years in-between elections. Black civic organizations were too inexperienced and unprepared for media war to provide a counter-balancing force to Dinkins's hesitancy to confront the racial undertones of conservative counter-mobilization against him. Dinkins had been elected with a coalition of middle- and upper-class white liberals, some business support, and strong African American support. The composition of his original electoral coalition, and pressure from his black and Latino supporters, forced him to mediate strong tensions within his coalition. But, the civic organizations that elected him, including community-oriented black nationalists, were disconnected from unemployed, angry, and rebellious youth in the city and Dinkins worried that his own racial rhetoric might be blamed in the event of a riot and loosen his hold on the liberal white voters essential to his hopes for reelection. Dinkins's ability to relate to the black poor was additionally weakened by his inability to establish an alternative political coalition (e.g., a viable and independent grass-roots majority coalition that could take on and organize around divisive racial and class issues), if indeed, a grass-roots community-labor coalition can be a strong enough countervailing force against a powerful network of financial and other interests. His proclivity for confronting racial conflicts directly was limited; over time Dinkins increasingly avoided deep racial discourse. The emergence of a progressive alternative to the liberal white-black coalition that elected Dinkins and then fragmented was essentially a black and Latino alliance willing to directly confront race and class issues and to seek support from working-class whites. It was a continuation, with some new leadership, of Dinkins's original majority coalition approach. What its chances would be for future political leadership of New York City is yet to be seen.

Views about racial conflict reflect basic differences in political perspectives regarding institutions and systems of law. Although many in the United States would strongly reject a view of the country as a racial state, many blacks (as well as others) view urban ghettos as officially condoned and carefully policed structures of blacks containment—a living legacy of the plantations and shantytowns of the last centuries (Wacquant 1997). Race continues to operate politically as a powerful force, on the one hand, justifying programs that differentially benefit middle- and working-class whites, and, on the other, as diverting those whites from challenging the privileges of the wealthy. Whether race or class is a more fundamental category of social stratification is a chicken/egg dilemma not of particular concern here. Most important is that the two kinds of stratification reinforce each other. Racism weakens class identification among whites and blacks, but nonracial concepts of class oppression hide and reinforce racial oppression.

The racial dynamics of the 1990 New York City crime wave is illustrative of the kind of harsh racial confrontations that confronted the first black mayor there. Crime hysteria gripped whites across the city in the year of David Dinkins's election. A columnist for the *Daily News* observed, "Dinkins seems psychologically unprepared for this whirlwind" (Newfield 1990). But though homicide levels were high, there was no extreme spike in crime when the media barrage on crime began. There *had been* a spike in crime some months earlier but without public outcry. Whites were the group expressing fear, but blacks and Latinos in that year accounted for 95 percent of the city's murder victims.[30] Polls showed that *whites,* but not blacks, were losing confidence in Dinkins's management of the city. Dinkins interpreted the mood among whites as suspicion that as a black, he was not committed to protecting whites against black criminals. After he reacted angrily to poll results showing declining white support, Bill Lynch asked Lee Jones, a senior white press aide to the Mayor, "Are white people really afraid in this city?" Yes, Jones said, there was genuine fear and a crisis of confidence in Dinkins's commitment to public safety.[31] The crime scare disoriented Dinkins and his senior African American aides. Jack Newfield argued in his *Daily News* column that Dinkins had to calm fears with the same "take charge" approach that John Lindsay and Fiorello LaGuardia had displayed as mayor when each walked the streets of Harlem during riots—

LaGuardia in the 1930s and Lindsay in the 1960s. But Dinkins had been convinced by the success of the moderate tone of his mayoral campaign that being a solid "public interest manager"—racially moderate, fiscally responsible, effective in reducing the homicide rates—*was the way* to calm skeptical white audiences about his leadership ability. As it happened, actual crime statistics were not significant here: deep-seated and unanticipated racial fears were at work (Lynch 2000). "Good government" was no longer "good politics," that is, if the mayor was black. Dinkins had suggested that the real problem was that crime had gone beyond the borders of the minority community. In the veiled racial rhetoric of white conservatives, such as the *New York Post,* New York was a city divided between the "good" and the "bad," "friend" and "foe."

Racial tensions extended to the budget. Dinkins opted for a racially even-handed approach to setting spending priorities, but actually tipped the budget to assuage white fears—at a time of budget crisis he had hired more than five thousand extra police officers and cut services in poor minority communities (see chapter 6). Yet he argued that white Democrats on the city council were insensitive to urgent needs of poor black and Latino neighborhoods such as reducing infant mortality rates, providing drug treatment and child health programs, and giving a higher priority instead to streetlights and the Central Park Zoo. Public officials tended to frame tourist attractions like the zoo as an economic development priority while labeling child-development programs "handouts." To the *Washington Post,* and in an editorial, Dinkins's budget priorities showed a misplaced sense of values; it quoted one of Ed Koch's former deputy mayors as viewing the budget battle as reflecting a competition of class, "between a family earning between $25,000 and $40,000 and the person below the poverty line, that's what's causing such tensions" (Weymouth 1991). It quoted Dinkins's opponent, Council Speaker Vallone: "We're not simply going to redistribute the wealth [from the middle and working class to the poor]." Said the *Washington Post,* "Dinkins and his allies . . . have failed to grasp the essence of the American dream. When immigrants arrived at Ellis Island a century ago, their goal was to become Americans, part of the melting pot—to join the mainstream through hard work and by embracing a common ethos." It wasn't only a class dispute, despite the *Post,* and to many blacks Ellis Island was a code word for "white."

Dinkins, the son of a domestic and a barber, an ex-Marine who had supported himself with hard work through law school and without any affirmative action, found charges that he had "failed to grasp the essence of the American dream" maddening. He often gave the local press corps impromptu history lessons on the experience of blacks of his generation. Children could not be accused of not working hard, or of being undeserving, for needy *children*—minority or not—so Dinkins thought, would trump less vital "quality of life" demands in better-resourced communities. Dinkins turned out to be wrong. The council majority's view was racially motivated; it did, in fact, distinguish between poor minority children and working- and middle-class white children.

Dinkins's proposed property tax increases would, indeed, hurt large real estate interests and impose minimal increases on middle-class homeowners, but the drive to raise real estate taxes would, he said, protect hardworking low income families. He reminded audiences that "black people pay taxes too." But so much popular symbolism had shored up the Horatio Alger myth of the brave and self-reliant white lad that Dinkins would not counter it effectively. Finding a new morality tale for New York that included blacks and Latinos as virtuous and worthy, without alienating whites in the process, was a frustrating enterprise. Dinkins's initially liberal pluralist approach to governing had not prepared him for this struggle; he had trusted that if he gained support of white elites he could serve the city's most needy. The kind of fundamental friend/enemy political division that Dinkins faced is precisely one the liberal pluralism's basic consensus framework denies.

In New York City, the ideological division on race, articulated or internalized, was the ultimate source of debates about who symbolized the American Creed, and who did not. Much of neo-Marxist and elite theory maintains that economic elites rule America, through control of capital and financial resources, which foster ownership and control of media, domination of politicians via large campaign contributions, and through control of development projects. But, while these forces do indeed influence policy they are not decisive in racially contested policy debates. The disputes between Dinkins and Vallone over deployment of resources, and between blacks and non-elite whites more generally, were not mere disputes of class, nor were they tugs-of-war between the Mayor and economic elites. Class was important but Marxist and neo-Marxist theories that give priority or sole agency to class over race fail to recognize the power accrued by non-elites over the last two centuries by virtue of being white. The argument for "deep pluralism" is that deepening the content and vigor of debates between civic actors, with candor addressing the divides between and among them, holds the most potential for equitable restructuring of power relations in the United States. So, too, the power of elites has been exaggerated when non-elites comprise the vast majority of potential voters, such voters hold the electoral power in a democratic republic. In New York City, it has been the public ideological debates among *non*-elites that have set the essential boundaries of elite deal making and determined the outcome, not the other way around.

The Crown Heights disturbance of 1991 had erupted soon after Dinkins's deputy mayor Bill Lynch initiated efforts to establish a progressive multiracial coalition (the majority coalition). The most racially divisive event during Dinkins's administration, it was viewed through contrary racial lenses; most blacks tended to see Crown Heights as an outcome of unemployment, racial discrimination, and police brutality; white leaders saw it as evidence of rampant, especially black, criminality, or even as a blatant black anti-Semitism. Dinkins's refusal to take sides in inflammatory street conflict probably avoided a major racially based escalation of violence, and was, in my opinion, a prudent and wise mayoral role. But the white community did not grant him this and, instead, defined him, simply by virtue of his being black, as an adversary who could identify with blacks alone. It was a no-win situation, a trap that Dinkins could not escape from except by being white. One might say that had Dinkins been a different personality, of stronger stature in the city as a whole, a man of greater charisma, more of a risk taker, he could have transcended that perception of himself as being defined only by race. If so, that would mean black mayors must be of far greater strength than must white mayors, since seldom has New York or any other American city had such a mayor. And so this is another trap. Black mayors do not speak for blacks or whites during racial confrontations; other civic organizations and leaders must play this role and they did not in New York. The Crown Heights incident reflected an urgent need to discuss and respond to the grievances of unemployed black youth, grave police-community tensions, and, at the same time, manage competition between low-income Jews and blacks for limited city resources, while working through reciprocal charges of white racism and black anti-Semitism. Jews and blacks in Brooklyn shared many common concerns, including reducing high crime rates and protecting property values, but though Crown Heights community discussions were often rich in subtlety and, occasionally, the basis of fruitful discourse and group cooperation across racial and ethnic divides, more often politicians and community activists on both sides resorted to simplistic racial narratives based on popular stereotypes about crime, race, and poverty. One meta-narrative, the "black narrative" expressed widely by black leaders and black media, argued that the Crown Heights disturbance, like previous ones, was the consequence of an institutional racism that had bred persistent poverty and despair in poor black communities, thereby legitimating street protests. A liberal pluralist white meta-narrative, identified "law and order" as the absolute priority for political leadership in American cities and it rejected the view that social causes explain, and even justify, lawbreaking and public disorder.

Summing-Up: Race and Political Change in New York City

Local charter reform strengthened power in the hands of the mayor and encouraged black organizational factions and leaders to combine their energies, to reach out to previously marginalized black community activist organizations in a campaign to elect David Dinkins. The local political structure influenced the structure of black politics. Not the national or regional political economy or even the resources available to black civic organizations, but the subtle rivalries encouraged by the five-way division of power in the city dissuaded black activists from building broad citywide black political coalitions.

Because New York City's Board of Estimate government provided substantial power to county Democratic machines outside of Manhattan, Brooklyn-based black nationalists were compelled to contest powerful borough officials for power and resources before moving beyond to organize in other boroughs. In Queens and the Bronx, black activists were dominated by white-majority county machines and made little effort to mobilize blacks. Manhattan, alone among the city's boroughs, had no political machine, and, therefore, Harlem officials could and did broker leadership positions in coalition with liberal white Democrats as an alternative to black mobilization. The result, as the 1977 mayoral campaign of black Manhattan Borough President Percy Sutton illustrated, was to confront the powerful white-dominated machines of the other boroughs. Black elected officials in those other boroughs focused on their own survival and avoided citywide black mobilization efforts. After the protest politics and urban turmoil of the 1960s, New York's fragmented political structure hampered black coalition building up to the late 1980s. Separate political arenas in the boroughs of Manhattan reinforced political differences among black factions. But in 1989, when municipal government became centralized within the mayor's office, fragmented black organizations formed citywide electoral coalitions. It took an intra-black citywide coalition to give black civic organizations the power to elect, and then later, to challenge Dinkins, New York City's first black mayor.

Charter reform had not been pursued by black activists as a means of building black solidarity or democratizing black participation; both were unforeseen by-products of charter reform. The black citywide coalition came together in 1989, the same year the old political structure was eliminated. The New York City experience supports Iris Young's argument (see introduction) that deep political differences may be bridged not necessarily by rational deliberation between actors but are, instead, the outcome of political structures forcing people into mutual dependence. Growing confidence among black activists in their ability to *lead* multiracial coalitions played a role in creating New York's black coalition, but structural change of the governing process was the necessary if not sufficient force that brought black politicians and activists together across ideological and factional divides. A unified diverse and expanded black activist community and electorate led to the election of David Dinkins, and with it increased black civic power and political capacity. Black democratization (strengthening internal black pluralism) leads to greater black civic power and capacity.

Greater black civic power and capacity, in turn, leads to greater accountability from black elected officials around issues of substance. New York City's blacks united across ideology and faction, with an expanded coalition of white liberals, to seek to compel the mayor to be accountable to them not through ideology, organizational loyalty, or intra-black trust, but through a convergence of interests. Crucial to democratic accountability is a skeptical distance between black mayors and black constituents, a certain *lack* of trust and focus on interests, and it was precisely a lack of trust in Mayor Dinkins that propelled New York's black civic organizations, among them trade union leaders and black nationalists, to monitor the progress of city hall on issues of substance such as economic need, changes in police practices, and patronage, and, when they concluded that their interests were being violated, to challenge him. Distrust without power creates cynicism and withdrawal from the political process. By contrast, black activists' confidence in challenging Dinkins was supported by the success of black civic organizations in electing Dinkins mayor. Internal black democratization, the first condition for deepening pluralism, led to greater black civic power, and that, in turn, strengthened civic organizations' ability, and the confidence in that ability, to hold their elected representative accountable to them.

Seeking to avoid offending white liberals, Mayor Dinkins had refused to stand behind young black Crown Heights protesters in the crisis that resulted from a long history of black/Jewish (Hasidic) conflict. The deep divide in response between blacks and whites in the city to that crisis, and the mayor's movement toward the center of white opinion put him far to the right of the black mainstream public, whom white political leaders had labeled extremists.[32] Dinkins's unwillingness to defend the black mainstream in the Crown Heights debate undermined the confidence of the black activists in his leadership, and, in consequence, weakened his own ability to sustain popular black support for his regime. The mayor, for his part, was, in effect, trapped between his unwillingness to repress black demonstrators with police force, angering the white-dominated police union and Hasidic groups, stimulating white political mobilization for Dinkins's Republican mayoral opponent, Rudolph Giuliani, and the frustration of the black mainstream who saw him as disloyal to their interests. Making matters worse, the mainstream (white) media seldom interpreted black community demands empathetically, and so the white public, therefore, had little access to a positive portrayal of the black narrative.

Black criticism of Dinkins conflated his role as a mayor and as a multiracial coalition leader with that of black community advocate. He could not perform these conflicting multiple roles simultaneously. A key source of the problem was an underdeveloped black civic capacity and a related lack of internal black civic democracy. Dinkins had virtually begged for a civic partner in Crown Heights to organize and represent black youth. Neither the churches, elected borough leaders, or community organizations represented Crown Height's young people, and Dinkins believed that as a matter of political or practical feasibility, he himself could not organize and speak for community youth and at the same time mediate tensions between them, the police, and the Hasidic community. Black civic organizations, strong enough to force Dinkins to consider their criticisms, were not strong enough to undertake the ongoing tasks of community organizing, formulating policy demands, and articulating local grievances.

There was no appropriate civic organization for Dinkins to be accountable to in the circumstance; the system of electoral representation simply did not work. The concept of representation embraced by Dinkins's black critics had relied on the city election's selection of black community leadership to fulfill the civic obligations of office and had undervalued the importance of civic organization and representation whether political leaders are black or white. The social capital literature notes the inadequacy of elections to sustain democratic participation on the part of citizens, and therefore, to sustain democracy itself (see discussion in chapter 2). Black mayors and voters may understand black needs and viewpoints better than many or most nonblack mayors, but being in office is not a substitute for sustained black civic participation.

Stronger internal black democratization followed by increased civic power and the resulting experience of being able to hold black elected officials accountable for matters of substance can lead to greater black civic openness to multiracial coalition building around substantive issues. Coalition building, in turn, can lead to changes in policies and structures that promote black community progress. Progress in bringing about changed policies and structures leads to greater internal democratization and racial deconstruction. The process becomes a virtuous cycle. This is the theory of how deep pluralism comes about. The examination of black mayors in large American cities provides considerable evidence to support such a theory. So, for example, in Chicago, years of black Democratic internal coalition building around a concrete community agenda led to increased black political capacity, to a clear understanding of what the community wanted from political partners and politicians, and to increased confidence in multiracial coalition building. The multiracial coalition's efforts led to the election of Harold Washington, who used the power of government to reward the movement and to encourage continued organizing and coalition building. Describing reasons for the Harold Washington administration's progressivism across black factions and interracial divisions, the black activist-scholar Doug Gills wrote:

> There was planning by a conscious leadership element. They had gained experience in successful coalition building and positioned themselves at critical vantage points on the political landscape that represented Chicago in the 1980–1983 period. The willingness to network, reach out, and develop common agendas and resistance efforts was a positive contribution of these early, fragile coalition efforts. They survived because the local agenda was

respected and the membership was tolerant of divergence from the generally accepted principles guiding local practices and because serious attempts were made to work out differences in healthy internal debate. (Gills 1991, 52)

In New York black democratization was far from complete, some segments of the black community were not represented in black civic organizations. Still, the overall direction of New York's black politics in the 1980s was toward greater democratization, more participation, and power building. Greater participation and power increased blacks capacity and confidence in leading multiracial political coalitions. The success of black activists in expanding black political mobilization during the Jesse Jackson campaign in 1984 led to a broadening of outreach efforts in the 1988 Jackson campaign. The multiracial campaign's ability in 1988 to defeat Mayor Ed Koch's favored presidential candidate in favor of the controversial black candidate made even dedicated black nationalists more willing to coalesce with whites. Grass-roots black political participation had boosted black activists' political efficacy and their confidence in their capacity to defend blacks' interests in coalitions with white organizations. Strong black civic participation had created conditions conducive to building a certain level of interracial trust, as seen in the 2001 black-Latino coalition in the Ferrer campaign, despite the fact that black civic organizations were initially separatist and altogether lacking racial trust.

Under grass-roots pressure from black groups, and in the face of a largely hostile white electorate, the Dinkins administration was compelled to pursue substantive changes in city policy. Black city council members' unwillingness to provide support for Mayor Dinkins's progressive tax and social spending proposals, because of their patron-client relationship to the council speaker, exposed the limits of black solidarity and of broader interracial support for black community demands. City hall's efforts to raise taxes to fund social-service programs for the poor and to rein in the police department polarized the city more deeply, though not along strictly racial lines. During budget negotiations with the city council, for example, all the black council members aligned themselves with the conservative and white council speaker to maintain conservative city policies, while a few Latino and white council members and activist organizations strongly supported progressive change. Dinkins's political strategists, and many black activists supporting Dinkins, reconsidered their view that intra-black coalitions would necessarily provide more support to substantive black community aspirations than multiracial coalitions—another example of the deepening pluralism process. In the process of deepening pluralism, Dinkins's political staff and black activists moved aggressively to pursue coalition strategies with Latinos and poor whites in order to make substantive improvements in the lives of their constituents; they attempted to use the power of the mayor's office to strengthen community organizing in poor neighborhoods (of all races) and in public housing and to weld a multiracial movement together in the majority coalition.

David Dinkins lost his campaign for reelection as New York City's mayor. The goals of his one administration, despite some successes in housing, after-school programs, and community health clinics, were, for the most part, not fulfilled in making substantive improvements in the lives of the poor. Deepening pluralism among blacks alone does not necessarily lead to politically successful interracial coalitions, or to realization of blacks' aspirations. The political disposition of black activists is not the only important variable in building effective interracial coalitions, the disposition of other group activists—majority and minority—is equally important.

From widespread calls for a police crackdown on protesting youth in Brooklyn's Crown Heights, to a movement for Staten Island succession from New York City, to a racially infused police riot at city hall, considerable white racial hostility was directed toward the city's black mayor. It frustrated building a progressive multiracial political coalition (the majority coalition) as well as the implementing of the mayor's reform proposals. New York's white city council leader mobilized substantial white opposition to even moderate increases in property taxes to pay for social programs for poor (mainly black and Latino) children. The council leader argued that social-welfare programs redistribute wealth from hard-working people to the undeserving poor, and hence that such programs violated the wholesome American value of just reward for honest effort. Around such invocations of the American Creed Mayor Dinkins encountered some of his greatest challenges with interracial communication during conflicts over spending programs. The American Creed was employed to silence racial claims for justice and to present misleading explanations for blacks' relative poverty and need (see chapter 6). Joshua Cohen and Joel Rogers make a similar point when they point out that for some subordinated groups, "their particular interests may not be well understood or included within conventional understandings of the common good" (Cohen and Rogers 2003, 246). Many whites viewed federal housing subsidies and subsidized transportation and utility services to suburbs that had been provided to whites over the decades and not to blacks, as "race neutral" rewards for a deserving middle class rather than historic racial preferences (Roediger 2002, 61).

Strong white voter support for a Republican mayor (and a conservative by New York City standards), Rudolph Giuliani, elected in 1993 to replace David Dinkins, did not bode well for the formation of multiracial coalitions. Angry protest-oriented black nationalists such as Al Sharpton surged in popularity in the black community. Black support for liberal-oriented coalitions, such as the 1997 mayoral campaign of Ruth Messinger, a white left Democrat, was extremely weak. Black political withdrawal helped Giuliani win two mayoral elections and to consolidate policies—such as harsh police tactics in black and Latino communities—that New York's first black mayor had been committed to change.

In 2001, a black-Latino political alliance committed to the campaign of a Puerto Rican, Fernando Ferrer, took the city by surprise, particularly in light of the long history of black-Latino political conflict in the Bronx (see chapter 5). The possibility of forging a core alliance between blacks and Latinos around substantive issues of mutual concern (in essence, a colored-class coalition) was a key factor. Such an alliance seemed a promising path for advancing Latino voter power in the city. Further, the potential of a black-Latino alliance—strengthened by a fast-growing Latino population—excited black activists and many black politicians as well. Ferrer rapidly built a solid base of black support from former Dinkins cadre (such as Bill Lynch, labor leader Gerry Hudson, and Congressman Charles Rangel) who had advocated the rebuilding of the majority coalition Dinkins had attempted to establish in 1991. The shift from an ethnic-bartering approach to politics to a multiracial coalition focused on results and to a coalition that did not back down from racial and class conflict is strong evidence of a new orientation in New York's black activists' politics. It is a world apart from the infighting and competition for individual political seats that characterized black-Puerto Rican politics of the past.

The process of deepening pluralism does not ensure winning elections. Ferrer narrowly lost the Democratic nomination in 2001. However, the process seemed to have considerable electoral potential for the future. Black activists' encouragement of Ferrer's deep pluralist approach had a demonstrable logic as well as a practical appeal. The logic was that: (a) mobilization of the Latino and black poor (expansion of the electorate through internal democratization) would provide a powerful bloc of votes that might/could win a citywide election; (b) maintaining a substantive focus (being accountable to the needs of their constituents) would provide incentives that could sustain black and Latino participation; and (c) a substantive focus and bent toward airing the voices of marginalized New Yorkers from all races and parts of the city had the potential to attract poor whites and white progressives and hence form a majority. Ferrer himself called his approach a "movement" approach to electoral politics, and likened it to the civil rights movement. By 2001 the approach had even more appeal—blacks and Latinos had become a majority of the New York City's population. A strong coalition might win election with the support of the city's poor and progressive white voters. Ferrer told his supporters, on the night of his defeat in the runoff election with Mark Green, "You opened a door that will never be closed" (Saltonstall 2001).

Conclusion

From Conflict

to Transformation

Black mayors, like other big-city mayors, are confronted with revenue short-falls needed to improve schools, deliver social and health services, and maintain and develop infrastructure. Part of their fiscal problems stem from reductions in federal aid to cities over the last two decades; another part comes from the fiscal isolation of wealthy suburbs from the urban poor and inner-city problems. Big-city fiscal problems are traceable, above all, to the political isolation of the inner-city poor in the larger body politic. Because the suburbs are mostly populated by whites and most big cities are predominantly black and Latino, overcoming the political isolation of big cities requires the formation of multiracial coalitions that span current city-suburban boundaries.

Nonetheless, black mayors cannot be counted upon to pursue such coalitions unless it is in their political self-interest to do so. Their political interests are influenced by local political factors such as whether black mayors actually need the black poor to win elections and whether the black poor are organized and focused enough to influence mayors' political orientation. These factors are shaped by the political and administrative structure of cities. Whether black mayors need the black poor to win elections, for example, depends largely on the racial composition of the city electorate, which is, in turn, politically determined; it should be remembered that cities have sometimes changed their municipal boundaries to alter their racial and class composition. The separation in racial composition between cities and suburbs has the double (ironic) benefit of protecting wealthy suburbs from urban fiscal problems and of making it easier for black mayors and other black officials to win citywide office. Maintaining the boundaries of majority-black cities, however, weakens the power of the black poor in local politics because it is easier for black mayors in such cities to win elections without them; the black poor are seldom a critical force in city elections with large black-majority populations such as Atlanta, Washington, D.C., or Detroit. Beyond political demography, the administrative structure of cities affects the political interest of mayors. Mayors of cities with a weak-mayor structure control little patronage (union contracts, contracts with non-profits, and direct agency hiring) that is "bread and butter" for maintaining black (and other) civic organizations; civic organizations focus their political attention on administrative bodies and politicians that control their budgets. Where administrative structures are fragmented and detached from mayoral control, so too are the civic organizations, thus making them harder to organize for mayoral elections. A third factor shaping the political interest of black mayors is the presence (or not) of strong municipal labor unions. Municipal labor unions, especially those in the service sector, are poor people's organizations. Though unions do not represent the poor as a whole and have an uneven presence in cities, they can exert strong pressure on black mayors particularly in strong-mayor cities and in racially contested cities (where the black population is neither overwhelming or negligible).

Different configurations of political demography, service-delivery systems, and unions create distinct incentives (or pressures) for black mayors to respond to the demands of black civic organizations. Once mayors encourage the black poor to participate in politics, they come under pressure to meet their substantive demands for jobs, health care, better housing, and quality schools. This, in turn, creates a political motive for black mayors to form and support coalitions among white progressives, poor whites, Latinos, and Asians in order to win critical policy changes in broader state and national politics. It is no accident that transformative black mayors supported such coalitions in Chicago, Baltimore, and New York; all three cities had strong-mayor systems, strong black civic organizations active in mayoral politics, and racially contested mayoral elections. However, the local structure of government rarely puts strong pressure on black mayors to mobilize the black poor and to engage in broad multiracial coalition building. In 2004, there were only five black mayors in racially contested big cities (with populations above 250,000)—in Memphis, Atlanta, Columbus, Ohio, Philadelphia, Newark, and Washington, D.C. The latter three cities are outside the South, where unionization of city workers is more prevalent. None were in the highly reformed Southwest. It is noteworthy, however, that Newark, Atlanta, and Washington, D.C., were all formerly more heavily (more than 65 percent) populated by blacks. This raises the possibility that cities previously considered certain to elect black mayors may become racially contested in the near future.

For black mayors wanting to mobilize and then sustain low-income black political participation, there is the problem of finding ways to do it; and there is the problem of handling racial conflict aroused by blacks' challenge to public policies that many whites strongly support. Unionizing city employees is one way to strengthen low-income blacks' political capacity; distributing administrative resources and decision-making authority to local community organizations is another.[1] Both measures address the problem raised by Frances Fox Piven and Richard Cloward that the poor are susceptible to elite control because elites command resources needed to maintain large-membership organizations (see chapter 2). But redistribution of resources is not enough; the mere presence of unions or strong community organizations does not ensure that they will cooperate with one another. Political coalitions among black organizations are called for to assemble sufficient power to influence mayors and to redirect urban policies. The formation of intra-black coalitions may be thwarted by fragmented governmental administration structures, or by patterns of intra-black ideological and organizational conflict in otherwise favorably centralized strong-mayor cities. The concept of deep pluralism recognizes that strong differences and internal hierarchies exist within marginalized and oppressed groups; that open and democratic engagement of internal conflicts are needed to assemble power among the oppressed; and that overcoming internal oppression enables marginal groups to more effectively challenge broader external oppression against the group. This approach is pluralist because it recognizes differences and conflict among all groups; it is "deep" in that it tackles oppression, as Lani Guinier and Gerald Torres put it, from the "inside out": it begins with an internal challenge for an oppressed group to confront its own prejudices and exclusions to create strong group unity needed to effectively challenge broader oppressions.

Practicing internal democracy not only helps poor or oppressed groups assemble power needed to confront broader oppressions, it provides the kind of political skills needed for oppressed groups to attract allies. Appealing to people of varied backgrounds and beliefs around issues of common substance, holding leaders accountable to the community's agreed upon agenda, and leaving open for revision resolutions about the framing of the community's agenda and its representation are not only useful methods for internal group organizing, they are positive approaches to building ties with others outside a community.

A dilemma for interracial organizing, as between blacks and whites, is how to handle conflict endemic to political contact between groups holding fundamentally opposed notions of fairness and governmental legitimacy. When the challenging group (in this case blacks) not only welcomes allies and open discourse but also recognizes oppression within the dominant group and includes oppressed members of the dominant group in its own appeals for justice, the problem can be reduced. For example, Harold Washington's reaching out to working-class white ethnics (including traditional machine leaders) demonstrated an awareness of class oppression underlying their traditional hostility to blacks. This is not to say that blacks or other oppressed groups have a special obligation to be virtuous; greater awareness of others' oppression by whites or wealthy groups would be of immense value. Yet if what blacks demand of the majority white society is inclusion and whites' openness to a fundamental revision of their concepts of fairness and racially identity, blacks endorse hypocrisy when not practicing these values internally.

Deliberation theorists promoting open discourse based on democratic principles that remove impositions of power might agree with deep pluralism's argument for more open deliberation both within and between groups. But, I also argue that as a practical matter power cannot be removed from discourse, it can only be countered. Deep pluralism requires, therefore, that oppressed groups assemble and deploy power to counter their more powerful and less democratic opponents. Power is not only an evil used to subjugate, it can be a good used to cement alliances that limit and overcome oppression. With power, marginal groups can offer valuable support to potential allies that creates trust and emotional commitments needed to bridge political differences. This occurred when Latino activists supported black sit-ins and demonstrations against police brutality in the late 1990s in New York, and when black activists went to jail in support of

Puerto Rican protests against the use of Vieques, Puerto Rico, for bombing exercises. In these cases, the offer of political support to another group was not based on agreement with the ultimate goals of the other, narrowly conceived self-interest, or suspension of reason. It was the expression of a desire for a political relationship based on awareness of interdependence between the groups: I cannot realize many of my goals without their help, and I cannot gain their help without supporting many of their goals, therefore, supporting others is thus part of my interest. The deployment of power to support the struggles of other oppressed groups might allow blacks to form coalitions that can encircle and politically isolate wealthy suburban elites who seek to isolate themselves from others. Other groups can use the same strategy. Some labor unions, for instance, have supported legalization and political rights for immigrants, and these efforts have reportedly improved labor's reputation among immigrants. Yet supporting the causes of others as a strategy for building alliances, as opposed to, for example, seeking to identify overlaps of narrow self-interests, is rarely applied in politics.

Social capital theorists might agree that establishing trust enables political coalitions among oppressed groups. But, like political deliberation theorists who lack a means of establishing the absence of power condition that they maintain is necessary for deliberation to occur, social capital theorists lack a means of evolving trust where group antagonism prevails. Social capital theorists overlook two aspects of group conflict that are the focus of deep pluralism: even tight-knit groups have internal divides that provide opportunities for outsiders to support marginalized subgroups, and, by recognizing that all groups have internal oppressions it follows that a member of an oppressed group may be oppressing even weaker subgroups. From this perspective, a better understanding and a form of identity can be developed with one's own oppressors. The oppressor group may then be seen as having internal divisions that create opportunities for building alliances with its marginalized subgroups. In addition, knowing that I too may be an oppressor provides a strong reason for me to limit attacks on my own oppressor, namely, to avoid licensing, by example, unlimited attacks on me by groups I oppress. If it is acceptable for black men to violently attack or dehumanize whites who oppress blacks, for example, then why should noncitizen Latino immigrants treat black officials who deny them government benefits differently? In short, by recognizing internal oppressions, deep pluralism makes it possible to expand the scope of struggle against external oppression while at the same time limiting its excess by providing an understanding of my own and my oppressors shared human vulnerability to oppressing others. This is pluralism in the deepest sense.

Deepening Black Pluralism
and Counterarguments in Other Cities

The value of black civic organization and mobilization has been questioned by urban scholars who suggest that a strengthened focus on black community mobilization will simply leave black elites in control of city institutions that can neither provide adequate resources to address local needs nor sustain local civic participation. For example, political scientist Marion Orr writes that, "people concerned about social conditions might do better to focus on making government more responsive and on strengthening government institutions rather than focusing on associational life" (Orr 1999, 6). Orr points out that the decisions of local government officials, "help cause anomie and social disintegration" and that, "without adequate public and private financial resources, local organizations and associations are ill-suited to address many of the challenges facing inner-city communities" (Orr 1999, 7, 8).

In addition to his question on lack of resources to support participation and problem solving in inner cities, Orr doubts whether black mobilization can lead to a broader, interracial, cooperation. He writes that

> [a] major flaw in the social capital argument is that it does not consider the difficulty in transferring intergroup competition into intergroup social capital. To appreciate the importance of social capital, especially in many of America's central cities, it is necessary to consider it within the context of intergroup competition and the distrust it built up over years of racial divisions and black subordination. (Orr 1999, 10)

Orr emphasizes the difficulty of building racial intergroup cooperation in cities like Baltimore, where whites are insensitive to the city's Jim Crow racial history and where black political activists fear restoration of white control of local black-run institutions. For Orr, black social capital is thus a double-edged sword, helpful in mobilizing blacks for self-improvement but inhibiting ties with other groups needed by blacks to support their own interests. Orr asks, "whether the operation of such [civic] groups and associations . . . contributes to the building of a society in which cooperation among all its members for all sorts of purposes—not just within the groups themselves—is facilitated" (Orr 1999, 196).

Orr's first point is that black communities, and majority-black cities like Baltimore, lack resources for civic organizing and civic problem solving. Orr's is a practical empirical statement that requires analysis of individual cities. In New York City, blacks' accession to power within municipal labor unions provided strong black civic capacity for collaborating with black community organizations. Baltimore, as Orr noted, also has a labor-community coalition with significant growth potential. *Double Trouble's* account of David Dinkins's administration of New York City demonstrates that resources already allocated by local city governments, such as housing funds directed to nonprofits and housing authorities, can be made available to community coalitions and tenant groups that directly engage community residents in civic affairs and politics. Yet, in contrast, some weak-mayor reform cities, such as Oakland, have a number of capacious black civic organizations that neither focus on city politics nor coalesce with other black civic organizations citywide because their political focus is fragmented across numerous administrative and political structures.

The decisive issue here is not whether or not there is a significant lack of civic resources but whether there is political fragmentation. Cities such as Atlanta in the formerly Jim Crow South, lack strong labor unions, have weaker government support for black social service organizations, and may have greater immediate resource problems than in the North and the West. Yet, despite all of these problems, the South was the center of strong black civic mobilization in the 1950s and early 1960s. It demonstrated that resources for civic organizing do not pose an insurmountable obstacle to black civic organizing and political engagement. Political engagement is not the same thing as changing social conditions in cities, which leads to the second of Orr's arguments.

Orr's second point is that insular social capital, especially where race is involved, discourages intergroup solidarity at the same time that it encourages intragroup solidarity, a conflict between "bonding" and "bridging" social capital (see chapter 2). The deep pluralist response is that building insular social capital, or "bonding," reflects a yearning for consensus politics (also seen in communitarianism) that is essentially apolitical and even potentially politically dangerous. In struggles among diverse groups over the meaning of the American Dream, there is no fundamental consensus about the United States's political, economic, and social structure, or about its values. In this sense, neither the country nor the black community is "bonded," even though in the latter case some black nationalists portray black communities as resembling a natural relationship akin to the bond of a mother and child. Used in this manner, social capital arguments edge toward conservative conformist politics. The notion of an internally unified black community is an oppressive concept that ignores power plays and oppression of subgroups within black communities. That the vast majority of blacks may agree on the status of blacks relative to whites or on the racially oppressive nature of U.S. institutions does not imply agreement on other issues, or that blacks have special love for other blacks.

Increasing black political solidarity across the black community necessitates engagement in internal politics to bridge deep differences, just as building coalition with whites requires bridging deep differences. Bridging deep differences, and fighting over them, is, from the perspective of a truly pluralist democracy, the definition of politics. Pluralist democracy, to be deeply or fully pluralist, is not for the expression of common social bonds or for the rational ordering of citizen preferences—these things are better done in church or in computer labs, respectively—it is for peaceful discourse over conflictual subjects.

The assumption of the deep pluralist argument is that the political skills that civic actors of a common group learn in contentious politics are transferable to political engagement with other groups, that it is a training ground. If this is so, there is no logical contradiction between blacks organizing internal politics and blacks engaging in external politics with other groups. The more likely contradiction is between forms of nationalistic rhetoric asserting unified black interests and a real politics that asserts the right to differ. As noted earlier, a second key postulate of deep pluralism is that the power gained through democracy building within marginalized communities provides greater political power, confidence, and leverage when engaging in coalitions with other groups. Rather than creating a reluctance to participate with others, black civic power building does the opposite.

A question remains as to whether or why poor or oppressed whites may want to engage in deep politics with blacks even though they belong to a more politically powerful group by virtue of being white. The evidence presented in *Double Trouble* does not offer a definitive answer, but the logical implication drawn from intra-black political coalitions is that whites will engage in political deliberation with previously adversarial blacks when conflicts over substance (e.g., class, gender, or other conflicts) with fellow white Americans undermine their confidence in the myth of the American Creed, leading them to identify themselves as an oppressed subgroup, and to rethink their alliances.

Orr maintains that to make government more responsive to urban problems and more capable of fixing them is preferable to focusing on black associational life. The argument advanced here is that because racial polarization has deepened since the Great Society programs and race riots of the 1960s, the white majority has little political will to come to the aid of cities, or to strengthen the capacity of local governments to solve urban problems. Orr is right to state that black communities do not have the financial resources to solve urban problems on their own, and that it is unfair to ask them to do so. However, the question of how then to make government more responsive to urban problems or how to finance programs to strengthen local government remains. Perhaps the greatest resource at the disposal of urban African Americans is democracy. Black civic organizations have the freedom, and, collectively, the resources, to develop the capacity of black community residents to participate in politics and to greatly expand the range of black organizations involved in politics. While political participation does not necessarily change social conditions, political development can lead to the formation of principled coalitions of substance (and broader democratization) among poor and otherwise oppressed groups of all races to alter the majority's political will, or to create a new political majority that can force government to aid cities.

The view that increased group political mobilization will only sharpen racial divisions between groups reduces democratic practice and fosters a reliance on governmental elites to steer society; for minorities and the poor, it can lead to a form of class and racial paternalism. Without a strong associational life, who will hold government accountable to respond to the needs of marginalized groups? The study of black mayors makes an opposite argument: without strong pressure from civic associations, mayors will avoid grass-roots political participation, for black mayors either because they fear the white majority's backlash or because grass-roots black participation threatens their own political dominance or survival. And, in the absence of black grass-roots participation, a white majority will likely continue to ignore racial claims for fair treatment and equality of services and risk that racial conflict will deepen. It is not intense black participation but the lack of it that poses the greater danger to interracial civic cooperation and black progress and the progress of metropolitan areas across race loyalties.

Arguments for Regionalism

A growing body of scholarly literature and political activism suggests that concentrated urban poverty and racial inequality can be alleviated through enhanced and improved metropolitan area governance, or regionalism (Altshuler et al. 1999; Orfield 1998a; Orfield 1998b). Interest in building movements for regional government has several sources, one is "frustration with the results of community-oriented approaches that have dominated policy for three decades" (Weir 1998, 1), a second is continuing state and federal government failure to provide adequate funding for cities, with substantial poor black and Latino concentrations, while enabling the wealthy to retreat to privileged outer-suburban environments that perpetuate social and economic advantage (Dreier et al. 2001). A third source is civil rights advocates' frustration with whites' use of municipal fragmentation to isolate poor minorities and to avoid racial integration of schools and housing. The black poor are concentrated in inner cities and inner-ring suburbs with poor schools, inadequate access to jobs, and associated negative stereotypes. Some civil rights advocates label this "the new face of racial subordination" (Regional Justice: The Framework for Achieving Civil Rights Objectives 2001). A fourth is a dawning pragmatism about the suburban dominance of the electorate. The literal geographic separation between minority poor and white middle-class areas hampers the formation of political coalitions and election of members of Congress committed to policies that could reduce growing income inequality (Massey and Denton 1993; Dreier et al. 2001).

Place Matters by Peter Dreier, John Mollenkopf, and Todd Swanstrom, posits that the key to Democratic control of Congress is both increasing political turnout in central cities and defeating Republican strategies aimed at splitting off suburban from central-city voters. Because a majority of voters now live in the suburbs and because central-city turnout is comparatively low, the battleground for control of Congress and the presidency has shifted to the suburbs. The authors believe that President Clinton's political success revealed new political possibilities, because he, like the Republicans, "got the bulk of his votes in predominantly suburban congressional districts, winning 800,000 more votes than Bush in 1992 and extending his margin to 2.7 million over Dole in 1996." Their advice to the Democrats is, "Whatever the obstacles, only when the party creates synergies between central-city and inner-suburban constituencies will it be able to build a durable electoral majority" (Dreier et al. 2001, 238, 240).

Place Matters asserts that suburban voters are amenable to central-city coalitions because they share many of the same problems as central-city residents. The core policy prescription of *Place Matters* is that metropolitan coalition builders make "clear, effective substantive policy appeals to white, Catholic, blue-collar suburbanites, whose once strong familial attachment to progressive positions has weakened, by addressing their actual needs, which revolve around the reality that they are working harder but not gaining a higher standard of living or achieving a more family-friendly workplace." Regarding blacks and Latinos, they advise, "Communicate with and mobilize emerging black and Hispanic suburban populations with nonracial appeals that speak to the same kinds of needs [as those of white suburbanites above"] (Dreier et al. 2001, 246). The authors also favor shifting some heavily Democratic [minority] urban precincts—that contribute, they argue, to a lack of political competition and voter demobilization—into suburban congressional districts where the precincts could tip the balance of votes in many districts to the Democrats.

Though many regionalists recognize the practical need for black political support to win metropolitan governance reforms in key urban areas, they tend to ignore the importance of Orr's discussion of deep black distrust of whites in cities (and of deep white distrust of blacks), and thus they do not consider whether strengthening blacks' political power in coalitions is a prerequisite to winning strong black support for common programs. Framing and control of the coalition agenda is what is at issue: there is no doubt that some suburban electorates will form political coalitions with central-city residents, as long as the agenda is focused on the needs of suburban residents. But, when, from the outset, regionalism advocates exclude issues of urgent concern to racial minorities themselves—such as policing, racial profiling by real estate brokers, or school integration—in favor of "nonracial appeals that speak to the same kinds of needs [as those of white suburbanites]" they do nothing to dispel the worries about racial subordination held by black grass-roots activists.

There are also differences in black activists' political orientations across cities that regionalists typically ignore. For distrustful blacks, regionalist proposals such as moving strong Democratic-voting minority voting precincts into white suburban districts look less like a political opportunity to elect racially sympathetic members of Congress than a scheme to empower white liberal Democrats at blacks' expense. As political scientist Margaret Weir has written, there are numerous examples of relatively resource-rich "elastic" cities that have maintained concentrations of poor black areas. Large jurisdictions, "create the possibility for a larger public pie because they have a larger tax base but in themselves ensure nothing about whether there will be a generous public sector or how the pie will be distributed" (Weir 1998, 10). Fear of whites' reassertion of control led the Leadership Conference on Civil Rights to state in a 2001 report on regionalism that, "the voice of communities of color cannot be absorbed into a coalition that is unresponsive or deleterious to concerns over integration, maintaining the social fabric of communities, and political power dilution" (Leadership Conference on Civil Rights and the Institute on Race and Poverty 2001). Regionalism might gain greater support among black activists in cities like Oakland, California, rather than in more deeply racially polarized Atlanta or Baltimore because Oakland's local government is fragmented, as are its black organizations. Unlike in deeply racially divided cities such as Atlanta or Chicago, Oakland's low-income black communities would probably realize *increased* political mobilization capacity and policy benefits from a centralization of political authority and resource allocation at the county or larger regional level. A change to metro-government in Oakland could quickly lead to greater convergence among black-led unions (or radical nonblack local unions) and black community groups and to a corresponding rapid increase in black organizational capacity for political mobilization. Black activists in Oakland tend to have strong historical relationships of trust with liberal and radical white groups as well as with Asian and Latino activists. As noted in chapter 4, these relationships date back to the formative Black Panther/antiwar period of the 1960s and continue to influence black activists in Oakland into the millenium. There are solid historically grounded prospects for a strong multiracial, anti-racist, and multidimensional coalition in the Oakland region. Black activists in Oakland are much more likely to interpret regionalism as a political opportunity than are activists in cities like Baltimore or Atlanta with strong Jim Crow legacies.

In cities like Oakland, prospects for multiracial regional coalitions are good, but, more typically, regionalists confront deep racial polarization and nonracial appeals fall on deaf ears among white and blacks. The assertion that, "there is an important class dimension to the problem [place-based inequality] that transcends its important racial aspect" (Dreier et al. 2001, 204), is a strongly ideological claim that has not yet been borne out in actual urban political coalitions. Efforts to organize class-based coalitions, such as Antonio Villaraigosa's 2001 mayoral campaign, did not transcend race but faltered on it. The problem with the binary of "confronting race/avoiding race" is that it reproduces the very racial conflict—blacks want racial justice, whites believe the society is already just and that racial claims are nonsubstantive—that the regionalism advocates seek to avoid. This presentation of race also avoids the internal politics of race, including the difficulties black communities have in civic organizing and holding leaders accountable, and the special racially defined dilemmas faced by blacks who are elected to office as mayors of cities. Such a view cannot see that the best way to strengthen interracial coalitions with blacks is to support blacks' capacity to organize and democratically define and advocate their own interests in order to provide them with more power and ability to attract allies and contend with opponents. Once they do that, blacks can themselves move beyond the white/black binary to differentiate friends and foes—based on their democratically self-determined and therefore irrefutable interests—with more fined-tuned concepts that reflect the complexities and submerged pluralities of racial groups in the United States.

Notes

Chapter 1

1. In 1991, Forbes ranked Atlanta the number one city in the United States in which to do business.

2. While all other U.S. cities come under the ultimate political and financial control of a state, Washington, D.C., the nation's capital, is unique in coming under the financial and political control of the U.S. Congress. Congress has ceded basic elements of home rule to local government in Washington, D.C., but it retains the power to revoke home rule.

3. Barry was arrested and convicted for his crime.

4. Michael Leo Owens and Michael J. Rich. 2003. "Is Strong Black Incorporation Enough? Black Empowerment and the Fate of Atlanta's Low-Income Neighborhoods," in *Racial Politics in American Cities*, ed. R. P. Browning, D. R. Marshall, and D. H. Tabb (New York: Longman, 2003). The city's deputy chief of operations pleaded guilty to accepting bribes from a company soliciting business from the city, and several of Campbell's key campaign contributors pleaded guilty to raising campaign funds in exchange for a promise of city contracts.

5. See Alan Berube, "Racial and Ethnic Change in the Nation's Largest Cities" in *Redefining Urban and Surburban America*, ed. B. Katz and R. E. Lang (Washington, D.C.: Brookings Institution Press, 2003); and William Frey, "Melting Pot Suburbs," in *Redefining Urban and Suburban America*, ed. B. Katz and R. E. Lang (Washington, D.C.: Brookings Institution Press, 2003). The white share of the population in America's 100 largest cities declined from 52 percent in 1990 to 44

percent in 2000. The top-five cities in the United States (New York, Los Angeles, Chicago, Houston, Philadelphia) together lost 1 million white residents.

6. Margaret Weir, "Central Cities' Loss of Power in State Politics," *Cityscape* 2, no. 2 (1996). The 1990 census showed that Arizona was the only state in which the combined population of central-city residents in cities with populations over fifty thousand constituted a majority of the state population. New York City's population constituted 81 percent of the metropolitan area population in 1950, by 1990 it was 64 percent. Chicago in 1950 was 70 percent of the metropolitan area population; in 1990 it was 32 percent.

7. William Julius Wilson, *The Declining Significance of Race: Blacks and Changing American Institutions* (1978; Chicago: University of Chicago Press, 1980). In 1947, the central cities' portion of all manufacturing employment was 66.1 percent; by 1970 it was less than 40 percent. A 1971 study of ten large metropolitan areas showed that 79 percent of employment growth in manufacturing between 1959 and 1967 occurred outside of central cities.

8. Source: Bureau of Labor Statistics. The figures are seasonally adjusted.

9. This statistic applies to the total population of black men; incarceration rates in poor urban neighborhoods are significantly higher.

10. Philip A. Klinker, "Bill Clinton and the Politics of the New Liberalism" in *Without Justice for All: The New Liberalism and our Retreat from Racial Equality*, ed. J. Adolph Reed (Boulder, Colo.: Westview, 1999). In 1992, for the first time in fifty years, the Democratic Party platform did not mention redressing racial injustice.

11. Conservative rhetoric championing laissez-faire free markets and attacking urban programs that aided blacks in cities became more powerful after the 1960s. Political leaders such as Barry Goldwater, Richard M. Nixon, and especially Ronald Reagan successfully invoked images of a virtuous white suburban nation defending itself against the unruly black masses of the inner city. A document entitled, "To Keep Our People Safe and Free," written when Ronald Reagan was governor of California not long after the 1965 Watts riot in Los Angeles, stated that "charges of brutality are being raised by a small but disruptive segment of society, which is constantly challenging the authority of the law. . . . For the law abiding, the policeman is a friend. For all our science and sophistication, for all our justified pride in intellectual accomplishment, the jungle is waiting to take over. The man with the badge helps to hold it back" (Quote is from "To Keep Our People Safe and Free: One of a Series of Creative Studies by the Reagan Administration," n.d. box 3, folder 4, California Republican Assembly (CRA) Papers and quoted in Lisa McGirr, *Suburban Warriors* (Princeton, N.J.: Princeton University Press, 2001, p. 204).

12. Martin Gilens, *Why Americans Hate Welfare* (Chicago: University of Chicago Press, 1999, 71). Gilens's survey research shows that even today, negative public perception of blacks, "continues to play the dominant role in shaping the public's attitudes toward welfare." Such conservative framing has been effective and lasting. Racist stereotypes remain widespread among whites. In a 1997 study, Lawrence

Bobo and James Kluegel reported that, when asked to compare blacks with whites, 54 percent of whites rated blacks as less intelligent, 62 percent rated blacks as lazier, 56 percent rated blacks as more prone to violence, and 78 percent rated blacks as preferring to live on welfare. See Lawrence Bobo and James R. Kluegel "Status, Ideology, and Dimensions of Whites' Racial Beliefs and Attitudes: Progress and Stagnation" in *Racial Attitudes in the 1990s: Continuity and Change,* ed S. A. Tuch and J. K. Martin (Westport, Conn.: Praeger, 1997).

13. Harold Meyerson, "Harvesting Voters," *The Washington Post,* November 12, 2003. Labor unions and union-affiliated voter outreach organizations (called 527s under the campaign finance law) allied with several local community groups and Rep. Chaka Fattah's (D-PA) political organization in Philadelphia in 2003 to register over 86,000 new voters, almost entirely in black and Latino neighborhoods The coalition effort supported Mayor Street and played a major part in his 59 to 46 percent victory over Republican Sam Katz, whom he defeated by a narrow nine thousand votes four years earlier in a highly racially polarized election. Even before the voter registration effort, Mayor Street, widely considered a machine politician and not a progressive, nonetheless endorsed a major low-income neighborhood revitalization proposal called the "Neighborhood Transformation Initiative" that was created through protest and negotiation by Philadelphia Interfaith Action, a community coalition of over thirty inner-city churches and synagogues affiliated with the Industrial Areas Foundation (IAF) and another ministerial group affiliated with the Center for Greater Philadelphia. See also Michael Powell, "Knock-Down, Drag-Out Urban Renewal; Philadelphia Program Targets Blighted Areas," *The Washington Post,* March 13, 2003.

14. Black non-mayors have not fared much better. There has been only one black governor, L. Douglass Wilder, elected in Virginia in 1989, in the history of the United States.

15. See the symposium on poor people's movements in the December 2003 issue of *Perspectives on Politics.* For similar arguments in black political studies see Adolph Reed Jr., "The Black Urban Regime: Structural Origins and Constraints," in *Comparative Urban and Community Research: An Annual Review* 1 (1986): 138–89; and Robert C. Smith, "'Politics' is not enough," in *From Exclusion to Inclusion: The Long Struggle for African American Political Power,* ed. R. C. Gomes and L. F. Williams (Westport, Conn.: Praeger, 1992).

16. It is not clear why Cloward and Piven thought black-led unions need to be "separatist" to be effective.

17. Cathy J. Cohen, *Black Political Participation* (New York: Aspen Roundtable on Comprehensive Community Development, 1998, 16–17). In summarizing a 1981 study of black voting by Richard Shingles, political scientist Cohen wrote that "it seems that although many blacks were willing to participate in potentially transformative (of the distribution of resources and power) political behavior, they were unwilling to engage in acts seen as largely symbolic and legitimizing of a political structure which they overwhelmingly distrusted." This finding seemed to go against a 1990 study by Bobo and Gilliam comparing black political par-

ticipation in high black-empowerment areas, such as cities with a black mayor, and low empowerment areas. Bobo and Gilliam found that blacks in high empowerment areas were more likely to participate in politics. See Lawrence Bobo, and Franklin D. Gilliam Jr. "Race, Sociopolitical Participation and Black Empowerment." *American Political Science Review* 84, no. 2 (1990): 377–93. However, Gilliam and Kaufman found in a subsequent 1998 study of cities having black mayors that black participation had declined, which seems to support Shingles's initial position. See Franklin D. Gilliam Jr. and Karen M. Kaufman. "Is There an Empowerment Life Cycle?" *Urban Affairs Review* 33, no. 6 (1998). The discrepancies highlight the difficulties of generalizing about black political participation across time and place. As Gilliam and Kaufman's later study shows, blacks' opinion about the substantive value of electoral participation has changed in some cities over time.

18. Robert D. Putnam, *Bowling Alone: The Collapse and Revival of American Community* (New York: Simon & Schuster, 2000, 409, 411). Putnam, a leading theorist of social capital, suggests that overcoming deep divisions like race "requires that we transcend our social and political and professional identities to connect with people unlike ourselves." He proposes that different groups join in team sports, and in the arts, as well as in community groups that attempt to "bridge the racial, social, and geographic cleavages that fracture our metropolitan areas." Yet in a democracy, a majority cannot be forced to do what it strongly opposes, and it is unlikely that metropolitan integration can be accomplished with unanimity. In the context of profound metropolitan segregation, white racial populism, and black withdrawal, these proposals do not seem realistic because conflicting groups need "bridging" social capital as a precondition to "bridge."

19. For the traditional pluralist view, see Robert A. Dahl, *Who Governs?: Democracy and Power in an American City* (New Haven, Conn.: Yale University Press, 1961); Paul E. Peterson, *City Limits* (Chicago: University of Chicago Press, 1981).

20. Lincoln quoted in David A. J. Richards, *Conscience and the Constitution: History, Theory, and Law of the Reconstruction Amendments* (Princeton, N.J.: Princeton University Press, 1993).

21. Pierre Manent, *An Intellectual History of Liberalism* (Princeton, N.J.: Princeton University Press, 1995). Majority rule aggregates the preferences of the many over the few. It is an ingenious combination of individual rights and authoritative rule in that it appeals to the strongest argument for individual liberty, that of natural equality between persons, to deny that liberty. That is, if all persons are equal, then the opinions of many persons must weigh more than the opinions of a few.

22. Robert Dahl, *Democracy and Its Critics* (New Haven, Conn.: Yale University Press, 1989, 207). Dahl corroborates this point in his discussion of the proper boundaries for a democratic state. He states that, "like the majority principle, the democratic process presupposes a proper unit." By "proper" unit, Dahl means that democracies embody, "two prior principles: that the interests of each person are entitled to equal consideration and that in the absence of a compelling

showing to the contrary an adult is assumed to understand his or her own interest better than any other person. . . . If the unit itself is not proper or rightful—if its scope or domain is not justifiable—then it cannot be made rightful simply by democratic procedures."

23. Frank Michelmen quoted in Jurgen Habermas, *The Inclusion of the Other: Studies in Political Theory,* ed. C. Cronin and P. D. Greiff (Cambridge, Mass.: MIT Press).

Chapter 2

1. Peter Dreier, John Mollenkopf, and Todd Swanstrom, *Place Matters* (Lawrence: University of Kansas Press, 2001). Lack of voter mobilization has been cited as a major contributing factor to anti-urban tilts in federal and state politics. Urban voter turnout for the 1992 presidential election was 5.8 percentage points lower than suburban turnout; in 2000 it was 9.8 points lower.

2. James B. Lane, "Black Political Power and Its Limits: Gary Mayor Richard G. Hatcher's Administration, 1968–87," in *African American Mayors: Race, Politics, and the American City,* ed. D. R. Colburn and J. S. Adler (Urbana: University of Illinois Press, 2001). Richard Hatcher, elected mayor of Gary, Indiana (population 170,000), in 1968 also made little effort to conceal racial antagonisms. Many white businesses responded by leaving Gary.

3. Manning Marable, *Black American Politics: From the Washington Marches to Jesse Jackson* (London: Verso, 1985, 185). According to historian Manning Marable, "in most U.S. metropolitan areas, the police department maintains its own intelligence units to track such leaders. By 1968, the Detroit Police Department had 75 officers in such a unit; Boston had 40; New York had 90 with an additional 55 undercover; and by 1970 Los Angeles had 167 agents." In 1984, the U.S. House Subcommittee on Civil and Constitutional Rights, chaired by former FBI agent Don Edwards, wrote about undercover operations: "The subcommittee learned a great deal about the pervasiveness of such operations, and the very disturbing impact they had had on the lives of innocent individuals. As the hearing process continued, the Subcommittee's concerns were compounded by the realization that the technique posed a very real threat to our liberties. Many of the values reflected in our Constitution are directly threatened by these operations." See U.S. Government Printing Office, FBI Undercover Operations, in *Subcommittee on Civil and Constitutional Rights* (Washington, D.C.: U.S. Government Printing Office, 1984, 2).

4. William J. Grimshaw, *Bitter Fruit: Black Politics and the Chicago Machine, 1931–1991* (Chicago: University of Chicago Press, 1992). Several black ward bosses broke publicly with the machine and endorsed Washington.

5. Amy Bridges, "Textbook Municipal Reform." *Urban Affairs Review* 33, no. 1, 1997, 98. Bridges found similarly that in constructing reform governments in the big cities of the Southwest, business-oriented "growth-machine" leaders aimed to minimize both voter participation and government redistribution. She wrote that "the Anglo middle class was the favored constituency not because their working-

class fellow citizens were self-regarding or abided corruption happily but because the political wish list of the middle class was short and admitted other social groups posed the threat of redistribution."

6. Charles Hamilton V, "Deracialization: Examination of a Political Strategy," *First World* 1 (March/April 1997): 3–5. Hamilton conceived of "deracialization" in the early 1970s as a means of rebuilding liberalism by emphasizing economic class issues as well as race. Following the rightward shift in politics led by Presidents Reagan and George H. W. Bush, however, the concept of deracialization (or crossover politics) took on a different meaning. It no longer referred to combining race and economic class appeals, but emphasized how urban black politicians could appeal to conservative white constituencies by downplaying race and the needs of the black poor. See also Paula D. McClain and Steven C. Tauber, "An African American Presidential Candidate: The Failed Presidential Campaign of Governor L. Douglass Wilder," in *African American Power and Politics: The Political Context Variable*, ed. J. Hanes Walton (New York: Columbia University Press, 1997); Joseph P. McCormick and Charles E. Jones, "The Conceptualization of Deracialization: Thinking through the Dilemma," in *Dilemmas of Black Politics: Issues of Leadership and Strategy*, ed. G. A. Persons (New York: HarperCollins, 1993). Studies show that black candidates use deracialization strategically to win elections. McClain and Tauber's study of former African American Virginia Governor L. Douglass Wilder's presidential campaign in 1992 found that in order to attract black voters, "he would have to change his position on some key issues. This, however, entailed a purposeful shift in constituency focus from conservative Virginia whites to a nationally diffuse black electorate. Therefore, Wilder abandoned his carefully developed and nurtured conservative, deracialized strategy in favor of more liberal and racially oriented themes." See Paula D. McClain and Steven C. Tauber, "An African American Presidential Candidate: The Failed Presidential Campaign of Governor L. Douglass Wilder," in *African American Power and Politics: The Political Context Variable*, ed. J. Hanes Walton (New York: Columbia University Press, 1997). Marcus Pohlmann and Michael Kirby's study of racial politics in Memphis similarly found that Mayor W. W. Herenton was able to win the black vote only by rejecting a deracialization strategy. See Marcus D. Kirby, and Michael P. Pohlmann, *Racial Politics at the Crossroads: Memphis Elects Dr. W. W. Herenton* (Knoxville: University of Tennessee Press, 1996).

7. David T. Canon, *Race, Redistricting, and Representation* (Chicago: University of Chicago Press, 1999). Recent studies of representation of black interests in Congress maintain that "white representatives are largely ignoring the interests of their black constituents" and that no more than a third of House Democrats support key items of the Congressional Black Caucus agenda. See also Robert C. Smith, *We Have No Leaders* (Albany: State University of New York Press, 1996, 189).

8. For a critical examination of the legal powers of local governments, see Gerald E. Frug, *City Making: Building Communities without Building Walls* (Princeton, N.J.: Princeton University Press, 1999).

9. For an exception to neglect of this issue, see chapter 4 in Lani Guinier, *The Tyranny of the Majority: Fundamental Fairness in Representative Democracy* (New York: Free Press, 1994).

10. McNeil noted similar dynamics among Latino politicians.

11. Registration figures from the New York Board of Elections in the early 1980s support Wooten's claims. Between 1982 and 1984, voter registration in majority-black assembly districts increased more in central Brooklyn districts represented by black nationalist activists than in any other districts in the city.

12. Also see Adolph Reed's discussion of development policy under Jackson in Adolph Reed Jr., "A Critique of Neo-Progressivism in Theorizing about Local Development Policy: A Case from Atlanta" in *The Politics of Urban Development*, ed. C. N. Stone and H. T. Sanders (Lawrence: Kansas University Press, 1987).

13. An estimate of AFSCME's local membership at the time was provided to the author in a phone conversation with Joe Alvarez, Northeast Director of the AFL-CIO, on May 12, 2001.

14. Georgia Ann Persons, "Atlanta: Black Mayoral Leadership and the Dynamics of Political Change" (PhD dissertation, Massachusetts Institute of Technology, 1978). Jackson continued to support unionization of municipal employees except police and firemen, although Georgia state law prohibited such unionization. The union, AFSCME, also may have angered Jackson by launching a national media campaign against the mayor even before he responded to their contract demands.

15. This remains the case despite the fact that Campbell has been described as a "technopolitician."

16. William J. Grimshaw, *Bitter Fruit: Black Politics and the Chicago Machine, 1931–1991* (Chicago: University of Chicago Press, 1992). Chicago established a "strong–mayor" system in 1955, when a Daley ally steered a bill through the state legislature transferring control of the city budget from the city council to the mayor.

17. For an example of this approach in Los Angeles, see Walter Julio Nicholls, "Forging a 'New' Organizational Infrastructure for Los Angeles' Progressive Community." *International Journal of Urban and Regional Research* 27, no. 4 (2003).

Chapter 3

1. Mark R. Warren, *Dry Bones Rattling: Community Building to Revitalize American Democracy* (Princeton, N.J.: Princeton University Press, 2001). Saul Alinsky founded the Back of the Yards Neighborhood Council in Chicago's Southwest Side in 1939, initially to support the CIO union-organizing drive in the stockyards and to address community concerns among a primarily Catholic constituency. With support from the Catholic Church and the philanthropist Marshall Field III, in 1940, Alinsky established IAF to expand community organizing to other communities.

2. Michael C. Dawson, *Black Visions: Roots of Contemporary African-American Political Ideologies* (Chicago: University of Chicago Press, 2001, 64). Dawson ar-

gues, in explaining black racial consciousness or the concept of blacks' sense of "linked fate," that, "if society is organized around race, and racial conflict is part of everyday life, and if our stories of the world are also organized around race, race is profoundly political and profoundly ideological, at least for blacks, and—one would suspect—for whites and others as well."

3. Manning Marable says that "much of the Black press" was subsidized by the Pullman Company to attack the Brotherhood of Sleeping Car Porters and Maids union, but he does not name specific newspapers other than the *Chicago Defender* and the *Pittsburgh Courier*. Historians Eric Foner and Ronald Lewis mention that the *Chicago Whip*, another leading black newspaper, encouraged black workers to join a company union established by the Pullman Company to fight Randolph's union. See Philip S. Foner and Ronald L. Lewis, *Black Workers: A Documentary History from Colonial Times to the Present* (Philadelphia: Temple University Press, 1989).

4. In a jibe at the National Negro Congress's (NNC) insistence on organizational independence, in 1940, Lewis told the NNC convention that "it was a great mistake for any class of laborers to isolate itself and weaken the bond of brotherhood." See Horne, Black, and Red (Albany: State Universtiy of New York Press, 1986).

5. Earl Ofari Hutchinson, *Blacks and Reds: Race and Class in Conflict 1919–1990* (East Lansing: Michigan State University Press, 1995). The apparent motivation for the Communist Party's support for an NNC alliance with the CIO was John Lewis's advocacy of U.S. neutrality in World War II after the 1939 Hitler-Stalin pact. Although supporting or opposing the U.S. war effort was probably not Randolph's principal concern, he attempted to organize protests for racial equality at home despite criticism that his racial advocacy was undermining the war effort.

6. Dawson's "black Marxist" category significantly differs from class-centered Marxist theories, but it is consistent with the "Third World" or nationalist-oriented black Marxist movements in the late 1960s and 1970s.

7. Robin D. G. Kelley, *Race Rebels: Culture, Politics, and the Black Working Class* (1994; New York: Free Press, 1996, 190). The well-known rap artist Ice Cube describes rappers as "underground street reporters. We just tell it how we see it, nothing more, nothing less." A 2001 National Urban League survey of black opinion found that 24.5 percent of African Americans between the ages of 18 and 24 believed that hip-hop and rap artists are good role models for children and teenagers, while 65 percent disagreed. See Walter W. Stafford, "The National Urban League Survey: Black America's Under-35 Generation," in *The State of Black America: 2001,* ed. L. A. Daniels (New York: National Urban League). Michael Eric Dyson and Cornel West are prominent supporters of rap. See Michael Eric Dyson, *Between God and Gangsta Rap: Bearing Witness to Black Culture* (New York: Oxford University Press, 1996).

8. Roger Waldinger, *Still the Promised City?: African Americans and New Immigrants in Postindustrial New York* (Cambridge, Mass.: Harvard University Press, 1996, 252). Waldinger points out another conflict that has been rarely publicized. He writes that "the black middle class largely works in government, the black

poor are its dependents. The interests of civil servants, regardless of ethnic stripe, leads them to push for higher wages and ever greater public jobs. The record shows that government has been extraordinarily responsive to these demands. . . . By contrast the poor did a good deal less well. . . . Public sector concentration thus pits the interests of the city's black middle class against the interests of its black poor." It is true that public-sector unions have usually focused on their member interests above those of the poor during budget negotiations, and that powerful unions have fared better in these negotiations than the poor. But some political and municipal labor leaders maintain that black and Latino union members should live in the same neighborhoods as the poor and suffer the consequences of cutbacks on the poor, and also that conservative attacks on the poor should extend to cuts on urban federal aid that funds union members providing services to the poor. These leaders advocate political alliances between black working- and middle-class government employees and the poor. See Gerry Hudson, interview by the author (New York, 2003).

9. Sowell is quoted in Lawrence M. Mead, *The New Politics of Poverty* (New York: Basic Books, 1992). The noted political scientists James Q. Wilson and Richard Herrnstein suggested that high rates of inner-city crime may be related not just to environmental factors but different physical constitutions created through heredity or poor parenting. See James Q. Wilson and Richard Herrnstein, *Crime and Human Nature* (New York: Simon & Schuster, 1985).

10. Margaret Weir, "Power, Money, and Politics in Community Development," in *Urban Problems and Community Development,* ed. R. E. Ferguson and W. T. Dickens (Washington, D.C.: Brookings Institution Press, 1999). Community Development Corporations (CDCs) grew substantially in the 1980s, particularly with congressional passage of the Home Mortgage Disclosure Act (HMDA) in 1975 and the Community Reinvestment Act (CRA) in 1977. The HMDA required banks to disclose information about their mortgage lending by census tract, while CRA established loose requirements for banks to lend in neighborhoods where they did business. The federal government did not actively enforce the legislation but allowed third parties like CDCs to collect data and file claims. The burden of enforcement of the legislation was thus put on resource-poor civic organizations in low-income communities.

11. Esther Fuchs, Robert Y. Shapiro, and Lorraine C. Minnite, "Social Capital, Political Participation, and the Urban Community," in *Social Capital and Poor Communities,* ed. S. Saegert, J. P. Thompson and M. R. Warren (New York: Russell Sage Foundation, 2001). In a study of the political activities of civic organizations (across race) in New York, Fuchs, Shapiro, and Minnite found that unions were by far the most politically active type of civic association, with 83 percent of the union members in their sample reporting that their unions were involved in politics,

12. Herbert Hill, "The Problem of Race in American Labor History." *Reviews in American History* 24 (2): 199. Hill who for twenty-five years served as labor secretary of the NAACP, and who later worked for the University of Wisconsin, has provided extensive documentation of strident racism within the United Mine

Workers and other CIO-affiliated unions. In criticizing a strong tendency among labor historians to overlook CIO racism, he wrote: "The fact that blacks were admitted into CIO unions because it was in the self-interest of whites to do so did not make it an 'inter-racial movement.' Interracial organization requires that fundamental shifts in institutional arrangements be made; above all it means sharing power. But the leaders of the CIO and their affiliated organizations were unwilling to accept blacks as equal partners in the leadership of unions, to share control with nonwhites and to permit them to share in the power that is derived from such institutional authority. In contrast to the craft unions of the AFL, [the] CIO admitted blacks, but CIO affiliates engaged in a variety of discriminatory practices after blacks had been admitted."

13. This data was taken from the 1984 National Black Election Study and did not include comparable surveys of white respondents.

14. Signithia Fordham and John Ogbu, "Black Students' School Success: Coping with the Burden of 'Acting White'" *The Urban Review* 18 (3) (1986): 176–206. On May 17, 2004, the African American comedian Bill Cosby was reported as saying, "The lower economic [black] people are not holding up their end in this deal. These people are not parenting. They are buying things for their kids— $500 sneakers for what? And won't spend $200 for 'Hooked on Phonics'. . . . They're standing on the corner and they can't speak English" (Lee, 2004). Cosby's comments reflected long-standing class and generational schisms within black communities, and his broad-brushed criticism of the black poor (as if all, or most, poor blacks do not "hold up their end") reinforced conservative arguments that blame the black poor for their conditions. Cosby's innuendo that the black poor waste money is not borne out in empirical studies; taking income into account, blacks' savings rate is at least as high as whites'. Blacks' lack of wealth is more accurately explained by the lack of inheritances among blacks as compared to whites, and this, in turn, can be traced to a history of exploitation. Another popular argument, that poor blacks are culturally opposed to working hard in school, rests on similarly weak empirical foundations, mainly an ethnographic study by Fordham and Ogbu in a single Washington, D.C., high school in the early 1980s.

15. A sense of this influence on the Southern Christian Leadership Conference can be found in Barbara Ransby, *Ella Baker and the Black Freedom Movement: A Radical Democratic Vision* (Chapel Hill: The University of North Carolina Press, 2003).

16. For empirical criticism of the "principled" racial opposition view, see Lawrence Bobo, "Race and Beliefs about Affirmative Action: Assessing the Effects of Interests, Group Threat, Ideology, and Racism," in *Racialized Politics: The Debate about Racism in America,* ed. D. O. Sears, J. Sadanius, and L. Bobo (Chicago: University of Chicago Press, 2000).

17. Leonard N. Moore, *Carl B. Stokes and the Rise of Black Political Power* (Urbana: University of Illinois Press, 2002). Stokes's strategy was to run a black candidate, his former aide Arnold Pinkney, in the general election against both Car-

ney (a weak Democrat candidate) and the Republican Ralph Perk, the same Republican Stokes had defeated in his 1969 reelection campaign. The strategy backfired as Stokes's intricate maneuvers confused black voters who split their votes between Carney and Pinkney. The split black vote enabled the Republican Ralph Perk to succeed Stokes as mayor.

18. Marion Orr, *Black Social Capital: The Politics of School Reform in Baltimore: 1986–1998* (Lawrence: Kansas University Press, 1999). On the contrary, Marion Orr's study of Baltimore argues that the city is plagued with resource problems and racial hostility.

19. Mark R. Warren, *Dry Bones Rattling: Community Building to Revitalize American Democracy* (Princeton, N.J.: Princeton University Press, 2001, 33). If consensus on an issue cannot be achieved, Warren writes, "divisive issues are typically dropped."

Chapter 4

1. Milton Street, brother of Philadelphia Mayor John Street (2000), is well known as a community leader and radical black separatist. He also served as a Pennsylvania state representative.

2. Dona Cooper Hamilton and Charles V. Hamilton. *The Dual Agenda: Race and Social Welfare Policies of Civil Rights Organizations* (New York: Columbia University Press, 1997). Hamilton and Hamilton provide evidence that black civil rights groups supported social democratic class transformation as well as civil rights from the 1930s through the 1960s, although they argue that the civil rights movement's dual agenda was blunted by white liberal civil rights allies who retreated from the broader economic agenda.

3. For a similar critique of pluralism and deep conflict, see James Bohman, "Public Reason and Cultural Pluralism." *Political Theory* 23, no. 2 (1995).

4. Wilbur C. Rich, *Coleman Young and Detroit Politics: From Social Activist to Power Broker* (Detroit: Wayne State University Press, 1989). Coleman Young regarded W. E. B. Du Bois and Paul Robeson as the primary influences on his intellectual development. Carl Stokes also was heavily influenced by Robeson's thinking and personal courage. See Carl B. Stokes, *Promises of Power: A Political Autobiography* (New York: Simon & Schuster, 1973).

5. Wilbur Rich, *Mayors, Images, and the Media: David Dinkins and Thomas Menino* (New York: Unpublished, manuscript, 2004). Blacks' views on race are expressed and interpreted largely through white-owned mass media. This is an area of continual complaint on the part of black mayors.

6. Jennifer L. Hochschild, *Facing Up to the American Dream: Race, Class, and the Soul of the Nation* (Princeton, N.J.: Princeton University Press, 1995). Political scientist Hochschild shows that middle-class African Americans, unlike their white counterparts, feel a shared responsibility to help the poor of their race. Hochschild roots this sentiment in African Americans' "shared past." Sociologist Lawrence Bobo's survey work on race shows that racial identity and attitudes are forced over a lifetime and are not based solely on individual status or experi-

ences, e.g., whether they are personally middle class or poor. Bobo's survey of racial attitudes in Los Angeles found that "feelings of threat and alienation are the product of social and collective processes that derive from the long-term experiences and conditions that cannot be reduced to the current status of individuals. ... Feelings of racial alienation reflect the cumulating personal, familial, community and collective experiences of racial differentiation, inequality and discrimination." See Lawrence Bobo, "Perceptions of Racial Group Competition: Extending Blumer's Theory of Group Position to a Multiracial Context," in *Russell Sage Foundation Working Paper no. 74: 12* (New York: Russell Sage Foundation, 1995).

7. Mary Summers and Philip A. Klinker, "The Election and Governance of John Daniels as Mayor of New Haven," in *Race, Politics, and Governance in the United States,* ed. H. L. Perry (Gainesville: University Press of Florida, 1996). The majority of black mayors in cities over 50,000 in population represent cities with fewer than 150,000 residents. Mayors of small cities, and small cities themselves, though important, are not focused on in this study and tend to be neglected in urban studies more generally. Some of the political studies of black mayors in small cities, such as that conducted by political scientists Mary Summers and Philip Klinker of Mayor John Daniels of New Haven, Connecticut, suggested that Daniels was a mobilizing mayor for similar reasons to those noted here.

8. Patrick Johnson, "Atlanta's First Woman Mayor Reflects New Era," *Christian Science Monitor* (January 16, 2002). Atlanta's current mayor, Shirley Franklin (2002–), is Atlanta's first woman mayor and the first black woman elected mayor in a major southern city. She won against two other black candidates by building a multiracial coalition of gays, Asians, and Hispanics, along with appeals to black women. Franklin said, "I don't think there's a move away from race, but a move toward inclusiveness." Franklin served as city manager under Maynard Jackson and Andrew Young, and it is yet to be seen whether Franklin reverts to the more traditional reliance on the black middle class and business coalition that undergirded previous black administrations.

9. For a notable exception, see Jeffrey M. Berry, Kent E. Portney, and Ken Thomson, *The Rebirth of Urban Democracy* (Washington, D.C: The Brookings Institution, 1993).

10. Three months later, the Black Panther Party brought shotguns to the steps of California's capitol building to symbolize their decision to protect black communities from overly aggressive police.

11. Huey Newton, "Huey Newton Talks to the Movement about the Black Panther Party, Cultural Nationalism, SNCC, Liberals, and White Revolutionaries," in *The Black Panthers Speak,* ed. P. S. Foner (Philadelphia: J. P. Lippincott, 1970). Huey Newton said in 1969 that, "we have an alliance with the [white] Peace and Freedom Party. The Peace and Freedom Party supported our program in full and this is the criterion for a coalition with the black revolutionary group. ... SNCC turned away from the white liberal, which was very good. I don't think they distinguished between the white liberal and the white revolutionary, because the

white revolutionary is white also and they are very much afraid to have any contact whatsoever with white people."

Chapter 5

1. Steven Gregory, *Black Corona* (Princeton, N.J.: Princeton University Press, 1998). Anthropologist Steven Gregory, conducting ethnographic studies of black activists in Queens, in 1998, made a similar observation about the exposure over time of New York black activists to multiple political influences—the Garvey movement, socialist radicalism, Black Power militancy, and black electoral politics. I am making a similar point about the influences of the distinct political environments across the boroughs.

2. Milton D. Morris, *The Politics of Black America* (New York: Harper & Row, 1975). The rise in the black power movement came at the same time as spontaneous episodes of violence and riots usually involving confrontations with the police and attacks on symbols of government authority or white-owned property in the ghetto. In 1964 Harlem experienced a bloody riot. In 1968 alone there were 329 major incidents in 257 cities leading to 52,629 arrests and 220 deaths, mostly of blacks. See Joe Feagan and Harlan Hahn, *Ghetto Revolts* (New York: Macmillan, 1973). By contrast, some middle-class blacks interpreted black power as conservative economic black nationalism. Vincent Harding, Robin Kelley, and Earl Lewis write that, "in an age when Black Power evoked fears of bomb-throwing militants and radicals with Afro hairstyles, it is interesting to note that the first Black Power conference was organized by conservative Republican Nathan Wright, and the second was cosponsored by Clairol, a manufacturer of hair care products. Even Republican Richard Nixon, who won the 1968 Presidential election, praised Black Power, since he, like the conservative business daily the *Wall Street Journal*, connected Black Power to black economic self-sufficiency." See Vincent Harding, Robin D. G. Kelley, and Earl Lewis "We Changed the World," in *To Make Our World Anew*, ed. R. D. G. Kelley and E. Lewis (New York: Oxford University Press, 2000, 531).

3. Lucius J. Barker, "Jesse Jackson's Candidacy in Political-Social Perspective," in *Jesse Jackson's 1984 Presidential Campaign: Challenge and Change in American Politics*, ed. Lucius J. Barker and Ronald W. Walters (Urbana: University of Illinois Press, 1989, 22). Barker attributed Rev. Jesse Jackson's decision to run for the presidency in 1984 largely to widespread black disappointment with the inability of black mayors to produce significant employment rewards for their participation in electoral politics and the sense among black political leaders that something needed to be done to rejuvenate interest in electoral politics. Barker said that black "frustration and restiveness" was especially strong in "view of the strong encouragement blacks received from their leaders and others to turn from 'protest to politics.'"

4. I use the term "radical" to denote a non-hierarchical combination of racial and interracial class advocacy. I distinguish "radical" from "leftist" groups that

did not embrace racial advocacy, or manipulated race to serve what they considered to be more important class-oriented imperatives.

5. After a split between the AFL and the CIO, the ALP was formed in 1936 by Sidney Hillman of the Amalgamated Clothing Workers Union, David Dubinsky of the ILGWU, and Max Zarinsky of the United Hatters, Cap and Millinery Workers, with the support of Eleanor Roosevelt and the Socialist Party. Mike Quill, head of the communist-led and heavily Irish Transit Workers Union (TWU), also joined.

6. Of Italian and Jewish heritage, LaGuardia was also a one-man ethnic coalition. LaGuardia won election in 1933 on a Republican/City Fusion ticket during a period of high voter dissatisfaction with Tammany government.

7. Martha Biondi, "The Struggle for Black Equality in New York City, 1945–1955" (PhD diss., Columbia University, 1997). An example of the work of the coalition is that in 1942 the radical Italian-American congressman from East Harlem, Vito Marcantonio, began attaching what he called "Harlem riders" to appropriations bills for armaments, housing, and education. Powell joined with the NAACP to sustain the practice of riders into the 1950s; they later became known as "Powell amendments." See Charles V. Hamilton, *Adam Clayton Powell, Jr.: The Political Biography of an American Dilemma* (New York: Atheneum, 1991).

8. Martha Biondi, *To Stand and Fight: The Struggle for Civil Rights in Postwar New York City* (Cambridge, Mass.: Harvard University Press, 2003). According to Biondi, in 1949 the Brooklyn NAACP accused Mayor O'Dwyer of helping to cover up police brutality against blacks, including the shooting of an unarmed black citizen, Hermon Newton, in the back. The NAACP twice petitioned New York's Republican Governor Thomas Dewey to appoint a special prosecutor to investigate police brutality and in October 1949 they demonstrated at City Hall against O'Dwyer's lack of action on police brutality. O'Dwyer also supported the Metropolitan Life Insurance Company against lawsuits that it illegally discriminated against blacks in its use of government subsidies the used to develop its huge housing complex, Stuyvesant Town, in Manhattan.

9. Martha Biondi, *To Stand and Fight: The Struggle for Civil Rights in Postwar New York City* (Cambridge, Mass.: Harvard University Press, 2003). Adam C. Powell's deal making with the machine runs against his image as a radical protest leader. Similarly, J. Raymond Jones's image as a machine Democrat runs against his support for Powell against the machine, with his cultivation of a political base independent of the machine. In his study of Powell, political scientist James Q. Wilson maintained that churches such as Powell's were politically important in the black community "only" where there was no African American political organization. Wilson contrasted Harlem to Chicago, where he described the machine as strong and centralized, with extensive patronage in the African American community, and thereby better able to control elections. Wilson argued that Powell gained power because Tammany failed to build a strong African American leadership in Harlem, thereby allowing Powell to fill the vacuum. Wilson's

own data, however, revealed that blacks in New York received substantially more patronage than did African Americans in Chicago. Wilson had difficulty explaining how, if the Tammany machine dispensed so much more patronage to blacks, the machine was not able to oust Powell in 1958–59, a period of machine strength. Wilson never considered that the black "machine" leader, J. Raymond Jones, could have harbored resentments against the white machine and outmaneuvered it, but that is exactly what Jones did. Recalling the 1950s, Jones said that "bosses, scoundrels and near criminals" ran the Democratic Party in New York City. Wilson also underestimated the appeal of Powell's outspoken radicalism. See James Q. Wilson, "Two Negro Politicians: An Interpretation." *MidWest Journal of Political Science* 4 (1960).

10. Martha Biondi, *To Stand and Fight: The Struggle for Civil Rights in Postwar New York City* (Cambridge, Mass.: Harvard University Press, 2003, 164). This was not an optimal choice sought by black political leaders. As Martha Biondi details in her history of New York's postwar civil rights movement: Cold war "repression had far reaching consequences. Most significantly, it dramatically slowed Black mobilization in New York City. It undermined the civil rights–trade union alliance, reduced civil rights leaders' calls for economic reform, and muted these leaders' criticism of U.S. foreign policy; it discouraged street protest and grassroots insurgency in favor of elite negotiations and lawsuits; it punished the most militant leaders, and imposed greater controls on more mainstream leaders; and above all else, the anticommunist crusade spread fear across American society" Clarence Taylor comes to similar conclusions in his study of postwar black civil rights protests in his book *Knocking at Our Own Door: Milton A. Galamison and the Struggle to Integrate New York City Schools* (New York: Columbia University Press, 1977).

11. Jones is quoted in Charles V. Hamilton, "Needed, More Foxes: The Black Experience," in *Urban Politics: New York Style*, ed. J. B. a. D. Netzer (Armonk, N.Y.: M.E. Sharpe, 1990).

12. Manning Marable, *Race, Reform and Rebellion: The Second Reconstruction in Black America, 1945–1982* (Jackson: University of Mississippi Press, 1984, 27). To Marable, the "breach" in civil rights advocacy occurred, in part, because, "in the face of growing racist opposition, the NAACP counseled . . . a general policy that spurned direct action. The failure and tragedy of this conservative approach to social change was in its parochial vision and tacit acceptance of Cold War politics. By refusing to work with Marxists, the NAACP lost the most principled antiracist organizers and activists." Marable asserts that similar purges of Troskyists and other leftists from the Congress of Racial Equality (CORE) in the late 1940s and early 1950s "seriously impeded CORE's growth." When the National Emergency Civil Rights Mobilization, initiated by the NAACP, held a meeting in Washington in 1950, 410 NAACP members, mostly from the Manhattan, Brooklyn, and Queens chapters, were barred by a CIO credentials committee from attending because of alleged communist sympathies. See also Martha Biondi, "The Struggle for Black Equality in New York City, 1945–1955," PhD dissertation, Co-

lumbia University, 1997; and Earl Ofari Hutchinson, *Blacks and Reds: Race and Class in Conflict 1919–1990* (East Lansing: Michigan State University Press, 1997). On January 21, 1950, Washington D.C.'s black newspaper, the *Afro-American* wrote of the incident, "the so-called civil rights mobilization was in fact a mechanism to demobilized the NAACP, weaken its leftist support and remove it from its position as the only powerful spokesman for the colored peoples." See Martha Biondi, *To Stand and Fight: The Struggle for Civil Rights in Postwar New York City* (Cambridge, Mass.: Harvard University Press, 2003).

13. Dona Cooper Hamilton and Charles V. Hamilton, *The Dual Agenda: The African American Struggle for Civil and Economic Equality* (New York: Columbia University Press, 1997, 101). The NAACP's decision to support the Powell amendments—that banned racial discrimination on federally funded contracts—elicited opposition from some of the NAACP's allies. Leslie Perry, head of the NAACP's Washington office, wrote Thurgood Marshall that their allies did not want even the use of the word "race" as it amounted to "waving a red flag." In 1955, Clarence Mitchell, director of the Washington bureau of the NAACP from 1950 to 1978, responded to one such charge, saying that, "We may as well face the fact that when reactionary elements try to kill legislation with civil rights measures they are stepping into the breach created because some liberals simply do not have the guts to make a good fight for this just principle."

14. Robert Goldstein, *Political Repression in America* (Cambridge, Mass.: Schenkman, 1978); Vincent Harding, Robin D. G. Kelley, and Earl Lewis, "We Changed the World," in *To Make Our World Anew,* ed. R. D. G. Kelley and E. Lewis (New York: Oxford University Press, 2000); Manning Marable, *Race, Reform and Rebellion: The Second Reconstruction in Black America, 1945–1982* (Jackson: University of Mississippi Press, 1984); and Doug McAdam, "The Decline of the Civil Rights Movement," in *Social Movements of the Sixties and Seventies,* ed. J. Freeman (New York: Longman, 1983). By the early 1970s militant black activists and street protesters had experienced intense engagement with the FBI and local police agencies with the arrest and prosecution of the "Panther 21" in New York, the killing of more than forty prisoners in the upstate New York Attica prison revolt of 1971, the disruption of militant black nationalist organizations by an FBI secret counterintelligence program, and stepped-up police "anti-riot" activities. The result, along with the assassination of Malcolm X and the urban "riots" of 1964 in Harlem, had a profoundly chilling effect on black protest politics in New York City of the late 1960s and early 1970s. Some black activists opted for working through "the system," satisfying themselves with the limited rewards of pluralist bargaining.

15. These debates are discussed in Manning Marable's *How Capitalism Underdeveloped Black America: Problems in Race, Political Economy, and Society.* (Boston: South End, 1983); and Robert C. Smith, *We Have No Leaders* (Albany: State University of New York Press, 1986).

16. Because Staten Island never had a large black population, and it has never elected a black person to political office, it is excluded from this analysis.

17. Charles V. Hamilton, "The Patron-Recipient Relationship and Minority Politics in New York City," *Political Science Quarterly* 94, no. 2 (1979). Hamilton once suggested that low-income black mobilization declined in the 1960s because government as "patron" increased social-welfare entitlements for the poor.

18. Thomas Bailey and Roger Waldinger, "The Changing Ethnic/Racial Division of Labor," in *Dual City: Restructuring New York,* ed. J. Mollenkopf and M. Castells (New York: Russell Sage, 1991). Government employment became increasingly important for native-born blacks in the 1970s, employing fully 36.1 percent of all native-born blacks working in New York City in 1980.

19. Martin Shefter, *Political Crisis/Fiscal Crisis* (New York: Basic Books, Inc, 1987); and Juan Williams, "Of Zulus, Watusis . . . ," *New York Times,* July 28, 1985. Koch highlighted his opposition to social-welfare programs run by "poverty pimps," his support for the death penalty (a state issue not within the purview of the mayor), and his willingness to stand up to the "Zulu warrior" in Congress, Rep. Ron Dellums (D-CA).

20. The other half of the planning board members were appointed by city council members.

21. Roger Waldinger, *Still the Promised City?: African Americans and New Immigrants in Postindustrial New York* (Cambridge, Mass.: Harvard University Press, 1996), 84. Native white New Yorkers have held a shrinking share of city jobs since mid-century, with whites leaving New York in increasing numbers during the economic crisis years of the 1970s. Sociologist Roger Waldinger estimates that 174,000 whites left New York in the 1970s because of job erosion, an additional 619,000 "for the suburbs and still greener pastures further afield."

22. Edwin R. Lewinson, *Black Politics in New York City* (New York: Twayne, 1974). The Reformers (mostly Jewish, liberal, and middle class) were considered by Harlem politicians less racist than the Italian or Irish political machines, but just as focused on their own group interests. Issues of traditional concern to Reform Democrats, such the elimination of patronage, were opposed by black politicians who did not object to patronage itself but rather blacks' lack of access to patronage. A 1975 study estimated that only 5 percent of black political club members belonged to Reform clubs. See Norman Adler and Blanche Davis Blank, *Political Clubs in New York* (New York: Praeger, 1975).

23. In New York City, if no candidate in the Democratic mayoral primary wins more than forty percent of the vote, the two candidates with the highest number of votes in the primary enter into a runoff (second) primary.

24. Vincent J. Cannato, *The Ungovernable City: John Lindsay and His Struggle to Save New York* (New York: Basic, 2001); and Roger Sanjek, *The Future of Us All: Race and Neighborhood Politics in New York City* (Ithaca, N.Y.: Cornell University Press, 1998). While he was not a racial conservative and was sharply critical of Koch's racial rhetoric, Mario Cuomo's rise to prominence as a mediator who convinced the Lindsay administration to scale down its plans to build fully racially integrated public housing in Forest Hills, Queens, led black politicians to eye him cautiously.

25. Edward I. Koch, *Politics* (New York: Simon & Schuster, 1985). Bill Banks, who worked on Sutton's campaign, told the author that many black politicians outside of Manhattan were taking direction from their county organizations. See Bill Banks, interview by the author on June 16, 1988 in Harlem, N.Y. However, it is difficult to gain a public record of which candidates black elected officials supported because machine politicians were not straightforward in announcing their preferences. For example, Koch deliberately requested that the Brooklyn County organization *not* endorse him publicly because he wanted to appear as an anti-machine candidate.

26. In 1964, Steingut offered Jones a civil court judgeship, and Jones accepted. Jones said in an interview with the author in 1988 that he had been "co-opted" by his acceptance of the judgeship.

27. Chisholm redirected her insurgent activism toward national politics, running as a candidate for president in 1972.

28. Although they supported community control, Chisholm and Fortune immediately made peace with the machine in the wake of community control's crushing defeat.

29. Alan Gartner, "Drawing the Lines: Redistricting and the Politics of Racial Succession in New York," January, at The Graduate School and University Center, City University of New York. In 1975, the Bronx, Manhattan, and Brooklyn counties were ordered by federal courts to comply with Section 5 of the Voting Rights Act (VRA), which mandated U.S. Justice Department approval of any new state legislative district boundaries in states found to have a history of political exclusion. New York was one of the first northern jurisdictions singled out for Section 5 coverage because of its egregious racial record concerning redistricting. In a 1981 challenge brought under the VRA, a federal court held that the allocation of two "at-large" city-council seats to each of the five boroughs violated the constitutional requirement of "one-person, one vote." Staten Island, a small and overwhelmingly white borough, had as many at-large seats as the much larger and majority-Latino and black Bronx.

30. Bill Banks, interview by the author June 16, 1988 in Harlem, N.Y; Esmerelda Simmons, interview by the author March 16, 1988 in Brooklyn, N.Y. Banks and CCE activist Esmeralda Simmons suggested that West Indians, coming from all-black Caribbean nations, were less attracted to CCE's black nationalism than were African Americans. Banks said that Caribbean blacks were more interested in "businesses and home ownership" than a heavy focus on race.

31. Bill Banks calculated that the Brooklyn machine had the support of nineteen district leaders, while CCE had the support of twelve minority district leaders and a good chance of winning the support of six anti-machine white reformers. CCE needed only to persuade one machine-aligned district leader to take control of the Brooklyn Democratic Party.

32. Former Congressman Rev. Floyd Flake, the principal exception, while not supported by the Queens County organization, received backing from Mayor Koch to defeat a black regular and a black reformer.

33. Hulburt James, interview by the author June 15, 1988 in Brooklyn, N.Y. According to the 1980 census, the congressional district was 47 percent black, 44 percent white, 8 percent Latino, and 1 percent Asian.

34. David Hatchett, "Where Is Queens Headed Politically?" *New York Voice* 1986. For Flake to win white support in Queens, he had to attract conservative white voters. "There is no liberal upper west side in Queens like there is in Manhattan," said Queens City Councilman Arthur Katzman, "and the Reform Democratic Movement has traditionally not been very strong." Flake's alliance with the then-popular and conservative Koch was, therefore, a shrewd tactical move.

35. Ronald W. Walters, *Black Presidential Politics in America: A Strategic Approach* (Albany: State University of New York Press, 1988). An October 1983 poll conducted by *Ebony,* the magazine then having the largest African American circulation in the United States, found that 67.1 percent of its readers approved of the idea of a black candidacy and 61.6 percent thought that Jackson should run.

36. Black turnout in the 1984 New York City Democratic primary was computed from the CBS News/*New York Times* 1984 Primary Exit Poll.

37. While Jackson did not win Jewish support, the low white turnout in the primary (41 percent) suggests that there was not a white (Jewish) mobilization against Jackson as a result of the "Hymietown" controversy, perhaps because his 1984 campaign was not taken very seriously in electoral terms.

38. Laura Blackburne, interview by the author (Manhattan, N.Y., 1988). The CJNY did not include Latino politicians or white elected officials.

39. A furious Vann continued to support Badillo, and the coalition immediately broke apart.

40. Blackburne maintained that the nearly all-male group could not countenance the idea of a black *woman* running for mayor ahead of them.

41. Estimates of voter turnout were calculated by the author based on election data taken from the Board of Elections.

42. Computerized listings of Jackson's contributors and contribution amounts were provided to the author by the Jackson '88 campaign.

Chapter 6

1. This is from a personal observation. I worked as deputy to Bill Lynch in the Manhattan Borough President's office from 1985 to 1989.

2. Christopher Quinn and Mark Vosburgh, White Hands Off a City That Bears His Stamp, *Cleveland Plain Dealer,* January 6, 2002. Unlike Stokes and Washington, Mike White was to the political right of the council. He ran a slate of candidates for city council in the fall of 2001 while at odds with many of the city's labor and community organizations. His preferred candidates lost in all but one race. The council's main complaint against White was that he ignored neighborhood issues like sidewalks, playgrounds, and parks.

3. For example, unions may have power when confronting a local mayor, and have little need to solicit the support of community groups. But when confronting Wal-Mart, the largest private employer in the nation, unions are rela-

tively powerless without the broad support of civic and community groups. The relations of power, the relative weight actors give different kinds of organizations, tend to change in relation to the task at hand.

4. Michael Herzfeld, *The Social Production of Indifference* (Chicago: University of Chicago Press, 1992). Dinkins's view was from a liberal pluralist managerial perspective, in which government administration is conceived as identifying and implementing rational (technical) solutions to problems. The thesis is that a mayor who is politically centrist and a good technician will be rewarded by reelection and that extensive mobilization by particular communities is not in the public interest because it compels elected officials to take sides and act less rationally. In a perspective that dates back, at least, to James Madison, liberals assume that large representative bodies will insulate legislators from discrete interests and make it easier to resolve conflicts in the interest of the public as a whole. See Peter Bachrach and Aryeh Botwinick, *Power and Empowerment: A Radical Theory of Participatory Democracy* (Philadelphia: Temple University Press, 1992).

5. John W. Kingdon, *Agendas, Alternatives, and Public Policies* (New York: Longman, 1995, 24). The ability to hire and fire key administrators is a coveted power of governmental executives. In a study of federal policy making, political scientist John Kingdon said, "To fill key policy making positions, the president nominates people who are responsive to his conception of the agenda for their agencies. If he discovers that his appointees are not responsive concerning items of major importance to him, they usually don't last long in the job." But Kingdon's executive argument did not hold for Dinkins.

6. Mayor Dinkins and Governor Cuomo's joint press conference (January 31, 1990). Friction between the mayor of New York City and governor of New York State has been a constant in New York history. The disputes center on the degree to which the state ought to control the city, and the degree to which city representatives dominate state policy making. See Gerald Benjamin "The Political Relationship," in *The Two New Yorks: State-City Relations in the Changing Federal System,* ed. G. Benjamin and Charles Brecher (New York: Russell Sage Foundation, 1987).

7. The FCB was composed of the governor, state comptroller, mayor, city comptroller, and three additional members appointed by the governor.

8. The black-owned *Amsterdam News* did not have a large circulation in comparison to New York dailies such as the *Daily News* or the *New York Post,* but like *El Diario* and other ethnic presses, it was closely read by political activists and by professional politicians.

9. According to the New York City Office of Collective Bargaining, the UFT eventually agreed to the deferral of somewhere between 20 to 30 percent of its wage increase to prevent layoffs. The settlement was, thereby, reduced to roughly 4.5 percent.

10. Author's conversation with UAW District 65 leader Jim Bell, May 12, 1990, at New York City Hall.

11. Bill Lynch, interview by the author June 25, 2000 in New York. To ensure an authentic labor voice in the public debates, Lynch said that he and Rivera even suggested a joint effort by DC 37 and Local 1199 to buy one of the city's daily newspapers

12. Wyatt T. Walker, for example, was secretary of Southern Christian Leadership Conference under Rev. Martin Luther King Jr., and was a key organizer in several historic civil rights campaigns.

13. The first phase of the project included 320 apartments for homeless, low-, and moderate-income families.

14. This is taken from my personal observation.

Chapter 7

1. Selwyn Raab, "Past Police Incidents Moved Blacks to Coordinate Protests," *New York Times,* June 23, 1978. In this *New York Times* article, New York City Deputy Medical Examiner Milton Wald was quoted as saying the autopsy showed "fatal force had been applied to the larynx of the businessman, Arthur Miller, the father of four children, by 'a forearm or a police stick.'"

2. From the JCRC archives.

3. Ibid.

4. Michael Kharfen, interview by the author on July 13, 2000 in Washington, D.C. The criticism from Lubavitcher leaders excluded, interestingly, the district attorney, Charles Hynes, who supervised Nelson's prosecution. Michael Kharfen, the former director of the city's Community Assistance Unit, maintained that because Hynes was normally attentive to Lubavitcher complaints, the Lubavitcher leadership made a political decision to blame Dinkins rather Hynes for Nelson's acquittal.

5. Ernest H. Wohlenberg, "The 'Geography of Civility' Revisited: New York Blackout Looting, 1977." *Economic Geography* 58, no. 1 (1977):29–44. It was incorrect to label Crown Heights the most extensive racial unrest in New York in over twenty years. Crown Heights, and several other parts of Brooklyn, was devastated by extensive rioting after an electrical blackout in 1977.

6. In the complicated maneuvering around this issue, Dinkins opposed a state legislative review of the referendum because, without such a review, it would have been easy to have the court declare the referendum unconstitutional. The state of New York (not borough voters) has the authority to set municipal boundaries. In Dinkins's view, Cuomo's action actually protected the referendum from a legal challenge.

7. Catherine S. Manegold, "Staten Island Secession More than Fringe Threat," *New York Times,* August 9, 1993. The 1990 census showed that Staten Island's population was roughly 70 percent Italian, Irish, or German descent; only 5 percent were black. The poverty rate was under 10 percent, compared with a roughly 25 percent rate elsewhere in the city. Richard Briffault, a Columbia University law professor, wrote that Staten Island secession posed the same kind of problem as suburban-central city unification efforts do in other regions: "that different groups

and interests in a complex urban setting cannot co-exist in one democratically governed local unit . . . being a part of New York City forces Staten Island, which in most demographic, economic and social senses is far more like a suburb, to come to grips with urban problems." See Chip Brown, "Escape from New York," *New York Times*, January 30, 1993, section 6, p. 22.

8. Marshal Ingwerson, "As Staten Island Goes, So Go Most Suburbs?" *The Christian Science Monitor* (October 19, 1993, 1). Secession advocates uniformly denied any racial motivation, however, Marshall Ingwerson, a writer for the *Christian Science Monitor*, wrote that, "the specter of race and racism is never far from talk of secession, since race is often intertwined with crime and drugs in many minds."

9. Author's personal notes. On October 28, 1991, Staten Island Democrats gathered at city hall to denounce Dinkins mainly because of his plan to build homeless shelters in Staten Island. See also James C. McKinley Jr., "Staten Island Democrats Warn Dinkins on Support," *New York Times*, October 29, 1991.

10. Ian Fisher, "O'Connor Again Praises Dinkins for Actions in Washington Heights," *New York Times*, August 21 1992. The article cited Cardinal O'Connor's column in *Catholic New York* the previous day.

11. This is my personal observation.

12. See Wilbur Rich, "Crime Coverage, Mayoral Images and Signaling" (unpublished manuscript, n.d.).

13. "Rumor and Justice in Washington Heights," *New York Times*, August 7, 1992. Giuliani said that Dinkins had repeatedly, "ceded neighborhoods to the forces of lawlessness" and that in Washington Heights, Dinkins had "used his office to make unjustified rumors and media reports of police brutality appear valid."

14. Jennifer L. Hochschild, *Facing Up to the American Dream: Race, Class, and the Soul of the Nation* (Princeton, N.J.: Princeton University Press, 1995, 60). In pre- and post-election polls, black and white opinion on the state of the city had moved in opposite directions before and after Dinkins's administration. Hochschild found that, "from 1988 to 1993 the proportion of African American New Yorkers who said race relations in their city were good increased from 19 percent to 34 percent. The corresponding proportion of white New Yorkers declined from 28 to 22 percent. In 1994, however, when Giuliani was mayor, a majority of whites who perceived any recent change thought New York's race relations had *improved* recently; a majority of blacks who perceived change thought relations had *worsened*."

15. Wilbur Rich, *Mayors, Images, and the Media: David Dinkins and Thomas Menino.* (New York: Unpublished manuscript, 2004, 298). Wilbur Rich, in a study of Dinkins's relation to the media, argued that Dinkins could not take credit for his anticrime achievements in part because of "*pre-packaged* [media] images of minorities as members of a criminal class." Rich maintains that Dinkins was initially socially constructed in the media as "the safe black man protecting us [whites] against the 'great undisciplined [black criminal element and black militants].'" But Crown Heights ruined that image. When Dinkins ran for reelection, Rich argues that the public was looking for "a strong man, not a concilia-

tor. This yearning for the man on a white horse brought a quick end to Dinkins's tenure."

16. Richard Girgenti, "A Report to the Governor on the Disturbances in Crown Heights, Volume I" (Albany: New York State Division of Criminal Justice Services, 1993, 13). The state's report did not analyze the political and historical context of events in Crown Heights. The report's conclusions about what police should have done in Crown Heights were therefore highly speculative and disconnected from local knowledge of Crown Heights and of black youth in the area in particular. The State report contends that, "The mobilization and deployment of officers to the accident scene occurred too slowly to prevent the spread of the disturbance." However, this view assumes that black community anger was *not* directed *at the police*. Had the State paid attention to Crown Heights's history of community conflict, or had it listened to community activists, it could not have ignored widespread community resentment against the police. Wilbur Tatum, the publisher of the *Amsterdam News*, wrote in an editorial that the state's report had followed "the lead of a white press corps in New York City that had already made it clear that Blacks were the culprits in this drama and that they would brook no interference with their interpretations and conclusion about events, no matter what information to the contrary was unearthed." See Wilbert Tatum, "Governor's Report on Crown Heights: A Redundancy at Best." *Amsterdam News* (July 24, 1993).

17. Former Councilwoman Alter blamed Dinkins for Democratic West Indian Councilwoman Una Clarke's election in Alter's former council district. Badillo was angry about what he saw as Harlem's sabotage of his own 1985 aborted mayoral candidacy (see chapter 5).

18. From the author's notes.

19. The campaign's minority community mobilization effort was further hurt by a $320,000 fine for a violation of the public campaign financing program and an unrelated agreement by the campaign to reimburse the State Democratic Committee $226,000 for anti-Giuliani ads. With less than two weeks left before the primary, these two actions cost the campaign more than $500,000. With little money left for field mobilization, the campaign went more "white" than intended.

20. The main beneficiary of the rise in nationalist influence was Al Sharpton, who without ever winning elected office, by the late 1990s was widely considered to be New York's principal black leader. In March 1999, Sharpton led daily protests at N.Y.P.D. headquarters against the February 4, 1999, police killing of an innocent African immigrant, Amadou Diallo. The protests led to twelve hundred arrests over two weeks. Those arrested included David Dinkins, nearly every black member of Congress, as well as prominent black business and civic leaders across the political spectrum.

21. Steven Greenhouse, "Takeover of City Union Will End Soon." *The New York Times*, January 10, 2002. Altogether, twenty DC 37 officials were convicted for stealing union funds and other crimes. Stanley Hill, who was the leader of DC 37, was never indicted, but critics maintained that Hill was grievously out of touch with the union's business.

22. Steven Greenhouse, "Vowing to Go from Scandal to Strength, City Union Looks for a Fight," *New York Times,* July 12, 1999. The new appointed leader of the union moved aggressively to reorient the union toward a protest of Giuliani's workfare program—that replaced city workers with welfare workers—and strengthen the union's political mobilization operations.

23. Dinkins's staff believed that Dinkins's strong support for additional Latino districts embarrassed Ferrer, who was rumored to have promised fewer Latino districts to appease white council members in the Bronx worried about losing their seats. The author observed this while serving as Dinkins's liaison to the Districting Commission.

24. The Hispanic Federation, Latino Political Participation in New York City: 2002. Latino voter registration swelled by 253,028 between 1990 and 2001. All but 57,000 of the city's nearly 700,000 registered Latinos were Democrats.

25. Author's conversation with Ferrer, New York City, April 19, 2001.

26. Taken from author's notes.

27. Celeste Katz and Joel Siegel, "Hopefuls Spar Over Who Is Being Divisive," *Daily News,* October 4, 2001. Green had also assiduously courted Al Sharpton the previous spring, organizing a series of private meetings with him, taking him to a Broadway play, and attending his marriage "recommitment" ceremony. But now, Green declared, "I never sought Al Sharpton's support."

28. Under federal law, each state must create provisional ballots to be used by qualified voters who declare that they are registered voters in a particular jurisdiction although their names do not appear on the official list of voters in that polling place. The provisional ballot is also known as an affidavit ballot because the voter must swear to her or his eligibility under penalty of perjury.

29. Scott Shifrel and Larry Cohler-Esses, "Green Aides Met With Dems on Ferrer-Sharpton Plan," *Daily News,* November 2, 2001. Green's campaign spokesperson, Joe DePlasco, noted that no one had established a link between the meeting Green's aides attended with the anonymous anti-Sharpton campaign. Although John Kest maintained that he objected to attacking Sharpton, several participants in the meeting disagreed with Kest's account.

30. Homicide statistics are from homicide data provided by the New York City Deptartment of Public Health.

31. Taken from author's personal observation.

32. Leaders such as Rev. Herbert Daughtry and Rev. Al Sharpton were in the black mainstream on the Crown Heights issue.

Chapter 8

1. A third approach is to organize consumer cooperatives and community-owned businesses. This approach was pursued by Marcus Garvey and subsequently championed by W. E. B. Du Bois, A. Philip Randolph, and Rev. Martin L. King Jr., yet for reasons that are unclear, this approach has seldom been implemented in cities.

References

Abbot, Alfreda. 1988. Interview by author June 28 in Atlanta.

Adler, Norman, and Blanche Davis Blank. 1975. *Political Clubs in New York*. New York: Praeger.

Alexander, Fritz II. 1992. Letter to the editor. *New York Times*. August 12.

Alexander, Kathy. 1997. Suburbs Loom Large for Atlanta's Mayor. *Atlanta Journal-Constitution*. November 23.

Alford, Robert C., and Eugene C. Lee. 1968. Voting Turnout in American Cities. *The American Political Science Review* 62 (3).

Altshuler, Alan, William Morrill, Harold Wolman, and Faith Mitchell, ed. 1999. *Governance and Opportunity in Metropolitan America*. Washington, D.C.: National Academy Press.

Amsterdam News. 1991b. Stanley Hill Tells Dinkins: We Must Avert Economic and Human Tragedy. June 22.

Amsterdam News. 1992. Editorial. February 29.

Anderson, John, and Hilary Hevenor. 1987. *Burning Down the House: MOVE and the Tragedy of Philadelphia*. New York: W.W. Norton.

Anekwe, Simon. 1990. Don't Blame Dinkins for Crimes, Pals Urge. *Amsterdam News*. September 22.

Applebome, Peter. 1993. The 1993 Elections: Mayoral Elections; Results Hint at Secondary Role for Race. *New York Times*. November 4.

Archer, Margaret S. [1988] 1992. *Culture and Agency: The Place of Culture in Social Theory*. Cambridge: Cambridge University Press.

303

Arian, Asher, Arthur Goldberg, John Mollenkopf, and Edward Rogowsky. 1991. *Changing New York City Politics*. New York: Routledge.

Bachrach, Peter, and Aryeh Botwinick. 1992. *Power and Empowerment: A Radical Theory of Participatory Democracy*. Philadelphia: Temple University Press.

Bailey, Thomas, and Roger Waldinger. 1991. The Changing Ethnic/Racial Division of Labor. In *Dual City: Restructuring New York*, ed. J. Mollenkopf and M. Castells. New York: Russell Sage.

Banks, Bill. 1988. Interview by author June 16 in Harlem, N.Y.

Barker, Lucius J. 1989. Jesse Jackson's Candidacy in Political-Social Perspective. In *Jesse Jackson's 1984 Presidential Campaign: Challenge and Change in American Politics*, ed. R. W. Barker Lucius. Urbana: University of Illinois Press.

Barrs, Rick. 2001. The Finger: The Hahn Campaign Played the Race Card again and again to Destroy a Latino Opponent. *New Times Los Angeles*. June 14.

Barry, Dan. 1999. Giuliani Says Diallo Shooting Coverage Skewed Poll. *New York Times*. March 17.

Bell, Jim. 1990. Interview by author May 12 in New York City.

Benjamin, Gerald. 1987. The Political Relationship. In *The Two New Yorks: State-City Relations in the Changing Federal System*, ed. G. Benjamin and Charles Brecher. New York: Russell Sage.

Bennett, Andrew. 1997. *Process Tracing in Case Study Research* http://www.georgetown.edu/bennett.htm. (assessed October 10 2001).

Bennett, Andrew, and Alexander George. *Research Design Tasks in Case Study Methods*. http://www.georgetown.edu/bennett, 1997.

Bernstein, Emily M. 1993. Neighborhood Report: Harlem; Reborn Brownstones: Phase I. *New York Times*. September 12.

Berry, Jeffrey M., Kent E. Portney, and Ken Thomson. 1993. *The Rebirth of Urban Democracy*. Washington, D.C.: Brookings Institution Press.

Berube, Alan. 2003. Racial and Ethnic Change in the Nation's Largest Cities. In *Redefining Urban and Suburban America*, ed. B. Katz and R. E. Lang. Washington, D.C.: Brookings Institution Press.

Best, Kathleen. 1994. NAACP Board Fires Chavis; Executive Director Calls Action a "Lynching." *St. Louis Post-Dispatch*. August 21.

Biles, Roger. 1992. Black Mayors: A Historical Assessment. *The Journal of Negro History* 77 (3).

Biondi, Martha. 1997. The Struggle for Black Equality in New York City, 1945–1955. PhD diss., Columbia Univ.

———. 2003. *To Stand and Fight: The Struggle for Civil Rights in Postwar New York City*. Cambridge, Mass.: Harvard University Press.

Blackburne, Laura. 1988. Interview by author April 20 in Manhattan, N.Y.

Bobo, Lawrence. 1995. Perceptions of Racial Group Competition: Extending Blumer's Theory of Group Position to a Multiracial Context. Faculty Working Paper 74, Russell Sage Foundation.

———. 2000. Race and Beliefs about Affirmative Action: Assessing the Effects of Interests, Group Threat, Ideology, and Racism. In *Racialized Politics: The*

Debate about Racism in America, ed. D. O. Sears, J. Sadanius, and L. Bobo. Chicago: University of Chicago Press.

Bobo, Lawrence, and Franklin D. Gilliam Jr. 1990. Race, Sociopolitical Participation and Black Empowerment. *American Political Science Review* 84 (2): 377–93.

Bobo, Lawrence, and James R. Kluegel. 1997. Status, Ideology, and Dimensions of Whites' Racial Beliefs and Attitudes: Progress and Stagnation. In *Racial Attitudes in the 1990s: Continuity and Change,* ed. S. A. Tuch and J. K. Martin. Westport, Conn.: Praeger.

Bobo, Lawrence, Melvin L. Oliver, James H. Johnson, and Abel Valenzuela Jr. 2000. Analyzing Inequality in Los Angeles. In *Prismatic Metropolis: Inequality in Los Angeles,* ed. L. D. Bobo, M. L. Oliver, J. H. Johnson, and J. Abel Valenzuela. New York: Russell Sage Foundation.

Bobo, Lawrence D., and Ryan A. Smith. 1998. From Jim Crow Racism to Laissez-Faire Racism. In *Beyond Pluralism: The Conception of Groups and Group Identities in America,* ed. W. F. Katkin, N. Landsman, and A. Tyree. Urbana: University of Illinois Press.

Bohlen, Christine. 1989. The New York Primary: Dinkins and Friends Exult in Victory. *New York Times.* September 13.

Bohman, James. 1995. Public Reason and Cultural Pluralism. *Political Theory* 23 (2).

Borden, Karen Wells. 1973. Black Rhetoric in the 1960s. *Journal of Black Studies* 3 (4).

Borstelmann, Thomas. 2001. *The Cold War and the Color Line: American Race Relations in the Global Arena.* Cambridge, Mass.: Harvard University Press.

Boyd, Herb. 1991. Labor leaders stand firm against layoffs, cutbacks: call for a progressive and just tax system. *Amsterdam News,* June 29.

Boyette, Michael. 1989. *"Let It Burn": The Philadelphia Tragedy.* Chicago: Contemporary Books.

Boyte, Harry. 1980. *Backyard Revolution.* Philadelphia: Temple University Press.

Bridges, Amy. 1997a. *Morning Glories: Municipal Reform in the Southwest.* Princeton, N.J.: Princeton University Press.

———. 1997b. Textbook Municipal Reform. *Urban Affairs Review* 33 (1).

Brooks, Joe. 2002. Interview by author January 5 in Oakland, Calif.

Brown, Chip. 1994. Escape from New York. *New York Times.* January 30.

Brown, Elaine. 1992. *A Taste of Power: A Black Woman's Story.* New York: Doubleday.

Brown, Michael K., Martin Carnoy, Elliott Currie, Troy Duster, David B. Oppenheimer, Marjorie M. Schultz, and David Wellman. 2003. *White-Washing Race: The Myth of a Color-Blind Society.* Berkeley and Los Angeles: University of California Press.

Browne, J. Zamgba. 1991a. All Across the City the Cry to Dinkins Is the Same: "Spare Us." *Amsterdam News,* May 18.

———. 1991b. Cuomo Backs Off Charges; Denies Rift with Dinkins. *Amsterdam News.*

———. 1991c. Top Labor Leaders Declare Dinkins "Betrayed" Workers. *Amsterdam News,* July 6.

Browning, Rufus, Dale Rogers Marshall, and David H. Tabb, eds. 1984. *Protest Is Not Enough.* Berkeley and Los Angeles: University of California Press.

Brownstein, Ronald. 1993. New York, New York; Whites Screaming at Blacks. Chasids Suing the Mayor. Latinos Grumbling They've Been Ignored. And Two Flawed Candidates Navigating the Edges of the Maelstrom. It's a Helluva Mayor's Race. *Los Angeles Times,* October 17.

Bullard, Robert D., and E. Kiki Thomas. 1989. Atlanta: Mecca of the Southeast. In *In Search of the New South.* Tuscaloosa: University of Alabama Press.

Bureau of Labor Statistics, U.S. Department of Labor, Middle Atlantic Regional Office. 1991. *News.* 27 March.

Bush, Rod. 1984. *The New Black Vote.* San Francisco: Synthesis Publications.

Bynoe, Audrey. 1988. Interview by author March 24 in Brooklyn, N.Y.

Byron, Peg. 1992. NYC Cops Mass at City Hall, Call for the Mayor's Ouster. *New York Times,* September 16.

Calhoun-Brown, Allison. 1996. African American Churches and Political Mobilization: The Psychological Impact of Organizational Resources. *The Journal of Politics* 58 (4).

Cannato, Vincent J. 2001. *The Ungovernable City: John Lindsay and His Struggle to Save New York.* New York: Basic.

Canon, David T. 1999. *Race, Redistricting, and Representation.* Chicago: University of Chicago Press.

Caraley, Demetrios. 1992. Washington Abandons the Cities. *Political Science Quarterly* 107 (1).

———. 1996. Dismantling the Federal Safety Net: Fictions Versus Realities. *Political Science Quarterly* 111 (2):253.

Carmichael, Stokely, and Charles Hamilton. 1967. *Black Power.* New York: Random House.

Carmines, Edward G., and James A. Stimson. 1989. *Issue Evolution: Race and the Transformation of American Politics.* Princeton: Princeton University Press.

Carson, Keith. 1988. Interview by author July 1 in Oakland, Calif.

Caruso, Phil. 1992. Letter to the editor. *New York Times.* September 25.

Chateauvert, Melinda. 1998. *Marching Together: Women of the Brotherhood of Sleeping Car Porters.* Urbana: University of Illinois.

Churchill, Ward, and Jim Vander Wall. [1988] 2002. *Agents of Repression.* 2nd ed. Cambridge, Mass.: South End.

City of New York Department of Housing Preservation and Development, Office of Development. 1990. Urban Renewal Plan: Saratoga Square Urban Renewal Project: Community District Nos. 3 and 16. Brooklyn. New York.

Clark, Kenneth B., and Jeanette Hopkins. 1970. *A Relevant War against Poverty.* New York: Harper & Row.

Clavel, Pierre, and Wim Wiewel. 1991. Introduction. In *Harold Washington and the Neighborhoods: Progressive City Government in Chicago, 1983–1987,* ed. P. Clavel and W. Wiewel. New Brunswick, N.J.: Rutgers University Press.

Cloward, Richard A., and Frances Fox Piven. 1974. *The Politics of Turmoil*. New York: Pantheon.

Cohen, Cathy. 2004. Deviance as Resistance: A New Research Agenda for the Study of Black Politics. *Du Bois Review* 1 (1).

Cohen, Cathy, and Michael Dawson. 1993. Neighborhood Poverty and African American Politics. *American Political Science Review* 87 (2):286–302.

Cohen, Cathy J. 1998. Black Political Participation. New York: Aspen Roundtable on Comprehensive Community Development.

———. 1999. *The Boundaries of Blackness: Aids and the Breakdown of Black Politics*. Chicago: University of Chicago Press.

Cohen, Joshua. 1997. Deliberation and Democratic Legitimacy. In *Deliberative Democracy*, ed. J. B. a. W. Rehg. Cambridge, Mass.: The MIT Press.

Cohen, Joshua, and Joel Rogers. 2003. Power and Reason. In *Deepening Democracy: Institutional Innovations in Empowered Participatory Governance*, ed. A. Fung and E. O. Wright. New York: Verso.

Cohler-Esses, Larry. 2001. Ferrer Tells Green: Fire 'Em. *New York Daily News*. November 5.

Colburn, David R. 2001. Running for Office: African-American Mayors from 1967 to 1996. In *African-American Mayors: Race, Politics, and the American City*, ed. D. R. Colburn and J. S. Adler. Urbana: University of Illinois Press.

Collins, Shiela D. 1986. *The Rainbow Challenge: The Jackson Campaign and the Future of U.S. Politics*. New York: Monthly Review Press.

Commission of Inquiry into the Black Panthers and the Police. Roy Wilkins and Ramsey Clark, chairmen. 1973. Search and Destroy. New York: Metropolitan Research Council.

Conason, Joe. 1985. Man vs. Machine. *Village Voice*, August 20, 1985.

Cooper, Andrew, and Wayne Barrett. 1984. Chisholm's Compromise. *Village Voice* October 30.

Cottman, Michael H. 1991. A Hammer of Hope in Harlem; City Revives Huge Redevelopment Plan. *Long Island Newsday*. April 8.

———. 1998. D.C.'s New Mayor, Against the Current; With Williams at Helm, Hope for a Sea Change. *The Washington Post*. November 8.

Crenshaw, Kimberlé. 1992. Whose Story Is It Anyway? Feminist and Antiracist Appropriations of Anita Hill. In *Race-ing Justice, En-gendering Power*, ed. T. Morrison. New York: Random House.

Dahl, Robert A. 1961. *Who Governs?: Democracy and Power in an American City*. New Haven, Conn.: Yale University Press.

———. 1989. *Democracy and Its Critics*. New Haven, Conn.: Yale University Press.

Danielson, Micheal. 1976. *The Politics of Exclusion*. New York: Columbia University Press.

Darnelle, Emma. 1988. Interview by author March 20 in Atlanta.

Daughtry, Herbert. 1997. *No Monopoly on Suffering: Blacks and Jews in Crown Heights (and Elsewhere)*. Trenton: Africa World Press, 169–221.

Davis, Darren W., and Ronald E. Brown. 2002. The Antipathy of Black Nationalism: Behavioral and Attitudinal Implications of an African American Ideology. *American Journal of Political Science* 46 (2).

Dawson, Michael C. 1994. *Behind the Mule: Race, Class, and African American Politics.* Princeton: Princeton University Press.

———. 1996. Black Discontent: The Report of the 1993–1994 National Black Politics Study: University of Chicago.

———. 2001. *Black Visions: Roots of Contemporary African-American Political Ideologies.* Chicago: University of Chicago Press.

Diamond, Randy, and Adam Nagourney. 1990. Dave Faces New Heat: Act Now, Urge Leaders. *New York Daily News.* September 11.

Dicker, Fredric, and Richard Steier. 1990. Cuomo and Morgy Call for More Cops Now! *New York Post.* September 11.

Dinkins, David. 1991. Remarks by Mayor David N. Dinkins, Press Conference to Present Fiscal Year 1992 Executive Budget, Public Hearing Room, City Hall. New York.

Dinkins, David N., and Peter F. Vallone. 1990. "Statement by Mayor David N. Dinkins and City Council Speaker Peter F. Vallone Regarding Agreement on Fiscal Year 1991 Budget.

Dionne, E. J Jr. 2002. Mr. Mayor, You Could Have Used a Machine. *The Washington Post,* July 28.

Douglass, William. 1993. Dole Pushes Reno for Decision on Crown Heights. *Long Island Newsday.* October 27.

Dreier, Peter. 1995. What Farrakhan Left Out: Labor Solidarity or Racial Separatism? *Commonweal,* December 15, 10–11.

Drier, Peter, John Mollenkopf, and Todd Swanstrom. 2001. *Place Matters: Metropolitics for the Twenty-First Century.* Lawrence: University Press of Kansas.

Dryzek, John S. 2000. *Deliberative Democracy and Beyond.* New York: Oxford University Press.

Du Bois, W. E. B. 1992. *Black Reconstruction in America.* New York: Atheneum.

———. 1995. Marxism and the Negro Problem. In *W. E. B. Du Bois: A Reader,* ed. D. L. Lewis. New York: Henry Holt.

Dudziak, Mary L. 2000. *Cold War Civil Rights: Race and the Image of American Democracy.* Princeton: Princeton University Press.

Duggan, Dennis. 1993. Yes, They Can Fight City Hall. *Long Island Newsday.* April 6.

Dyson, Michael Eric. 1996. *Between God and Gangsta Rap: Bearing Witness to Black Culture.* New York: Oxford University Press.

Edmonds, Patricia. 1993. Race Is Driving Issue in Detroit. *USA Today.* October 29.

Edsall, Thomas B. 1993. Conflicting Trends Seen in Whites' Willingness to Vote for Blacks. *The Washington Post,* December 19.

Eisinger, Peter. 1998. City Politics in an Era of Federal Devolution. *Urban Affairs Review* 33 (3).

Elliot-Banks, Manley. 2000. A Changing Electorate in a Majority Black City: The

Emergence of a Neo-Conservative Black Urban Regime in Contemporary Atlanta. *Journal of Urban Affairs* 22 (3).

English, Merle. 1988. Jackson Allies Criticize His City Campaign. *Long Island Newsday,* April 18, 1988.

Fears, Darryl. 1997. Mayor's Race Exposes Old Rift between Lighter, Darker Blacks; Remarks Embarrass Many. *Atlanta Journal-Constitution.* November 22.

Fenno, Richard E. 2003. *Going Home: Black Representatives and Their Constituents.* Chicago: University of Chicago Press.

Ferguson, Karen J. 1996. The Politics of Inclusion. PhD diss., Duke University.

Ferman, Barbara. 1996. *Challenging the Growth Machine.* Lawrence: University of Kansas Press.

Fettmann, Eric. 2001. The "Other" Other New York. *New York Post.* September 9.

Finder, Alan. 1993a. The 1993 Campaign: The Incumbent; Dinkins and Giuliani Grapple for Voters—Mayor Aims Efforts at Reinvigorating Vote Coalition. *New York Times,* November 1.

———. 1993b. New York Poll Sees Grim View of Life in City. *New York Times,* October 8.

Fine, Janice. 2000–2001. Community Unionism in Baltimore and Stamford: Beyond the Politics of Particularism. *WorkingUSA* 4 (3):59–85.

Fine, Janice R. 2003. Community Unions in Baltimore and Long Island: Beyond the Politics of Particularism. PhD diss., Massachusetts Institute of Technology.

Fiorina, Morris P. 1999. Extreme Voices: A Dark Side of Civic Engagement. In *Civic Engagement in American Democracy,* ed. T. Skocpol and M. P. Fiorina. Washington, D.C.: Brookings Institution Press.

Fireman, Ken, and William Murphy. 1988. Koch Wars: The Reverend Strikes Back. *Long Island Newsday,* April 12.

Fisher, Ian. 1992. "O'Connor Again Praises Dinkins for Actions in Washington Heights." *New York Times,* August 21, 3.

Flateau, John. 1988. Interview by author April 28 in New York.

Foner, Philip S., and Ronald L. Lewis. 1989. *Black Workers: A Documentary History from Colonial Times to the Present.* Philadelphia: Temple University Press.

Ford, Pat. 1988. Interview by author July 3 in Oakland, Calif.

Fordham, Signithia, and John Ogbu. 1986. "Black Students' School Success: Coping with the Burden of 'Acting White'" *The Urban Review* 18 (3): 176–206.

Franklin, Jimmie Lewis. 1989. *Back to Birmingham: Richard Arrington, Jr., and His Times.* Tuscaloosa: The University of Alabama Press.

Frey, William. 2003. Melting Pot Suburbs. In *Redefining Urban and Suburban America,* ed. B. Katz and R. E. Lang. Washington, D.C.: Brookings Institution Press.

Fried, Joseph P. 1979. U.S. Inquiry Acquits Police In '78 Death of a Black Leader. *New York Times,* August 3.

Frug, Gerald E. 1999. *City Making: Building Communities without Building Walls.* Princeton: Princeton University Press.

Frump, Bob. 1978a. Rizzo Warns of Radicals. *Philadelphia Inquirer.* September 22.

————. 1978b. Rizzo's Message As Clear As Black and White. *Philadelphia Inquirer.* September 24.

Fuchs, Esther R., Robert Y. Shapiro, and Lorraine C. Minnite. 2001. Social Capital, Political Participation, and the Urban Community. In *Social Capital and Poor Communities,* ed. S. Saegert, J. P. Thompson and M. R. Warren. New York: Russell Sage Foundation.

Fung, Archon, and Erik Olin Wright. 2003. Countervailing Power in Empowered Participatory Governance. In *Deepening Democracy: Institutional Innovations in Empowered Participatory Governance,* edited by Archon Fung and Erik Olin Wright. New York: Verso.

Gaines, Kevin K. 1996. *Uplifting the Race.* Chapel Hill: University of North Carolina Press.

Garrow, David J. 1986. *Bearing the Cross.* New York: William Morrow.

Gartner, Alan. 1993. "Drawing the Lines: Redistricting and the Politics of Racial Succession in New York," January, at The Graduate School and University Center, City University of New York.

Gilens, Martin. 1999. *Why Americans Hate Welfare.* Chicago: University of Chicago Press.

Gilliam, Franklin D. Jr., and Karen M. Kaufman. 1998. Is There an Empowerment Life Cycle? *Urban Affairs Review* 33 (6).

Gills, Doug. 1991. Chicago Politics and Community Development: A Social Movement Perspective. In *Harold Washington and the Neighborhoods: Progressive City Government in Chicago, 1983–1987,* ed. Pierre Clavel and Wim Wiewel. New Brunswick, N.J.: Rutgers University Press.

Giloth, Robert. 1991. Making Policy with Communities: Research and Development in the Department of Economic Development. In *Harold Washington and the Neighborhoods: Progressive City Government in Chicago, 1983–1987,* ed. Pierre Clavel and Wim Wiewel. New Brunswick, N.J.: Rutgers University Press.

Girgenti, Richard. 1993a. A Report to the Governor on the Disturbances in Crown Heights, Volume II. Albany: New York State Division of Criminal Justice Services.

————. 1993b. A Report to the Governor on the Disturbances in Crown Heights, Volume I. Albany: New York State Division of Criminal Justice Services.

Gittell, Marilyn. 2002. Community-Based Organizations and Civil Society. New York: The Howard Samuels State Management and Policy Center, The Graduate Center of the City University of New York.

Gittell, Marilyn, Kathy Newman, and Francois Pierre-Louis. 2001. Empowerment Zones: An Opportunity Missed. New York: The Howard Samuels State Management and Policy Center.

Giuliani, Rudolph W. 1992. Rumor and Justice in Washington Heights. Opinion editorial. *New York Times.* August 7.

Glasser, Ira. 1999. American Drug Laws: The New Jim Crow. *Albany Law Journal* 63 (703).

Goddard, Bruce. 1988. Interview by author June 30 in Oakland, Calif.

Goldfield, Michael. 1997. *The Color of Politics: Race and the Mainsprings of American Politics.* New York: The New Press.

Goldstein, Robert. 1978. *Political Repression in America.* Cambridge, Mass.: Schenkman.

Gomes, Ralph, and Linda Faye Williams. [1992] 1995. Coalition Politics: Past, Present, and Future. In *From Exclusion to Inclusion,* ed. R. Gomes and L. F. Williams. Westport, Conn.: Praeger.

Gonzalez, Juan. 1992. Breaking Rules, and Then Our Hearts. *New York Daily News.* February 22.

———. 2001. Mark Must Take Blame. *New York Daily News.* November 8.

Goode, W. Wilson, and Joann Stevens. 1992. *In Goode Faith.* Valley Forge, Pa.: Judson.

Greenberg, Cheryl Lynn. 1991. *"Or Does It Explode?"* New York: Oxford University Press.

Greene, Judith A. 1999. Zero Tolerance: A Case Study of Police Policies and Practices in New York City. *Crime and Delinquency* 45 (2):171–87.

Greenhouse, Steven. 1999. Vowing to Go from Scandal to Strength, City Union Looks for a Fight. *New York Times.* July 12.

———. 2002. Takeover of City Union Will End Soon. *New York Times,* January 10, 2002.

Gregory, Steven. 1998. *Black Corona.* Princeton: Princeton University Press.

Grimshaw, William J. 1992. *Bitter Fruit: Black Politics and the Chicago Machine, 1931–1991.* Chicago: University of Chicago Press.

Gross, Jane. 1986. Queens Legislators Looking to a Future without Manes. *New York Times,* March 19.

Grossman, James R. 2000. A Chance to Make Good. In *To Make Our World Anew: A History of African Americans,* ed. R. D. G. Kelley and E. Lewis. New York: Oxford University Press.

Guinier, Lani. 1994. *The Tyranny of the Majority: Fundamental Fairness in Representative Democracy.* New York: Free Press.

Guinier, Lani, and Gerald Torres. 2002. *The Miner's Canary.* Cambridge, Mass.: Harvard University Press.

Gumbs, Maurice. 1993. Crown Heights. *Amsterdam News.* July 26.

Habermas, Jurgen. 1987. *The Theory of Communicative Action.* Vol. 2. Boston: Beacon.

———. 1998. The Inclusion of the Other: Studies in Political Theory, ed. C. Cronin and P. d. Greiff. Cambridge, Mass.: MIT Press.

Hahn, Joe, and Harlan Feagan. 1973. *Ghetto Revolts.* New York: Macmillan.

Hamblin, Ken. 2002. No Black Governors? Here's Why. *The Denver Post.* January 27.

Hamilton, Charles V. 1977. Deracialization: Examination of a Political Strategy. *First World* 1 (March/April):3–5.

———. 1979. The Patron-Recipient Relationship and Minority Politics in New York City. *Political Science Quarterly* 94 (2).

———. 1990. Needed, More Foxes: The Black Experience. In *Urban Politics: New York Style*, ed. J. B. a. D. Netzer. Armonk, N.Y.: M. E. Sharpe.

———. 1991. *Adam Clayton Powell, Jr.: The Political Biography of an American Dilemma*. New York: Atheneum.

Hamilton, Dona Cooper, and Charles V. Hamilton. 1997a. *The Dual Agenda: Race and Social Welfare Policies of Civil Rights Organizations*. New York: Columbia University Press.

Harding, Vincent, Robin D. G. Kelley, and Earl Lewis. 2000. We Changed the World. In *To Make Our World Anew*, ed. R. D. G. Kelley and E. Lewis. New York: Oxford University Press.

Harms, William. 1994. Blacks Pessimistic about Future, Dawson Says. *The University of Chicago Chronicle*. April 28.

Harris, Art. 1988. Mr. Atlanta: Andy Young. *Long Island Newsday*, July 16.

Harris, Fredrick C. 2001. Religious Resources in an Oppositional Civic Culture. In *Oppositional Consciousness*, ed. J. Mansbridge and A. Morris. Chicago: University of Chicago Press.

———. 1999a. *Something Within: Religion in African-American Political Activism*. New York: Oxford University Press.

———. 1999b. Will the Circle Be Unbroken?: The Erosion and Transformation of African-American Civic Life. In *Civil Society, Democracy, and Civic Renewal*, ed. R. K. Fullinwider. New York: Rowman & Littlefield.

Hart, Duane. 1988. Interview by author April 4 in Queens, New York.

Hatchett, David. 1986. Where Is Queens Headed Politically? *New York Voice*.

Hayduk, Ronald Joseph. 1996. Gatekeepers to the Franchise: Election Administration and Voter Participation in New York. Ph.D diss., City University of New York Graduate Center.

Henry, Keith S. 1977. The Black Political Tradition in New York: A Conjunction of Political Cultures. *Journal of Black Studies* 7 (4).

Herbert, Bob. 1990a. Another Chance for Dave. *New York Daily News*. September 6.

———. 1990b. Emergency: Ferrer Calls It a Crime to Live Like This. *New York Daily News*. August 5.

Herring, Mary, Thomas B. Jankowski, and Ronald E. Brown. 1999. Pro-Black Doesn't Mean Anti-White: The Structure of African-American Group Identity. *The Journal of Politics* 61 (2).

Herzfeld, Michael. 1992. *The Social Production of Indifference*. Chicago: University of Chicago Press.

Hicks, Johnathan. 1993. Disappointed Black Voters Could Damage Dinkins's Bid. *New York Times*. October 4.

Higginbotham, Evelyn Brooks. 1993. *Righteous Discontent: The Women's Movement in the Black Baptist Church, 1880–1920*. Cambridge, Mass.: Harvard University Press.

Hill, Herbert. 1996. The Problem of Race in American Labor History. *Reviews in American History* 24 (2):189–208.

Hill, Robert A., and Barbara Bair, eds. 1987. *Marcus Garvey: Life and Lessons.* Berkeley and Los Angeles: University of California Press.

Hispanic Federation. Latino Political Participation in New York City: 2002. 2002.

Hochschild, Jennifer L. 1995. *Facing Up to the American Dream: Race, Class, and the Soul of the Nation.* Princeton: Princeton University Press.

Hollander, Elizabeth. 1991. The Department of Planning under Harold Washington. In *Harold Washington and the Neighborhoods: Progressive City Government in Chicago, 1983–1987,* ed. P. Clavel and W. Wiewel. New Brunswick, N.J.: Rutgers University Press.

Holli, Paul M. and Melvin G. Green. 1989. *Bashing Chicago Traditions: Harold Washington's Last Campaign.* Grand Rapids: William B. Eerdmans.

Holmes, Robert. 1995. Atlanta City Politics and the Bill Campbell Administration. In *The Status of Black Atlanta: 1995,* ed. R. Holmes. Atlanta: Southern Center for Studies in Public Policy, Clark-Atlanta University.

Honey, Michael K. 1993. *Southern Labor and Black Civil Rights: Organizing Memphis Workers.* Urbana: University of Illinois Press.

Horne, Gerald. 1986. *Black and Red: W. E. B. Dubois and the Afro-American Response to the Cold War: 1944–1963.* Albany: State University of New York Press.

———. 1994. *Black Liberation/Red Scare: Ben Davis and the Community Party.* Newark: University of Delaware Press.

Hudson, Gerry. 2003. Interview by author July 10 in New York.

Huen, Floyd. 1988. Interview by author June 29 in Oakland, Calif.

Hutchinson, Earl Ofari. 1995. *Blacks and Reds: Race and Class in Conflict 1919–1990.* East Lansing: Michigan State University Press.

Ingwerson, Marshall. 1993. As Staten Island Goes, So Go Most Suburbs? *The Christian Science Monitor.* October 19.

Jackson, Kenneth. 1985. *Crabgrass Frontier.* New York: Oxford University Press.

James, George. 1992. Police Dept. Report Assails, Officers in New York Rally. *New York Times.* September 29.

James, Hulburt. 1988. Interview by author June 15 in Brooklyn, N.Y.

Jennings, James. 1990. *The Politics of Black Empowerment.* Detroit: Wayne State University Press.

Jetter, Alexis. 1987. The Numbers, But Not the Votes. *Long Island Newsday.* 5 November.

Johnson, Patrick. 2002. Atlanta's First Woman Mayor Reflects New Era. *Christian Science Monitor.* January 16.

Johnston, David. 1994. *The Idea of a Liberal Theory: A Critique and Reconstruction.* Princeton, N.J.: Princeton University Press.

Jones, Thomas. 1988. Interview by author April 8 in Brooklyn, N.Y.

Joseph, Cecil. 1988. Interview by author April 7 in New York.

Judd, Dennis R. 1999. Symbolic Politics and Urban Policies: Why African Americans Got So Little from the Democrats. In *Without Justice for All: The New Liberalism and Our Retreat From Racial Equality,* ed. A. Reed. Boulder, Colo.: Westview.

Judd, Dennis R., and Todd Swanstrom. 2003. *City Politics: Private Power and Public Policy.* 3rd ed. New York: Longman.

Katz, Celeste, and Joel Siegel. 2001. Hopefuls Spar over Who Is Being Divisive. *New York Daily News.* October 4.

Katznelson, Ira. [1973] 1976. *Black Men, White Cities: Race, Politics and Migration in the United States 1900–30, and Britain, 1948–68.* Chicago: University of Chicago Press.

———. 1981. *City Trenches: Urban Politics and the Patterning of Class in the United States.* Chicago: University of Chicago Press.

———. 1989. Was the Great Society a Lost Opportunity? In *The Rise and Fall of the New Deal Order: 1960–1980,* ed. S. Fraser and G. Gerstle. Princeton, N.J.: Princeton University Press.

Kaufman, W. S. 1960. *Governing New York City.* New York: Russell Sage Foundation, 626.

Kearney, Richard. 1992. *Labor Relations in the Public Sector.* New York: Marcel Dekker.

Keiser, Richard A. 1997. *Subordination or Empowerment: African-American Leadership and the Struggle for Urban Political Power.* New York: Oxford University Press.

Kelley, Robin. 2000. Into the Fire: 1970 to the Present. In *To Make Our World Anew: A History of African Americans,* ed. R. D. G. Kelley and E. Lewis. New York: Oxford University Press.

Kelley, Robin D. G. [1994] 1996. *Race Rebels: Culture, Politics, and the Black Working Class.* New York: Free Press.

———. 2002. *Freedom Dreams: The Black Radical Imagination.* Boston: Beacon.

———. 1998. Building Bridges: The Challenge of Organized Labor in Communities of Color. Paper written for the Aspen Institute Roundtable on Comprehensive Community-Building, July.

Kharfen, Michael. 2000. Interview by author. Washington, D.C.

Kiely, Kathy. 2002. These Are America's Governors. No Blacks. No Hispanics. *USA Today.* January 21.

Kihss, Peter. 1978. N.A.A.C.P. Seeks Federal Inquiry in Miller's Death. *New York Times.* July 18.

Kilson, Martin. 1987. The Weakness of Black Politics. *Dissent,* Fall: 523–29.

———. 1996. Anatomy of the Black Political Class. In *The Politics of Minority Coalitions,* ed. W. C. Rich. Westport, Conn.: Praeger.

King, Martin Luther Jr. 1986a. If the Negro Wins, Labor Wins. In *A Testament of Hope: The Essential Writings of Martin Luther King, Jr.,* ed. J. M. Washington. San Francisco: Harper & Row.

———. 1986b. The Drum Major Instinct. In *A Testament of Hope: The Essential Writings of Martin Luther King, Jr.,* ed. J. M. Washington. San Francisco: Harper & Row.

———. 1986c. *Playboy* Interview: Martin Luther King, Jr. In *A Testament of*

Hope: The Essential Writings of Martin Luther King, Jr., ed. J. A. Washington. San Francisco: Harper & Row.

———. 1986d. A Testament of Hope. In *A Testament of Hope: The Essential Writings of Martin Luther King, Jr.,* ed. J. M. Washington. San Francisco: Harper & Row.

———. 1986e. The Trumpet of Conscience. In *A Testament of Hope: The Essential Writings of Martin Luther King, Jr.,* ed. J. M. Washington. San Francisco: Harper & Row.

King, Mary. 1988. Interview by author June 21 in Oakland, Calif.

Kingdon, John W. 1995. *Agendas, Alternatives, and Public Policies.* New York: Longman.

Kirby, Marcus D., and Michael P. Pohlmann. 1996. *Racial Politics at the Crossroads: Memphis Elects Dr. W.W. Herenton.* Knoxville: University of Tennessee Press.

Klinkner, Philip A. 1999. Bill Clinton and the Politics of the New Liberalism. In Without Justice for All: The new Liberalism and Our retreat from Racial Equality, ed. J. Adolph Reed. Boulder, Colo.: Westview.

Koch, Edward I. 1985. *Politics.* New York: Simon & Schuster.

Kramer, Marcia. 1988. Mr. Ed says "Woe!" *New York Daily News.* April 20.

Lane, James B. 2001. Black Political Power and Its Limits: Gary Mayor Richard G. Hatcher's Administration, 1968–87. In *African American Mayors: Race, Politics, and the American City,* ed. D. R. Colburn and J. S. Adler. Urbana: University of Illinois Press.

Larkin, Brent. 1993. Critics Missed the Political Shift. *Cleveland Plain Dealer.* November 7.

———. 2001. The Legacy of Mike White; A Look at What It Is after 12 years, and What It Might Have Been. *Plain Dealer.* December 16.

Leadership Conference on Civil Rights and the Institute on Race and Poverty. Regional Justice: The Framework for Achieving Civil Rights Objectives. 2001.

Lee, Felicia R. 2004. Cosby Defends His Remarks about Poor Black's Values. *New York Times,* May 22, 7.

Levy, Frank. 1998. *Dollars and Dreams: American Incomes and Economic Change.* New York: Russell Sage Foundation.

Lewinson, Edwin R. 1974. *Black Politics in New York City.* New York: Twayne.

Lewis, David Levering. 1993. *W.E.B. Du Bois: Biography of a Race 1868–1919.* New York: Henry Holt.

———. 2000. *W.E.B. Du Bois: The Fight for Equality and the American Century, 1919–1963.* New York: Henry Holt.

Lewis, Earl. 1991. *In Their Own Interests: Race, Class and Power in Twentieth Century Norfolk.* Berkeley and Los Angeles: University of California Press.

Lewis, Zoltan L., and Paul G. Hajnal. 2003. Municipal Institutions and Voter Turnout in Local Elections. *Urban Affairs Review* 38 (5).

Liff, Bob. 1987. Black Leaders Present Koch with Crown Heights Plan. *Long Island Newsday.* July 23.

Lin, Wendy. 1993. A Lone Island: SI Secession Feasible, Report Says. *Long Island Newsday*. February 2.

Lincoln, C. Eric, and Lawrence Mamiya. 1990. *The Black Church in the African American Experience*. Durham: Duke University Press.

Liu, Baodong. 2003. Deracialization and Urban Racial Contexts. *Urban Affairs Review* 38 (4).

Locke, Alain. 1968. *The New Negro: An Interpretation*. New York: Arno.

Long Island Newsday. 1993. Dinkins Nixes Claim Playing Race Card in Staten I. August 10.

———. 1991. Fourth Night Brings More Violence. August 23.

Lowery, Mark. 1991. Sharpton Calls for a Boycott of Classes. *Long Island Newsday*. August 18.

Lucas. 1988. Interview by author May 3 in Atlanta.

Lueck, Thomas. 1993. Secession Could Avoid Big Tax Rise. *New York Times*, October 13.

Lynch, Bill. 1999. Interview by author July 10 in Harlem, N.Y.

———. 2000. Interview by author June 25 in New York.

Lynn, Frank. 1985. Black Political Leaders' Divisions Appear Again after New York Primary. *New York Times*. September 14.

———. 1986. Bronx, as Usual, Unruffled by Scandal. *New York Times*, December 7.

———. 1987a. Bids to Fill Simon Seat Are Started. *New York Times*. March 17.

———. 1987b. Borough Chief Contest Splits Hispanic Politicians in Bronx. *New York Times*. March 25.

Mahoney, James. 2000. Strategies of Causal Inference in Small-*N* Analysis. *Sociological Methods and Research* 28 (4):387–424.

Manegold, Catherine S. 1992. Rally Puts Police Under New Scrutiny. *New York Time.*, September 27.

———. 1993. Staten Island Secession More than Fringe Threat. *New York Times*. August 9.

Manent, Pierre. 1995. *An Intellectual History of Liberalism*. Princeton, N.J.: Princeton University Press.

Mangcu, Xolela. 1997. Harold Washington and the Cultural Transformation of Local Government in Chicago. PhD diss., Cornell University.

Marable, Manning. 1983. *How Capitalism Underdeveloped Black America: Problems in Race, Political Economy, and Society*. Boston: South End.

———. 1984. *Race, Reform and Rebellion: The Second Reconstruction in Black America, 1945–1982*. Jackson: University of Mississippi Press.

———. 1985. *Black American Politics: From the Washington Marches to Jesse Jackson*. London: Verso.

———. 1995. *Beyond Black and White*. London: Verso.

———. 1999. *Black Leadership: Four Great American Leaders and the Struggle for Civil Rights*. New York: Penguin.

Marks, Alexandra. 2002. "Hip hop mayor" Aims to Rev Motor City Engine. *Christian Science Monitor*. August 7.

Martin, Waldo E. 1984. *The Mind of Frederick Douglass*. Chapel Hill: The University of North Carolina Press.

Massey, Douglas S., and Nancy A. Denton. 1993. *American Apartheid: Segregation and the Making of the Underclass*. Cambridge, Mass.: Harvard University Press.

McAdam, Doug. 1983. The Decline of the Civil Rights Movement. In *Social Movements of the Sixties and Seventies*, ed. J. Freeman. New York: Longman.

McClain, Paula D., and Steven C. Tauber. 1997. An African American Presidential Candidate: The Failed Presidential Campaign of Governor L. Douglass Wilder. In *African American Power and Politics: The Political Context Variable*, ed. J. Hanes Walton. New York: Columbia University Press.

McCormick, Joseph P. 1997. The Message and the Messengers: Opinions from the Million Men Who Marched. *National Political Science Review* 6.

McCormick, Joseph P., and Charles E. Jones. 1993. The Conceptualization of Deracialization: Thinking through the Dilemma. In *Dilemmas of Black Politics: Issues of Leadership and Strategy*, ed. G. A. Persons. New York: HarperCollins.

McDougall, Harold A. 1993. *Black Baltimore: A New Theory of Community*. Philadelphia: Temple University Press.

McGee, Hansel. 1988. Interview by author April 7 in Bronx, N.Y.

McGirr, Lisa. 2001. Suburban Warriors. Princeton, N.J.: Princeton University Press.

McKinley, James C. Jr. 1991a. Staten Island Democrats Warn Dinkins on Support. *New York Times*. October 29.

———. 1991b. Money Talked in Race, But So Did Volunteers. *New York Times*. September 15.

———. 1992. Officers Rally and Dinkins Is Their Target. *New York Times*. September 17.

———. 1993. Dinkins Retains Financing from Groups of 4 Years Ago. *New York Times*. October 29.

McKinney, Charles. 1989. Interview by author February 1 in Harlem, N.Y.

McNeil, Larry. 2004. Interview by author February 20 in Palm Springs, Calif.

Mead, Lawrence M. 1992. *The New Politics of Poverty*. New York: Basic.

Meeks, Greg. 1988. Interview by author April 21 in Queens, N.Y.

Meier, Mark. 1987. *City Unions: Managing Discontent in New York City*. New Brunswick, N.J.: Rutgers University Press.

Meislin, Richard J. 1986. Friedman Mixes Instinct, Contacts and Illusion. *New York Times*. January 27.

Meyerson, Harold. 2001a. City of Tomorrow. *American Prospect*. April 9.

———. 2001b. L.A. Story. *American Prospect*. July 16.

———. 2003. Harvesting Voters. *Washington Post*. November 12.

Miley, Nate. 1988. Interview by author July 1 in Oakland, Calif.

Miller, Alton. 1988. *Climbing a Great Mountain: Selected Speeches of Mayor Harold Washington*. Chicago: Bonus Books.

———. 1989. *Harold Washington: The Mayor, The Man*. Chicago: Bonus Books.

Miller, Denene. 1996. Hip Hop Regroups and Beats Macho Rap. *New York Daily News.* January 31.

Mitchell, Alison. 1993. Giuliani Ads Accuse Dinkins of Using Race Issue. *New York Times.* October 6.

Mollenkopf, John. 1997. New York: The Great Anomaly. In *Racial Politics in American Cities,* ed. R. Browning, D. Marshall, and D. Tabb. New York: Longman.

———. 2003. New York: Still the Great Anomaly. In *Racial Politics in American Cities,* ed. R. Browning, D. Marshall, and D. Tabb. New York: Longman.

Mollenkopf, John H. 1983. *The Contested City.* Princeton, N.J.: Princeton University Press.

Mollenkopf, John Hull. 1992. *A Phoenix in the Ashes: The Rise and Fall of the Koch Coalition in New York City Politics.* Princeton, N.J.: Princeton University Press.

Montgomery, Lori. 2004. Williams Reserves Right to Change Familiar Agenda. *Washington Post.* September 20.

Montgomery, Lori, and Yolandee Woodlee. 2004. Barry In; 3 D.C. Councilmembers Out. *Washington Post.* September 15.

Mooney, Mark. 1990. Dinkins: No, This Is Not Dodge City. *New York Post.* August 1.

Moore, Leonard N. 2002. *Carl B. Stokes and the Rise of Black Political Power.* Urbana: University of Illinois Press.

Morris, Aldon D. 1984. *The Origins of the Civil Rights Movement.* New York: Free Press.

Morris, Milton D. 1975. *The Politics of Black America.* New York: Harper & Row.

Morrison, Toni. 1992. Introduction: Friday on the Potomac. In *Race-ing Justice, En-gendering Power,* ed. T. Morrison. New York: Random House.

Murphy, William. 1990. Dinkins Popularity Is Polarized. *Long Island Newsday.* July 9.

Nagourney, Adam. 1997. More at Play in Runoff than Vote Outcome. *New York Times.* September 15.

———. 2001a. Campaigning for Mayor: The Democrats; Vallone Asserts Ferrer's Campaign Is Polarizing City. *New York Times.* September 10.

———. 2001b. Entering Race, Ferrer Focuses on Giuliani. *New York Times.* June 28.

———. 2001c. Political Memo: Heated Race Revisited, Amid Claims of Racism. *New York Times.* October 16.

Nelson, William E. 1982. Cleveland: The Rise and Fall of the New Black Politics. In *The New Black Politics: The Search for Political Power,* ed. M. B. Preston, L. J. Henderson, and P. Puryear. New York: Longman.

———. 1990. Black Mayoral Leadership: A Twenty-Year Perspective. *National Political Science Review* 2.

Netzer, Dick. 1990. The Economy and Governing of the City. In *Urban Politics New York Style,* ed. J. Bellush and D. Netzer. Armonk, N.Y.: M. E. Sharpe.

New York Times. 1978. Accounts Vary Widely on Beating of 16-Year-Old Youth in Brooklyn. June 21.

———. 1991. After the Voting; Highlights of the Primary. September 14.

————. 1992. Rumor and Justice in Washington Heights. August 7.

————. 1993. A Second Term for Mayor Dinkins.

————. 2001. Ferrer Defines the "Other New York," and He Discusses His Plans to Help It. July 27.

Newfield, Jack. 1990. Slow-mo Dinkins Missing the Beat. *New York Daily News.* September 16.

Newton, Huey. 1970. Huey Newton Talks to the Movement about the Black Panther Party, Cultural Nationalism, SNCC, Liberals, and White Revolutionaries. In *The Black Panthers Speak,* ed. P. S. Foner. Philadelphia: J. P. Lippincott.

Nicholls, Walter Julio. 2003. Forging a "New" Organizational Infrastructure for Los Angeles' Progressive Community. *International Journal of Urban and Regional Research* 27 (4): December 2003.

Noel, Peter. 2001. What Black Vote? *Village Voice.* September 11.

O'Clairiecain, Carol. 2000. Interview by author January 15 in New York.

Oden, Robert Stanley. 1999. Power Shift: A Sociological Study of the Political Incorporation of People of Color in Oakland, California, 1966–1996. PhD diss., University of California, Santa Cruz.

Office of Management and Budget, New York City. 1990. Background on the City Fiscal Outlook.

Office of Mayor David Dinkins. 1990. Statement by Mayor David N. Dinkins at Press Conference to $75 Million in Actions to Keep the City's 1990 Budget in Balance between Now and June 30. Press Release.

Office of the City Comptroller, New York City. 1992. *Economic Notes.* 13 January.

Office of the Mayor. 1990. Cops and Kids: An Omnibus Criminal Justice Program for the City of New York.

Oreskes, Michael. 1988. Jackson Troops Say They Won Future. *New York Times.* 4 April.

Orfield, Gary, and Carole Ashkinaze. 1991. *The Closing Door: Conservative Policy and Black Opportunity.* Chicago: University of Chicago Press.

Orfield, Myron. 1998a. Atlanta Metropolitics: A Regional Agenda for Community and Stability. Atlanta: The Turner Foundation.

————. San Francisco Bay Area Metropolitics: A Regional Agenda for Community and Stability. San Francisco: Urban Habitat Program.

Orr, Marion. 1999. *Black Social Capital: The Politics of School Reform in Baltimore: 1986–1998.* Lawrence: Kansas University Press.

Osterman, Paul. 2002. *Gathering Power: The Future of Progressive Politics in America.* Boston: Beacon.

Owens, Michael Leo, and Michael J. Rich. 2003. Is Strong Black Incorporation Enough? Black Empowerment and the Fate of Atlanta's Low-Income Neighborhoods. In *Racial Politics in American Cities,* ed. R. P. Browning, D. R. Marshall and D. H. Tabb. New York: Longman.

Pagano, Michael A. 1991. City Fiscal Conditions in 1991: National League of Cities.

Page, Susan. 1988. Clear the Air, Urge Advisors. *Long Island Newsday.* April 6.

Palmer, Louise. 1998. D.C.'s New Mayor: He's No Barry; Williams's Backers See Technocrat with Vision. *The Boston Globe*. November 9.

Parker, Heather R. 2001. Tom Bradley and the Politics of Race. In *African-American Mayors: Race, Politics, and the American City*, ed. D. R. Colburn and J. S. Adler. Urbana: University of Illinois Press.

Pattillo-McCoy, Mary. 2000. The Limits of Out-Migration of the Black Middle Class. *Journal of Urban Affairs* 22 (3).

Patrick, Reginald. 1992. Did Media Push Blackburne Out? *Staten Island Advance*. February 23.

Payne, J. Gregory, and Scott C. Ratzan. 1986. *Tom Bradley: The Impossible Dream*. Santa Monica, Calif.: Roundtable Publishing.

Peirce, Neil. 1993. Detroit's New Mayor Aims to Reinvent the Inner City. *New Orleans Times-Picayune*, December 6.

Perez-Pena, Richard. 1999. Police May Have Understated Street Searches, Spitzer Says. *New York Times*. March 23.

———. 2001. A Democrat's Mandate: No More Racial Division. *New York Times*. November 14.

Perlstein, Daniel Hiram. 1994. The 1968 New York City School Crisis: Teacher Politics, Racial Politics and the Decline of Liberalism. PhD diss., Stanford University.

Persons, Georgia A. 1993. Black Mayoralities and the New Black Politics: From Insurgency to Racial Reconciliation. In *Dilemmas of Black Politics: Issues of Leadership and Strategy*, ed. G. A. Persons. New York: HarperCollins.

Persons, Georgia Ann. 1978. Atlanta: Black Mayoral Leadership and the Dynamics of Political ChangePhD diss., Massachusetts Institute of Technology.

Peterson, Paul E. 1981. *City Limits*. Chicago: University of Chicago Press.

Pierce, Neal. 1993. Latest Mayoral Victories Signal a New Urban Politics. *New Orleans Times-Picayune*, November 8.

Pinderhughes, Dianne M. 1997. An Examination of Chicago Politics for Evidence of Political Incorporation and Representation. In *Racial Politics in American Cities*, ed. R. P. Browning, D. R. Marshall, and D. H. Tabb. New York: Longman.

Piven, Frances Fox. 2004. Retrospective Comments. *Perspectives on Politics* 1 (4):709.

Piven, Francis Fox, and Richard A. Cloward. 1999. *Poor People's Movements*. 2nd ed. New York: Vintage.

Polletta, Francesca. 2002. *Freedom Is an Endless Meeting*. Chicago: University of Chicago Press.

powell, john. 2002. Sprawl, Fragmentation, and the Persistence of Racial Inequality. In *Urban Sprawl*, ed. G. D. Squires. Washington, D.C.: The Urban Institute Press.

powell, john A. 1999. Addressing Regional Dilemmas for Minority Communities. Unpublished manuscript.

Powell, Michael. 2003. Knock-Down, Drag-Out Urban Renewal; Philadelphia Program Targets Blighted Areas. *Washington Post*. March 13.

Pryce, Vinette K. 1991. Caruso's 'lazy, shiftless' tirade spurs Flake's welfare jobs plan. *Amsterdam News.* November 2.

Purdum, Todd. 1993a. Rudolph Giuliani and the Color of Politics in New York. *New York Times.* July 25.

Purdum, Todd S. 1990. Dinkins Talks of Crime Fear and of Race. *New York Times.* September 20.

———. 1991. Tension in Brooklyn; A Frustrated Dinkins Appeals for Peace: "I Alone Cannot Do It." *New York Times.* August 23.

———. 1993b. Dinkins and Giuliani Make Closing Appeals for Votes in Rematch. *New York Times.* November 2.

———. 1993c. Giuliani Campaign Theme: Dinkins Isn't Up to the Job. *New York Times.* October 24.

Purnick, Joyce. 2001. For Ferrer, a Bloc Is a Hard Place. *New York Times.* May 2.

Putnam, Robert D. 2000. *Bowling Alone: The Collapse and Revival of American Community.* New York: Simon & Schuster.

Quinn, Christopher, and Mark Vosburgh. 2002. White Hands Off a City That Bears His Stamp. *Cleveland Plain Dealer* January 6.

Raab, Selwyn. 1978. Past Police Incidents Moved Blacks to Coordinate Protests. *New York Times.* June 23.

Ransby, Barbara. 2003. *Ella Baker & the Black Freedom Movement: A Radical Democratic Vision.* Chapel Hill: The University of North Carolina Press.

Reed, Adolph Jr. 1986a. *The Jesse Jackson Phenomenon: The Crisis of Purpose in Afro American Politics.* New Haven, Conn.: Yale University Press.

———. 1986b. The Black Urban Regime: Structural Origins and Constraints. *Comparative Urban and Community Research: An Annual Review* 1:138–89.

———. 1987. A Critique of Neo-Progressivism in Theorizing about Local Development Policy: A Case from Atlanta. In *The Politics of Urban Development,* ed. C. N. Stone and H. T. Sanders. Lawrence: Kansas University Press.

———. 1999. *Stirrings in the Jug: Black Politics in the Post-Segregation Era.* Minneapolis: University of Minnesota Press.

Rich, Wilbur C. 1982. *The Politics of Urban Personnel Policy: Reformers, Politicians, and Bureaucrats.* Port Washington, N.Y.: National University Publications.

———. 1989. *Coleman Young and Detroit Politics: From Social Activist to Power Broker.* Detroit: Wayne State University Press.

———. 1996. *Black Mayors and School Politics.* New York: Garland Publishing.

———. 2004. Mayors, Images, and the Media: David Dinkins and Thomas Menino. New York.

———. n.d. "Crime Coverage, Mayoral Images and Signaling." Unpublished manuscript.

Richards, David A. J. 1993. *Conscience and the Constitution: History, Theory, and Law of the Reconstruction Amendments.* Princeton, N.J.: Princeton University Press.

Riles, Wilson. 1988. Interview by author June 23 in Oakland, Calif.

Roberts, Sam. 1984. New York Democrats Gain Black and Hispanic Voters. *New York Times*. April.

———. 1985. New York Blacks Take a Big Step Toward Political Clout. *New York Times*. April 8.

———. 1992. Dinkins and the Police: A Campaign Issue. *New York Times*. September 20.

———. 1993a. The Murky Mix of Race, Competence, and Politics. *New York Times*. October 4.

———. 1993b. Staten Island Packs One-Two Punch. *New York Times*. February 1.

Robinson, Cedric J. 1997. *Black Movements in America*. New York: Routledge.

Robinson, Dean E. 2001. *Black Nationalism in American Politics and Thought*. New York: Cambridge University Press.

Roediger, David E. 2002. *Colored White: Transcending the Racial Past*. Berkeley and Los Angeles: University of California Press.

Ross, Bernard H., and Myron A. Levine. 2001. *Urban Politics: Power in Metropolitan America*. 6th ed. Itasca, Ill.: F.E. Peacock Publishers.

Ross, Catherine E., John Mirowsky, and Shana Pribesh. 2001. Powerlessness and the Amplification of Threat; Neighborhood Disadvantage, Disorder, and Mistrust. *American Sociological Review* 66 (4).

Rubin, Victor. 1988. Interview by author June 30 in Berkeley, Calif.

Sack, Kevin. 1991. New Group to Support Insurgents Is Divided as Council Vote Nears. *New York Times*. September 10.

———. 1993. If Staten Island Votes to Secede, What Will Albany Do? *New York Times*. October 24.

Saltonstall, Dave. 2001. Ferrer's Camp Proud of Way It Ran the Race. *New York Daily News*. October 12.

Samama, Jabari. 1988. Remarks by Jabari Samama. Atlanta. FM-90 WABA. Tape recording April 10.

Samuel, Terence. 1997. A "New Breed of Mayor" Is Saving American Cities. *St. Louis Post-Dispatch*. August 17.

Sanjek, Roger. 1998. *The Future of Us All: Race and Neighborhood Politics in New York City*. Ithaca, N.Y.: Cornell University Press.

Schnieder, Craig, and Carl Campanile. 1993. Sour Apple: Staten Island Ready to Drop N.Y. *Newhouse News Service*. October 24.

Seifman, David. 1991. Beat the Clock. *New York Post*. July 1.

Self, Robert Owen. 1998. Shifting Ground in Metropolitan America: Class, Race, and Power in Oakland and the East Bay. PhD diss., University of Washington.

Shapiro, Thomas M. 2004. *The Hidden Cost of Being African American: How Wealth Perpetuates Inequality*. New York: Oxford University Press.

Sharkey, Mary Anne. 1994. For Stokes, Time to Look Ahead and Back. *Cleveland Plain Dealer*. September 4.

Shefter, Martin. 1987. *Political Crisis/Fiscal Crisis*. New York: Basic.

Shepherd, Peggy. 1988. Interview by author March 10 in Harlem, N.Y.

Shifrel, Scott, and Larry Cohler-Esses. 2001. Green Aides Met with Dems on Ferrer-Sharpton Plan. *New York Daily News.* November 2.

Shinholster, Earl. 1988. Interview by author May 2 in Atlanta.

Shipp, E. R. 1991. Harlem Battles over Development Project. *New York Times.* July 31.

Siefman, David. 1990. Stein: Call in National Guard. *New York Post.* August 3.

Simmons, Esmerelda. 1988. Interview by author March 16 in Brooklyn, N.Y.

Sims, Calvin. 1992. A Commissioner Done In by a Staff She Offended. *New York Times.* March 1.

Skenazy, Lenore. 2003. Mike Gets It Right on Rudy's Divisiveness. *New York Daily News.* November 9.

Smith, Malcolm. 1988. Interview by author Arpril 7 in Queens, N.Y.

Smith, Robert C. 1992. "Politics" Is Not Enough. In *From Exclusion to Inclusion: The Long Struggle for African American Political Power,* ed. R. C. Gomes and L. F. Williams. Westport, Conn.: Praeger.

————. 1996. *We Have No Leaders.* Albany: State University of New York Press.

Smith, Rogers M. 1997. *Civic Ideals: Conflicting Visions of Citizenship in U.S. History.* New Haven, Conn.: Yale Press.

Smith, Steven Rathgeb, and Michael Lipsky. 1993. *Nonprofits for Hire: The Welfare State in the Age of Contracting.* Cambridge, Mass.: Harvard University Press.

Sniderman, Paul, Gretchen C. Crosby, and William G. Howell. 2000. The Politics of Race. In *Racialized Politics,* ed. D. O. Sears, J. Sadanius, and L. Bobo. Chicago: University of Chicago Press.

Sonnenshein, Raphael. 1993. *Politics in Black and White: Race and Power in Los Angeles.* Princeton: Princeton University Press.

Stafford, Walter W. 2001. The National Urban League Survey: Black America's Under-35 Generation. In *The State of Black America: 2001,* ed. L. A. Daniels. New York: National Urban League.

Stokes, Carl B. 1973. *Promises of Power: A Political Autobiography.* New York: Simon & Schuster.

Stone, Clarence N. 1989. *Regime Politics: Governing Atlanta 1946–1988.* Lawrence: University Press of Kansas.

————. 1993. Urban Regimes and the Capacity to Govern: a Political Economy Approach. *Journal of Urban Affairs* 15 (1):1–28.

————. 2004. It's More Than the Economy After All: Continuing the Debate about Urban Regimes. *Journal of Urban Affairs* 26 (1).

Stone, Clarence N., Jeffrey R. Henig, Bryan D. Jones, and Carol Pierannunzi. 2001. *Building Civic Capacity: The Politics of Reforming Urban Schools.* Lawrence: University of Kansas Press.

Summers, Mary, and Philip A. Klinker. 1996. The Election and Governance of John Daniels as Mayor of New Haven. In *Race, Politics, and Governance in the United States,* ed. H. L. Perry. Gainesville: University Press of Florida.

Sutton, Chuck. 1988. Interview by author March 17 in Harlem, N.Y.

Sviridoff, Mitchell. 1994. The Seeds of Urban Revival. *Public Interest* 114 (8):8.

Swain, Carol. 1993. *Black Faces, Black Interests: The Representation of African Americans in Congress.* Cambridge, Mass.: Harvard University Press.

Swanstrom, Todd, Colleen Casey, Robert Flack, and Peter Dreier. 2004. Pulling Apart: Economic Segregation among Suburbs and Central Cities in Major Metropolitan Areas. In *The Living Cities Census Series.* Washington, D.C.: The Brookings Institution.

Tate, Katherine. 1994. *From Protest to Politics: The New Black Voters in American Elections.* 2nd ed. Cambridge, Mass.: Harvard University Press.

———. 2003. *Black Faces in the Mirror.* Princeton, N.J.: Princeton University Press.

Tatum, Wilbert. 1993. Governor's Report on Crown Heights: A Redundancy at Best. *Amsterdam News.* July 24.

Taylor, Clarence. 1977. *Knocking at Our Own Door: Milton A. Galamison and the Struggle to Integrate New York City Schools.* New York: Columbia University Press.

Teixeira, Ruy, and Joel Rogers. 2000. *Why the White Working Class Still Matters.* New York: Basic.

Thompson, J. Phillip. 1990. David Dinkins' Victory in New York City: The Decline of the Democratic Party Organization and the Strengthening of Black Politics. *PS: Political Science and Politics* 23 (2).

———. 1996a. The Election and Governance of David Dinkins as Mayor of New York. In *Race, Politics, and Governance in the United States,* ed. H. L. Perry. Gainesville: University Press of Florida.

———. 1996b. The Failure of Liberal Homeless Policy in the Koch and Dinkins Administrations. *Political Science Quarterly* 111 (4).

———. 2004. What Are Labor's True Colors? *New Labor Forum* 13 (2).

Tomasky, Michael. 1991. "Public Enemies." *Village Voice.* July 9.

Treaster, Joseph B. 1978a. Brooklyn Businessman Strangled in a Struggle with Police Officers. *New York Times.* June 17.

———. 1978b. Excessive Force in Brooklyn Man's Death Is Denied. *New York Times.* June 18.

Tucker, Cynthia. 1997. Leadership: In Progressive Atlanta, the Mayor Lives in the Past. *Atlanta Journal-Constitution.* July 9.

———. 1998. City Disappointment: Atlanta Hopes for Improved Campbell. *Atlanta Journal-Constitution.* June 3.

U.S. Department of Commerce, Bureau of the Census. 1983. General Social and Economic Characteristics, Vol I, Chapter C. Washington D.C.

U.S. Government Printing Office. 1984. FBI Undercover Operations. In *Subcommittee on Civil and Constitutional Rights.* Washington, D.C.

Vaca, Nicolas C. 2004. *The Presumed Alliance: The Unspoken Conflict between Latinos and Blacks and What It Means for America.* New York: HarperCollins.

Valentine, Paul W. 1995a. Schmoke Victory Reveals Baltimore's Racial Polarization. *Washington Post.* September 15.

———. 1995b. Schmoke, City Council President Square Off in Baltimore Mayoral Race. *Washington Post.* April 2.

Vann, James. 1988. Interview by author June 20 in Oakland, Calif.

Vidal, Avis C. 1997. Can Community Development Re-invent Itself? The Challenges of Strengthening Neighborhoods in the 21st Century. *Journal of the American Planning Association* 63:429–38.

Vincent, Theodore G. 1971. *Black Power and the Garvey Movement.* Palo Alto, Calif.: Ramparts.

Viterritti, Joseph P. 1990. The New Charter: Will It Make a Difference? In *Urban Politics New York Style,* ed. J. Bellush and D. Netzer. Armonk, N.Y.: M.E. Sharpe.

Wacquant, Loic. 1997. Three Pernicious Premises in the Study of the American Ghetto. *International Journal of Urban and Regional Research* 21 (2): June 1997.

Waldinger, Roger. 1996. *Still the Promised City?: African Americans and New Immigrants in Postindustrial New York.* Cambridge, Mass.: Harvard University Press.

Walters, Ronald W. 1988. *Black Presidential Politics in America: A Strategic Approach.* Albany: State University of New York Press.

Walton, Hanes Jr., and Robert C. Smith. 2000. *American Politics and the African American Quest for Universal Freedom.* New York: Longman.

Ware, Alan. 1985. *The Breakdown of Democratic Party Organization, 1940–1980.* Oxford: Clarendon.

Warren, Mark R. 1998. Race, Religion and Community Activism: Developing Effective Strategies and Institutions to Address Structures of Racism. New York: Aspen Institute Roundtable on Comprehensive Community Initiatives.

———. 2001. *Dry Bones Rattling: Community Building to Revitalize American Democracy.* Princeton, N.J.: Princeton University Press.

Washington, Preston. 2000. Interview by author July 20 in Harlem, N.Y.

Weills, Annie. 1988. Interview by author June 30 in Oakland, Calif.

Weir, Margaret. 1992. *Politics and Jobs: The Boundaries of Employment Policy in the United States.* Princeton: Princeton University Press.

———. 1996. Central Cities' Loss of Power in State Politics. *Cityscape* 2 (2): May 1996.

———. 1998. Race and the Politics of Metropolitanism. New York: Aspen Roundtable on Comprehensive Community Initiatives.

———. 1999. Power, Money, and Politics in Community Development. In *Urban Problems and Community Development,* ed. R. E. Ferguson and W. T. Dickens. Washington, D.C.: Brookings Institution Press.

Weiser, Benjamin. 2001. New York Will Pay $50 Million in 50,000 Illegal Strip-Searches. *New York Times.* January 10.

Welch, Susan, and Timothy Bledsoe. 1988. *Urban Reform and Its Consequences.* Chicago: University of Chicago Press.

Weymouth, Lally. 1991. Who Will Save New York City? *Washington Post.* August 19.

Williams, John. 2004. Houston Says It's Mayor White. *Houston Chronicle.* March 4.

Williams, Juan. 1985. Of Zulus, Watusis . . . *New York Times.* July 28.

———. 1995. Why Brimmer Won't Blink. *Washington Post.* December 3.

Williams, Linda, and Lorenzo Morris. 1989. The Coalition at the End of the Rainbow. In *Jesse Jackson's 1984 Presidential Campaign,* ed. L. J. Barker and R. W. Walters. Urbana: University of Illinois Press.

Williams, Lorrie, and Linda Faye Frasure. 2002. Civic Disparities and Civic Differences. College Park: The Democracy Collaborative, University of Maryland.

Williams, Pete. 1988. Interview by author March 9 in Brooklyn, N.Y.

Williams, Vanessa. 1998. A City Wonders: What Now?; D.C. Laments Its Lagging Political Development. *Washington Post.* September 13.

Wilson, Basil, and Charles Green. 1989. *The Struggle for Black Empowerment in New York City.* New York: Praeger.

Wilson, James Q. 1960. Two Negro Politicians: An Interpretation. *MidWest Journal of Political Science* 4 (4): November 1960.

Wilson, James Q., and Richard Herrnstein. 1985. *Crime and Human Nature.* New York: Simon & Schuster.

Wilson, William Julius. [1978] 1980. *The Declining Significance of Race: Blacks and Changing American Institutions.* Chicago: University of Chicago Press.

———. 1987. *The Truly Disadvantaged: The Inner City, the Underclass, and Public Policy.* Chicago: University of Chicago Press.

———. 1996. *When Work Disappears.* New York: Knopf.

———. 1999. *The Bridge over the Racial Divide.* Berkeley and Los Angeles: University of California Press.

Wohlenberg, Ernest H. 1982. The "Geography of Civility" Revisited: New York Blackout Looting, 1977. *Economic Geography* 58 (1):29–44.

Wooten, Paul. 1988. Interview by author March 12 in Brooklyn, N.Y.

Zannes, Estelle. 1972. *Checkmate in Cleveland: The Rhetoric of Confrontation during the Stokes Years.* Cleveland: The Press of Case Western Reserve University.

Zuber, Paul. 1969. Parties and Politics in Harlem. In *Harlem: A Community in Transition,* ed. J. H. Clarke. New York: Citadel.

Zukin, Sharon. 1998. How "Bad Is It?: Institutions and Intentions in the Study of the American Ghetto." *International Journal of Urban and Regional Research* 22 (3).

Index

black politics in, 173–76
Brownsville, 86–87, 174, 215, 242
Coalition for Community Empowerment, 175–76, 182–85, 189
common concerns of Jews and blacks in, 255
Crown Heights incident, 212, 221–27, 236, 250, 251, 255–56
and Dinkins campaigns, 184, 239
infighting with Harlem politicians, 184
and Jackson campaign, 183
machine power in, 158, 166
Saratoga Square, 215–16
voter registration in, 57–58
Brooklyn Bridge, 232, 233
Brooks, Joe, 71
Brooks, Leo, 116
Brotherhood of Sleeping Car Porters and Maids, 81, 92
Brown, Elaine, 148, 149
Brown, Jerry, 70, 71, 151–52
Brown, Kenneth, 177
Brown, Lee, 134, 197
Brown, Ronald, 84
Brown, Roscoe, 242
Brown, Willie, 151
Browning, Rufus, 149
Brownsville (Brooklyn, N.Y.), 86–87, 174, 215, 242
BUILD. *See* Baltimoreans United in Leadership Development
Bunche, Ralph, 122
Burns, Clarence "Du," 76
Bush, George, 275
business development, 40–41, 63–64, 71, 137
Butler, Jim, 205
Butts, Calvin, 85, 225
Bynoe, Audrey, 57, 103

California, 17, 68, 69, 134, 140, 151
Campbell, William "Bill," 7, 9, 13, 14, 46, 60, 145
Canason, Joe, 174
Capelli, Allen, 228
Caraley, James, 11
Carey, Hugh, 170, 171
Carmichael, Stokely, 95–96, 97–98, 100, 125
Carney, James, 107, 108
Carter, Alprentice "Bunchy," 99
Caruso, Phil, 230, 233
Catholic Charities, 78
Catholic Church, 195
CBOs. *See* community-based organizations
CCE. *See* Coalition for Community Empowerment

CDCs. *See* community development corporations
Central Freeway project (San Francisco), 40
Charles A. Hayes Labor and Educational Center, 44
Chatterjee, Partha, 49
Chavis, Ben, 104
Chicago (Ill.), 17, 276
black and Latino percent of total population, 51, 134, 135
black coalition in support of Washington, 107, 108
black mayors in, 51, 110
civic activity in, 26
deracialized strategy in, 53
Empowered Participatory Governance case studies, 26–27, 28
job loss in, 165
lack of black civic coalitions, 79
multiracial coalition, 259, 266
patronage in, 62–63
racial polarization in, 71
under Mayor Washington, 21, 39, 41–46, 65, 72, 73, 85, 105, 145, 194, 195, 259
unionization in, 16, 65
after Washington's death, 74, 107, 109
Chicago Defender, 81
Chicago Federation of Labor, 65
children, 254, 261
Chisholm, Shirley, 148, 173
churches, 23, 93–95, 162, 187, 214
CIO (Congress of Industrial Organizations), 82, 91
Cisneros, Henry, 134
cities
administrative structure of, 266
black and Latino percent of total population in, 51–53, 135
"civil rights" mayors in, 4, 10, 12, 13
downtown development in, 40, 41, 64, 71
federal aid to, 4
fiscal and political isolation of, 10, 265
patronage, 62–71, 108, 158, 163, 164, 250, 266
pro-growth coalitions, 40
service delivery, 68
union density in, 66–67
See also municipal unions; *specific cities*
City Sun, 188, 225
civic coalitions, 73–74, 85, 195, 250
civic organizations, 12, 75–113, 158, 195–96, 251, 257, 258, 260, 266, 270–71
civic participation, 85–88, 89, 257, 259, 260